AREA HANDBOOK

for

GUINEA

Coauthors

Harold D. Nelson

Margarita Dobert
James McLaughlin
Barbara Marvin
Donald P. Whitaker

Research completed February 1975

Second Edition

Published 1975

DA Pam 550–174

Library of Congress Cataloging in Publication Data

Nelson, Harold D.

Area handbook for Guinea.

"One of a series of handbooks prepared by Foreign Area Studies (FAS) of the American University."

"DA Pam 550-174."

A revision of the 1961 ed. issued by Foreign Area Studies Division, American University.
Bibliography: p. 343–361.
Includes index.

1. Guinea. I. American University, Washington, D.C. Foreign Area Studies. II. American University, Washington, D.C. Foreign Areas Studies Division. Area handbook for Guinea. III. Title.

DT543.N44   1976   966'.5205   75-26515

For sale by the Superintendent of Documents, U.S. Government Printing Office
Washington, D.C. 20402 - Price $7.00

FOREWORD

This volume is one of a series of handbooks prepared by Foreign Area Studies (FAS) of The American University, designed to be useful to military and other personnel who need a convenient compilation of basic facts about the social, economic, political, and military institutions and practices of various countries. The emphasis is on objective description of the nation's present society and the kinds of possible or probable changes that might be expected in the future. The handbook seeks to present as full and as balanced an integrated exposition as limitations on space and research time permit. It was compiled from information available in openly published material. An extensive bibliography is provided to permit recourse to other published sources for more detailed information. There has been no attempt to express any specific point of view or to make policy recommendations. The contents of the handbook represent the work of the authors and FAS and do not represent the official view of the United States government.

An effort has been made to make the handbook as comprehensive as possible. It can be expected, however, that the material, interpretations, and conclusions are subject to modification in the light of new information and developments. Such corrections, additions, and suggestions for factual, interpretive, or other change as readers may have will be welcomed for use in future revisions. Comments may be addressed to:

The Director
Foreign Area Studies
The American University
5010 Wisconsin Avenue, N.W.
Washington, D.C. 20016

PREFACE

At independence in late 1958 the Republic of Guinea occupied a special position among the new African states that had emerged out of the rising tide of nationalism in the years after World War II. It alone of France's West African territories had opted in a referendum for independence outside the French Community proposed by General Charles de Gaulle. The choice, which suddenly cut off sorely needed French technical and material assistance, established the new republic as an enviable pioneer in the African quest for nationalism—a position it retained during its early years of sovereignty. By the early 1970s, however, its prominence as a revered spokesman for pan-Africanism had waned.

When the first edition of the *Area Handbook for Guinea* was written in 1961, no other comprehensive study of the country had been published. The continuous process of interaction between the new and the old within the young republic was only beginning to form a coherent national pattern out of the people's differing attitudes, values, and institutions. In the fifteen years that have elapsed, much of the specific information contained in the earlier handbook has been modified by time and events; a revision, therefore, seems appropriate.

The first edition of the handbook was prepared by a research team composed of Robert J. Catto, John P. Heawood, Elliot Liebow, Frederica M. Bunge, Teresa Rakowska-Harmstone, Frances Chadwick Rintz, and Harvey H. Smith under the chairmanship of George L. Harris. The revised edition, in a somewhat different form, seeks—like the earlier work—to provide a compact and objective exposition of the dominant social, political, and economic aspects of Guinean society. It is designed to give the reader an understanding of the forces operating within the society. There remain, however, a number of gaps in information on certain subjects to which the reader's attention has been directed at appropriate places in the text.

The spelling of place names conforms to the standard established by the United States Board on Geographic Names in its gazetteer published in June 1965 and its supplement of April 1972. All textual references to tonnages are expressed as metric tons, unless otherwise noted. Conversion factors for Guinean currency appear in the Glossary, which is included as an appendix for the reader's convenience.

The authors wish to thank those persons who gave of their time, documents, and special knowledge of the country to help improve this work.

COUNTRY SUMMARY

1. COUNTRY: Formal name, Republic of Guinea; short form, Guinea. Former French colony; date of independence, October 2, 1958. Capital, Conakry.

2. SIZE: Land area of 94,925 square miles; greatest west-east distance about 450 miles, north-south maximum about 350 miles; claimed territorial waters extend to 130-nautical-mile limit, approximate edge of continental shelf.

3. TOPOGRAPHY: Four diverse topographical regions: narrow coastal plain and foothill area rising eastward to central region of dissected plateaus averaging over 3,000 feet in elevation; plateaus slope on the east to broad expanse of level savanna averaging about 1,000 feet above sea level; southern interior mainly of rounded mountains having general elevation between 1,500 and 3,000 feet but with peaks up to 5,000 feet including Mount Nimba, country's highest point at 5,748 feet.

4. CLIMATE: Tropical to subtropical, characterized by distinct wet and dry seasons. Hot and humid in coastal zone and forested southern interior; central plateaus relatively comfortable; eastern savanna has long dry season accompanied by uncomfortably low humidity. Rainfall from less than sixty inches in savanna region to over 100 inches in southern and coastal areas; principal period of rains, April to November.

5. POPULATION: Over 5 million in Guinean census of 1972, including estimated 600,000 to 1 million outside national territory; more than 80 percent rural. Most growth-rate estimates about 2.3 percent, but some as high as 3.5 percent by mid-1970s. Three major ethnic groups— Malinké, Peul, and Soussou—constitute about 75 percent of population. Principal minor ethnic groups live in southeast and are relatively homogeneous in customs and social organization.

6. LANGUAGES: Guinea has one official language—French—and eight national languages: Poular, Malinké, Soussou, Kissi, Guerzé, Toma, Coniagui, and Bassari.

7. RELIGION: From 75 to 90 percent of the people profess Islam; Christian churches claim from 30,000 to 40,000 members; rest of population adheres to indigenous, locally based religious beliefs.

8. EDUCATION: Nationalized school system offering instruction from primary school to university. Free at all levels, and compulsory through lower secondary school (ninth grade). In 1975 schools in process of

conversion to combination study-work institutions with about 40 percent of time devoted to productive activities. National languages used in lower primary school classes; French as language of instruction gradually being replaced throughout educational system. Enrollment growing steadily; about 184,000 primary school students, 71,000 secondary-level students, and 2,900 university students in 1972. Functional literacy rate low; less than 10 percent in French, negligible in national languages.

9. HEALTH: Malnutrition, lack of adequate sanitation, insufficient modern health services, and existence of a number of communicable diseases present severe health problems. Chief endemic diseases are malaria, venereal diseases, and tuberculosis.

10. GOVERNMENT: Constitution in effect since 1958 with few amendments; serves only as source of government's legitimacy rather than as basis for actual authority; governmental system is parliamentary with authority vested in National Assembly and president. In reality all authority vested in single Democratic Party of Guinea (Parti Démocratique de Guinée—PDG) under control of President Ahmed Sékou Touré and small leadership nucleus within PDG Central Committee. Country is divided into twenty-nine administrative regions; outlet for popular expression provided at village level through combined local unit of party and government. No opposition or criticism tolerated, contributing to flight of many Guineans into exile.

11. JUSTICE: Legal system of French origin considerably altered after independence; law largely based on French-style codes, but judges given degree of discretion to apply precedent; judiciary specifically forbidden to be independent from state and governing party. Three lower levels of people's courts; criminal courts for more serious cases and courts of appeal located at Conakry and headquarters of four geographic regions; highest court is Superior Court of Cassation, which has no power of judicial review. Political crimes often tried before several kinds of largely ad hoc judicial bodies of the PDG or National Assembly.

12. ECONOMY: Smallholders predominate in population and produce largely for subsistence. Critical urban food shortage, rapid inflation, and lagging growth have fueled black market in scarce food, consumer goods, and foreign exchange; smuggling trade exists on widespread scale. Government has monopoly on trade and banking, owns most factories, and has effected half-share takeover in fast-growing bauxite mining and alumina production supported by foreign firms or governments.

13. PRINCIPAL EXPORTS: Bauxite, alumina, coffee, pineapples, palm kernels; declining exports of bananas and diamonds.

14. PRINCIPAL IMPORTS: Probably petroleum products, rice, machinery and equipment, raw materials for industry.

15. CURRENCY: Until March 1, 1960, country used African Financial Community franc (Communauté Financière Africaine franc—CFAF) tied to French franc (CFAF50 equaled one French franc); separate

Guinean franc (GF) introduced March 1, 1960. On October 2, 1972, currency was changed to Guinean syli (GS), equivalent to ten Guinean francs. One syli consists of 100 cauris; not convertible, not accepted on most exchange markets; black market rate of five to eight times official rate has prevailed. For currency conversion factors, see Glossary.

16. COMMUNICATIONS: Domestic postal, telephone, and telegraph service provided by central government. Service was poor in early 1970s but was under improvement. Mass media poorly developed and completely under government control. Domestic radio broadcasts reached less than one-half of the population. Printed media numbered fewer than five regular publications, including one daily newspaper and one weekly magazine, both organs of the country's single political party. No television in early 1975.

17. RAILROADS: Government-operated meter-gauge railroad from Conakry to Kankan in poor operating condition in 1974. Three modern railroads in operation to bauxite mines—one meter gauge, two standard gauge. Financing being sought in early 1975 for 745-mile railroad to planned iron ore and bauxite mining areas.

18. INLAND WATERWAYS: Limited shallow-draft barge traffic on Niger and Milo rivers in July and August; most traffic confined to poled barges and canoes.

19. PORTS: New ore port built at Kamsar for bauxite shipments. Most other traffic through port of Conakry; in 1974 traffic subject to delays because of poorly maintained loading equipment. Loan sought for reconditioning.

20. ROADS: Main highway from Conakry to southeast paved by 1975. Remaining roads mostly dirt surfaced, seasonal, in poor condition.

21. CIVIL AVIATION: Government-owned Air Guinea serves eight small domestic airfields. Scheduled flights of other airlines call at Conakry-Gbessia airport, which is of international standard.

22. INTERNATIONAL-MEMBERSHIP AND AGREEMENTS: Organization of African Unity (OAU); United Nations and most of its specialized agencies; International Bank for Reconstruction and Development (IBRD, commonly known as the World Bank); International Development Association (IDA); International Bauxite Association (IBA). Known defense treaties with Sierra Leone and Libya.

23. SECURITY FORCES: In early 1975 military forces numbered approximately 5,500 officers and men; organized into army of 5,000, air force of 300, and navy of 200. Army organized mainly as infantry with supporting armored and engineering units but utilized largely in civic action programs to aid national development. Security forces included variety of police services, totaling about 3,500 officers and men, and Cuban-style militia with personnel strength estimated variously at 5,000 to 15,000. Total paramilitary capability estimated at about 8,000 officers and men. All security forces dependent on foreign sources for equipment;

mainly supplied by Soviet Union, Czechoslovakia, People's Republic of China (PRC), and Cuba.

GUINEA

TABLE OF CONTENTS

LIST OF ILLUSTRATIONS

LIST OF TABLES

SECTION I. SOCIAL

CHAPTER 1

GENERAL CHARACTER OF THE SOCIETY

The Republic of Guinea entered the growing list of sovereign African states on October 2, 1958, after existing more than half a century as part of the French colonial empire. Its independence, viewed with pride as a great moment in African self-achievement, followed quickly after the referendum of September 28, 1958, when the Guinean people and the other members of the twelve-year-old French Union went to the polls to vote for or against continued association with France in the French Community proposed by General Charles de Gaulle. Alone among the former French African colonies, Guinea rejected membership in the new alliance and voted instead for complete independence. Behind the Guinean response lay not only accumulated resentments against colonial rule but also aspirations formed under French influence and political experience gained during the period of colonial reform after World War II (see ch. 2).

During the first years of its national life, the young republic served as a testing ground and showcase for anticolonialism and, as such, achieved a political importance far out of proportion to its strategic location, size, population, and the nature of its economy. Under the leadership of President Ahmed Sékou Touré, who was personally responsible for the people's decision to break away from France, the government and the sole political party—the two practically synonymous—sought to bring Guineans into an African form of political socialism and a collectivist economy.

By the early 1970s, however, the aura surrounding the country's anticipated success as a model of African political and economic development had lost much of its pristine attraction. Plagued by myriad economic difficulties, elements of local dissatisfaction, and a perennial climate of real or imagined security threats, Guinea in early 1975—sixteen years after independence—remained on the United Nations list of the world's twenty-five least developed countries.

Lying on the great bulge of West Africa between the seventh and twelfth parallels north of the equator, the Republic of Guinea covers an area of nearly 95,000 square miles. From its western extremity on the Atlantic Ocean the country curves inland in a broad, narrow southeasterly arc, sharing borders with Guinea-Bissau, Senegal, Mali, Ivory

1

Coast, Liberia, and Sierra Leone (see fig. 1). Maximum distances within the territorial boundaries are about 450 miles from west to east and approximately 350 miles from north to south.

The country is divided into four topographical regions (see ch. 3). In the west the region of Lower Guinea begins in a series of wide marshes that give way inland to a narrow coastal plain. In the adjoining region of Middle Guinea, foothills rise to an area of high central plateaus riven by narrow valleys that is known as the Fouta Djallon. Eastward the region of Upper Guinea is one of broad savannas, and in the Forest Region to the southeast the land becomes a mixed area of plains and mountains.

In 1972, according to the latest government census, the country was the home of approximately 5.1 million people, a population that was increasing at an annual rate generally estimated at 2.3 percent. Densities were greatest on the coast near the capital city of Conakry, in the central portion of the Fouta Djallon uplands, and in the southern part of the Forest Region.

Approximately twenty-four ethnic groups are represented within the Guinean population, but three of them constitute about 75 percent of the total (see ch. 4). Middle Guinea is the traditional domain of the Peul, the largest group; the Malinké predominate in Upper Guinea; and the Soussou are preponderant in Lower Guinea. French, a legacy of the country's colonial past, is the official language. In choosing a national language after independence, however, the government did not wish to offend any of the ethnic groups by giving one of the many spoken vernaculars preeminence over the others. The national languages, therefore, are the country's eight major vernaculars: Poular, Malinké, Soussou, Kissi, Guerzé, Toma, Coniagui, and Bassari.

Islam is the religion of 75 to 90 percent of the people, including nearly all members of the three major ethnic groups (see ch. 5). Membership in Christian churches—mainly Roman Catholic—was estimated in the mid-1970s at 30,000 to 40,000; the rest of the people adhered to locally based traditional religious beliefs, which had by no means disappeared among the adherents of the other religions. The Muslim community is growing at the expense of other faiths, particularly Christianity, which in Guinea is associated with white people, an attitude reinforced particularly by memories of the country's former colonial experience.

Except in the towns and at the sites of mining activity, the people are scattered in more than 4,000 agricultural villages. More than 80 percent of the active population is believed to be engaged in such rural activities as cultivation, herding, forestry, or fishing. The urban minority, which has shown marked increases since independence, is associated with the growing desire for wage employment. Its members work largely for the government in the civil service or the public enterprises (including commerce, transport, or the still embryonic manufacturing enterprises), but many are engaged in small-scale private activity. A few thousand are employed in mining and associated activity, a sector with strong growth

2

potential. During the 1960s political disillusionment and economic pressures had induced 600,000 to 1 million Guineans to depart their country in a search for better economic opportunities and living conditions (see ch. 8; ch. 10).

Guinea acquired its present territorial boundaries early in the twentieth century. Less than 100 years before, the French, pushing down from their older base in Senegal, had established trading posts on the estuaries of the swampy coast. In the mid-1800s the aggressive colonial policies of France's Second Empire added the motive of military and political expansion to commercial incentive. The advance into the interior in the succeeding decades was a record of military expeditions and treaty making with local chiefs. In one region after another, trading rights were converted into powers of protectorate and finally into outright French sovereignty.

The early French traders, soldiers, and civil officials encountered in this area a diverse collection of peoples. Beyond the similarities of village living patterns and subsistence farming with primitive tools, the population was divided ethnically and linguistically. Social organization varied from the highly stratified class system of the cattle-breeding Peul to the simple cultivating communities of some of the coastal groups.

Among the Peul and the Malinké a complex hierarchy of hereditary chiefs suggested the centralized and autocratic structure of the early West African kingdoms and empires. By contrast, on the coast and in the Forest Region the authority of the chief did not usually extend beyond the village or cluster of villages, and he was expected to act with the consensus of the community expressed through a council of elders.

Throughout the whole area the extended family was important, but the forms of its organization varied with marriage and residence patterns. Although most groups reckoned descent through the male line, some were matrilineal. Most of the people were nominally Muslim, but an indigenous pattern of locally based religious beliefs prevailed in the forests and on the coast.

Although strong local opposition was sometimes encountered, French rule eventually imposed a unity on this human diversity. Within the arbitrarily drawn boundaries of the colony, the people were not only members of this or that ethnic group or local community but also inhabitants of French Guinea and subjects of France. Not until after World War II was any concentrated effort made to develop the territory. The European impact—strongest on the coast—nonetheless was felt throughout the colony.

Under the French system of direct administration, the chiefs were replaced by the colonial bureaucracy or converted into its agents and charged with tax collection, labor and military recruitment, and the dispensation of justice in the spheres left to customary law. French, the language of the administration, had to be learned by any who aspired to service on the lower levels of the colonial bureaucracy open to Africans.

The export of agricultural products to world markets did not much affect the subsistence farming practices throughout the territory, but it caused the development of banana and coffee plantations, introduced wage labor, and commercialized the gathering of forest products. With these developments, money transactions were introduced into an economy in which goods and services formerly had been exchanged almost exclusively by barter or through the traditional forms of cooperation among kinsmen or obligation of serf or slave to master. The French ban on slavery and feudal tribute finally became effective and, although barter continued to predominate in the villages, the impersonal money nexus permanently undermined the traditional economic relationships.

The decisive years in the formation of modern Guinea, however, came after World War II. During that period internal and external events coincided to transform the territory into a national entity. This process, in which Guinea acquired a political personality and a leadership that was to propel it into independence, was a particular expression of the general rise of African nationalism.

Throughout Black Africa the basic nationalist motive was—and is—self-rule and equality with the former colonial powers. In Guinea that motive was to be translated into political attitudes, concepts, and goals that ultimately not only separated it from France but also made it a spokesman for nationalism among the other emerging African states. The clearest and most persuasive voice was that of Sékou Touré. The principles he advocated primarily for Africa and generally for all underdeveloped areas were: unqualified rejection of all vestiges of colonial control; alertness against what he saw as the threat of "neocolonial" domination by developed Western nations employing economic means; "positive neutralism" in the field of international relations, which tended to be more infused with indignation against the West than with doubts about communist countries; and the creation of an economically self-sufficient union of African states.

Power generated in Europe had made Guinea a colony. Not surprisingly, the concepts and organizational techniques that were employed by the young Guineans who led the country to independence were also European. But they were acquired under the influence of the French left-wing labor confederations and political parties that became active in French West Africa after World War II. The early labor unions were modeled on the French confederations with which most of them were affiliated. The strongest proved to be the communist-influenced General Confederation of Labor, and it was as leaders of the union's Guinean branch that Sékou Touré and his closest associates first gained a mass following. With the founding in 1947 of the Democratic Party of Guinea (Parti Démocratique de Guinée—PDG), they had a political instrument that would reach beyond the town-centered membership of the unions into the scattered and generally agricultural population.

4

By early 1975, after more than sixteen years in office as the republic's first and only head-of-state, President Touré remained the undeniable center of all political, social, and economic authority. As head-of-government and leader of the country's sole political party, his voice has remained persistent in exhorting the people to strive for national development, an effort he has chosen to label the "Guinean revolution."

The theories, goals, and methods of the PDG, which has not tolerated any political opposition, touch every sphere of public and personal life. They are projected directly into the community by the party committees in the towns and villages and indirectly by the government and numerous parapolitical mass organizations in which party members occupy all the key positions. President Touré, in his dual position of authority, has impressed his philosophies and personality on the whole structure. As products of a particular experience of colonial rule, he and his colleagues reveal in what they have done and hope to do the selective utilization of European and African elements for national purpose.

A number of outside observers have likened the discipline of the PDG—and the conception of its relationship to the government and all other Guinean institutions—to those of the communist parties in various other countries of the world. President Touré, however, describes the rule of the PDG as a popular dictatorship based on the will of the whole people and contrasts it with the class dictatorship of the communist states. In rejecting the Marxist concept of class struggle during the first decade of independence as inapplicable to Guinea, he asserted that he and the PDG were not interested in theoretical doctrines but rather in practical needs. By the early 1970s, however, his opposition to the principle of class struggle had lessened as he warned the people that a fifth column (agents of foreign interests) in Guinea represented a serious threat to the country's revolutionary goals (see ch. 8; ch. 13).

Since independence the party-state has sought to minimize the political and social implications of ethnic differences by exhorting the people to strive for national unity as Guineans rather than as competitive members of particular ethnic groups. In a contest that has been principally one between the local communities and the central government, national leaders have made decided inroads in their assault on the traditional social system (see ch. 5). Increasingly, traditional functions have been taken over by elements of the governing regime, generally lifting the individual out of a world in which family and kinship ties formerly defined his place in society and placing him in one where new group loyalties have assumed a position of primacy and where such values as education, skills, and national solidarity are repeatedly asserted. The national leadership, which has the power to reward its friends and punish its enemies, has succeeded in involving almost everyone in one way or another. Such pressures have been particularly successful among the young.

Nonetheless, in early 1975 there were indications that obvious differences in language, custom, and religion continued to exist to some degree in everyday affairs, despite party efforts to dispel them. This appeared to be particularly true of the uneducated masses of subsistence cultivators whose isolation defied widespread ethnic interaction. Although the PDG extols national unity as the answer to Guinea's problems, the traditional assurance arising from membership in the family and larger kin group remains the subsistence cultivators' major guarantee against economic disaster. Moreover, traditional ethnic alliances with peoples in neighboring countries—ties that for centuries have ignored territorial boundaries—complicate the efforts to achieve national unity.

Before independence in 1958 Guinea was regarded as the most favorably endowed territory of French West Africa in agricultural, mineral, and hydroelectric potential. Relatively little had been done, however, to develop this potential, and the difficult conditions under which Guinea had obtained its independence had brought new setbacks, requiring an entirely fresh start. In the wake of France's immediate withdrawal of assistance, the new republic's short-term economic difficulties were overcome to some degree by foreign aid from other countries, notably communist states. Economic well-being, however, was short lived (see ch. 10).

In the early years of sovereignty, initial progress toward the goal of economic autonomy was made through the pervasive efforts of the party and government machinery—a system that, in its political context, was described by many observers as one of the best organized in Africa. The pervasive government machinery was less effective, however, in exercising its far-reaching economic functions (see ch. 12). The proclaimed objective was to organize the economy along noncapitalist lines with state control of production and trade.

In early 1975 satisfaction of the country's long-range economic needs was yet to be resolved. The rate of economic growth since independence was thought to have barely kept pace with the growth of population. Agricultural production for the official market had stagnated, and the processing industries installed by foreign aid were mostly operating below capacity. Moreover, the government had to a large extent lost control over the level of economic activity and had been unable to curb inflation and maintain the value of its currency. Widespread rural underemployment, limited urban employment, an extreme shortage of consumer goods, and a flourishing black market and smuggling trade were all evidence of the country's economic malaise.

As an alternative the government has become more and more reliant on exploitation of Guinea's rich bauxite resources, estimated by some experts as surpassing in size and purity all of the world's known deposits except those of Australia and Brazil. Typical of the pragmatic policies adopted by the regime of President Touré, exploitation of the bauxite has been made possible by resorting to capitalistic methods involving agreements with foreign investors whose companies have provided the

6

technological and financial assistance required. In early 1975 similar plans to exploit large untapped iron ore deposits in southeast Guinea were being negotiated (see ch. 12).

The character of Guinean society is marked to a great degree by the social and economic distinction that exists between citizens in positions of authority and those who are not. High social status, prestige, and privilege come from participation in the government, the political party, and the parapolitical mass organizations. At the other end of the societal spectrum are the Guinean masses, who exist largely at a subsistence level. Contrasting patterns of living, conditioned largely by divergent economic means, have yet to experience the promise of balance inherent in the goals of the "Guinean revolution" (see ch. 6).

Since independence the major lines of the republic's foreign policy have generally been determined by pragmatic considerations, a situation generated largely by the need for external assistance (see ch. 9). Moreover, Guinea's relations with other countries have been affected by actions that the government has often regarded as threats to its security. In periods of internal crisis, President Touré has imposed a policy of extreme isolationism. In contrast his foreign policy has been more outward looking when domestic conditions have been relatively stable. For many foreign nations, particularly neighboring African states, the "Guinean revolution" that had raised such hopes when it was initiated in 1958 had by 1975 lost much of its idealistic attraction.

CHAPTER 2

HISTORICAL SETTING

The region of West Africa constituting the present Republic of Guinea has been inhabited since well before the Christian Era. The earliest dwellers included the ancestors of some coastal and forest peoples of modern Guinea. The forebears of the present principal ethnic groups, the Malinké and Peul, came in considerable numbers, however, only after A.D. 1000. The origins of the Soussou, the third major group, were still uncertain in the mid-1970s (see ch. 4).

The Malinké and the Peul have both played major roles in the history of West Africa in an area far larger than the territory of the modern state. These two peoples attained a high degree of social development, and both created large, centralized political entities. In the case of the Malinké, political control was expanded into an extensive empire known as Mali, which at the peak of its power in the fourteenth century encompassed much of the western Sudan (see Glossary) savanna, including the savanna region of the present republic. Guineans consider their country's entry into history to have begun with that empire. Much later, in the latter 1800s, the Malinké of Guinea helped forge another empire under the leadership of Samory Touré, now a national hero. This empire, however, was short-lived, being destroyed by the French during the 1890s.

The Peul became a major part of Guinean history only in the late seventeenth century after they conquered the Fouta Djallon, the mountain region that takes up most of Middle Guinea, and subsequently established there an independent theocratic Muslim state (see ch. 3). That state maintained its independence until the end of the 1800s, when sovereignty in the Fouta Djallon passed into the hands of the French.

The formation of Guinea as a distinct political entity was made without the participation of any of the peoples of the modern state in the decision. It stemmed from the European division of Africa during the great power scramble for territory of the late 1800s and, more immediately, from the carving up by the French of their West African conquests into administrative units of convenience. For over half a century thereafter the French governed Guinea, utilizing amenable indigenous chiefs (who became little more than French agents) to assist them. At the same time the French pursued a general policy of imparting French culture on the theory that at some date in the future the colony would merge with Metropolitan France into a single community.

World War II engendered new ideas and brought demands for greater

9

particpation by the indigenous population in Guinean affairs. In 1946 a beginning of local representation was offered—to all French Black Africa—through membership in the newly established French Union. Thereby Guinea and the other French overseas territories became integral parts of the French Republic. World War II also brought a growth of political parties. Among these was the Democratic Party of Guinea (Parti Démocratique de Guinée—PDG), which evolved, under the leadership of Ahmed Sékou Touré from the early 1950s, into a mass organization having wide popular support.

In 1956 France made further concessions to its former colonies that implied the eventual granting of autonomy. In the following year elections in Guinea for a territorial assembly having new internal legislative powers placed de facto control in the hands of the PDG, which had a large majority in the assembly. Then, in 1958, France offered a new relationship to its overseas territories in the proposed French Community (Communauté Française), an association of the members of the French Republic in a federation of equals. Guinea's leaders, however, tended to favor a confederal setup, which would include a strong federated West African entity that could deal with Metropolitan France more effectively than its individual members. They also wished that the basic right to national independence be guaranteed.

The French president, General Charles de Gaulle, refused to agree to a strong federation. More important, he strongly implied that independence would mean total severance from the community. Faced by rejection of what were considered reasonable requests, the Guinean people, led by the PDG, voted for independence in September 1958. France immediately dissociated Guinea from the community, and the former colonial territory began a new course as the Republic of Guinea.

PREHISTORY IN GUINEA

Through the mid-1970s only limited archaeological studies had been made of the area of West Africa constituting modern Guinea. Stone tools had been found in several localities in the country and were identified as belonging to Late Stone Age cultures, but few of the sites had been dated. Styles of workmanship indicated that at least some of the early toolmakers had probably come from the Sahara region to the north and northeast. The time of this movement was unknown, but it was speculated that changing living conditions brought on by the gradual desiccation of the Sahara, which had become quite noticeable by the third millennium B.C., were an important factor in the migration.

By A.D. 1000 peoples in the coastal region of present-day Lower Guinea, believed to have been mainly speakers of West Atlantic languages at that time, were generally cultivators (see ch. 4). These groups experienced little pressure from outside their own communities, and the development of political organization was minimal. Mostly they lived in small, independent or loosely associated villages and hamlets.

The staple crop was rice, which had been introduced from the Niger River valley sometime during the first millennium A.D. Fishing was also an important occupation for some, and cured fish and salt obtained by solar evaporation were probably trade items.

In the forested areas behind the coastal zone, in parts of the Fouta Djallon, and in the Forest Region of modern Guinea, other speakers of West Atlantic languages and presumably some Mandé languages roamed as hunters and gatherers. By A.D. 1000 many such groups had settled in isolated farming villages in forest clearings, where they also practiced slash-and-burn agriculture. Their adoption of a sedentary life had been encouraged by the new knowledge of iron smelting and forging that brought replacement of earlier stone farming implements by iron ones and made cultivation easier and more productive. As in coastal areas there was little stimulus for the development of central political controls, which was further discouraged by the difficulty of communications.

In contrast to the coastal and forest areas, the open land of the savanna was conducive to the early development of settled agricultural communities. During the first centuries of the Christian Era, technological advances in agriculture resulted in the growth of such communities in the broad savanna zone between the upper Niger River basin and the southern limits of the Sahara—a zone that includes the savanna region of modern Upper Guinea. This growth was accompanied by the gradual development of more complex societies in which social classes became differentiated and highly organized political institutions appeared that evolved into hereditary kingdoms.

HISTORICAL ANTECEDENTS

Important in the rise of centralized kingdoms in the savanna area was the expansion of trans-Saharan trade, between Mediterranean North Africa and the western Sudan, that occurred after the introduction of the camel at about the beginning of the Christian Era. Certain caravan terminals in the western Sahel zone on the Sahara's southern edge developed into commercial centers. Control of the trade through these points—principally the export of gold and slaves to North Africa in exchange for salt and some other commodities—led by about the middle of the first millennium A.D. to the emergence in this area of a powerful black kingdom peopled or dominated by the Soninké, who belong like the Malinké of modern Guinea to the Manding group.

During the next several centuries this kingdom absorbed or reduced to tributary status neighboring states, including some Berber groups in the southern Sahara. It expanded in the process to a politically well-organized, militarily powerful, and economically wealthy empire. Generally known as Ghana (although apparently called Wagadu by the Soninké), the empire covered a large area roughly northeast of modern Guinea. Its borders did not encompass any present Guinean territory, but the empire's influence certainly extended at the peak of its power in

11

the eleventh century well into the savanna area of the modern Guinean state (see fig. 2).

The decline of Ghana started abruptly in the latter eleventh century. In the 1050s Berber groups to the north were swept up by the Almoravid movement—a militant Muslim religious community and their supporters in Berber West Africa. Fired in part by Islamizing zeal and perhaps to a greater degree by visions of Ghana's riches, the Almoravids invaded the empire and subdued it in 1076. After several decades the Soninké regained control, but the imperial power had been weakened, and many of the vassal states broke away. Among them was the kingdom of Soso, lying to the south of Ghana, which expanded aggressively throughout the twelfth century. Soso was decisively defeated in the early 1200s, however, by the rising Malinké state of Mali, which soon made itself the successor empire to Ghana.

Oral traditions have placed the origin of Mali on the upper Niger River in about the eighth century A.D. Growth into an empire began, however, only some three centuries later when the emergence of the Bouré goldfields (on the headwaters of the Bakoye River in present-day Upper Guinea) as the major source of gold and the extension of trade routes southward to the Niger provided favorable economic conditions.

The expansion of Mali dates from Sundiata (ruled 1230–55), who defeated the Soso kingdom in 1235 and founded the empire. Northward, control was obtained of the trans-Saharan trading centers, and over time the empire's boundaries were pushed westward, eventually reaching the Atlantic Ocean and including within them approximately the northern half of modern Guinea. The height of power was reached in the fourteenth century under Mansa Musa, who reigned from 1307 to 1332.

Toward the end of the fourteenth century, weakness and dissension within the regime led to a decline of central authority. Vassal states gradually threw off Mali's sovereignty and acquired part of its territory. During the fifteenth century disintegration continued, and a large area was lost to Songhai, formerly a tributary state along the middle Niger River, which expanded into an empire, largely at Mali's expense, during this period. Songhai continued to expand in the 1500s to become the largest unified state in the western Sudan until establishment of French West Africa (Afrique Occidentale Française) at the beginning of the twentieth century.

In the sixteenth century Songhai in turn was weakened by relatively constant warfare and the problems of dynastic succession. During that century gold and slaves began moving toward new outlets on the Atlantic coast as European traders entered the market (see The European Arrival and Its Aftermath to 1900, this ch.). The possibilities of increasingly declining trade across the Sahara caused concern in Morocco, which attacked and conquered Songhai in 1591. Moorish controls proved ineffective, and political disintegration of the empire occurred rapidly. From then until the nineteenth century the western Sudan was

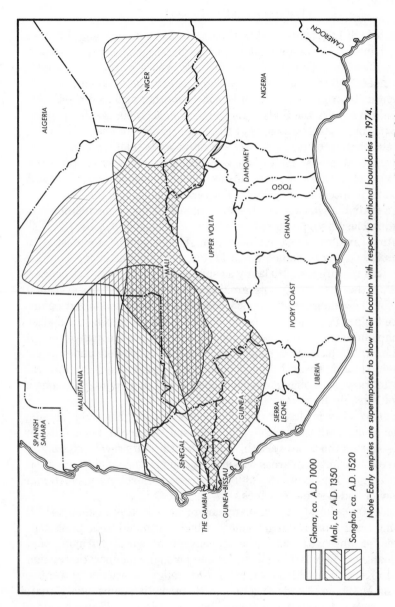

Source: Adapted from Roland Oliver and J. D. Fage, *A Short History of Africa*, Baltimore, 1962, p. 87.

Figure 2. Early West African Empires

Note–Early empires are superimposed to show their location with respect to national boundaries in 1974.

Ghana, ca. A.D. 1000

Mali, ca. A.D. 1350

Songhai, ca. A.D. 1520

characterized politically by small, frequently warring states. New migrations into the Guinea area resulted, perhaps the most significant for the modern state being the arrival of the Peul in the seventeenth century (see The Peul Islamic Theocracy, this ch.).

THE SPREAD OF ISLAM

Islam, which was to become in time a binding force among different ethnic groups in the western Sudan, probably reached Ghana about, or not long after, the Arab conquest of North Africa in the early eighth century A.D. It did not arrive as a proselytizing force, however, but as a coincidental factor in the efforts of Berber and other arabized merchants to expand trade with the Sudan. By the year A.D. 1000, Muslim traders were living in separate sections of the main trading towns. They were permitted complete freedom of worship, and some actually held important court posts. At the time Islam appears to have had little general appeal and spread principally as a class religion of the aristocracy; it had been adopted by the rulers of several small kingdoms—although the ruler of Ghana was apparently not then a Muslim. Some members of the trading class had also accepted it.

The Almoravid conquest of Ghana brought conversion of almost all of the Soninké. Ghana remained powerful for some time after the Soninké dynasty was restored, and Islam was spread among the subject peoples still within the empire. No reversion occurred when Mali succeeded Ghana, for the ruling Keita dynasty had already been Islamized before the state began its expansion. Islam was not officially spread until after establishment of the empire, when the country took on the appearance of a Muslim state. Koranic schools and mosques flourished under royal sponsorship, and several rulers made the pilgrimage to Mecca. Ambassadors were exchanged with Morocco, and that country became a center of learning for scholars from Mali.

Islam was also professed by the rulers of Songhai, and Muslim practices continued to spread. The diffusion occurred peacefully in general—during the time of the three empires the state rarely attempted to enforce conformity. In areas outside the main towns its dissemination was carried out principally through the personal efforts of those African traders who had become Muslims.

The acceptance of Islam at first appears to have been as a belief parallel to existing traditional religious beliefs, which continued to be practiced. This was in line with the African concept of social harmony and accommodation. Eventually Islam became for many a syncretic religion combining Koranic teachings and indigenous religious practice. After the decline of Mali and the destruction of Songhai, it seems likely that, although Koranic teaching remained influential at courts of some residual states, the religious practices of rulers and chiefs tended gradually to give greater emphasis to traditional observances. Many individuals nominally Muslim, mainly in agricultural areas but also in towns, apparently reverted completely to indigenous religious beliefs.

Efforts to enforce the doctrines and practices of Islam to the exclusion of other religious beliefs began in the modern Guinea region with the jihads (see Glossary) of the Peul theocracy founded in the Fouta Djallon in the 1700s. During the following century Islam attained its greatest militancy in the jihad of Al Haj Omar in the savanna area of Guinea, which started about 1850, and from about 1880 in that of Samory, which encompassed most of eastern Guinea and continued until the French conquest in the 1890s.

THE PEUL ISLAMIC THEOCRACY

The plateau areas of the Fouta Djallon have long offered attractive grazing land for the nomadic Peul pastoralist, and during the early centuries of the second millennium A.D. some Peul groups migrated to this region. The historical importance of the Peul in Guinean history dates, however, only from the seventeenth century, when considerable numbers arrived in the Fouta Djallon from Macina (Massina), a state in the upper Niger River basin.

The Peul newcomers, then only nominally Muslims, were accompanied by devout religious teachers. By about 1725 the teachers had converted the Peul into strong believers, as well as converting some of the surrounding Dialonké, a branch of the Soussou. In that year a jihad was launched under the cleric Ibrahim Musa against other nonbelievers. Despite early successes the jihad was at the point of failure when Ibrahim Musa died in 1751. He was succeeded by Ibrahim Sori, a secular military leader, who managed finally to establish firm Peul control over the Fouta Djallon and some surrounding territory in the latter 1770s.

A theocratic governmental system was instituted by the Peul under which the state, divided into semiautonomous provinces, was ruled by a Muslim aristocracy under an *almamy* (a military, religious, and spiritual leader) chosen by a select body of clerics and acclaimed by a general assembly of free Peul. Sori's early dictatorial attitude when war leader had caused concern and led to selection of a descendant of Ibrahim Musa as *almamy*. After Sori's victories in the 1760s, however, he ruled jointly with Ibrahim Musa until his death in 1784. The system of having joint *almamy* was then continued, and a sometimes bloody struggle ensued between the two groups of descendants until agreement was reached in 1837 for each *almamy* to rule for two years alternately. Refusal to hand over power resulted from time to time in further dissension, however, and this situation was not finally resolved until the French seized control of the Fouta Djallon in 1896 and a pro-French *almamy* was elected in the following year.

Although not particularly strong militarily, the Peul theocratic state substantially influenced some of the peoples around it. The practice of government based on Islamic legal and ethical principles offered reassurances that law and justice would be relatively uniformly applied.

15

This tended to encourage trade through the Fouta Djallon, which appears to have become a crossroads for traffic between the forest zone and the savanna.

THE EUROPEAN ARRIVAL AND ITS AFTERMATH TO 1900

Early Activities to the Mid-1800s

The first European explorers to reach the area of modern Guinea were Portuguese, who sailed along the coast in the mid-1400s. The voyages were part of a long-range exploration plan of Prince Henry the Navigator that included as one goal the bypassing of Muslim North Africa in order to secure direct access to trade in West Africa, particularly to the sources of gold. Little gold was found on the early voyages, but West African captives were taken to Portugal for training to assist in future explorations. Portuguese merchants saw in the captives, rather, a source of slave labor, and exploitation of the market was actively under way by the latter 1400s.

During the 1500s British and French business ventures occasionally sought trade along the West African coast; but by the latter part of the century the plundering of Spanish shipping from the New World proved more profitable, and West African trade was left largely to the Portuguese. The principal exception was filling the need for slaves for the new West Indian plantations, which resulted in some British and French activity. During the century Portuguese trading posts were established at various points along the Guinean coast, but few records of their early operations remain. It is known, however, that from sometime in the 1500s slaves and ivory were being sent out via the Rio Nunez estuary.

The seventeenth century was a period of intense commercial competition between the Dutch, British, and French. Much of Portuguese authority along the West African coast disappeared during this time. The Dutch, initially strong, were eliminated from that coast by about the end of the century, and the area from present-day Sierra Leone to north of Senegal was generally under French domination.

French and other European commercial interest was centered on Senegal in the 1700s. The coast of modern Guinea, greatly indented and difficult to navigate, offered little attraction, and throughout the century trade conducted there was largely in the hands of stateless Portuguese and Portuguese half-castes who had settled permanently and had become part of the indigenous societies. British-French wars from about midcentury brought loss of important French settlements in Senegal. They were restored in 1783 only to be lost again during the Napoleonic Wars (1793–1815), which also brought a complete halt to French trade with West Africa.

The Treaty of Paris of 1814 returned France's West African holdings and established equal French trading rights with the British and the Portuguese. Until the mid-1800s, however, British economic influence was dominant all along the coast of Guinea, and there was considerable sentiment in Sierra Leone for annexation of the coastal zone, but the idea received little support from the home government. In 1818 the British obtained the Iles de Los by treaties with local chiefs, although for other purposes, and continued to hold them until 1904. In 1816 the British had also attempted, unsuccessfully, to establish political and trade ties with the Fouta Djallon.

During the early decades of the 1800s, French influence and French trading activities developed slowly in the coastal area of modern Guinea. Agreements were made with local chiefs for trading privileges in exchange for payment of fees. Among the early agreements was one with the Landouma, a people living upriver from the Rio Nunez estuary, on which a French trading post had been established. Another was concluded with the neighboring coastal Nalou. Most arrangements were made directly by private traders, although some agreements or treaties may have involved official participation.

In 1837 a French mission recommended that official French trading activities be limited to north of the Casamance River in southern Senegal. Two years later, however, a new Landouma chief raised trading fees; the traders refused to pay, and their houses were destroyed. British and French warships arrived, and the customary fees were reinstated. But trouble over fees continued during the next ten years, and in 1849 a French ship bombarded Boké, the principal Landouma center. This resulted in local acceptance of French sovereignty, the first such instance in the modern Guinea region.

Exports during these years consisted of various locally produced goods and of hides and some gold that came from the Fouta Djallon. Slaves were also an item of trade. The slave trade was made illegal by the French in 1818, and in 1831 France further allowed British naval vessels to stop and search suspected slave ships. The trade was officially abolished in 1848; but the many inlets and estuaries of the Guinea coast offered excellent hiding places for slave ships, and the trade continued until about 1865.

The French Conquest of Guinea (1850–1900)

Until the mid-1800s French power in West Africa was largely centered in Saint-Louis and the Ile de Gorée in Senegal, other French holdings being little more than trading areas occupied or used by French merchants. There was little enthusiasm in France for the acquisition of colonies although, after the accession of Napoleon III in 1848, the government announced that it would actively promote the development of trade in Senegal and extension of French influence toward the interior.

In 1854 Captain (later General) Louis Faidherbe arrived in Senegal as governor. Faidherbe was convinced that access to the Sudan hinterland and its trade and French control of such access were vital to the development of a viable French commerce in the region. This aim, which he pursued throughout his long tenure (1854–61 and 1863–65), had an important influence on the military officers who later led the way in the acquisition of the French West African colonies.

Faidherbe's arrival coincided with a period of militant Islamic revival and the formation in the western Sudan of the Toucouleur Empire of Al Haj Omar. Originally from the Fouta Toro, Al Haj Omar had established himself at Dinguiraye in present-day Upper Guinea in 1850. Using this as a base, he organized a large military force, which included many Toucouleur people, and began the conquest, partly by conversion and partly by arms, of native states lying to the north and northeast. Although Al Haj Omar appears to have been interested in cooperation with the French, recognizing the value of their trade to provide him with arms, Faidherbe perceived militant Islamism as a threat to his own goal and the safety of the coastal settlements. In 1857 his forces halted the Muslim advance at Médina (at which a French fort had been built in 1855) on the upper Sénégal River, and Al Haj Omar's main thrust then turned eastward. Al Haj Omar was killed in 1864, but his son Ahmadu continued to hold areas of eastern Guinea until the Toucouleur Empire was defeated by the French in 1893.

The French drive toward the interior of West Africa ended for a time, however, when Faidherbe left Senegal in 1865. His immediate successor favored extension of activities along the present Guinea coast, and in 1866 a French military detachment was sent to garrison Boké; the following year a military post was established at Benti. French political control of the coastal area of Guinea was strengthened, meanwhile, when the ruler of Forécariah placed himself and his people under French suzerainty and protection in 1865, and similar actions were taken by the Landouma and Nalou in treaties in 1866.

During this time in Metropolitan France, Napoleon III's Second Empire was experiencing increasing financial problems. There seemed little profit in pursuing an active policy of annexation of colonial territories, and a new governor sent to Senegal in 1869 was instructed to emphasize the peaceful consolidation of trade. The French interest in colonial expansion was further weakened by defeat in the Franco-Prussian War of 1870 to 1871; it remained largely dormant until the end of the decade.

The 1880s—the decade in which the so-called scramble for Africa by the principal European powers started—and the 1890s brought a major division of West Africa between Great Britain and France. Individuals directly involved in this action included several French military officers in West Africa who were imbued by Faidherbe's vision of empire and who conducted campaigns and political intrigues frequently without prior approval from the civilian authorities in France. Moreover, in contrast to British goals, which were for a long time basically concerned with the protection of economic spheres of interest, French operations were in fact military conquests aimed at securing colonial territory.

18

The goal of these French officers ruled out any accommodation with indigenous states other than as a temporary expedient. In the Guinea area it resulted in a major and lengthy conflict with the powerful Manding Empire of Samory Touré, a Malinké, that began in the mid-1880s and ended only in 1898. In the early 1800s the Manding descendants of the Mali Empire inhabited a large area centering generally in the old Manding heartland between Siguiri in modern Guinea and Bamako in Mali. They were only loosely organized politically but possessed an underlying feeling of national cohesion and a pride in their history stemming from the glories of the Mali Empire. By about 1870 several small Manding states had been welded together by Samory, a former trader and a convert to Islam, who set up his capital at Bissandougou, near present-day Kérouané.

By the mid-1880s Samory's empire covered most of present-day Upper Guinea and the Forest Region, as well as parts of Mali and Ivory Coast. In 1885 the French attempted to occupy the Bouré gold-producing region held by Samory but were forced to withdraw. The next year, however, Samory signed a treaty of friendship with France in which he gave up all territory (mainly in Guinea) north of the Niger River. Although subsequently refuted by Samory, the French claimed that he had accepted a protectorate status; this turned out to be an important point in later British-French negotiations and in British decisions not to help Samory.

In the latter 1880s French penetration into Guinea was essentially peaceful. The British and the French governments, their economies and their French West African trade seriously affected by an international recession, had little interest in military ventures and sought to resolve colonial problems by compromise. During this time Samory, concerned over future French ambitions, approached the British for a mutual agreement. Merchants in Sierra Leone favored collaboration as offering possibilities for access to trade in the interior, but Samory's offer appears to have been given little consideration in Great Britain. In 1889 a British-French boundaries agreement established an interior demarcation line for Sierra Leone, in effect leaving the western Sudan interior to the French.

The relative lull in French West African military operations after 1885 was broken by an attack on the Toucouleur Empire in 1889. The attack was mounted by one of the so-called Sudan officers, French military men who during the next decade often took matters into their own hands but whose military exploits brought them national acclaim from a public that became increasingly colony-minded during the 1890s. As part of their effort to conquer the western Sudan interior for France, an attempt was made to induce the king of Sikasso to attack Samory's empire, which was seen as a major obstacle to their goal. Samory, upon learning of this, repudiated his earlier treaty with the French. The French then advanced into Guinea and took Bissandougou in 1891. A Samory offer to cede his empire to the British in return for their help was of no avail, and a bloody, destructive, and societally highly disruptive war was fought during which his forces finally withdrew eastward completely out of Guinea. The war ended only with the capitulation of Samory in 1898.

Modern African attitudes toward Samory have been described as ambiguous by West African scholars. His earlier conquests and especially his later resistance to the French advance are remembered for the great suffering, and in some places the considerable depopulation, they caused, which included selling captives into slavery to obtain funds for arms and cavalry horses. There is little question, however, of his military and administrative abilities, and he has been given great credit for his struggle to maintain independence. In modern Guinea Samory is popularly regarded as a national hero and as a symbol of resistance to colonialism.

A significant feature of Samory's empire was the spread of Islam among the Manding and other peoples included in it. Samory himself originally held indigenous religious beliefs (although his ancestors had at one time been Muslims) but was converted to Islam, probably around the mid-1800s. His Islamic belief was to some extent pragmatic, and it was not until about 1880, several years after acquiring broad political power, that he began a jihad to convert unbelievers. During the succeeding years, however, Islamic practices were introduced throughout the area under his control, and by the empire's demise in 1898 a substantial number of individuals had been brought into the faith.

Formation of French Guinea

Initially all French settlements in West Africa were under the authority of Senegal, but in 1845 French possessions were divided into Senegal, having its administrative center in Saint-Louis, and Rivières du Sud, which was placed under a naval commander in chief with headquarters at Ile de Gorée. The latter's authority included all French centers (at that time coastal only in nature) from Ile de Gorée to Gabon.

In 1859 Senegal assumed direct administration of the Rivières du Sud colony. The following year the Peul in the Fouta Djallon ceded rights to a large area around Boké (actually occupied by the Landouma but tributary to the Peul). Some twenty years elapsed, however, before the French officially secured a foothold in the interior of Guinea. This was effected through a treaty of friendship, concerned mainly with French trading rights, concluded with the almamy in the Fouta Djallon in 1881. In return the French engaged to pay agreed upon fees on a regular basis. This treaty in fact established a protectorate over the Fouta Djallon, although effective implementation of this provision did not occur until after the mid-1890s.

In 1882 Rivières du Sud was again made a separate political unit under a lieutenant governor who was, however, subordinate to the governor of Senegal. In 1890 greater administrative autonomy was acquired by the colony, which included Dahomey and Ivory Coast. Separate budgets and staff were authorized, the latter to be located in Conakry. A lieutenant governor remained in charge, but he had direct access to the government in Paris and was only required to report to Senegal. The colony was also given responsibility for the Fouta Djallon protectorate. Then in 1891 an independent governor was authorized, and the colony was officially designated French Guinea and Dependencies. Two years later, the holdings in Dahomey and Ivory Coast were separated from the new political unit.

In 1893 the colony of French Guinea actually included only the Maritime Region and the Fouta Djallon protectorate (still nominal, although a new treaty in 1888 had reaffirmed its existence). This was only about one-half of the area encompassed by the Republic of Guinea in 1975 (see fig. 3). A firm hold existed only over the coastal zone, except for the Iles de Los, which were in British hands.

The 1888 treaty failed to provide continued payment of fees to the *almamy*, causing resentment. Upon the death of the incumbent *almamy* in 1889, a civil war erupted between pro- and anti-French chiefs—the latter suspected supporters of Samory—over his successor. Disturbances continued during the next several years until finally a French military contingent occupied Timbo, capital of the Peul state, in 1896. A new pro-French *almamy* was elected, and a treaty, signed by the *almamy* with the French in early 1897, gave France effective sovereignty. A French resident administrator was appointed, and the French acquired the right to set up civil and military posts freely. Local chiefs continued to be elected, but they had to have the approval of French administrators, and they ruled with French advice. The treaty also established local taxes in the amount of two francs per head or ten francs per household. This head tax was later extended to the rest of the colony.

The area to the east of the Fouta Djallon was the province of the French Sudan military administration in the 1890s but was not brought under effective control until after the expulsion of Samory's forces. In 1895 a section along the Sierra Leone frontier corresponding roughly to the present-day Faranah Administrative Region was transferred to Guinea. Most of the remainder of present-day Upper Guinea was detached from French Sudan and added to the colony in 1899.

In 1892 a frontier agreement with Liberia had accorded the colony a considerable area in the Forest Region of modern Guinea. Operations against Samory led to French entry into the area, however, and it was in effect made part of Guinea in 1899, organized as a separate military district; confirmation of French possession occurred in a French-Liberian agreement in 1911. The various ethnic groups in the forest resisted the French advance, and it was not until 1911 that the last group, the Toma, was pacified.

The French possessions in the western Sudan, including the new colony of French Guinea, were grouped together into one large administrative unit, French West Africa, in 1895. French Guinea remained a part of that body until establishment of the French Union in 1946 (see French Rule to World War II; From World War II to Independence, this ch.).

FRENCH RULE TO WORLD WAR II

French Colonial Policy

Public discussion of colonial policy in France during the latter 1800s and into the twentieth century revolved around two principal concepts, one labeled assimilation, the other association. The assimilation policy was based on the assumption that all men are equal and thus should be treated alike and reflected the universalist and egalitarian ideas of the French Revolution. At the same time, however, the idea of universalism was tied to French culture, which proponents of assimilation indirectly maintained was superior to all others. Thus in practice assimilation meant the extension of the French language and French institutions, laws, and customs to the people of the colony.

In contrast, under the concept of association Africans were to keep their own customs—insofar as these were compatible with French aims—and different systems of laws and institutions would be applied in the colonies to the French and the Africans. Advocates of the concept left no doubt, however, that the French were to be the rulers and the Africans the subjects.

In actual practice colonial policy as applied in Guinea (and other West African colonies) was one neither of assimilation nor of association. The assimilation concept of French cultural superiority was embraced by most colonial administrators, who saw themselves as the instruments of a civilizing mission and felt that the African subject should be happy to accept the free gift of French culture. The idea of equal citizenship implied in assimilation was not in general accepted, however; and although provision for citizenship was made, the procedure and requirements resulted in its being granted to relatively few individuals.

The concept of association also soon became a hollow term describing French-developed procedures that increasingly relegated the African to an inferior status and concentrated more and more power in French hands. Some colonial administrators did advocate continuance of the traditional chieftainships, but nothing came of this. Early in the colonial era chiefs who opposed the French were eliminated, and others willing to accept a subordinate status were appointed. The administrative authority of such chiefs was reduced to the execution of French orders, and their judicial powers were curtailed and brought under French supervision. Parallel with their loss of temporal power occurred a diminution of their religious role and prestige. Eventually, except in

22

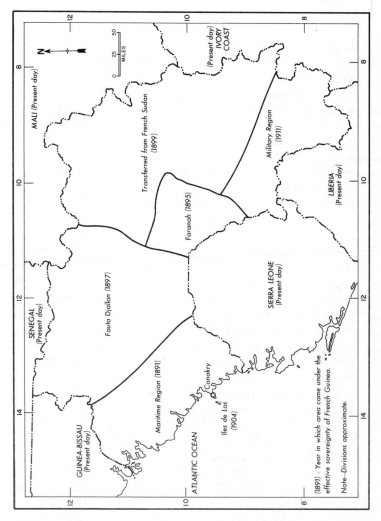

Figure 3. Guinea, Formation of the Colony of French Guinea

23

remote villages, the French ruled either directly or through chiefs who functioned essentially as French agents.

French African colonial policy in general was best described as highly pragmatic. The real aim of the colonial administration was to integrate the colony into an imperial system that would bring the greatest benefit and glory to the mother country. There was no change in this policy from the late nineteenth century to World War II as businessmen and bureaucrats developed vested interests in the system and successfully resisted any real liberalization of policies, despite the agitation against colonial exploitation that developed in France in the 1930s.

In general, French public opinion was too preoccupied most of the time with domestic affairs to take great interest in colonial matters. These were the special domain of the bureaucracy under the Ministry of the Colonies, which administered all overseas possessions except Algeria (treated as part of Metropolitan France) and the protectorates of Morocco, Tunisia, and the Levant. The only concessions made by bureaucracy to liberal public opinion were minor reforms that led to administrative decentralization, the establishment of consultative councils on which Africans had a few seats, and the granting of French citizenship to a few Africans on an individual basis.

The Colonial Administration

In 1895 French Guinea became a part of a larger West African colonial administrative grouping, French West Africa, which was constituted that year by decree of the president of the French Republic. French West Africa was headed by a governor general, but the several colonies retained substantial autonomy, including their own fiscal systems and services. In 1904 a new federal structure was established, and defined powers and responsibilities were assigned to the federal government. The colonial governments had separate budgets, but certain revenues and the provision of specified services were reserved to the federal government. The governor general and governors (lieutenant governors from 1902 to 1937) were appointed by the French president on the recommendation of the minister of the colonies, under whose jurisdiction French West Africa fell.

The Ministry of the Colonies was assisted by several councils. Of these, the Supreme Council for Overseas France (Conseil Supérieur de la France d'Outre-Mer), until 1937 known as the Supreme Council for the Colonies, was the most important for West Africa. The council was composed of a small number of parliamentary deputies from the colonies—including one from West Africa (from Senegal)—delegates elected by French citizens in the colonies, and a few representatives of African interests nominated by colonial governors.

Each colony had its own Council of Administration whose members, at first appointed, were elected after 1925. In French Guinea, the council consisted of two French citizens elected by the local chambers of agriculture and commerce and two subjects elected by an electoral college drawn from seven categories of Africans, such as civil servants, persons with prescribed property or educational qualifications, and those who had been officially cited for loyalty to France.

French Guinea, like other colonial components of French West Africa, was divided into administrative districts *(cercles)*. The basic unit of territorial administration, the district was headed by a district commandant *(commandant de cercle)*, a civil official with extensive powers, who was directly responsible to the governor. Some districts were divided into subdivisions headed by assistant administrators. The urban centers of Conakry, Kankan, and Kindia were given separate administrative status as communes in 1920. They were headed by appointed French mayors assisted by appointed councils, half of whose members were French citizens and half African subjects.

French administrative officials belonged to a career colonial service made up of colonial administrators and a lower category of civil servants. The first were graduates of a special school in Paris; most colonial governors and district commandants came from this group. Below them were civil servants who were recruited, trained, and employed locally to serve as assistants and clerks; they could not rise higher than the post of chief of a subdivision. Educated Africans were admitted to this category.

The district and subdivision were the smallest units directly administered by French officials. Below them was the province under an African chief. The province in turn was divided into cantons and villages—each also under an African chief, all of whom had been reduced to adjuncts of the colonial administration. The provincial chief—the office was not everywhere present—nominally had authority over the chiefs of the cantons in his province and, through them, over the village chiefs in the area. Some villages, however, were outside this pyramidal scheme, their chiefs being directly under the French authorities. The French apparently were not altogether satisfied with the office of provincial chief—reminiscent in rank of the once-powerful independent regional chieftainships—and sought to dispense with it whenever possible.

Chiefs were chosen from among those Africans believed to be loyal to the French. A traditional chief might be confirmed in office, but appointment frequently went to individuals who had been clerks or interpreters in the French service or to graduates of the School for the Sons of Chiefs and Interpreters at Saint-Louis, Senegal (founded in 1856 by General Louis Faidherbe, when governor of the colony).

The main responsibilities of the chiefs were to collect taxes, to supply the French authorities with the labor required for public works and other activities, and to provide men for military service. Provincial and canton chiefs were paid a salary. Village chiefs were remunerated with a share of the taxes they collected. Their share was progressively reduced with delay in the collection of taxes, and the chief received nothing if taxes were not in by a certain date.

As agents of an alien authority, the chiefs were distrusted by the community and had no power beyond that derived from their French superiors. They were mainly distrusted, however, because of their reputation, which many of them deserved, for maladministration and corruption.

In 1919 councils of local notables (conseils de notables indigènes) were established in the districts to advise the commandants on such matters as taxation and labor conscription. The councils were intended to help create native understanding of government policies and support for them but, having only limited advisory power and being dominated by the French (district commandants were council presidents), the councils had little value as channels of African opinion.

The Administration of Justice

Justice was administered separately for French citizens and African subjects. For French citizens primary civil jurisdiction was exercised by a court of the first instance in Conakry and criminal jurisdiction by the Court of Assizes, also located in Conakry. Their decisions could be appealed to the West African Court of Appeal in Dakar and, further, to the Court of Cassation in Paris. For African subjects the administration of justice, at first in the hands of the chiefs, was gradually brought under French supervision. In 1912 the judicial powers of village chiefs were completely abolished, and customary courts (tribunaux indigènes) were created in district and subdivision headquarters. District courts sat under Europeans, but African judges could preside in the subdivisions.

In 1925 almost all judicial functions were brought under French supervision. As finally reorganized in 1931, the system of justice for African subjects consisted of customary courts of the first degree composed of two African assessors (lay judges) usually under the presidency of the district administrative officer. The vote of the assessors was, however, deliberative in that at least one assessor had to vote with the president for a decision to be made. These courts had primary jurisdiction in civil actions involving limited sums and in criminal cases in which penalties did not exceed a fine of 2,000 francs or ten years' imprisonment or both. Customary courts of the second degree ordinarily sat in district headquarters and had original and appellate civil jurisdiction but no criminal jurisdiction. They were composed of a French district official, who presided, and two native assessors with a deliberative vote.

Unlimited original criminal jurisdiction in serious offenses, with the right to impose the capital penalty, was exercised by a criminal court in each district. Presided over by a district administrator, the criminal court usually had four assessors—two Africans and two Europeans—half of

26

whom had to agree for a judgment to be rendered. The colonial Court of Appeal in Conakry was composed of two senior French officials and two African notables. It had appellate jurisdiction in civil and criminal customary law cases coming from the courts of the first and second degree. The Supreme Customary Court of Appeal (Chambre d'Annulation) in Dakar had final appellate jurisdiction in all customary and civil and criminal cases.

The basic drawbacks in the system of justice for African subjects were the absence of a unified penal code, the ignorance of many of the French officials of African concepts and customs, and the cumbersome appellate procedure, which made appeal practically impossible in criminal cases (where appeals had to be initiated by the procurators) and extremely difficult in civil ones. There was a shortage of courts and of judicial officials. Many offenses were not brought to court, whereas others might be punished too severely or too lightly by African standards. In civil cases local customary law was frequently misunderstood and misapplied. No attorneys were allowed to practice in the customary courts.

A particular source of dissatisfaction was the *indigénat*, a system of summary disciplinary measures under which French administrators had discretionary power to punish their African subjects for minor infractions. Penalties could not exceed a fine of fifteen francs or five days' imprisonment (before 1925 the limits had been 100 francs and two weeks). Besides being arbitrary, the system could be—and often was—abused as a means of discouraging "insolence" or as a device for securing free labor.

Social Change

French rule brought important changes in the structure of society through the dismantling of the indigenous political and administrative hierarchies. From the early 1900s efforts to suppress serfdom and the slave trade struck at the economic power of a leisured aristocracy (see ch. 5). Many former slaves and serfs, however, had no claim, or only tenuous ones, to land or had to pay high rent and remained economically and psychologically dependent on their former masters; this was particularly true in the Fouta Djallon.

Trade, a principal purpose of the colony, created opportunities for new employment for individuals apart from the traditional traveling merchant. The poorly financed African was generally relegated, however, to a secondary role, providing domestic goods to European and Levantine companies and selling consumer items imported by such firms. The introduction of plantation production for export also created new occupations in the late 1930s. Urbanization, although very slow, brought the development of new service requirements and new jobs, as did the expansion of the colonial government. Before World War II the wage economy grew only slowly, however, and the vast majority of the population, which had been recorded at somewhat over 2 million in a census made in the latter 1930s. continued to engage mainly in subsistence agriculture.

The French, in the field of culture even more than in that of the economy, brought changes—some deliberately, some indirectly. The French language, culture, and ideas and particularly the introduction of a Western educational system resulted in the emergence of a new elite group, the so-called *évolués* (individuals who had become as much French as they were African). By the 1920s and 1930s this group was largely self-sustaining and self-perpetuating. Children of the members were sent to schools operated for the French and emerged with an outlook vastly different from that of the great mass of Guineans.

The first school in Guinea was opened by the Holy Ghost Fathers at Boffa in 1878. In 1890 the school was moved to Conakry, where three years later the first girls' school was opened by the Sisters of Saint Joseph of Cluny. The Holy Ghost Fathers opened five more schools during this period. By 1900 the missionary schools had a total enrollment of about 360 children.

Anticlerical pressures in France for the secularization of schools in the colonies resulted in the introduction of a state school system in French West Africa in 1903 and led in 1906 to a withdrawal of government subsidies to mission schools that halted their progress. The new system called for separate primary schools for Africans and for French and certain assimilated Africans and children of mixed parentage. The African system was to include rural village schools and regional schools, the latter located at district administrative centers.

In Guinea the development of African schools proceeded slowly; three village and twelve regional schools, plus two schools in Conakry, had been established by 1906. The total enrollment was fewer than 1,400. In 1918, after the end of World War I, the French government announced that education was the basis of its policy for Africans and essential to economic progress in the colonies. A broad development plan was laid out, but the cost of implementation was to be met by the colonies; and in Guinea, largely for reasons of expense, educational expansion continued at a slow pace. The worldwide depression of the 1930s also seriously affected expansion, and by 1938 only fifty-five primary schools for Africans (forty-three of them village schools) having an enrollment of under 7,700 students were operating. In addition one government higher primary school and one vocational school accommodated about 200 other African students. There were also three private mission schools having an enrollment of over 900.

The chief task of the village schools, which provided three to four years of education, was to spread a knowledge of spoken French and of personal hygiene practices. Reading and writing in French and some arithmetic were also taught. The regional schools offered five to eight years of more formal French, and introduction to practical agriculture, and some vocational training using facilities, if available, at nearby civil or military installations. A primary certificate could be acquired at the regional schools, although scholastically it was well below that offered by the French schools.

The academic content of the instruction, which was entirely in French, was of French origin and largely irrelevant to African life. In 1932 a Paris intercolonial conference pointed out that teachers recruited from France had no knowledge of Africa or Africans and that African teachers were trained exactly as those in France were. Moreover, African teachers often taught in rote manner metropolitan subject matter they had learned in order to pass teacher training examinations. Almost all textbooks used in African schools were from France or French Algeria.

Guinea's single African higher primary school and an African vocational school, the Georges Poiret School (Ecole Georges Poiret), opened in Conakry in the early 1930s offering two to four-year courses to those who had earned primary certificates. The former turned out junior administrators, the latter foremen or artisans. Both schools accepted only as many pupils as would be required to fill the administration's needs, as they existed solely for this purpose and the French avoided giving instruction to those who would not be able to use it. In 1933 a small agricultural school was opened at Tolo, near Namou, and offered adult classes in the vernacular in agriculture, crafts, and hygiene. This completed the French educational system in Guinea for the African population until after World War II.

FROM WORLD WAR II TO INDEPENDENCE

Prelude to Change

After the fall of France and the creation of the German-allied Vichy government in 1940, most of the administration, as well as leaders of the armed forces, in French West Africa accepted the authority of the new regime. Included were the governor of French Guinea and the French colonial staff in the colony. French residents in general also gave support to the Vichy government. Later in 1940 the position of that government was strengthened by the appointment of Pierre Boisson, who was personally loyal to Marshal Henri Philippe Pétain, head of the Vichy regime, as governor general of French West Africa.

In November 1942, after the Allied landings in North Africa and Admiral François Darlan's declaration for the Allies, Boisson and other French West African government leaders declared their allegiance to General Charles de Gaulle, head of the Free French, and to the French Provisonal Government in Algiers. In 1943 a French consultative assembly called by this government meeting in Algiers replaced Boisson, the colonial governors, and some other senior administrative staff. In general, however, the administration in Guinea and the other colonies continued as before.

The war brought hardships for the indigenous population of French

Guinea. Imported consumer goods were in short supply, and requirements to deliver foodstuffs and strategic raw materials, such as wild rubber, were imposed. Decreases in administrative staff resulted in the use of arbitrary means to solve growing problems. Under the Vichy regime racial discrimination came into the open, although this affected the small group of *évolués* more than the ordinary person, who had long been openly subjected to this practice. The use of forced labor also increased greatly. The situation did not improve after the changeover from Vichy to the Free French. If anything, the demand for materials to support the Allied war effort rose, and methods used to recruit troops and to obtain laborers and porters continued to be equally repressive.

Most of the African population showed little if any political interest in the struggle in Europe. From about 1943 the educated minority came to some extent under Marxist influences propounded by French Communists serving as teachers and labor organizers. In Conakry a branch of the Communist Studies Groups (Groupes d'Etudes Communistes) offered an opportunity for young African intellectuals to discuss African problems in Marxist terms. No effort appears to have been made, however, to encourage the formation of a domestic African communist party. Such political activity as existed in the colony was largely confined to small groups concerned with local or self-interest issues. The germ of nationalism was present, but it was not until after the end of World War II that present-day Guinean nationalism took root in the political ferment of the times and began to spread with the development of major political parties in the latter 1940s.

In early 1944, in the confused situation that existed in French Africa after the ousting of Vichy control, the French National Liberation Committee, of which General de Gaulle was president, called the French African Conference to consider a program of reform. Better known as the Brazzaville Conference—it met in Brazzaville, Congo—the gathering was composed of French colonial governors and administrators, parliamentarians, and labor leaders; despite its name the French African Conference included no Africans.

Various political, social, and economic recommendations were made that in overall character were a compromise between the old assimilationist and a new federalist point of view. It was proposed that the colonies send representatives to the French Constituent Assembly—the representatives would include Africans—when it convened after the war and that they be granted political representation in a future federal assembly. No express provisions were made for an African franchise, but it was recommended that each colony have a consultative assembly composed of Europeans and Africans. Decentralization was envisaged in the postwar administrative structure. The conference recommended that industrialization be undertaken, that tariffs and customs be liberalized, that local customs be respected and safeguarded, that the *indigénat* be abolished (but not until the end of the war), and that a new penal code be adopted. Health and education facilities were to be improved, and labor conscription was to be ended (after five years). It also proposed that colonial administration be opened to Africans.

The Brazzaville Conference signaled the beginning of a new era in French colonial policy. The general tenor, however, anticipated not independence but a degree of autonomy and a more real assimilation. It had little immediate effect, except for the passage of a law in August 1944 granting labor in French West Africa the right to organize.

In November 1945 the postwar First Constituent Assembly convened in Paris, charged both with drafting a new constitution for the Fourth Republic and also with carrying on regular legislative activities. As part of the latter it abolished the *indigénat* and forced labor, adopted a new penal code for French West Africa, and approved funds for economic and social development. In May 1946 it passed the Lamine-Guèye Law (named for an African socialist deputy from Senegal), which extended French citizenship to all the inhabitants of the French colonies. It failed to define closely the new rights of citizenship, however, with the result that African inhabitants of the colonies were not admitted to the full exercise of civil rights on the ground that they were not yet ready.

The draft constitution prepared by the First Constituent Assembly was rejected in a popular referendum, and the Second Constituent Assembly met in Paris in June 1946. Differences of opinion, evident in the first assembly, sharpened. A few deputies, from North Africa and Madagascar, demanded political independence. The deputies from French Black Africa (including the socialist Yacine Diallo from Guinea), supported by the French political Left, favored the establishment of a French Union, in which each member state would have political autonomy and there would be political equality of Frenchmen and the colonial people. White colonial interests and the French political Right and Center inclined toward a nominally federalist system, within which France would preserve its dominant position.

A compromise was finally reached, and the plan for the French Union was written into a new draft constitution. This was adopted by the assembly on September 28, 1946; all deputies from French Black Africa voted for it. It was then approved as the Constitution of the Fourth Republic in a referendum held throughout France and the overseas possessions on October 13, 1946.

The French Union—Early Years

The preamble of the new 1946 constitution stated that the French Union was founded on equality of rights and duties without prejudice with respect to race or religion and that it was France's role to lead the peoples of the French Union toward democratic self-government. Overseas possessions were divided into three categories: overseas departments, administratively organized on the pattern of departments of Metropolitan France and legally a part of it; overseas territories, including the former colonies of French West Africa, all considered part of the French Republic and as such entitled to send deputies to the French National Assembly; and associated territories and states, which were juridically members of the French Union but not a part of the French Republic.

The president of the French Republic was president ex officio of the French Union, the organs of which were a high council and an assembly. As before, Metropolitan France dominated; the French government exercised all legislative and executive powers, and the administration of the overseas possessions continued in a centralized pattern. Despite its federal trappings, it was in fact a unitary and, in many respects, a strongly assimilationist system. Laws, administration, citizenship, and the educational system were all French; and the basic premise of economic planning was full integration of the colonial economy with that of France. The first steps toward political autonomy were taken, however, by giving some administrative and financial powers to the elective General Council in each territory, by granting limited suffrage, and by removing the ban on political association.

The General Council established for Guinea consisted initially of forty members elected by two separate colleges; sixteen members were chosen by citizens under French law and twenty-four by citizens under customary law. In 1952 the number was increased to fifty, eighteen elected by persons under French law and thirty-two by enfranchised persons under customary law. At this time the council was also redesignated the Territorial Assembly. The increase in representatives of the customary law electorate reduced somewhat the disproportion between representation for the two groups, but it still remained heavily weighted in favor of voters under French law, who constituted only a very small percentage of total voters.

The council (later assembly) had chiefly a regulatory and advisory function, as the French government possessed the exclusive right to legislate for the overseas territories. Despite its limited powers, however, the council played a significant role through its broad authority to make inquiries and the authority it had relative to land and property disposal, economic development, and matters concerned with education, health, and social welfare. It also proved to be a training ground for individuals who later became members of the Republic of Guinea government.

The deputies sent to the French National Assembly (there were three from Guinea by 1954) were elected directly by all enfranchised citizens in one college. Guinea's two members of the French Council of the Republic were chosen indirectly by the territory's General Council, whose members voted in two colleges, each electing one senator. Four representatives to the assembly of the French Union were elected indirectly by the General Council voting in one college, as were the territory's five deputies to the Grand Council of French West Africa.

No basic changes were made in the organization of local administration in the territory. The three existing communes—Conakry, Kankan, and Kindia—were advanced a step toward self-government by being granted elective councils, although their mayors continued to be appointed. In 1953 three other towns—Labé, Mamou, and Siguiri—were raised in status to communes with appointive councils.

During these years the reorganization of procedures for the administration of justice was carried out, based on the reform of April 1946. The French penal code was extended to all inhabitants of French West Africa, and the customary courts were deprived of their competence in criminal matters. Jurisdiction in minor transgressions was transferred from the customary courts of the first degree to appointed justices of the peace. A French court of the first instance in Conakry was given jurisdiction in all major crimes committed by citizens under both French and customary law. Customary courts were retained, however, for civil litigation involving citizens under customary law. In 1950 the Second Lamine-Guèye Law admitted Africans to certain higher posts in the civil service hitherto reserved for Europeans. Another change, in 1952, was the introduction of a new labor code patterned on the code in force in Metropolitan France.

Political Development

In late 1945 the political party scene in Guinea was characterized by organizations made up of the French and local African elite that had relations with parties in France (of which they were in fact affiliates) and local indigenous organizations that were basically ethnic and regional in orientation. Significant among the former was the affiliate of the French Socialist Party called the Socialist Democracy of Guinea (Démocratie Socialiste de Guinée—DSG). Headed by Yacine Diallo, the party appealed for support mainly to the elite. The party's power reached a peak in elections in 1946 and 1947 but began to decline thereafter. After an expansion of the electorate effective in 1951, its relative strength dropped considerably, and party support was reduced still further by the death of Diallo in 1954.

In 1945 the four principal indigenous parties were centered in different geographic regions and, although ethnic differences had lost some of their significance under French rule, each party tended to represent a particular group. The four parties included the Committee of Lower Guinea (Comité de la Basse-Guinée), which was Soussou dominated; the Gilbert Vieillard Association of Friends (Amicale Gilbert Vieillard) of Middle Guinea, principally grouping the Peul of the Fouta Djallon; the Manding Union (Union du Manding) in Upper Guinea, representing Mandé-speaking peoples, including the large Malinké group; and the Forest Union (Union Forestière), which combined the articulate political elements of the various ethnic communities in the Forest Region. During the first few post-World War II years most of the African electorate were members of these four parties. Their several leaders displayed little interest in territory-wide problems, however, and little effort was made at cooperation.

In 1946, on the initiative of the African deputies elected to the constituent assembly in France, among whom was Diallo, and with the cooperation of other African leaders in the territories making up French West African and French Equatorial Africa, a general conference was called at Bamako to unite the multitude of territorial political groups and formulate a common policy for French Black Africa. From this emerged the African Democratic Rally (Rassemblement Démocratique Africain—RDA). Guinea delegates to the conference included Sékou Touré, but Diallo did not attend although he had signed the original manifesto calling for the meeting. Nor did Diallo later join the Guinea branch of the RDA, the Democratic Party of Guinea (Parti Démocratique de Guinée—PDG), but went his separate political way as head of the socialist cause.

The PDG was formed in May 1947; it introduced a new political force that was eventually to become dominant in Guinea. The PDG's early years were marked by little strength, however, the diverse ethnic and political elements among its leadership often tending to go their own way. Government opposition arose that stemmed from the association of a small group of younger, dedicated leaders (who in effect kept the party alive during the first years) with the French Communists. Opposition also developed in other groups, including the village chiefs, over what were considered extremist positions. During this time the party drew little mass support, as was demonstrated by its failure to secure any of the seats in the French National Assembly in 1951 or in the Territorial Assembly in 1952.

In 1952 Sékou Touré became secretary general of the party and began actively to recruit members from the labor unions belonging to the communist-dominated General Confederation of Labor (Confédération Générale du Travail—CGT), in which he held a prominent position. In the early 1950s rising mining production and some new industries had increased the relative size of the industrial labor force; and by 1953 the CGT had about 2,600 members, many of whom joined the PDG, adding materially to the party's organizational strength. In September of that year the CGT began a territory-wide strike with PDG backing that continued for over two months, largely through Sékou Touré's persistent efforts, to a successful conclusion. The strike achieved a substantial increase in minimum wages, not only in Guinea but also in the rest of French West Africa. Sékou Touré's image, as well as the party's, was tremendously enhanced, and CGT membership rose dramatically to 10,700 in 1954 and 39,000 in 1955.

In August 1953 Sékou Touré won a country-area by-election to the Territorial Assembly, improving his personal stature in the process by defeating a well-known fellow Malinké politician and demonstrating his ability to attract the rural vote. Sékou Touré's strength and that of the PDG were then put to a wider test in the election held in mid-1954 to fill the French National Assembly seat of the deceased Diallo. This became an open contest with African conservatives—supported by the establishment, the traditional chiefs of the Fouta Djallon, and the white residents—who backed Diawadou Barry, a Peul from the Fouta Djallon and head of the African Bloc of Guinea (Bloc Africain de Guinée—BAG). A third candidate, Ibrahima Barry (in Guinea usually called Barry III), ran under the DSG banner. Diawadou Barry was declared the winner by the government. Sékou Touré, who had received enthusiastic receptions throughout most of Guinea except the Fouta Djallon, protested, and charges of irregularities were rampant, being voiced even in France. Nothing came of these, however.

From sometime in 1955 the PDG adopted a new program of political action designed to bring into the party a broad segment of the population. The membership base was declared to be the peasant class; a new dignity was to be accorded women; and youth was to become an active participant in party affairs. Labor would collaborate with the other elements of society in the effort to make the party representative of all Guineans regardless of regional or ethnic origin. PDG membership expanded, and in the election for the three seats in the French National Assembly held in January 1956 PDG candidates took two (one by Saïfoulaye Diallo, the other by Sékou Touré); the third was narrowly won by Diawadou Barry of the DSG, who was reelected.

In June 1956 passage by the French National Assembly of the so-called *loi-cadre* (enabling act) for French West Africa and French Equatorial Africa introduced a new dimension into the political situation. This law established universal suffrage, voting in one college. Of greater significance, however, was the law's provision for the devolution of legislative powers to the individual territorial assemblies from the French National Assembly. The existing federal structures (west and equatorial) were to cease to exist other than as consultative groupings. In essence the basic political relationship would be between the French Republic and the individual territory. The balkanization of French Black Africa that would result was opposed by Sékou Touré. It was to become a major factor in the decision of Guinea's leaders to vote against membership in the French Community two years later.

The changes approved implied that the Territorial Assembly would eventually evolve into a sovereign government. Control of the assembly, therefore, became of paramount party importance, and the PDG further extended its efforts to broaden its membership. In the process it reduced substantially the proportion of intellectuals and government officials, and the party became in fact more genuinely indigenous and more fully representative of the rank and file of the population. This contrasted with the association of the DSG and BAG in many minds with parties in

Metropolitan France, although in January 1957 the DSG had become a member of the new Africa Socialist Movement (Mouvement Socialiste Africain—MSA), restricted to Africa and founded to improve the strength of the territorial socialist parties. BAG, initially associated with General de Gaulle's Rally of the French People (Rassemblement de Peuple Française—RPF), later affiliated itself, and continued its connection, with the Radical Socialists in France.

Highly united and tightly organized, the PDG took an aggressive stand on territorial and colonial reforms in the campaign for the crucial assembly elections, set for March 1957. Its militant cadres were articulate and fired with a spirit of mission. The two other parties were far less assertive and less clear on their goals. PDG candidates received over 75 percent of the vote, gaining fifty-seven of the sixty seats. The socialists won only three seats—although this was apparently in part because some of their candidates ran as independents—bringing to an end the party's role as a major force in Guinean politics. BAG secured no seats. Implementation of the *loi cadre* in Guinea thus came fully into the hands of Sékou Touré and the PDG.

Changes Under the Loi Cadre

Under the *loi-cadre* the French governor remained head of the territorial government. He was to be assisted, however, by the Government Council chosen by the newly elected Territorial Assembly, and provision was made for an African vice president, to be selected from among the assemblymen. Council members were not responsible to the assembly and could be dismissed only by a decree of the French Council of Ministers with the assembly's concurrence. Regulations issued by the council could be set aside by the governor, now designated the chief of the territory, but only if they exceeded the council's competence.

The PDG had complete control of the Territorial Assembly, and the twelve members of the first council were from the leadership of the party; Sékou Touré was elected vice president. In effect the council members functioned as ministers, each in charge of a sphere of local administration. The French governor of Guinea, who was sympathetic to African aims for autonomy, was president ex officio of the council. But from the beginning he permitted Sékou Touré to preside, and the latter for all practical purposes assumed the functions of a prime minister. In July 1958 a French decree officially made the African vice president in the various territories the council president.

The governor also cooperated closely in the reforms proposed by the PDG, which included the takeover of as much of the territory's administration as possible and the africanization of the civil service. One of the first actions of the council was to abolish the system of government-appointed chiefs and to establish elective councils in the villages, communes, and districts—the latter were redesignated circumscriptions *(circonscriptions)*. Elections to local councils were held in

November 1957, when some 40,000 councillors were elected to 4,123 village councils. These local councils, elected by universal suffrage for five years, replaced the village chiefs. Additionally, 526 councillors were elected to twenty-five district councils. Most of the deputies were PDG members.

The PDG, through the Government Council and the Territorial Assembly, continued to press for measures calculated to limit the powers of the French administrators and increase Guinean initiative. Several more towns were elevated to the status of communes, and a plan was approved for establishing over 100 administrative posts to be staffed by Guineans in parts of the country long neglected by the authorities. The new administrators were taken from the first students of the Territorial School of Administration (Ecole Territoriale d'Administration), established in 1957 (see ch. 7).

By mid-1958 the government of the territory was thoroughly reorganized and largely in African hands, and the Government Council had become the central executive authority. Locally the PDG, which had over 4,000 village committees, maintained effective control through its members in the elected local councils and the steadily increasing number of Africans serving as appointed administrators. French local administrators were largely bypassed and their complaints generally ignored.

Independence

In June 1958 General de Gaulle returned to power in France and, in the draft Constitution of the Fifth Republic, the French Union was replaced by the French Community, a new kind of association between France and its overseas possessions. The draft envisaged a free association between France and its former colonies, in which the former would serve as senior partner.

The federal powers of the French Community—foreign affairs, defense, and basic policies on the economy, finance, strategic raw materials, and higher education—were clearly delineated. Its organs, under an elected president (who was also the president of the French Republic), were the Executive Council (composed of the president, the prime ministers of member states, and the French ministers concerned with the community's affairs); the Senate (with a membership elected indirectly by each member state in proportion to its population); and the Court of Arbitration. The draft constitution was submitted to Metropolitan France and all overseas components of the French Union in a general referendum on September 28, 1958. A free choice to accept or reject the draft constitution was given, but in a speech in Conakry in August 1958 General de Gaulle had stated that rejection would result in complete independence—outside the community—and strongly implied that undesirable consequences might well stem from a "no" vote.

Sékou Touré expressed great opposition to the lack of provision in the new constitution for a federal structure for French West Africa (and also for French Equatorial Africa), which he felt necessary to establish equality with Metropolitan France in a possible confederation of equals. Nor did the proposed constitution otherwise provide for a strong federal legislative body of supranational character but left final control in the hands of the French National Assembly.

The French refusal to consider formation of what Guinean leaders considered a genuine federal community or to acknowledge the right of each state to opt (in essence at some future date) for independence led to a call by a PDG territorial conference in mid-September 1958 for a nationwide "no" vote. Leaders of the BAG and DSG joined Sékou Touré in a communiqué asking for a "no" vote. The result was an overwhelming ballot for independence (over 1.1 million "no" votes against about 57,000 "yes" votes) that reflected in part the growth of nationalism in Guinea since the 1950s and in part the attainment of political ascendancy achieved by the PDG, notably the control secured in the election of village and district councils in 1957.

On October 2, 1958, independence was formally proclaimed by the Territorial Assembly, and the country was named the Republic of Guinea. The assembly was transformed into the National Sovereign Constituent Assembly to draft a constitution; the Government Council resigned; and Sékou Touré, as leader of the majority party, assumed the task of forming a new government.

POSTINDEPENDENCE

The new republic's leaders had apparently not anticipated the severity of the French reaction to the declaration of independence. In fact Sékou Touré, before the date of the vote, had informally applied through the French governor of Guinea for association with the French Community under the terms contained in the constitution being put to referendum. This application was subsequently ignored by the French government, which notified the new state of its severance from the French Community immediately after the ballot. French personnel were permitted to remain for two months to assist in the transfer of authority, but at the same time the French government let such personnel know that they would be given another post in French West Africa if they left Guinea. Only certain technical and security staff were actually directed to stay at their jobs. Moreover, the favored-nation status of Guinean exports to France was rescinded, and French government investments—under way and projected—and assistance to the Guinean budget were cut off.

The French government also refused to give de jure recognition to the Guinean government. Meanwhile, French administrative staff, military units, most teachers, and others left Guinea taking equipment with them and reportedly destroying items that had to be left behind. But Sékou Touré persisted in attempts to get French acceptance; and finally in January 1959 several agreements were signed—without, however, providing for de jure recognition—that included an exchange of

38

diplomatic representatives, acceptance of French as the official language of Guinea, and continuance of Guinea in the French franc zone. Technical assistance and cooperation were also agreed on, but continued strained relations resulted in nonimplementation of this provision.

French failure to recognize Guinea had little influence on most independent countries outside the North Atlantic Treaty Organization (NATO). Neighboring Liberia and Ghana extended recognition immediately, and similar action by the Soviet Union and other members of the Eastern European communist bloc followed rapidly. At the end of October 1958 Great Britain became the first Western state to recognize Guinea, and the Federal Republic of Germany (West Germany) extended recognition the next day. By late December over sixty countries, including the United States, had recognized the new state. The United States action, like that of Great Britain and West Germany, was obviously delayed, however, until consultations were held with France; in the United States case, the first American ambassador did not actually arrive in Conakry until mid-1959. In December 1958 Guinea was admitted to the United Nations.

Although the shortage of Guinean administrative personnel, emphasized by the departure of the French, was a pressing problem, the economic situation was much more serious. Imports, which regularly considerably exceeded exports, and the export trade itself had been very largely with either France or other countries of the franc zone. Deficits incurred by Guinea as a colony had been covered by France through the Franc Zone Stabilization Fund. This was no longer the case. Substantial funds had also been put into development in Guinea by the Investment Fund for the Economic and Social Development of the Territories (Fonds d'Investissement pour le Développement Economique et Social des Territoires—FIDES.) This source of aid was also cut off at independence.

For whatever reasons, little immediate financial help was forthcoming from other Western nations. Hard pressed, the Guinean government then turned to barter agreements offered by the Eastern European communist bloc. The first assistance of any significance, however, came from Ghana in the form of a loan equivalent to US$28 million extended in early 1959 (see ch. 10).

Guinea's leaders decided early that lack of financial resources could be made up to a considerable extent by so-called human investment. This involved unpaid voluntary labor utilized on a variety of projects much as it was in traditional village communal activities. Tremendous initial enthusiasm was generated through the efforts of Sékou Touré and the PDG cadres, and during the program's first year (1959) numerous real accomplishments were recorded. These continued into 1960, but then enthusiasm started to wane as planning caused problems and other difficulties arose—for example, in obtaining supplies and needed materials—and especially when local government and party officials began using work groups for their own or party aims. Ultimately many participants worked only because of threats and other pressures. The program continued to be eulogized, but after the first years its importance in economic plans was greatly deemphasized.

CHAPTER 3

GEOGRAPHY AND POPULATION

Guinea is situated on the southwestern edge of the great bulge of West Africa, between roughly 7° and 12.5° north of the equator. From its westernmost limit bordering on the Atlantic Ocean, the country curves inland in a great southeasterly-bearing arc that averages some 150 to 200 miles in width (see fig. 1). The maximum west-east distance is about 450 miles, that from north to south about 350 miles, and the country's total area is 94,925 square miles. On the arc's inner perimeter lie Sierra Leone and northern Liberia, and on its outer edge are the states of Guinea-Bissau, Senegal, Mali, and Ivory Coast.

The country has a varied terrain that ranges from wide coastal marshes and an inner lying plain along the Atlantic Ocean to high central plateaus, a region of broad savannas in the east, and a combination of mountains and plains in the southeast. In early 1975 these areas were tied together by a network of roads, but communications were generally far from modern and in many places difficult during periods of heavy rain.

Less than one-third of the country's total area is considered suitable for cultivation. Soils are relatively poor, the result in many instances of adverse actions by man over many centuries. Guinea is fortunate in other natural resources, however, having large deposits of bauxite and iron ore and considerable hydroelectric potential.

Guinea's location places it in a favorable position for rainfall, which is generally adequate but limited over most of the country to a rainy season alternating with a dry one. The climate ranges from tropical to subtropical. Sustained heat and humidity are characteristic of the coastal lowlands and the forested area of the southern interior. In contrast, the climate of the central plateaus is more refreshing. Particularly noticeable in the eastern savannas are the heat and the low humidities experienced during the rather long dry season.

Vegetation is affected by the climatic variations and in its natural state included rain forest in the southeast, deciduous and broadleaf evergreen forest in the areas west of the central plateaus, and deciduous forest on the plateaus and the plains of eastern Guinea. Human activities have brought extensive changes, however, and present-day vegetation includes large areas of savanna grassland, woodland, and bush.

The population is essentially young, growing rapidly in size, and predominantly rural. The urban segment grew markedly during the 1960s, and this trend presumably continued into the early 1970s. There

41

was no evidence of any measures by the government to introduce family planning.

Foreign observers estimated the size of the de facto population at 4.2 million in early 1973. A Guinean census of 1972 indicated a total of over 5.1 million, but this figure appeared to be for the de jure population, thus including people involved in the large, semipermanent emigration that took place mainly during the 1960s when an estimated 600,000 to 1 million individuals, including family members, departed from Guinea. This outward movement consisted of people whose motivation fell into two principal categories: political disillusionment resulting from the increasingly totalitarian aspects of the government; and economic reasons, principally the great shortage of consumer goods and the belief that living conditions and work opportunities were better outside Guinea (see ch. 8).

MAJOR GEOGRAPHIC REGIONS

The government distinguishes four geographic regions each of which is characterized by different morphological features and a somewhat different climate. Additionally, in each of three regions a different major ethnic group predominates, and in the fourth region are groups having cultural and organizational similarities (see ch. 4). The regions include Lower Guinea (also known as Maritime Guinea); Middle Guinea, consisting principally of the central highland area (the Fouta Djallon); Upper Guinea, a region of savannas; and the Forest Region, which includes the Guinea Highlands and rain forests of southeastern Guinea (see fig. 4).

Lower Guinea

Lower Guinea stretches inland from the Atlantic Ocean to the main mass of the Fouta Djallon. The coast is of the submerged kind lined by broad marshes through which drowned rivers (estuaries) open onto the sea. This coastal strip is broken at only two points where spurs of resistant rock formations jut into the ocean; one is found at Cape Varga in the north, and the other is the Camayenne (or Kaloum) Peninsula on which Conakry is situated. Tides are high along the entire coast, reaching fifteen or more feet, which results in brackish water in estuaries many miles inland.

Behind the coastal swamps lies an alluvial plain averaging about thirty miles wide but considerably narrower in its central section. Soils tend to be soggy during periods of heavy rain, but the continuous, generally humid heat favors agriculture. Crops consisted of rice, fonio (a variety of millet), and maize (corn); kola trees and oil palms were also widely grown, the latter being a characteristic feature of the landscape. Banana plantations have been developed in the southern part, and pineapples were also cultivated there.

To the east of this plain, the region rises in a series of foothills that

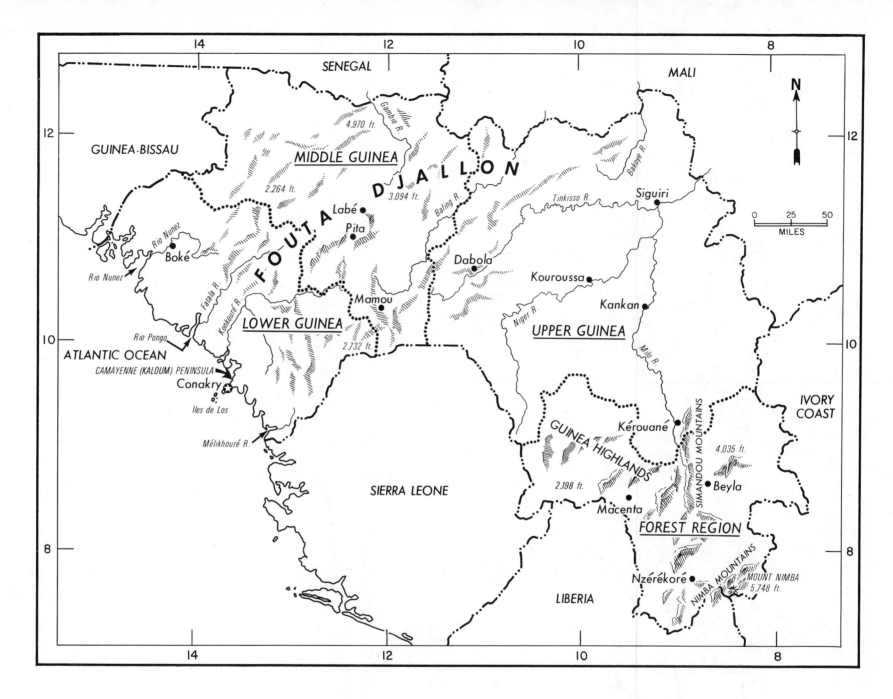

Source: Adapted from W.B. Morgan and J.C. Pugh, *West Africa*, London, 1969,
pp. 266-270.

Figure 4. Guinea, Geographic Regions

merge into the Fouta Djallon. In the south, in particular, these foothills occur in steep steps having escarpments from several hundred to well over 1,000 feet high. The foothills area was included in the maritime region primarily because of the greater ethnic and economic relationships it has with this region than with the Fouta Djallon.

Middle Guinea

The Fouta Djallon highland mass constituting most of Middle Guinea consists of a complex of elevated, relatively level plateaus. About 5,000 square miles of this area are over 3,000 feet above sea level. The plateaus are deeply cut in many places by narrow valleys, many of which run at roughly right angles, giving the region a checkerboard appearance. A number of major valleys extend for long distances, providing important lines of communication; the railroad from Conakry to Kankan runs in part through one of these valleys.

Much of the plateau area is inhabited by the Peul, who raise large numbers of cattle there (see ch. 4). Agriculture is frequently difficult because of the hard lateritic soil crust, and the main crops are grown in the valleys. In certain places, as near Labé, soils derived from igneous rocks are rich and permit cultivation of coffee, bitter oranges, and jasmine (used in perfumes). In some areas pineapples are grown, and banana plantations exist in wetter valleys able to provide adequate moisture for growth throughout the dry season.

Upper Guinea

The principal feature of Upper Guinea, which lies to the east of the Fouta Djallon, is the extensive lightly wooded, tall grass savannas. This savanna area is interrupted, however, by a long rocky spur extending eastward along the Mali border, from the Fouta Djallon, for over 100 miles. Shorter spurs are also found east of Dabola, and in the area west of Siguiri rounded granite domes rise above the plain. The southern limit of the region is generally marked by the northwest-southeast trending Guinea Highlands.

The region has an average altitude of about 1,000 feet. Hard lateritic crust underlies much of the savanna, and agriculture is practiced mainly in the river valleys, which in the case of the principal tributaries of the Niger River extend for hundreds of miles. The main crops include wet rice, fonio, groundnuts (peanuts), and sweet potatoes. Cattle raising is an important industry on the savanna but comparatively less so than in the Fouta Djallon.

Forest Region

The Forest Region encompasses the southeastern corner of Guinea. Its major feature is the Guinea Highlands, which have general elevations ranging from about 1,500 feet above sea level in the west to over 3,000 feet in the east; peaks at several points attain 4,000 feet and above. The topography, consisting mainly of rounded and dome-shaped surfaces, contrasts sharply with the plateau terrain of the Fouta Djallon. The difference is emphasized further by the dense rain forest—now largely secondary growth—that is the usual cover in areas below 2,000 feet. Higher areas are more lightly forested, and some detached hills have crests of bare rocks.

The areas around Beyla and Nzérékoré consist of rolling plains. At one time probably covered by rain forest, the plains' present vegetation is mainly derived savanna. Southeast of Nzérékoré are the Nimba Mountains on the Liberian and Ivory Coast frontiers. Guinea's highest point, Mount Nimba (5,748 feet), is in this range.

Agriculture in the Guinea Highlands includes the cultivation of rice, maize, cassava, kola and oil palm trees, bananas, and coffee. Tobacco is also grown in the plains areas, and cattle are also raised. The arbitrary nature of the colonial political division of West Africa is well illustrated in the Forest Region, where the easiest lines of communication to the coast are through neighboring Liberia and Sierra Leone rather than through the rest of Guinea. The borders with those two countries also artificially divide peoples of the same principal ethnic groups in the area (see ch. 2; ch. 4).

DRAINAGE

Guinea is the source of over one-half of West Africa's principal rivers and many of their tributaries, which rise either in the Fouta Djallon or the Guinea Highlands of the Forest Region. The two highlands, moreover, form the drainage divide between the upper Niger River basin and the rivers that flow westward through Guinea, Sierra Leone, and Liberia to the Atlantic Ocean. In the north the Fouta Djallon also separates the watersheds of the Niger, Gambie (in The Gambia, known as the Gambia), and Sénégal rivers. The Gambie actually rises in the Fouta Djallon, and a major tributary of the Sénégal, the Bafing (in reality the upper course of the Sénégal), also has its origin there.

The fan-shaped system of the Niger River, which originates in the Guinea Highlands, drains over one-third of the country's total area including most of Upper Guinea and the Forest Region. In the west Lower Guinea is crossed by many usually short rivers, which originate either in the Fouta Djallon or in its foothills. Among the more important for navigation purposes are the Rio Nunez, which debouches through the Rio Nunez estuary; the Fatala, emptying into the Rio Pongo estuary; and the Mélikhouré, near the Sierra Leone border. In the mid-1970s the Konkouré River, situated north of Conakry, had little navigation value but had important potential for hydroelectric power development (see ch. 12).

CLIMATE

The climate is characterized by wet and dry seasons that vary in length in different parts of the country. In the far south the wet season begins in February or March but in the northeast may not begin until June. In general, however, the period of heaviest rains in most areas is from April or May to October or November. The dry season usually falls between November and April. The greatest rainfall is experienced everywhere during July and August.

The country's varied elevations affect the amount of rain and produce considerable climatic diversity. The principal determining factors in the length of the seasons, however, are the tropical maritime monsoon, which carries moisture-laden air from the southwest over West Africa during the wet season, and the dry, hot, and dusty harmattan, which originates over the Sahara region and blows from the northeast during the dry period.

These two air masses move regularly in response to the apparent movement of the sun back and forth across the equator. At the peak of its northward course the monsoonal air mass covers, and brings rain to, all of Guinea. The harmattan, however, usually pushes southward just through the Forest Region, and its effect there is pronounced for at most two months. The zone of contact of the two air masses is characterized by violent thunderstorms and squalls that move across the country with each advance and retreat of the front. In the coastal area the turbulence may result in tornadoes.

Lower Guinea has wet and dry seasons of roughly equal length. Because of the western escarpments of the Fouta Djallon and the effects they cause atmospherically in increasing precipitation, the region has a mean average rainfall of 110 inches or more annually, the highest anywhere in the country. In some places the total rainfall may far exceed this average; for instance, at Conakry it is usually close to 170 inches and may in some years be over 200 inches.

The wet season in the Fouta Djallon rarely exceeds four months, but some rainfall occurs during most other months. A mean average of about 100 inches falls in areas close to Lower Guinea's coastal region, seventy or more inches in the more central part of the highland, and about sixty inches in the eastern part. East of the Fouta Djallon the savannas of Upper Guinea have a rainfall that rarely exceeds sixty inches. Rain falls there principally between June and September, but storms may occur during any month; less than one-half inch is usually registered monthly, however, between December and March.

In much of the Forest Region precipitation occurs throughout most of the year; only in January is there usually less than one-half inch of rainfall. The average annual precipitation is somewhat less than in Lower Guinea, but the more extended period of rainfall permits growth of a rain forest vegetation in the region (see Vegetation, this ch.).

Temperatures and relative humidity are usually high in the coastal zone at all times and result in a generally enervating climate that becomes even more trying for the region's inhabitants during the rainy season. In

Conakry, where sea breezes bring some amelioration, temperatures generally remain between 90°F and 75°F. The relative humidity ranges from about 70 to nearly 100 percent—the annual mean minimum is above 73 percent in the early afternoon and 89 percent in the early evening. In the Boké area away from the sea breeze, the annual mean maximum temperature is about 93°F, and during March and April daily mean maximums are 100°F or above. The humidity in Boké is usually above 90 percent by early evening throughout the year. The effects of the harmattan during the dry season, however, occasion a definite lowering of humidity in daytime to between 40 and 50 percent.

In the Fouta Djallon temperature readings are lower, and the range of humidity percentages is wider than in the coastal zone. Daily mean temperatures may range between 54°F and 94°F during the dry period, and the mean relative humidity may vary from 93 percent in early morning to, at some points, as low as 29 percent by late afternoon. In July and August daytime mean maximum temperatures, lowered by the rains, do not exceed 80°F, and at night they may drop to 65°F. The relative humidity during this time fluctuates between 95 percent in the morning and 84 percent in the early evening.

In Upper Guinea temperatures and especially the humidity are strongly influenced by the harmattan, when temperatures are over 90°F during the day—toward the end of the dry season they often exceed 100°F—and drop to 60°F or below at night. During the dry period relative humidities of 70 percent or above at night decline to under 40 percent at midday and may be between 20 and 30 percent by late afternoon. During the rainy season temperatures usually are between 70°F and 90°F. Relative humidities remain comparatively high during this time, generally between 70 and 90 percent or over.

SOILS AND MINERALS

The alternation of wet seasons having a high rainfall and dry seasons lasting several months has resulted in extensive leaching of nutrient soil minerals and formation of a hard subsurface crust of laterite over large areas of the country. This laterite, detrimental to crop growing, consists mainly of a mixture of iron and aluminum oxides and hydroxides. In some areas of Guinea the aluminum compounds greatly predominate, giving rise to large deposits of economically valuable bauxite, a major source of aluminum (see ch. 12).

Soils in the coastal zone are composed mostly of workable sandstone gravels washed down from the Fouta Djallon. A lateritic layer has developed between the upper soil and the granitic-gneissic bedrock and causes waterlogging during the wet season. Laterite is also common in the Fouta Djallon and covers considerable areas with a hard crust that supports only minimal vegetation. This soil, however, produces pasturage during the wet season. Soil conservation is a particularly serious problem on the plateaus as the lateritic crust makes for rapid runoff of rainwater, which cuts deep gullies and washes the soil down to lower levels. Moreover, in places where the crust is loosened for cultivation, the soil tends to lose quickly any organic materials by leaching.

The lateritic covering disappears in the Guinea Highlands. The more even distribution of rainfall throughout the year and the resultant luxuriant vegetation bring a greater accumulation of organic materials in the soils that have originated from decomposition of the underlying granites, gneisses, quartzites, and schists. The heavy foliage also helps prevent excessive leaching or evaporation and preserves the richness of the soil.

The savannas of Upper Guinea are underlain by rocks similar to those of the Guinea Highlands. The pronounced wet and dry seasons, however, have leached the soil, and a lateritic crust is widespread, greatly hampering cultivation. Humus is scarce, and fires are regularly lit during the dry season to increase soil fertility. When the rains begin, tall grasses quickly reappear, and the scattered trees put forth a rich foliage.

In 1975 the variety of minerals reported to have been found was limited, but several having great economic importance existed in large quantity. These included bauxite, iron ore, and diamonds. Major deposits of bauxite have been located in the Fouta Djallon and its foothills, the principal known deposits being at or near Dabola, Fria, Kindia, Sangarédi (in Boké Administrative Region), and Tougué. Bauxite deposits also exist in the Iles de Los, but exploitation had practically exhausted these by the mid-1960s (see ch. 12).

Iron ores have been found in several parts of the country. Among the more important were a large limonite-rich deposit discovered on the Camayenne Peninsula near Conakry early in the 1900s. Major deposits of magnetite have been found in the Nimba Mountains along the Liberian border and in the Simandou Mountains, which lie in the eastern part of the Guinea Highlands. A significant deposit of hematite ore reportedly existed at an unidentified location along the Sierra Leone frontier.

The presence of gold has been known since ancient times, and the alluvial Bouré goldfield north of Siguiri—now very largely worked out—was an important source of wealth for the ancient Mali Empire (see ch. 2). Gold occurs in the gravel of streams in the Niger River valley in the area of Siguiri and Kouroussa; traces of gold are found also near Nzérékoré. In the 1950s gold-bearing quartz veins were worked in present-day Dinguiraye Administrative Region. There were no reports of major gold-mining operations in early 1975.

Economically important diamond-bearing gravels are found at various places within an area encompassed by Macenta, Kérouané, and Beyla. Diamond-bearing geologic pipes have also been discovered in that general area and were under exploitation. Stones include both industrial and gem varieties.

Information on the presence of other minerals was scanty. The iron ore deposits on the Camayenne Peninsula also contained chromite and nickel.

The presence of graphite and at least small quantities of marble has been reported. Limestone occurs in quantity in the Mali Administrative Region. Surveys in the 1960s reportedly uncovered exploitable deposits of both common and rare minerals, but further action had not been taken as of early 1975.

No known deposits of mineral fuels, either coal, petroleum, or natural gas, existed in late 1974. Guinea, however, has a broad continental shelf, part of which extends over 100 miles out to sea, and the possibility that petroleum deposits might be found there led to agreement with United States oil interests in 1974 for exploration (see ch. 12).

VEGETATION

Temperatures throughout Guinea are sufficiently high at all times for continuous plant growth. Variations in the amount of precipitation and in particular the length of the dry season have resulted, however, in the development of several differing natural vegetation zones to which, in a general way, the country's four geographic regions correspond. Considerable modification in vegetation has occurred, however, as the result of human activity. Extensive areas are under permanent cultivation, and slash-and-burn agriculture over the centuries has brought the degradation of forests. The practice of repeated burning to fertilize the ground and especially to promote the growth of grass for pasturage has also caused forested areas to be replaced by savanna parkland, grassland, or brush (see fig. 5).

The natural vegetation of most of Lower Guinea apparently consists of mixed deciduous and broadleaf evergreen forest. Rain forest occurs in favored localities, for example, as gallery forests along waterways, but more extensive development is precluded by the length of the dry season—up to six months—despite the region's high total rainfall and rather constantly high humidity. The sunken nature of the coast has promoted the growth of extensive mangrove swamp forests along the seafront. Mangroves also border the numerous creeks that interlace the coastal marshes and penetrate inland along estuaries to the limit of tidal flow, in some cases as much as twenty miles.

Human action has brought significant changes in the vegetation of Lower Guinea. In many areas it has resulted in replacement of the original forest by savanna woodland or brushland. As a result also the oil palm has become a dominant feature of the landscape, in the lower plains particularly. To a limited extent areas of mangroves have been deforested and the land converted to wet-rice culture.

Notable changes in vegetation have occurred in the Fouta Djallon. Upland open forests are believed to have existed at one time on many plateau areas but were degraded to grassland, brush, or open savanna woodland marked by scattered fire-resistant trees as a result of clearing and cultivation. Regrowth of the forest has been inhibited by regular burning of the plant cover, but remnants are found in wide stream valleys

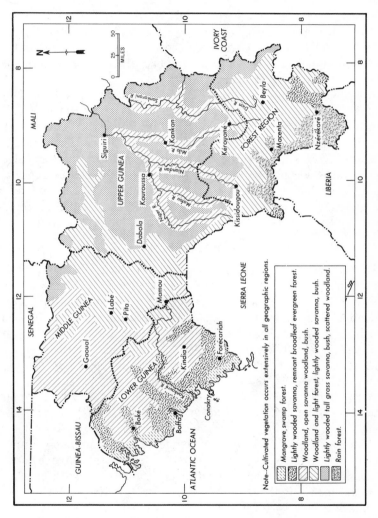

Figure 5. Guinea, Present-Day Vegetation

Note—Cultivated vegetation occurs extensively in all geographic regions.

Mangrove swamp forest.
Lightly wooded savanna, remnant broadleaf evergreen forest.
Woodland, open savanna woodland, bush.
Woodland and light forest, lightly wooded savanna, bush.
Lightly wooded tall grass savanna, bush, scattered woodland.
Rain forest.

and in a few protected spots. Heavily forested areas still existed in the Mamou area in the early 1960s; later information was not available.

The natural vegetation of Upper Guinea has also undergone great change as the result of man's activity. Much of the region was probably covered at one time by open deciduous forest consisting of trees of medium height. Over the centuries, however, the spread of cultivation and regular burning reduced large areas to open savanna woodland or parkland with tree species having thick, fire-resistant bark. Large areas also have been degraded to grasslands, in which grasses attain a height up to about ten feet during the rainy season, and still other areas have a mixed cover of bush and grass. The economically valuable shea tree is found throughout the region, as is the baobab, which grows to a large size, especially along streams.

A large section of the Forest Region, where appreciable amounts of rain fall during a nine-to ten-month period, has a natural cover of dense humid or rain forest. Primitive agricultural practices, however, have brought replacement of most of the original three-tiered canopy of treetops, typical of the virgin rain forest, by a lower, and economically less valuable, secondary growth; in 1975 primary forest was found only in a few places, mainly in forest preserves. Human activities have reduced the vegetation in some places to grass-woodland, and in parts of the region cultivation has completely eliminated the forest cover.

WILDLIFE

Human encroachment and hunting have reduced the wildlife and, in particular, the numbers of larger animals. The latter found in Guinea include the hartebeest, bongo, reedbuck, waterbuck, gazelle, buffalo, and other animals typical of the western Sudan savanna. Bush pigs, warthogs, leopards, and lions (relatively rare) are among other larger animals found in different parts of the country. Small herds of elephants also exist. The larger rivers contain some hippopotamuses—pygmy hippopotamuses are found in the Forest Region in the area of the Liberian border—and manatees are occasionally encountered in larger estuaries. Chimpanzees and several kinds of monkeys inhabit forest areas.

Reptiles include crocodiles, which infest the swamps and waters near the mouths of streams along the coast, and both nonvenomous and venomous snakes. Among the latter are the deadly green mamba and various vipers. Pythons reportedly grow to a length of twenty to twenty-five feet.

Freshwater fish, a supplemental item of the diet in Upper Guinea and along the lower sections of the coastal rivers, include numerous species, mostly small, among which are various tilapias. Saltwater species include barracuda, sharks, Spanish mackerel, skipjacks, yellowfin tuna, tarpon, mullet, various flatfish, shrimp, and oysters.

Birdlife is plentiful and diverse, ranging from colorful finches to parrots, birds of prey—including vultures—and water birds, such as egrets and herons. Game birds include bush and Guinea fowl, doves, and quail.

INTERNATIONAL BOUNDARIES AND POLITICAL SUBDIVISIONS

Guinea has a land frontier of almost 2,050 miles that borders on six other countries. In addition Guinea has a coast, measured in a roughly straight line, of about 190 miles on the Atlantic Ocean. Three of the land borders, with Guinea-Bissau (240 miles), Liberia (350 miles), and Sierra Leone (405 miles), were determined by international agreements during the colonial period. The remaining three, Ivory Coast (312 miles), Mali (534 miles), and Senegal (205 miles), were established by administrative actions within former French West Africa. In all cases boundaries were drawn with few considerations for the distribution of the ethnic groups residing in the area through which the demarcation line passed.

The frontier with Guinea-Bissau was based on an 1886 convention between France and Portugal; demarcation was completed in 1905. For most of the distance this boundary follows arbitrarily established straight-line segments or the midpoint of rivers. Similarly, straight lines delimit numerous sections of Guinea's border with Liberia. In the latter case, however, where rivers constituted the demarcation line, the Liberian bank formed the actual boundary. A convention on the Guinea-Liberia border was originally agreed upon between France and Liberia in 1892; but neither side then had physical control of the border area, and the agreement proved impractical. A new convention in 1907 assigned to French Guinea a large strip of territory that formerly had been part of Liberia; this strip had meanwhile been occupied by French military forces engaged in pacification operations (see ch. 2). Delimitation of this boundary was made in 1911.

The border between Guinea and Sierra Leone was established mainly by a series of Anglo-French agreements in the 1890s that were intended to delimit the spheres of influence of the two colonial powers. Although straight lines were used, natural features were employed for a considerable part of the delimitation—rivers formed about one-half of the border, and the dividing line between the Niger River basin and the basins of rivers flowing into the Atlantic Ocean constituted another principal part.

In early 1975 the first-order divisions of the country's administrative hierarchy consisted of twenty-nine administrative regions (*régions administratives*). These were divided into about 220 administrative districts (*arrondissements administratifs*). At the third level were about 7,800 units combining local administrative and party organs. Each unit is known as the Local Revolutionary Power (Pouvoir Révolutionnaire Local—PRL) (see ch. 8).

In early 1975 Guinea claimed territorial waters that extended to 130

53

nautical miles. This distance is approximately the outermost point of the continental shelf off Guinea.

SETTLEMENT PATTERNS AND MAN-MADE FEATURES

The basic settlement pattern is the cluster hamlet or village. Climate, soil, and cultural factors have influenced the location of the settlements. For example, many forest people of southeastern Guinea, who have no strong tradition of large political groupings, reside in generally isolated villages in forest clearings. In Lower Guinea, villages of the Baga may be found having houses in a linear arrangement along a dry ridge near of among the marshy coastal lands used for wet-rice culture. In the Fouta Djallon the degradation of the soil in many places, which has resulted from regular burning of grasses and destruction of the forest cover, has brought a concentration of agricultural villages in the valleys where better soil conditions exist. In the Fouta Djallon, however, many of the plateaus also have numerous scattered hamlets of cattle-raising Peul. In certain areas having especially favorable growing conditions, for instance around Labé and Pita, a large number of villages dot the countryside, many only a few hundred yards to one or two miles apart.

In Upper Guinea large numbers of villages are found in the great valleys of the Niger River and of its major tributaries, as well as in the valleys of smaller rivers. This is partly because of the greater fertility of the valley soils, but large areas of the region have also been abandoned because of their reduction through human practices to laterite underlain or encrusted savanna grassland and bush of poor agricultural value.

Guinea's present-day towns have developed in a number of ways. Some grew from villages at road crossings that came to serve as area and regional market centers, such as Nzérékoré and Dinguiraye. Others were focal points along the coast for seagoing trade. Siguiri in Upper Guinea was the center for operations in the Bouré goldfields, and Kouroussa developed along the Niger River where rapids halted upstream navigation. Construction of the Conakry-Kankan railroad in the early 1900s also brought growth to certain larger villages along its route.

The French colonial administration and various non-African trading interests introduced Western-style structures into the emerging towns. The trend toward using such structures for administrative and business purposes, and also for housing, has continued since independence in 1958, and many of the smaller and medium-size towns in 1975 presented a mélange of Western and African elements. Conakry and a few large towns had areas completely Western in appearance, and surrounding sections had African features.

In early 1975 Guinea's principal, man-made features were those constructed to facilitate transportation or intercommunication between different parts of the country. They included about 2,000 to 3,000 miles of main roads and several thousand miles of roads described as improved, which formed a network connecting the capitals of the administrative regions or tied local towns to this network (see ch. 12).

Railroads totaled under 700 miles, and regularly operating lines were confined to Lower Guinea. A line from Lower Guinea (Conakry) ran through the Fouta Djallon to Kankan roughly in the center of the savanna of Upper Guinea but was in disrepair and little used in 1975. Several seaports existed, but the only ones of significance were at Conakry and Kamsar. A number of airfields were also located at various points throughout the country.

Irrigation was practiced along the Niger River floodplain, but associated construction was not extensive and consisted mainly of flood control structures. Dams that impounded varying quantities of water had been built at several places for the development of hydroelectric power. Information was not available on the size of the lakes formed.

POPULATION

A census conducted on December 31, 1972, determined the country's population to be 5,143,284. This figure differed substantially from the estimates of the United Nations (UN) and foreign governmental organizations, which placed the total between 4.1 million and 4.2 million in 1972. The substantial difference may relate to the inclusiveness of the enumeration. The presidential decree ordering the census directed that all habitual residents, both those within and those without the country, were to be counted, although through early 1975 the government had not publicly stated whether individuals absent from Guinea were included in the published figure. In the case of the UN and foreign government estimates, the totals were for the de facto population only.

Population Dynamics

With the exception of the distribution of the population by administrative region, other demographic data obtained in the 1972 census had not been made available to the general public through early 1975. This lack of published detail also applied to an earlier census carried out in May 1967 that reportedly counted 3,784,786 inhabitants. As a result demographers in analyzing Guinea's population dynamics have generally relied on the information secured in a rather extensive sample survey conducted by the French colonial administration in early 1955, which determined the de facto population to be 2.57 million. More than 77,000 other Guineans were outside the country at the time, making the de jure population about 2.65 million.

Rate of Growth

In the latter 1950s the average annual population growth rate was estimated at about 2.2 percent. The UN continued to use that rate for estimates of growth during the 1960s, and the United States Bureau of the Census placed the rate at about 2.3 percent in the mid-1970s. According to the 1955 sample survey, births were then estimated to be averaging sixty-two per 1,000 of the population nationwide and deaths forty per 1,000 nationally. UN estimates for the period 1965 to 1970 placed the birthrate at 47.2 per 1,000 and the mortality rate at 25.1 per 1,000, and the United States Bureau of the Census estimated the rates at forty-seven births and twenty-four deaths per 1,000 in 1974. A somewhat higher birthrate of fifty per 1,000 was estimated in a study of sub-Saharan Africa published in 1972. There was little doubt that the birthrate was remaining high and nothing to indicate a change from the observation made in the latter 1960s that all but a very small percentage of women were married by age twenty and that during the reproductive period those married women who had children bore close to ten, of whom at least five or six survived. Guinea's high death rate was owing in large part to infant mortality, which was reported at 216 deaths per 1,000 births before reaching one year of age in 1955.

Sex and Age Distribution

In 1955 the male-female ratio in the de facto population was ninety-one males to every 100 females. This considerable difference was explained by the greater number of males among the over 77,000 Guineans then outside the country. The 1972 census indicated a ratio of more than ninety-nine males to every 100 females.

The apparent age distribution reported in 1955 was typical of developing countries in general. Over two-fifths of the population then in French Guinea was in the age-group from birth to fourteen years, whereas the age-group from fifteen through sixty-four years contained more than one-half of the total population. According to an estimate made by the UN for the year 1965, the proportionate number in the younger age-group had increased slightly, and individuals in the age-group from fifteen to sixty-four years had declined to just below 50 percent. The proportion in the age-group of sixty-five and above doubled, presumably reflecting improved health conditions. The 1972 census proportions varied little from the 1965 estimates (see table 1).

Density

Based on official Guinean estimates that placed the total population at approximately 2.75 million in late 1958, the average population density was twenty-nine per square mile about the beginning of 1959. The subsequent 1967 census indicated that the density had risen to forty per square mile, but this figure had to be considered in the light that information was unavailable as to whether the census totals were for the de facto or de jure population. The 1972 census showed a density of fifty-four per square mile. In view of the likelihood that published totals were for the de jure population, the actual density at the time may have been lower.

In 1959 the most heavily populated areas were in the Fouta Djallon in Middle Guinea, and the greatest densities were found in the Labé and Pita administrative regions, both of which enjoyed a generally agreeable climate and favorable soil conditions. In the intervening years to 1972

Table 1. *Guinea, Age Distribution of the Population, Selected Years, 1955-72*
(in percent)

Age in Years	1955[1]	1965[2]	1972[3]
Birth to 14	42.1	43.7	43.1
15 to 64	54.5	49.5	49.5
65 and over...............................	3.3	6.8	7.4
TOTAL	99.9[4]	100.0	100.0

[1] Sample survey.
[2] United Nations estimate.
[3] Population census.
[4] Does not add to 100 because of rounding.

various other administrative regions experienced population increases at a higher rate, but according to the 1972 census the Labé and Pita regions remained the most densely inhabited. In 1959 parts of the Forest Region were also heavily populated, in particular the agricultural areas centering in Guéckédou and Nzérékoré; both areas also had the region's highest population densities in 1972 (see table 2).

Upper Guinea remained relatively the most lightly inhabited geographic region, having a density of only twenty-seven per square mile, or one-half of the indicated national average, in 1972. Although this region encompassed two-fifths of Guinea's total territory, its vast grassy savannas and savanna woodlands were less fertile than other parts of the country, and these areas had little apparent attraction for individuals seeking new land. Despite the overall low density, however, certain areas of the region, especially along the Niger and Milo rivers, had some of the highest rural concentrations in the entire country.

The population density of Lower Guinea, excluding Conakry, doubled between 1959 and 1972 from thirty to sixty-one per square mile. The growth rate was particularly great in the Dubréka and Fria administrative regions, whose combined density rose from thirty-eight to ninety-one per square mile during the thirteen-year period. This was probably attributable in part to the development of bauxite mining and processing in the Fria region but perhaps owed more to the fact that Dubréka was immediately adjacent to Conakry, received spillover from the latter, was the location of small new manufacturing establishments, and also contained the food-growing areas for the city's population.

Migration and Urbanization

There was little current information on seasonal migration in the mid-1970s. It was known that in the early 1960s farmers, mainly from Upper Guinea, went periodically to The Gambia and Senegal to grow or harvest groundnuts. Young men also went to Liberia and Sierra Leone to work for a period for cash wages, returning home thereafter. Within Guinea Malinké from Upper Guinea regularly went to the Forest Region,

Table 2. Guinea, Areas, Populations, and Average Population Densities of Geographic Regions and Their Subdivisions, 1959 and 1972

Geographic Regions and Their Administrative Subdivisions	Area (in square miles)	Population[1] 1959	Population[1] 1972	Average Density (per square mile) 1959	Average Density (per square mile) 1972
Lower Guinea					
Conakry	119	78,388	525,671	659	4,417
Boffa	2,317	66,199	121,134	29	52
Boké	4,266	85,750	178,574	20	42
Dubréka	2,191	83,154	145,322	38	
Fria (in 1959 included in Dubréka)	n.a.	n.a.	54,398	n.a.	91
Forécariah	1,785	64,800	132,184	36	74
Kindia	3,408	110,448	224,396	32	72
Télimélé[2]	3,109	110,211	190,981	35	61
Total	17,195	598,950	1,572,660	35	91
Middle Guinea					
Dalaba	2,220	101,729	149,667	46	67
Gaoual	4,439	71,818	129,693	16	29
Labé	2,980	257,155	418,648	86	140
Mali	3,419	122,817	193,973	36	57
Mamou	2,377	81,700	184,633	34	78
Pita	1,583	125,300	206,064	79	130
Tougué	2,316	69,840	112,295	30	48
Koundara (formerly Youkounkoun)	2,000	54,816	88,427	27	44
Total	21,334	885,175	1,483,400	41	70
Upper Guinea					
Dabola	3,474	32,448	83,070	9	24
Dinguiraye	2,817	50,079	109,162	18	39
Faranah	5,057	74,154	135,466	15	27
Kankan	10,610	157,662	264,684	15	25
Kérouané[3]	n.a.	n.a.	44,850	n.a.	...
Kouroussa	6,332	84,200	121,338	13	19
Siguiri	9,023	154,771	253,758	17	28
Total	37,313	553,314	1,012,328	15	27
Forest Region					
Beyla	6,736[4]	141,500	192,212	21	...
Guéckédou	1,605	118,926	173,915	74	108
Kissidougou	3,424	127,975	177,607	37	52
Macenta	3,362	114,500	167,749	34	50
Nzérékoré	3,931	211,209	290,743	54	
Yomou (in 1959 included in Nzérékoré)	n.a.	n.a.	72,670	n.a.	92
Total	19,058	714,110	1,074,896	37	56
GRAND TOTAL	94,900	2,751,549	5,413,284	29	54

n.a.—not available.
[1] 1959, estimates; 1972, census totals. It was not known whether 1972 totals were for the de facto or de jure population.
[2] In 1959 part of Middle Guinea.
[3] In 1959 included in the Beyla subdivision of the Forest Region.
[4] The 1972 area of the Beyla subdivision was unknown. See also footnote 3.

Source: Adapted from "Décret No. 145 PRG du 2 Juillet 1973," Journal Officiel de la République de Guinée, September 1973, p. 187; Ray Autra (Mamadou Traoré), Connaissance de la République de Guinée, Dakar, 1960, pp. 20-21.

where they engaged in small-scale trade; changes in national economic policies during the 1960s and early 1970s greatly affected this practice, but to what extent was unknown in early 1975 (see ch. 12). A seasonal movement of large scale, which continued in the 1970s, was the migration of Peul cattle raisers and their herds to the plateaus of the Fouta Djallon during the rainy season from valley pastures to which they returned when the dry weather set in.

The population in urbanized areas was estimated by UN and United States government sources at about 12 percent in the early 1970s. The number of inhabitants of Conakry alone, as reported by the 1972 census, raised a question concerning this percentage since the population of the city itself constituted 10 percent of the national population in 1972. (The Conakry total, however, appeared to be for the de jure population, and the number in actual residence was uncertain.) The census provided no additional information on cities and towns, and current data from other sources were practically nonexistent. Urbanization in general and the size and rates of growth of other urban centers were, therefore, largely a matter of conjecture.

The 1955 sample survey classified nineteen populated places as urban. Together they had 213,000 inhabitants, constituting slightly over 8 percent of the total population. Four years later, in 1959, another estimate counted seventeen towns having populations over 5,000 and a total of more than 243,000 inhabitants. Subsequently, during the 1960s, movement to the towns appears to have gone on at an accelerated rate in all parts of the country, as shown by estimates for various towns in 1967. For example, Conakry grew from over 78,000 in 1959 to 197,000 in 1967. In Middle Guinea Labé increased during the same period from 12,500 to 30,000; in Upper Guinea Kankan reached 40,000, compared with an earlier 29,000; and in the Forest Region Nzérékoré more than doubled from 10,500 to 23,000. Smaller towns that attained importance became the destination of migrants and also took part in the rapid increase. Thus Koundara, which was made capital of the then Youkounkoun Administrative Region in 1964, grew from about 1,500 in 1959 to 6,000 in 1967. An even greater expansion was experienced by Télimélé—a new, postindependence administrative region capital—from a small village in 1959 to a population of 12,000 in 1967.

CHAPTER 4

ETHNIC GROUPS AND LANGUAGES

There are about two dozen ethnic groups in Guinea, ranging in size from a few thousand to nearly 1 million people. Three major groups constitute about 75 percent of the total, and each one predominates in a particular geographical region. The Soussou are preponderant in Lower Guinea, the Peul in Middle Guinea, and the Malinké in Upper Guinea (see fig. 6). Many minor groups in these three regions tend to be assimilated by the dominant one. No single group predominates in the Forest Region, but the various peoples who live there are similar in culture and social organization.

Many ethnic groups are known by various names. In some cases people call themselves by a different name from the one given them by their neighbors. The Peul are a case in point. Peul is the name used by French speakers, whereas English speakers refer to them as Fulani. Their own name is Fulbé (sing., Pullo) or some variant of that name. A name often used in Guinea is Foulah. Generally, differences in spelling or pronunciation result from different ways of handling the same sound.

Language is an obvious feature distinguishing the ethnic groups in Guinea from one another, and the names of the principal ethnic groups are the same as, or similar to, the languages they speak. Retained notions of ethnic identity and objective variations of cultural patterns often accompany and reinforce differences in languages. In some instances, however, groups with similar cultural patterns speak different languages, as for example in the Forest Region. In others, groups with distinctive cultural patterns may speak the same language, as in the Fouta Djallon (the mountainous region that takes up most of Middle Guinea).

The last sample population survey listing ethnic affiliation was carried out in 1954 and 1955. At that time the Peul were the largest group numerically, constituting 28.6 percent of the population, followed by the Malinké with 22.4 percent. The Soussou were the third largest with 13.1 percent. The forest groups together made up 18.1 percent of the total. Since that time the proportions have changed, although precise figures were not available in early 1975. Both the Malinké and the Soussou have increased in numbers because they assimilated members of smaller ethnic groups living among or near them. Thus, according to tentative estimates, the Malinké and the Peul each accounted for about 30 percent of the population in the early 1970s. The Soussou share had grown to 16 percent, and the proportion of forest peoples had remained stable at approximately 18 percent. The fact that no single group could attempt to dominate the entire country helped create an equilibrium, but the predominance of one group in three of the four geographical areas created a definite tendency toward regionalism.

There were indications in early 1975 that differences in languages, custom, and religion, which for centuries have set the people off from—and often against—one another, continued to intrude in everyday affairs. Neither the government nor the ruling party could ignore the persistence of group loyalties and ethnic identification. This was demonstrated on the one hand by concessions to traditional practices and on the other by the apparent failure of some governmental measures that did not or could not take ethnic differences into account. Nevertheless, ethnic factors seemed to be less important in Guinea than in many other parts of Africa. Increasing numbers of people began regarding themselves as sharing a single Guinean and African heritage, largely as a result of the cohesive force of the country's single political party (see ch. 8).

PEOPLES OF LOWER GUINEA

The Soussou

The Soussou (Sosso or Susu) speak a language that is almost indistinguishable from that of the Dialonké in Middle Guinea. This close linguistic relationship supports a hypothesis that the Soussou and the Dialonké were once members of the same group in the Fouta Djallon, that they were separated by Peul invaders, and that the Soussou moved southward, absorbing other people in the process.

The economic and political preeminence of Lower Guinea in general and Conakry in particular gives the Soussou a special importance apart from their numerical size. Throughout Lower Guinea they have tended to assimilate other small groups. Soussou culture has supplanted some traditional features of the social system of other groups, such as the matrilineal organization of the Landouma and the land tenure system of the Nalou. Soussou is the lingua franca of Lower Guinea, and almost everyone speaks it either as a first language or in addition to his or her mother tongue.

The Soussou are primarily cultivators and traders who dominate the commerce between the coast and the interior. Those on the coast are fishermen who also rely heavily on coconut palms and oil palms for their livelihood.

The Baga

The Baga, largest of the minor groups in Lower Guinea, live scattered along the coast from Conakry and the Camayenne Peninsula to the Rio Nunez estuary, a distance of about 160 miles. Most of them are cultivators and fishermen. Although most Baga remember their history no further

back than to the founder of their village, they were reported by sixteenth-century Portuguese explorers to be living in that area. A tradition survives among them that they originally inhabited the western part of the Fouta Djallon, from where they were driven out first by the Dialonké and later by the Peul.

Northwest of Boffa in the coastal swamps around Monchon live the Baga Foré (Soussou for black Baga, meaning possibly pagan Baga), who are mostly rice cultivators. They seem to have been among the earliest Baga to reach the coast and have been strongly influenced by their more powerful Nalou neighbors. Their language is related more closely to that of the Nalou than to that of other Baga.

The Baga are under pressure from the expanding Soussou. Young men often go to work in the towns, marry girls from other ethnic groups, give up their local religion, adopt Islam, and begin referring to themselves as Soussou. They are a good example of a small ethnic group melting easily into a larger one.

The Nalou

The Nalou live on the lower Rio Nunez and Kogan River and on the Tristão Islands. Like the Baga they are said to have come originally from the Fouta Djallon. The Nalou are cultivators and artisans. Among the latter group, blacksmiths are the most important. As they were not involved in the early conflicts with Peul nomads, some stayed in the Fouta Djallon and are considered the ancestors of the still-existing caste of blacksmiths in Peul society (see ch. 5). Others, who had become serfs of Peul masters, left them and went south or west when domestic slavery was outlawed in 1905.

The Landouma, the Tyapi, and the Mikhiforé

The Landouma (Landoma) are closely related to the Baga and speak a dialect of the same language. They live inland from the Nalou between the Rio Nunez and the estuary of the Fatala River and west of Gaoual, along the Guinea-Bissau border.

Some groups in the Gaoual Administrative Region are called Tyapi (Tiapi), although they refer to themselves as Cocoli. They belong to the least studied people of Guinea. They speak the same language as the Landouma and consider themselves related to them. Portuguese explorers mentioned them as being in the Guinea-Bissau area as early as the fifteenth century. According to their tradition, they came orginally from the Fouta Djallon.

Between the Landouma and the Baga live the Mikhiforé. They are a small Mandé-speaking group related linguistically to the Malinké in Upper Guinea.

The Mmani

The Mmani (sing., Manil; the Soussou call them Mandenyi) live between the Kolente (Great Scarcies in Sierra Leone) and Forécariah rivers. They are rice cultivators; but the gathering of nuts from oil and coconut palms, fishing, and salt extraction are important subsidiary activities. The Mmani seem to have been latecomers to the coastal area. Several Mmani place names are apparently of Baga origin. Their language is dying out and is being replaced by Soussou in many villages.

PEOPLES OF MIDDLE GUINEA

The Peul

The Peul belong to a large ethnic group spread through much of West Africa from Senegal to Lake Chad. Their language, Poular, is spoken by about 7 million people. More than 80 percent of the Guinean Peul live in the Fouta Djallon. Their principal concentrations are in the Labé, Pita, Dalaba, and Mamou administrative regions, but they constitute the majority in most of the Fouta Djallon. Outside of Guinea they live mainly in the Fouta Toro of Senegal, in the Macina region of Mali, and in the Adamawa highlands of Nigeria and Cameroon. Smaller groups are located elsewhere in West Africa. Each speaks a distinctive, though mutually intelligible, dialect. The Peul have used arabic script to create a vernacular, essentially religious, literature. The Koran, for example, has been translated word for word into Poular the way it is spoken in the Fouta Djallon, and there is also a body of secular poetry and prose.

The ultimate point of Peul origin is still at issue, but their nomadic ancestors are thought to have come from the area north of the Sénégal River and to have moved gradually south and eastward during the last 400 or 500 years. The Peul started coming to the Fouta Djallon during the sixteenth century and perhaps earlier. They lived among the sparsely settled indigenous cultivators and hunters, such as the Soussou and Dialonké, with whom they seemed to have had amicable relations. Nomads and settled cultivators developed a symbiotic relationship that was advantageous to both. The Peul supplied milk and animal products from their herds in exchange for produce from cultivators' fields. In return for caring for the villagers' livestock, the nomads were allowed to pasture their own herds in the cultivated fields after the annual harvest, thus providing fertilizer. Gradually many of the Peul became sedentary or semisedentary cultivators as well as stockraisers. Some had already become partially sedentary in Macina before coming to the Fouta Djallon.

During the eighteenth century an Islamic holy war started in the Fouta Toro of Senegal. Under its impetus many more Peul came to the Fouta Djallon of Guinea, and great numbers of the Muslim converts then turned on the unbelievers in their area. Eventually, after a long series of alliances and internal struggles, most of what is present-day Middle Guinea was brought under direct Peul control. Most of the original inhabitants who did not leave became serfs to Peul masters. In present-day Guinea at least one-third of the people of the Fouta Djallon are descendants of Dialonké, Malinké, and others who were subjugated by the Peul.

Although most Peul consider themselves Muslims, many differ little from their non-Muslim neighbors in religious practice. According to legend, the Peul are descended from four sons of Omar ibn Assi, reputedly the first to bring Islam to the Macina region in what later became Mali. Each son is considered to be the founder of one of the four great tribes into which the Peul are traditionally divided—Dialloubé, Ourebé, Ndayébé, and Ferobé. Historically prominent tribal names; such as Diallo, Ba or Baldé, Bari, and So, are still current but no longer signify organized kin groups.

Under the influence of sedentation and Islam, a social hierarchy developed among the Peul with a hereditary nobility at the top and hereditary slaves at the bottom. It no longer exists, but the attitudes associated with this system survive in attenuated form. Social, economic, and psychological habits of dependency, built up over generations, have given way only slowly. The severance of traditional dependency relationships has left a patchwork of Peul, Dialonké, Malinké, and other settlements in the Fouta Djallon. Communities that once were integral parts of a feudal hierarchy dominated by the Peul have become formally independent. The closeness of the feudal past, with all the class and caste consciousness it generated, is still an obstacle to the equitable political and social integration of these communities (see ch. 5).

The Dialonké

The Dialonké (Djallonké, Dyalonké), who call themselves Jallonké, are considered by some simply a branch of the Soussou. They are said to be indigenous to the south and central part of the Fouta Djallon, which the Peul named after them. During the holy war, which began about 1727, most were reduced to serfdom. Those few who accepted Islam remained free and were allowed to keep their land. Many, however, left, going either south to the foothills of the mountains in Mamou Administrative Region or east to live among the Malinké of Upper Guinea, especially in the administrative region of Faranah. Smaller concentrations are found in the Kouroussa Administrative Region. Additional Dialonké are located in Senegal.

The main activity of the Dialonké is cultivation, but they also raise a few animals and engage in trade. There exists among them a caste of ironsmiths, whose women are potters, and a special caste of professional bards.

The Diakhanké

The Diakhanké live in an enclave at Touba and in a satellite village called Toubanding (little Touba) in Peul country in the Middle Guinea administrative region of Gaoual. The ancestors of this group came there in the late 1700s from Mali and were probably partly Soninké, the ethnic group that had constituted the basic population of the Ghana Empire (see ch. 2). Diakhanké men are respected by the Peul as greatly learned and deeply religious. Some of their ancestors are reputed to have adopted Islam in the eighth century. In contemporary times at least one son in each family spends many years in Koranic studies with a noted Islamic scholar.

The economic situation of the Diakhanké gradually deteriorated in the first half of the twentieth century after the 1905 government decree freeing the slaves who had worked their land. From then on the Diakhanké had to cultivate their fields and could devote less time to religious teachings, which had been their primary source of income. Some teachers, whose students pay for tuition by working in the fields, however, continue to be fairly wealthy. Some Diakhanké have moved to the urban environments of Boké and Conakry.

The Tenda

The name Tenda covers five groups and seems to have been applied by the Peul to the Coniagui, Bassari, Badyaranké, Boeni, and Mayo. The five groups share some cultural traits that they have retained in the midst of very different societies, either Malinké or Peul. Ethnologists range them among the original inhabitants of that region who were once much more widespread but were pushed long ago into a few recesses by other ethnic groups.

The Coniagui, Bassari, and Badyaranké live around Youkounkoun in the northern part of Middle Guinea. The Coniagui and the Bassari straddle the Guinea-Senegal border, and many have migrated toward the Senegalese towns. Some also live in Guinea-Bissau. Both groups are matrilineal, tracing succession through females. The Badyaranké, who are related to both the Coniagui and the Bassari, seem to have been influenced by the Manding and might even be part Manding. The Boeni might be Bassari who have become Muslims. There is little difference between them and the Mayo.

PEOPLES OF UPPER GUINEA

The Malinké

The Malinké are one of the three most important groups among the cluster of linguistically and culturally related people called Manding by English speakers and Mandingue by French speakers. They are distributed among several West African countries in an arc of some 800 miles from the mouth of the Gambia River in the northwest to the interior of the Ivory Coast in the southeast. The other two groups are the Bambara, who live mainly in Mali, and the Dyoula, who are known as traders over a large part of West Africa and are scattered in Guinea among the Malinké and the forest peoples.

The ancestors of almost all Manding groups were once united in the great Mali Empire, the successive capitals of which were located in the traditional heartland known as Mandé or Mandin on the upper Niger River between Bamako and Siguiri (see ch. 2). The Malinké are said to have been in Guinea as early as the thirteenth century.

Most Malinké live in Upper Guinea. The largest concentrations are in the administrative regions of Kankan, Siguiri, and Kouroussa, where such old clan names as Keita, Camara, Traoré, and Kourouma still predominate. The Malinké are not only cultivators but also traders and as such have profited from cultural contacts. Their adaptability and their strong social structure have led to their hegemony over other peoples or to the absorption of smaller ethnic groups who live close to them. They are gradually spreading into the Forest Region to the south, where their language is becoming a lingua franca.

The Malinké are almost all Muslims, but their earlier religious practices, centering on ancestor cults and a supernatural relationship to the land, persist. The Maninka-Mory, a Malinké subgroup centered in the Kankan area, are perhaps the most Islamized of all Malinké groups and are known as tradesmen and religious functionaries. Their name for other Malinké—Sounounké—means pagan, perhaps dating back to the seventeenth and eighteenth centuries, when the Maninka-Mory led a religious revival in the area (see ch. 5). Although their speech is not distinctive, the names of some of their villages (such as Karfarmoria, Tassiliman, Fodecariah, and Foussé) and their principal clan names (Cissé, Diakité, Diane, and Kaba) support their claim of having been originally part of the Soninké (Sarakollé or Sissé), a Mandé-speaking people from the western Sudan (see Glossary).

The Ouassoulounké

The Ouassoulounké (Wasulunka) live west of Kankan in the southeastern part of Upper Guinea on both sides of the Mali border. Although they are culturally akin to the Malinké and speak their language, they consider themselves a separate ethnic group.

Recent research indicates that they are the Peul who were conquered by Samory Touré and that they carved out a small principality for themselves after his defeat in the last decade of the nineteenth century. They still have Peul patronymic names, such as Diallo, Sidi Bey, and Sangaré.

PEOPLES OF THE FOREST REGION

The Kissi

The Kissi are concentrated in the Guéckédou and Kissidougou administrative regions. There are some Malinké and Kouranko in the north and northwest of Kissidougou Administrative Region, but the dense forest farther south is inhabited only by the Kissi. Some Kissi live on the other side of the borders of Sierra Leone and Liberia.

In the seventeenth century the Kissi were driven out of the southeastern part of the Fouta Djallon by the Dialonké. Originally they raised fonio (a variety of millet), resulting in widespread deforestation as they shifted their fields. In the eighteenth century they adopted the practice of rice cultivation (for which they use the Malinké word *malo*) from their eastern neighbors. When Asian varieties were introduced from Sierra Leone during the second half of the nineteenth century, the Kissi fully launched into the cultivation of rice. They planted their rice in the bottom of marshy valleys or on deforested hillsides. Since then they have become famous as expert growers. The Malinké call them "people of the ricefields."

Although their region borders on the savanna, the Kissi are people of the forest. The young go to work in the cities, banana plantations, or other enterprises in Lower Guinea in order to earn money, but they remain attached to their village and almost always go back there to live.

They are culturally and linguistically closely related to the Mmani of the coast of Lower Guinea. The northern Kissi are in regular contact with the Malinké and increasingly adopt their language and customs. One of the principal Kissi families has taken the name Keita, which is traditionally associated with a ruling Malinké family.

The Toma

In Macenta Administrative Region to the east of the Kissi live the Toma, who call themselves Loma. A greater number of Toma live in Liberia, where they are known as Busi or Buzi. The Toma in Guinea are geographically divided into two sections by a number of Malinké villages. The Toma are said to have been in the country before the arrival of the Kouranko, Kissi, and Guerzé. The northwestern section is being assimilated by Malinké.

The Guerzé

East of the Toma live the Guerzé (Nguerze, Ngere). They are mainly concentrated in Nzérékoré Administrative Region, but just as many live across the border in Liberia, where they are known under the name Kpelle (Pele). Most of the Guerzé are cultivators, but they rely less on rice and more on root crops, food gathering, and hunting than do the Kissi. They are said to live in the region that their ancestors chose in the seventeenth century in order not to be troubled by the Malinké.

Other Forest Groups

To the east of the Guerzé are two smaller groups, the Mano (Manon) and the Kono. Both speak Mandé languages. The majority of the Mano live in Liberia. The Konianké (Konuak) constitute a small subgroup of the Malinké, in whose midst they live in the north of Beyla Administrative

Region. They came as conquerors to this area in precolonial times and have since lived peacefully as cultivators and merchants, usually in administrative centers and important markets. The Kouranko (Koranko) live in the northern part of Kissidougou Region amid the Malinké, to whom they are distantly related. Around the city of Macenta lives a small mixed group, the Toma-Manian, who are the descendants of Toma women and immigrant Malinké men. They speak Toma.

FOREIGNERS

No figures were available in early 1975 for the number of foreigners living in Guinea. French, and Lebanese and Syrians with French passports, had constituted the largest group. In the early 1970s, however, there were only about fifty Frenchmen reported to be living in the country, most of them in Conakry, and an unknown number of Lebanese and Syrians had either left the country or had become Guinean citizens.

The Lebanese (the majority of them Christians) and the Syrians (who are mainly Muslims) have been in the country since the end of the nineteenth century. Until the socialist philosophy of the postindependence government began to curtail their economic activities seriously, they played a preponderant role in commerce.

The diplomats, teachers, and various experts working in aid projects came from both western and eastern countries. Russians, Czechs, and Yugoslavs were fairly numerous. Chinese from the People's Republic of China (PRC) constituted the majority of this group. They worked in rice cultivation and various infrastructure projects, notably rural electrification. The number of Africans from other countries who were in Guinea in early 1975 was not known. They included the Balantes, who have come across the sparsely settled border with Guinea-Bissau in increasing numbers since the beginning of the armed resistance against the Portuguese in the middle 1950s.

LANGUAGES

Guinea has one official language—French—and eight national languages because the regime does not wish to offend some of its citizens by giving one language preeminence over others. The national languages are the country's major vernaculars: Poular, Malinké, Soussou, Kissi, Guerzé, Toma, Coniagui, and Bassari. In 1962, with the help of the United Nations Educational, Scientific and Cultural Organization (UNESCO), a literacy campaign was begun. The program was designed to teach people to read and write in their own language. Because the African languages spoken in Guinea do not have their own scripts, they were transcribed into a modified Latin alphabet. Even government employees who were literate in French were required to become literate in their native language under penalty of being dismissed. Lack of funds for books and teachers, however, soon slowed down the campaign. In 1975 literacy efforts concentrated mainly on Poular, Malinké, Soussou, and Guerzé.

The Voice of the Revolution, Conakry's radio station, has daily ten-minute broadcasts in all the national languages, using French the rest of the time. Theatrical presentations are always given in one of the national languages in line with the official policy of emphasizing the cultural heritage of the various ethnic groups.

Guinean languages belong either to the West Atlantic family of languages, which are spoken in the coastal areas from Senegal to Liberia, or to the Mandé languages prevalent in much of the savanna area and in the interior forests of West Africa from the Atlantic Ocean to the Black Volta River in Ghana and in parts of western Nigeria. Both language families are part of the larger Niger-Congo linguistic group (see table 3).

It has been estimated that about 8 million people in West Africa speak a Mandé language as either their first or second language. In geographic spread, Mandé ranks with Hausa and Swahili. The Mandé languages spoken in Guinea either belong to a subgroup called Manding or are marginally related to Manding. David Dalby, who has made a detailed study of Manding people and languages, has ranked them in terms of relatedness. Of those spoken in Guinea, according to Dalby, Malinké and Dyoula are closest. At the next level he places Kono, which is not strictly

Table 3. Guinea, Classification and Geographic Distribution of Languages

Geographic Region	West Atlantic Languages		Mandé Languages
	Southern Branch	Northern Branch	
Lower Guinea	Baga Landouma Mmani	Nalou	Soussou Mikhiforé
Middle Guinea	....	Poular Badyaranké Coniagui Bassari	Dialonké Diakhanké
Upper Guinea	....	....	Malinké Ouassoulounké
Forest Region	Kissi	....	Guerzé Toma Mano Kono Konianké Kouranko Toma-Manian

part of the Manding group, although Kono is closer to Manding than to any other language. Manding and Kono speakers can understand each other to some degree. More distantly related are Soussou and Dialonké; still less, Guerzé and Toma; and least of all, Mano.

Adoption of a major language by members of a smaller group is often the first step toward cultural assimilation. In Lower Guinea—including Conakry, which is Baga territory—Soussou is increasingly becoming the lingua franca. Its influence reaches in the north to the neighborhood of Boké, in the east to Mamou, and in the south to part of Sierra Leone. During the first phase of this development, Soussou is used only for communication with people of other ethnic groups. In the next phase the young generation speak their parents' language imperfectly and adopt Soussou as a first language. Eventually the old generation dies out, and entire villages of Baga, Nalou, and others speak only Soussou. The same process can be observed in the Forest Region, where Malinké, the language of well-to-do traders, is more and more becoming the lingua franca among Kissi, Toma, and Guerzé.

French fills a need for administrative, technical, and business communications inside the country and for inter-African and international relations. It is understood by about 20 percent of the population and is used as a lingua franca between educated Guineans of varying ethnic affiliation. It is the language of instruction beginning with the fifth year of school.

INTERETHNIC RELATIONS

The years before independence were marked by intense rivalry among political groups that were, until the founding of the Guinean branch of the African Democratic Rally (Rassemblement Démocratique Africain-—RDA) in 1947, primarily formed on the basis of ethnic and regional affiliation (see ch. 2). Since independence the government has sought by all official means to minimize the political and social implications of ethnic differences, making it difficult to assess their present-day importance. President Ahmed Sékou Touré reiterates that there are no longer Peul, Malinké, Soussou, and other ethnic distinctions in the country but Guineans who differ only in their revolutionary fervor.

Whatever ethnic tensions survived in the 1970s had their roots in ancient histories of conquest, subjugation, harassment, and exploitation of one group by another. In the 1970s not all Coniagui, Bassari, and Badyaranké had forgotten that their ancestors were routed from their territory by the Peul during the nineteenth century and were forced to pay tribute to Peul rulers. Soussou, Dialonké, and others also remembered that their ancestors were enslaved or displaced by the Peul.

During colonial times the administration strengthened its position by exploiting ethnic tensions, such as the opposition between Peul masters and Dialonké serfs, competition between Nalou and Landouma chiefs, and other latent rivalries. It increased the power of traditional chiefs, thus emphasizing ethnic divisions. The administration's economic measures, however, eventually led to a breakdown of barriers between ethnic groups. The exploitation of mineral resources and the establishment of banana plantations in Lower Guinea, which began in the middle 1930s, attracted people of different regions who then lived and worked in close proximity. After World War II Peul from the Fouta Djallon began going to Upper Guinea to work among the Malinké as stockraisers, butchers, and tailors or south to Lower Guinea where they earned their living as small-scale vendors, as domestic workers, and in other occupations.

In the course of modernization a bourgeoisie that was open to contacts evolved. Teachers, doctors, employees of the administration and private enterprises, and members of the army had common interests that often proved stronger than ethnic ties. The ideology of the ruling Democratic Party of Guinea (Parti Démocratique de Guinée—PDG), which preached equality of all races, appealed first to the intellectuals among this group. It was particularly successful in Lower Guinea, where the cash economy had taken root and where traditional society was less structured than in the Fouta Djallon or Upper Guinea. Malinké cultivators, however, did begin to enter the party in 1954. In the following years the Kissi, Toma, Guerzé, Mano, and Kono in the Forest Region flocked to the PDG when it began to fight the chiefs who had been discredited as tools created by the colonial regime and who had enriched themselves at the expense of the people. The feudal, seminomadic society of the Fouta Djallon, which had remained largely in the subsistence economy, held out longest against the PDG. But in the elections for the Territorial Assembly in March 1957, the PDG, without appealing to local ethnic loyalties, won fifty-seven of sixty seats.

After independence, integration of ethnic groups became the avowed aim of the regime. Members of all ethnic groups were promised an equal chance in the political, economic, and social arena by President Touré. All the features of the Guinean constitution—one party, one legislative chamber whose members are elected on a single national slate, one executive head, one criminal and civil law code, one flag, and one anthem—were designed to foster national rather than ethnocentric feelings, as were public speeches and slogans, education in public schools and youth organizations, and the practice of rotating public officials. Administrators, party officials, teachers, and members of the army and militia were frequently posted outside their native area, a policy that encouraged interethnic marriages.

More than 80 percent of all Guineans, however, are rural inhabitants, and their isolation defies attempts at ethnic fraternization. Economic stagnation has driven the majority back into the subsistence economy, restricting their social ties to those within their local community. For the poor cultivator, membership within the family and the larger kin group remains the major guarantee against economic disaster. Outside Conakry interethnic marriages amount to less than 1 percent of the total, according to unofficial estimates. Within Conakry interethnic marriages usually involved educated partners and, particularly, government officials. A study conducted in 1967 showed that Malinké officials sometimes took Peul wives but that it was rare to find a Peul man marrying a Malinké or Soussou woman.

In the administrative regions of Boké and Kindia, quarrels between herders and cultivators correspond to ethnic divisions between the Peul and the Soussou. In the Forest Region growers of export crops feel exploited by enterprising Malinké, who after World War II began buying up their coffee, palm products, and cola nuts. Kissi, Toma, and Guerzé who experience economic difficulties blame them on the Malinké merchant, on the Malinké immigrant who often cultivates his crops with more success, or on the Malinké administrator or party official.

Despite government and party injunctions against nepotism, even people in salaried employment depend on a relative to find a job or to get a share in the distribution of imported goods. Urban dwellers, especially the unskilled and semieducated, tend to have friends mainly among those of the same ethnic group or even from the same village. In Conakry the sections called Dixinn-Ecole and Hafia are inhabited mostly by Peul; Dixinn-Port is inhabited mainly by Soussou. Malinké, Soussou, and Peul live in different parts of the town of Mamou. Kindia, which is in Soussou territory, has a special Peul section; and Kissidougou, in Kissi country, has a special Malinké section.

Ethnic differences are buttressed by disparate self-conceptions. The Peul are said to see themselves as more aristocratic than others, the Soussou as better educated, the Malinké as possessing a special flair for business and being therefore richer, and the peoples of the Forest Region as working harder than others.

Another factor that militates to some degree against the building of Guinean nationalism is the attachment that exists with people across the country's borders. There are Coniagui and Bassari in Senegal and Guinea-Bissau, Kouranko and Kissi in Sierra Leone, and Guerzé and Toma in Liberia. The Peul of the Fouta Djallon have ties with Peul in Senegal and Mali. Malinké have commercial and family ties in Senegal, Mali, and the Ivory Coast.

Continuous official accusations of racism and regionalism attest to their persistence. In 1965 a decree was issued that deals harshly with persons convicted of using ethnic connections in procuring a post or of favoring members of one's own ethnic group over those of another. The penalty may be ten years in prison.

The government has tried to deal with the ethnic problem by proportioning government jobs and appointments to the tribunals of conciliation within each party committee on the basis of ethnic affiliation and by giving recognition and support to different cultures. Schoolbooks emphasize the traditional values and qualities of all Guinean peoples. The twice-a-year national dance competition between performers from all parts of Guinea is designed to keep alive the special cultural heritage of each participating group.

Ethnic and local loyalties, however, are more a restraint than an impediment to the creation of national unity. The principal contest is not so much between one ethnic group and another as it is between the local community and the central government. In other words, it is between those who have vested political, economic, or emotional interests in a traditional order that emphasized, among other values, ethnic loyalty and those who are committed—in tune with party ideology—to building a modern national state. The competition between local groups and the government is, however, an unequal one. The chief weakness of the local communities is that they no longer have the traditional structure and machinery to keep alive the historic cultural and emotional ties among their members.

Traditional functions have steadily been taken over by soldiers, policemen, judges, labor unions, cooperatives, women's and youth organizations, and agencies of the government. The national leadership, which controls the schools, the press, and the radio—and has the power to reward its friends and punish its enemies—has succeeded in involving almost everyone in one way or another. People are encouraged- —sometimes forced—to identify themselves as Guineans, rather than as Malinké or Soussou, and to call each other "comrade." Such pressures are especially successful among young people.

CHAPTER 5

THE SOCIAL SYSTEM

The principal social distinction within Guinean society is between those who are in positions of public power and authority and those who are not. High social status, prestige, and privilege are attainable only through participation in the government, the sole political party, and the parapolitical mass organizations—trade unions, youth groups, women's organizations, and various cooperatives.

In the past the large kin group—the basis of village organization and the individual's social world—tended to be a corporate body, responsible for the actions of its members. Subsistence, regulation of marriage, education of the young, care of the old, the paying of taxes and tributes, and the maintenance of law and order were the group's collective concerns. A man's place in society was determined by his family's status and other circumstances of birth. Power and prestige were monopolized by the older generation.

Social and economic changes after World War II affected the traditional structures. Many villagers were drafted into labor or military service and taken from their communities; others, especially young people, often left of their own volition, drawn by the opportunity for wage labor and personal freedom. The physical dispersion of village members made it difficult for the kin group to function as a corporate entity, however strong the affective bond between kinsmen remained. Colonial administrators, acting through appointed territorial chiefs, took over many of the legal, educational, and police functions of the kin community. Indigenous religious beliefs, too, were weakened by social and economic changes. The cash economy rendered the earth less sacred and the ancestor cult less vital for the migrants and the urbanized. The range of individual loyalties and obligations began to shrink from remotely related kinsmen to individual households.

Since 1957, when Guineans effectively began to govern themselves, the national leaders have directed a many-sided assault on the traditional social system, aiming at a complete metamorphosis of human relations. New laws were passed regulating marriage, divorce, and inheritance. The party took over some of the functions of land distribution that had formerly been performed by lineage elders. Generally an attempt was made to lift the individual out of a world in which family and kin group define his place in society into one in which education, skills, and national citizenship take precedence.

The major tool in this task has been the Democratic Party of Guinea (Parti Démocratique de Guinée—PDG), particularly the party committee. Two years after independence some 26,000 local committees, varying in size from a few to several hundred people, were in operation. Hamlets that had been isolated since they were founded were suddenly thrust into the mainstream of national life. In 1964 the number of committees was drastically reduced because of changing party membership policies, but it has been estimated that in that year one person in eleven, including children, held an elective office either in the government or in the party apparatus (see ch. 8). In principle at least, during committee meetings each member's voice carries equal weight, regardless of social distinction, sex, age, or ethnic or religious affiliation.

In some communities the changeover has been considerably slower than in others, and social stratification continues to reflect earlier social divisions. In the Fouta Djallon area, for example, aristocratic Peul families, although they sometimes live less well than their former serfs, persist as a social elite in their local communities and continue to provide much of the religious and even political leadership, despite the government's attempt to break their hold on the area. The trend there too, however, is toward social leveling.

Generally the change has been most effective in the urban communities and probably least in the remote areas of the interior. In a genuine break with the past, the party has since 1954 enlisted the support of young people and women. It has also attempted to influence religious beliefs. A persuasive propaganda campaign was launched during which some aspects of Islam were castigated and certain Koranic teachers denounced as fakes. The Roman Catholic clergy were condemned as agents of French colonialism who had supported the opposition during the struggle for independence. Official efforts were particularly harsh regarding indigenous religions, which—in the party view—were tied to archaic social structures and considered a handicap in the development of a dynamic modern society. Masks, some sacred forests, and other symbols were systematically destroyed.

In areas of religious activity that pose no threat to its exercise of full power, however, or that provide an opportunity to extend its power, the government has been willing and even eager to identify itself with the Muslim majority. The construction of mosques, for example, is explicitly provided for in economic planning, and the government arranges annually for charter flights to Mecca.

Outside observers have pointed out that the attempts at total transformation of the social system reflect only the wishes of a small minority and that participation in and enthusiasm for party activities has waned as the desired economic gains have failed to be realized. The exodus from Guinea of a large part of the intelligentsia as well as other segments of the population seems to bear this out. In early 1975 it was impossible to estimate with accuracy how much of the traditional social system had survived or whether the changes that had been undertaken since independence were permanent or tied to the fortunes of President Ahmed Sékou Touré's regime.

TRADITIONAL ELEMENTS IN THE SOCIAL SYSTEM

The small, relatively isolated community of ten to 100 families was traditionally the principal unit of social organization for the majority of Guineans. Within most Guinean villages the basis of organization was the patrilineage, consisting of all the descendants in the male line of a known common ancestor. Among a few peoples, such as the Coniagui, the Bassari, and other small ethnic groups, social organization was based on the matrilineage, which consisted of all the descendants through the female line of a common female ancestor. In either case an individual's closest friends and neighbors were also his closest kinsmen. Friendship, cooperation, and mutual assistance followed the network of kinship ties.

Lineages were ranked according to the length of time they had been settled in the area, highest status being accorded to the descendants of the village founder. The founder of a lineage—usually no more than four or five generations removed—was one of the principal objects of reverence, for it was he who first cleared the land and established the rights to ownership and use. Indeed, it was traditionally only through membership in a lineage that the individual had rights to land, the right to demand help in working it, and the right to a share of its products. To an outsider a lineage appeared to be at different times a large family, a landowning corporation, a religious sect, a cooperative work group, or simply a local community. Typically the senior male, acting with the lineage elders, was alternately patriarch, trustee and administrator of lineage property, chief priest, labor coordinator, and village headman.

Hamlets and small villages usually consisted of a single lineage. Larger villages often had two or more lineages. Their members usually considered themselves related to each other but could not trace the connection. The composition of wards or quarters of towns generally corresponded to similarly organized kin groups.

Lineages usually retained the names of their founding ancestors. Even when there was no real kinship connection, members of lineages of the same name assumed that they were descended from a common ancestor and were therefore kinsmen. Where related lineages resided in the same community, they usually acted as a single corporate group, the senior male of the senior lineage acting as head of the whole kin community. Where the related lineages were settled in different communities, they had no common corporate existence, but their members were expected to be hospitable and friendly to each other. In general, however, the recognition of kinship and of mutual obligation was extended only to those relatives in other lineages with whom the individual had established a personal relationship.

Among the Peul, the dominant ethnic group in Middle Guinea, a clear distinction was made between maximal lineages *(lenyol)*, major lineages *(gorol)* and, at the lowest level of segmentation, minimal lineages (*suudu*, which also means house), consisting of the male or female descendants of the same paternal grandfather. Members of maximal lineages were usually geographically dispersed, but the major lineage was a corporate economic and social entity. Members held land collectively and gave each other social and physical support, especially during life-cycle ceremonies.

Typically an individual married outside his or her own lineage. Among patrilineal peoples marriage to a member of one's mother's patrilineage was frequently the preferred form. Thus the Malinké, Soussou, and Kissi preferred marriage with a mother's brother's daughter but forbade it with a father's brother's daughter, who was, of course, of one's own patrilineage. An exception occurred among some strongly Islamized Peul and Malinké families. Here, according to Muslim laws, marriage inside the patrilineage—especially with a father's brother's daughter—was preferred.

Among the patrilineal peoples the most general form of the family was the extended family, consisting of a senior man, his wife or wives, his sons and unmarried daughters, his sons' wives and children, and possibly his younger brothers and their wives. At the death of the grandparent generation, it would consist of a senior man and his younger brothers, their wives, children, and unmarried daughters. Residence was patrilocal; at marriage daughters left the family and went to live with their husbands and their husbands' kinsmen. The typical extended family in matrilineal societies consisted of a senior man, his wife or wives, their young children, and one or more of his sisters' sons, their wives, and their children. When descent was traced through females, a person inherited property and other rights from a maternal uncle. A man's heirs thus were not his own sons but those of his sister.

The nuclear family (a husband, his wife or wives, and their unmarried children) within the extended family had rights and interests that were distinguished from those of the larger group. Husband and wife, jointly or separately, often had rights to their own piece of land and to other personal property for which they were accountable to no one. They formed the principal unit of consumption and production. But even where the nuclear family constituted a separate residential unit, it was only as a member group of the extended family that it participated in lineage and community affairs.

Succession to positions of authority was the primary concern of the lineage and the extended family. Within the lineage authority rested ultimately with the senior man of the senior generation. Individual, family, and lineage rights to property frequently overlapped. Traditional inheritance patterns were seldom clear cut, and conflicting claims of inheritance were the most common cause of litigation.

Within each community people were commonly grouped by age, the major divisions or age-groups corresponding roughly to the three living generations: young boys, young unmarried or married men who lived with their parents, and the mature. A group formed spontaneously among boys born within the span of a few years. Its members then moved together throughout life from one social state to another. Circumcision, special initiation rites and, among Muslims, the complete reading of the Koran by age thirteen to fifteen marked the transition from the first age-group to the second. The division between the second and third age-groups was not as clear cut as that between the first and the second. A man joined the mature group when he established his household and became responsible for his own domestic group. Only then did he fully take part in the village's economic and social life. There were parallel age-groups for females.

Those who were initiated at the same time were subordinate to those who were initiated before and thus were superior to those who followed. The senior age-group held the important positions in the society. Frequently the individuals who held these offices were also the heads of the lineages and members of the councils of elders. Men and women usually chose their closest friends from those in their own age-group. Age-groups, along with kin groups, were commonly used as the basis for organizing mutual help associations and cooperative work parties.

In the Forest Region, among some coastal groups, and in parts of Upper Guinea, men's and women's secret societies were widespread and performed important functions, especially in education and law enforcement. Such societies usually included all adult men or women in the community, and they supervised the extensive training and elaborate rites connected with initiation.

Almost everywhere in Guinea there were endogamous groups who were specialists in certain crafts, such as metalworking, carpentry, dyeing, and praise singing. The wives of metalworkers were usually potters. The economic situation of these artisans was not unfavorable because they worked at their specialty during the dry season and cultivated land during the rains. Techniques were transmitted from one generation to the next.

Some ethnic groups developed social and political units beyond the village level. An outstanding example are the Peul of Upper Guinea, who created complex social structures on a large scale based on domination of the area's more simply organized peoples. This domination assumed various forms. During the eighteenth and nineteenth centuries some conquered people were assimilated and absorbed; others were enslaved. A highly stratified feudal society evolved in which Peul overlords frequently claimed both the land and the cultivators. In this society four main social strata existed. There were chiefs and their patrilineal kinsmen, free Peul, Peul of the bush, and serfs.

The chiefly lineages furnished the rulers of the nine territorial districts into which the Fouta Djallon was divided (see ch. 2). Chiefs ruled in conjunction with the elders of the free lineages, whose members were descendants of those who had chosen to fight in the jihad (see Glossary). The free lineages supplied the chiefs for the *misside* (a village or cluster of villages with a mosque). *Misside* chiefs were concerned with marriage, divorce, inheritance, distribution of land, and the recruitment of men for the jihad. Their decisions were made with the help of lineage elders and the judges of the mosque. The Peul of the bush were descendants of those who either had not participated in religious campaigns or had actively hindered them. Consequently they were forced to pay tribute and, when they died, a fairly substantial part of their property (cattle, land, or gold) was given to the *misside* chief.

Serfs were descendants of earlier non-Peul inhabitants of the Fouta Djallon, such as the Dialonké and Soussou. Their numbers steadily increased with the acquisition of prisoners of war. The proportion of serfs in the Fouta Djallon, who had constituted about one-half of the population in the beginning of the twentieth century, remained until independence at about one-third. Serfs lived in their own villages, which did not have a mosque. They were economically self-sufficient, cultivating fields and gardens that had been put at their disposal by their masters. In return they worked five days each week on their masters' fields and gave him 10 percent of their own harvest, except maize (corn). Serf wives cultivated their own gardens and also those of their masters' wives, fetched water, washed clothes, cooked for their masters' households, and cared for their children. Serf children helped with domestic work in the masters' households. The masters paid their serfs' taxes and were held responsible for any infractions of the law the serfs might commit.

Serfs were regarded as belonging to the maximal and major lineages of their masters because their own origins were uncertain. The distinction between chiefly and nonchiefly lineages became blurred under French colonial rule, and the main distinction in Peul society has become that between descendants of serfs and freeborn Peul.

SOCIAL CHANGE AND MODIFICATION

Modernizing Influences

The suppression of domestic slave trading in 1905, the development of plantation production of export crops in the late 1930s, the beginning of modern mining and industry after World War II, and the introduction of Western ideas and practices deeply affected social structures. Village headmen, paramount chiefs and, in the Fouta Djallon, regional rulers were made part of the colonial administration. They collected taxes and ensured the fulfillment of conscription quotas for military service and various forms of forced labor. Where traditional chiefs demonstrated a willingness to carry out French policies, they were permitted to remain in office. Where they did not, more compliant ones were appointed, often from outside dominant families or from collateral lines who had only tenuous claim to legitimacy. Where large-scale chiefdoms had been nonexistent, as in the Forest Region, or wherever the existing structure did not match the colonial pattern, new chiefdoms were created.

The Peul aristocracy of the Fouta Djallon largely collaborated with the French colonial administration. In return their social system was left comparatively untouched, although certain chiefs were replaced. Serfdom, which was the economic base, persisted to the eve of independence. Nevertheless, traditional Peul society was indirectly undermined. No significant mineral resources were discovered in the Fouta Djallon before World War II, nor was the land suited for large-scale cultivation; a poor soil was slowly exhausted and could no longer meet the demands of a growing population (see ch. 3). The creation of job opportunities elsewhere made it possible to escape from economic stagnation and low social status. Many serfs departed to work on southern plantations or in the cities in Guinea, Senegal, Sierra Leone, and Ivory Coast. Thus labor became the main export of the Fouta Djallon. When serfs departed with their families, wives of their former masters had to do the cooking, fetching of water, and other tasks formerly performed by serf women. No longer were free Peul able to demand a serf's daughter as a concubine or wife.

Serfs also performed military service in World War II and sent money home to their families. Later, as veterans, they drew pensions and were able to acquire cattle, which had hitherto been a prerogative of free Peul. They bought land, plows, and trucks and went into trade. They attended school and found jobs in the administrative and the private sector. Money created a new kind of equality. Increasingly decisions regarding serf marriage, inheritance, and other internal affairs were made by the elders of serf villages. Although serf elders assumed neither an economic nor a political role, their influence and prestige grew.

Social distinctions between free Peul and former serfs were still significant in the early 1970s, especially in the conservative regions of Pita, Labé, and Dalaba. Serfs were contemptuously referred to as "Peul of the twenty-eighth of September" (the day of the vote for independence in 1958) by their former masters, who thus underlined their different ethnic origin. The usual form of addressing a free Peul—prefacing his name with the term *modi* or *modibo* (meaning mister or sir)—was not used when speaking to a former serf, nor did former serfs use this form when addressing each other. Although all labor obligations had formally ended at independence, some serfs continued to pay the 10-percent tribute to their former masters, asked permission to enlarge their homesteads, or tried to buy land from them despite the fact that since independence they were considered to own the land they cultivated. When the land had to lie fallow, they usually borrowed fields from their former masters, who felt obligated to comply.

Everywhere else in Guinea labor migration, urbanization, better communication, and the political activity that began after World War II also weakened traditional social structures. New divisions appeared in the social fabric, between the educated and the illiterate, the urban and the rural, the progressive-minded young people and the conservative older generation. Greater mobility and a wider choice of occupation led members of specialized artisan families to abandon the profession into which they were born. Minstrels and woodcarvers, for example, often became merchants. A small bourgeoisie emerged, composed of clerks, teachers, medical and military personnel, and owners of shops, trucks, and small plantations.

The process continued after independence despite an official ideology preaching equality. Actually, modernizing efforts brought forth a spirit of individual ambition that was at odds with the regime's socialist orientation. As the traditional structures weakened, their communal aspects disappeared as well. Use and ownership of land were examples. Traditionally land had belonged to the lineage and was parceled out for use to its various members. The French encouraged private ownership but succeeded only in certain areas, particularly where cash crops replaced subsistence farming, as among the Soussou, who grew bananas, pineapples, palm tree products, and vegetables for sale, the Baga and the Kissi, who went into commercial rice cultivation, and the Guerzé and the Toma, who planted coffee. After independence land was supposed to belong to the person who worked it. Otherwise it reverted to the state. This has enabled those who can hire labor and buy farm machinery to gain control of large tracts.

In Upper Guinea where the availability of labor was the most important factor limiting agricultural production, chiefly families in Malinké society have been able to appeal successfully to members of the traditional age-groups to work for them in return for food and a little money and have thus gained effective control of much land. They also often benefited from government projects because their social position allowed them to put pressure on the administration. In Lower Guinea, too, members of the new upper classes have reaped economic benefits from land. On Kabak, a small island south of Conakry where the fertile soil is suited to rice cultivation, a large part of the harvest is given to merchants or government officials in Coyah or Conakry in return for the loan of tractors during the time of cultivation.

Family relations also were affected. The existence of labor markets was the most important factor undermining the authority of the older generation. Generally the power of the head of the family increased at the expense of that of the lineage head. Some sons no longer built their houses near those of their fathers. Brothers often still had fields next to each other, but they worked them individually and helped each other only in case of need. Many went away to avoid a life that revolved around kin obligations and farm labor, although they usually returned to get married. Often they left again when their wives became pregnant.

Social Role of the Political Party

Complete social change has been the avowed aim of Sekou Toure's government, and even before independence the party became the chosen instrument for remodeling Guinean society. Party committees began to replace all former local institutions. A local committee was formed for each cluster of villages or for each quarter in towns and cities. These groupings did not correspond to former divisions, such as the *misside* in the Fouta Djallon, where the party committee began supplanting the mosque as the key local political institution. During committee meetings—in contrast to traditional polite usage—neither rank nor age was respected. Old and young, highborn and lowborn Guineans addressed each other freely, meeting on equal terms.

Many functions that had formerly been the preserve of lineage or family elders were taken over by the party. The work was directed by a chosen administrative official, not the descendant of a prestigious lineage. Directives were issued in Conakry and were transmitted to local party leaders who discussed them during weekly meetings and supervised their enforcement. In 1959, for example, it was decided that initiation rites should no longer interfere with schooling. Dates and length of such rites were set, and party committees watched over the strict application of these rules. Among the Toma, who were most fervently attached to indigenous beliefs, there were strong protests. A group of women—members of secret societies that had traditionally supervised these rites—refused to hold any initiation whatever, and for the first time a young generation married without having previously been initiated. Throughout the country joining the party youth wing became the substitute for former initiation rites or was at least considered more significant by many. The civic service and militia groups took over some of the functions formerly performed by the age-groups of young men.

Arbitrating disputes regarding marriage, divorce, inheritance, or land, which formerly had been one of the main functions of chiefs and councils of elders, became the prerogative of the committees of reconciliation, which were established in 1964 at all levels of the party apparatus. Disputes that could not be solved by the reconciliation committee of the local party cell were referred to its counterpart at the regional or, in rare cases, the federal level. These committees, however, could not impose fines, render judgments, or otherwise assume juridical functions. They could only attempt to reconcile quarreling parties.

In the absence of an heir, land that formerly had gone back to the lineage reverted after independence to the state and was administered by party officials. No information was available in early 1975 to indicate how fairly this regulation was handled, whether the president of the committee was truly accountable to the committee members who had elected him, whether he was subservient to former heads of prestigious lineages, or whether he used his position to personal and family advantage.

Another important task of local party committee members was to ascertain whether taxes were collected from all households listed by census officials. The actual collection, however, was usually done at the home of someone who could read and write in French.

The party also was entrusted with implementing a program called human investment, which was popular during the first years of independence. In towns and villages citizens voluntarily and enthusiastically built schools, dispensaries, roads, and party headquarters and undertook cleanup campaigns and other projects with tangible results. They felt less keen about the cultivation of so-called collective fields. These fields were started in 1961 in line with the government's communitarian ideology and were supposed to continue the old African tradition of cultivating fields for the heads of extended families or lineages. Traditionally the harvest had been used for ceremonies and the entertainment of guests. In contrast benefits to the community from the collective fields often seemed doubtful, the work rather being reminiscent of forced labor during the colonial times.

For the implementation of his programs, President Touré depended heavily on the young and on women. To both of these groups he assigned roles not held by them in the traditional social system, and both were represented as separate entities within the organizational structure of the party. President Touré has said that 100 percent of the younger generation and 95 percent of the women were ready to espouse his revolutionary ideas. In fact those of the younger generation who had gone to school, particularly to college, had been the first to rebel against the authority of the elders and the first to flock to the PDG. During various crises members of the party's youth wing and of the militia, which is staffed by young men and women, have been called upon to defend the regime.

Support by women has been an important factor in Guinea's social evolution. To court their allegiance, several changes in family law were introduced. An ordinance of April 15, 1958, set the minimum age for marriage at seventeen, reduced the amount of bridewealth to a symbolic minimum, and made registration of marriage before civil authorities and consent of both parties mandatory. A decree published in *Horoya* in February 1968 prohibited new polygynous marriages.

Women enthusiastically embraced the party slogan of absolute equality between men and women. They flocked to the party from its inception and, after independence, became instrumental in spreading party directives. Even in conservative Fouta Djallon, Muslim women of aristocratic families defied tradition by being active party members, leaving their homes to become market traders and, in some cases, tailors—an occupation formerly reserved for men.

The National Society

As far as could be determined by outside observers, the majority of Guineans, in the mid-1970s, remained primarily oriented toward their local communities despite party efforts to draw them into national life. In contrast party and government officials constituted an emerging national society.

The men and women who have represented the central organs of the party and the government since independence constituted a political and social elite whose authority reached down to the smallest village and whose prestige and status were recognized by everyone. As leaders of the PDG they made national policies and, as heads of the various ministries, agencies, trade unions, youth wings, and women's groups, they carried them out. No French-appointed former chiefs or high officials were represented among them. A few were known to be descendants of precolonial aristocratic families, but this link had little if any connection with their national positions or prestige.

Typically they were sons of small farmers or of lower level civil servants, and they had a background of years of common experience and long personal knowledge of each other. With few exceptions they were Malinké, Peul, or Soussou and, in name at least, were Muslims. But always in public these men and women drew their basic identification from the party rather than from any ethnic, religious, regional, or other affiliation. All had primary and secondary school training, and the number of university-trained scholars and professionals among them was growing. All spoke French, wore European-style clothes, and had adopted Western styles of living. Nevertheless, they were among the most vigorous and articulate proponents of African values.

The party leaders and higher civil servants serving at the regional level were in direct personal contact with the national leaders at Conakry. They shared their values and commitment to national goals. At the apex was the governor of the administrative region. Under him were the key party officials, the members of his staff, and other specialists under his direct command—the chief of police, the regional health officer, the treasurer, the principal of the secondary school, labor coordinators, directors of youth and sports activities, and agricultural or animal husbandry extension agents (see ch. 8).

The top regional administrators and specialists were almost invariably members of the PDG. Ordinarily they did not come from areas in which they served. Professional administrators were moved regularly from one post to another. Policemen, schoolteachers, military officers, technicians, clerks, and other assorted functionaries also considered themselves and were considered by others representatives of the central apparatus and gained their basic orientation from their superiors rather than from the local population. This was reinforced by the government's policy of transferring them periodically from one town or region to another. The great majority of these civil servants were probably members of the PDG, but education and experience were the principal prerequisites for their jobs.

The backgrounds of these regional officials were varied. Some were the sons or daughters of men who had filled similar jobs under the French. Whatever their origins, they were all salaried employees—that is, town dwellers who could read, write, and converse in French and who had at least a primary school education.

Even at the local level high status and even authority were passing from those who were invested with traditional status based on lineage, seniority, and inherited rank to the men and women who represented the local sections of mass organizations. Members of the political party, trade unions, youth groups, cooperatives, and women's organizations represented no single occupational or other social group. Their fathers may have been cultivators, tradesmen, civil servants, laborers, or religious functionaries. They may have come from towns or hamlets and from the whole range of occupational, religious, and ethnic groups. They were the leaders and organizers of community life, who had been selected for their roles according to criteria that in large part were established by the PDG. They were generally young and perhaps better educated than most other Guineans.

RELIGIOUS LIFE

In the mid-1970s Islam was the religion of 75 to 90 percent of the people, embracing almost all members of the three major ethnic groups, the Peul of the Fouta Djallon, the Malinké of Upper Guinea, and the Soussou of Lower Guinea. The Muslim community, which was growing at the expense of other faiths, also included important segments of minor ethnic groups throughout the country. Christian churches, which were encumbered by their past association with whites in general and French colonialism in particular, had only from 30,000 to 40,000 members. The rest of the Guineans adhered to indigenous, locally based religious beliefs. Whatever their formal religious affiliation, Guineans regarded themselves as living in intimate association with the supernatural world. Followers of Islam and Christianity in urban as well as rural areas had not entirely renounced their commitment to the ancestral and nature cults but had attempted to fit them into the framework of their adopted religion.

The Constitution assured freedom of religion. The secular-minded regime used this principle to separate the supernatural strictly from the social and political spheres.

Islam

Antecedents of Guinean Islam

Islam is a universal, monotheistic, revealed religion founded in the seventh century A.D. by the Prophet Muhammad. The sacred book, the Koran, comprises the inspired teachings of the prophet. The Hadith (tradition) records his noninspired sayings and actions and those of the original community of believers. Together they make up the core of the Muslim belief. Associated with them are a large body of interpretive commentaries and an elaborate system of Islamic canon law *(sharia)*, of which there are four schools. In Guinea, as in West Africa generally, Muslims belong to the Sunnite sect, the largest branch of Islam, and recognize only the Malikite version of Islamic law.

Islam was first carried into West Africa by North African Muslim traders probably as early as the eighth century. By the eleventh century it had become the principal religion of many traders and ruling groups. The great mass of rural cultivators, however, remained largely untouched (see ch. 2).

The Fouta Djallon had been almost entirely converted to Islam by the time of the jihad of Al Haj Omar, which began in about 1850. In Upper Guinea and parts of the Forest Region, Samory Touré forcefully imposed Islam by destroying the symbols of indigenous religions in the jihad beginning about 1880. He forbade the drinking of fermented drinks and built mosques. In the twentieth century the growth of Islam was encouraged by French colonial administrators during a period of antagonism to the Roman Catholic hierarchy. Moreover, colonial penetration favored communication and exchanges and thus helped to disseminate Islam. From then on Islam was spread along commercial routes by Malinké and Dyoula traders in salt, kola nuts, and rice. Only the forest peoples resisted Islam because they identified it with Malinké domination. There were, however, Muslim islands in Kissi territory along the kola routes or wherever the Malinké had settled. In the region of Nzérékoré some Guerzé were converted after they intermarried with Muslim Konianké (see ch. 4).

The spread of Islam was favored by the fact that it had no organized church and required no formal adherence to an elaborate system of dogma and belief. The convert needed only to assert his belief in the unity of God, the mission of the prophet, and the promise of eternal life. He did not need to break with traditional customs or upset his family structure. His social prestige was enhanced by joining a world fraternity of believers reputed to be literate, learned, and law abiding.

Muslim Beliefs and Practices

Prayer, fasting, alms, pilgrimage, and the profession of faith constitute the Five Pillars of Islam—the basic duties of Muslims everywhere. The fundamental tenet is the public profession of faith *(shahada):* "There is no God but God and Muhammad is His prophet." This is usually abbreviated in West Africa to "There is no God but God," and for some Muslims the declaration is their only formal observance.

Muslims are enjoined to pray five times a day: at dawn, twice in the afternoon, at dusk, and later in the evening. Prayer consists of recitations from the Koran accompanied by a series of prescribed body movements oriented toward Mecca. Ritual washing preceding prayers, although usually perfunctory, remains an important part of the ritual. Only the very pious and various religious officials usually perform the daily prayers. These include the *imam* (leader), teachers or generally learned men, and several other variously titled officials, such as those qualified to interpret canon law or to adjudicate difficult cases. Midday prayers on Friday are considered more important than others and are everywhere well attended, especially by the older men of the community. Among the Peul the Friday service typically concludes with a sermon, which is then translated from Arabic into their own language.

Communal prayer is held at the mosque under the leadership of the *imam*. It is traditionally the center of religious as well as secular activities of the community. In Guinea the distinctive and imposing mosques familiar in the Middle East are absent, and in villages and small towns the mosque may be a round hut that looks like an ordinary dwelling or may consist of no more than a special area marked off by stones or a low wall. Women are excluded from the mosque, with the occasional exception of the aged.

The requirement for fasting is commonly observed. It requires abstention from all drink and worldly pleasures between dawn and dusk of each day of the month of Ramadan, the ninth month in the Muslim lunar calendar. During Ramadan religious practices are more strictly observed than at any other time, and the mosques are generally crowded with men who neglect weekday prayer at most other times of the year. Daily prayer is also observed regularly on two other occasions—the festival that marks the end of Ramadan and the Great Festival, popularly known as *tabaski* (great year-end festival), which falls on the tenth day of the twelfth month.

Each festival lasts two or three days and is marked by feasting, visiting, and the giving of gifts especially to children. Strict Muslims generally frown on the parades and nightlong drumming and dancing that are conspicuous elements of the celebrations at the end of Ramadan. During the Great Festival more time is given over to rest and quiet visiting. Other festivals, such as Muhammad's birthday (the twelfth day of the third month) and the commemoration of the prophet's visit to the seven heavens and the seven hells (the twenty-sixth day of the third month), are less widely celebrated.

The pilgrimage to Mecca is more an ideal goal than a practical possibility for most people. Those who go are mainly elderly people who come from families long Islamized. The title Haj borne by the returned pilgrim is highly respected but confers no special privileges.

In becoming a Muslim a convert often also becomes a member of one of the brotherhoods that play an important role in the organization and practice of Islam. Their rise was closely connected with the development of Sufism, a mystical approach in Islam seeking a closer personal relationship to God through special spiritual disciplines, such as poverty and seclusion. The term Sufism derives from the Arabic word *suf* (wool), from which the crude garment worn by the Muslim holy man was made. His piety and inspiration attracted a number of disciples. Out of these groups evolved brotherhoods organized along hierarchical lines.

One of the oldest and most widespread of these brotherhoods is the Qadiriya, whose African branch was founded by a Maure, Sidi Ahmad al Bekkaye, in the late fifteenth century. In Guinea in the present day only the Diakhanké at or near Touba belong to the Qadiriya. The Peul belong to the Tidjaniya brotherhood, which is more tolerant, flexible, and individualistic. Its roots go back to a dream that Si Ahmad ben Muhammad al Tidjani, a North African, had in 1781 while on a pilgrimage to Mecca. The dream revealed the rules and the path to God of a new order. It spread rapidly in the second half of the nineteenth century under the impetus of Al Haj Omar's jihad. Tidjanism guarantees more to its followers and demands less than Qadiri Islam. It does not require esoteric learning or elaborate ritual. It does, however, demand absolute loyalty. Malinké Muslims usually do not belong to brotherhoods.

Trends in Guinean Islam

The purity and fervor of Guinean Islam vary greatly among different Guinean people, diminishing from the Diakhanké to the Peul to the Malinké to the Soussou to the Baga and the forest people. Everywhere, in the process of being adopted by the great majority of Guineans, Islam has undergone important changes. Even among the Peul and Malinké—more deeply Islamized than other ethnic groups—indigenous practices and beliefs have not entirely disappeared, and Islam takes on a specifically local quality. The result of accommodating a wide range of beliefs and practices has been a synthesis of Muslim and pre-Muslim elements that is the characteristic feature of religious belief and practice in Guinea.

In several important instances, as in the acceptance of polygamy and marriage payment, Islamic law clearly fits traditions and requires no important change in attitude or practice of either system. In the majority of cases, however, the two systems are sufficiently far apart to require a shift in one or both.

Circumcision, for example, is sanctioned both by local cults and by Islam. It is an integral part of ritual of the former; in Islam it is a strong, unvarying custom but lacks any supernatural sanction. Among those with a superficial Muslim orientation, circumcision tends to be seen as in accordance with the will of God and takes on the added quality of a purification rite. Furthermore, although Islam encourages early circumcision—on the seventh day, the fortieth day, or in the seventh year—most Guinean groups delay it until puberty or later, and it thus retains much of its former significance as an initiatory rite.

Other indigenous practices are preserved and given Islamic respectability. A pre-Islamic Malinké taboo against cutting down a certain variety of tamarind persists, but it is now explained by a reworked legend that this tree provided shade for the prophet when he prayed. Similarly, an old taboo against eating monkeys—observed by certain coastal groups—is now justified on the grounds that monkeys were once people who had to be punished for not observing Friday prayers.

Islamic belief and practices are also reshaped. Most Muslims observe the injunction against eating pork, but the superficial converts do so in the belief that a pig once befriended Muhammad; the pig is therefore sacred rather than, as to the more genuine Muslims, unclean.

In general, traditional practices have been retained but reinterpreted and fitted, however loosely, into an Islamic framework, particularly in regard to specific religious and magic practices. Islam condemns the worship of spirits or spirit forces, for example, but does not condemn belief in them. Monotheism is combined with ancestor cults and with a belief in horoscopes and in spirits (either benevolent or malevolent) who live in special places or in animals. Indeed, Islamic tradition in Guinea gives explicit recognition to a host of angels and *jinn* (Arabic, terrestrial spirits), which frequently become counterparts of, or are identified with, specific local deities. At both ends of the Muslim indigenous spectrum, man continues to recognize the spirit world through ritual prayer and sacrifice. But the more Muslim he is, the more he sees himself as worshiping God while seeking only to control or bargain with the lesser spirits.

Christianity

In 1974 the Christian community, overwhelmingly Roman Catholic, was concentrated mainly in the Boké, Boffa, Conakry, and other areas of Lower Guinea. Smaller groups were scattered throughout Upper Guinea and the Forest Region. It was estimated that Christians constituted less than 1 percent of the Guinean population. An archbishop at Conakry and two bishops at Nzérékoré and Kankan presided over the Roman Catholic community. Protestants, numbering perhaps no more than 1,000, included an Anglican community (the Church of England's Society for the Propagation of the Gospel) on the Iles de Los and some dispersed converts of a few American missions.

Christian missionaries who came in the wake of colonial penetration achieved little success largely because of the inroads previously made by Islam on the country's major ethnic groups, the Peul, the Malinké, and the Soussou. Consequently they confined themselves almost entirely to work among ethnic minorities. The first Christian mission was established in 1877 at Boffa by the Holy Ghost Fathers, and the mission of Boké was founded in 1897. From these posts missionaries reached the savanna region of Upper Guinea, circumventing the Fouta Djallon and going through Senegal and Mali to the Niger River basin. The Forest Region was penetrated by the White Fathers only after it had been militarily subdued in 1920. Christian missionaries had some success among the Guerzé and somewhat less among the Kissi. The Toma, however, remained a closed society, resisting all foreign influences.

After World War II Christian missions won few new converts. Islam was then spreading at the expense of indigenous religious beliefs, and competition between Roman Catholic and Protestant efforts—the latter emanating from Sierra Leone—hurt the Christian cause. At any given time there probably were never more than 200 foreign clergymen and other church personnel in Guinea, but their rudimentary schools and small dispensaries often had been the first agents to introduce modern ideas and practices. Many of the country's leaders, both before and since independence, received their initial formal training at mission schools.

Indigenous Religious Systems

Despite differences in detail, all indigenous religions share a belief in a creator God or Supreme Being who is omnipotent, timeless, and remote from man but who is rarely worshiped. In contrast intermediary powers are considered to be amenable to prayer and appeasing sacrifice.

Everything in the world—animate or inanimate, living or dead—is believed to have its own *nyama* (soul or spirit, in Malinké) whose existence is independent of its material form. To believers the *nyama* is not a diffuse and impersonal spirit; it is distinct and personal, a property of concrete objects and specific phenomena. For them there is a *nyama* for each tree but not for trees generally; there is a *nyama* for each man but not for mankind. According to the belief, each distinct plot of ground has its *nyama*, as does every rock or rain cloud and every growing thing. Each object is believed to have a will, a personality, and a distinctiveness. Depending on differences in geographic regions and economic activities, such beliefs concentrate on various aspects of nature. For example, the wet element predominates among fishermen along the coast, where belief in a water genie, Sata-Bo, is prevalent. Surviving pre-Islamic beliefs among the Peul center on the bull and the use of sour milk in life-cycle ceremonies. In Malinké country all rites have some connection with the earth. In many villages the crocodile is worshiped. According to this view, the natural and the supernatural are integral parts of the everyday world.

The Cult

Spirits of founding ancestors and of natural phenomena associated with ancestral land are considered most important, and the principal responsibility for dealing with them rests with the family or the lineage. They are not only objects of the family cult, but they are also the *nyama* of men or of things.

The ancestral cult is generally the most important bond uniting a kin group. The head of the family lineage is also its chief priest, who attempts to bring about or to maintain a desirable relationship with the

93

supernatural. Accordingly he alone has the right to communicate with the *nyama* of the ancestors, and he does so on behalf of the members of the group. Thus to be successful every undertaking of the group—clearing the land, sowing, reaping, hunting, housebuilding—required the previous consent and goodwill of the deities concerned, each of which must be approached through invocation, sacrifice, prayer, or other appropriate ritual.

Family rites are usually carried out at sites where the deities are thought to reside. The sacrifice to an ancestor may be conducted in the center of the family compound or in the house in which he died or was buried. A sacrifice to the *nyama* of ancestral land is conducted in the field itself or at a distinctive rock or tree close by. A particular spot on a riverbank or a place struck by lightning is thought to be a likely residence of a nature deity. The *nyama* of land, water, and other major phenomena are sometimes represented, indirectly and by extension, by objects that usually appear in close association with them. Thus an animal may be regarded as sharing the power and sacred character of the forest or river in which it lives, or a rock may come to symbolize the *nyama* of the field that surrounds it.

The particular form of the ritual depends on the deity involved and on what is wanted from him. The invocation may follow one of several formulas; the sacrificial victim may be a cow, sheep, goat, dog, chicken, or even an egg; and the offering itself may be a piece of flesh or some blood, hair, skin, or other part of the animal. Palm wine, millet beer, or other fermented drinks are common libations. The altar may be a small clay table, a flat stone, a conical clay mound, a tree or tree stump, or simply a designated area of ground. A bowl is always placed on the altar to receive the offering or libation.

Ancestral spirits are represented in tangible form by a wide variety of objects: small statues, generally made of wood or clay but occasionally of stone or metal; personal possessions, such as a drum or some other item owned by the ancestor during his lifetime; and bones or other relics of the deceased. The relationship of such objects to the spirit forces with which they are associated may vary from group to group or from person to person. In theory the distinction between the objects and *nyama* is clear; in practice the symbol tends to become confused with what is symbolizes.

In addition to general participation in ancestral cults, the men of a community—and sometimes the women—may belong to mystery cults, the so-called secret societies. The best known are the Poro society for men and the Sande society for women, which are most active in the southern and coastal areas of the country. Membership is by initiation rather than birth, and the same cult may have members in several different communities.

Typically the cult object is an animal or nature spirit. Each cult has its own sanctuary (generally a grove or a clearing in the bush), altars, and other ritual paraphernalia. Members of particular cults may be identified by characteristic tattoos, dress, dance steps, songs, secret passwords, emblems, or other special feature. Initiation into a mystery cult, or secret society, ordinarily takes place at puberty. Men's and women's societies are separate, and each is secret with respect to members of the opposite sex and uninitiated children. The identity of the officials of the society is known only to the initiates and sometimes not to all of them. When appearing in their official capacities, the officers wear masks that represent the cult object. Such masks are among the most sacred and carefully tended ritual objects in the community.

The chief executives of the societies usually are senior persons in the community, and frequently they are also members of the council of elders. Some secret societies, especially in the Forest Region and along the Sierra Leone and Liberian borders, have been sufficiently powerful to exercise an important voice—occasionally a controlling one—in local affairs.

The Individual

Ancestral and mystery cults aim principally at the collective security and general well-being of the group. With regard to personal matters, an individual must look out for himself and the members of his immediate family by establishing a favorable personal relationship with the spirit world. According to traditional belief, nothing happens of itself; there is no such thing as an accident. Personal fortune or misfortune, the failure or success of an enterprise, the contraction and course of a disease, all are thought to come about through the action of the spirit forces of the universe.

In large part these forces are considered amenable to manipulation by humans who may use them for good or ill. Thus, the man who wants to get along must deal with them, either directly or with the help of a variety of persons who are believed to have special knowledge or special power in such matters. According to believers, perhaps the greatest threat to the individual comes from witches or sorcerers—men and women endowed with the power, perhaps unconscious and involuntary, of directing sickness, death, or other misfortunes toward others. Trial by ordeal is one of the principal traditional techniques for identifying sorcerers, but even rumor or suspicion is frequently sufficient to indict a person for sorcery and expose him to the wrath of the community. Often, however, individuals who feel threatened defend themselves by enlisting the aid of private practitioners of the occult.

Almost everyone has regular recourse to diviners, healers, spell casters, makers of protective amulets and charms, or other specialists in the supernatural. Each practitioner has his own way of dealing with the supernatural and is apt to have more or less regular clients who hire his services whenever the need arises. Treated on a private, individual basis, each case must be separately analyzed and prescribed for. Thus in addition to observing the taboos, cult objects, sacrifices, and other rituals of his ancestral or other local cult (which are fixed by custom and are uniform for all members), the individual lives with a whole complex of personal taboos, sacred objects, and sacrificial and ritual observances that he has either discovered for himself or that have been prescribed for him.

President Touré's "Debunking" Campaign

Differences between Islamic, Christian, and indigenous beliefs were less deep than the gulf separating a religious from a nonreligious outlook. In the late 1950s, in line with its rationalist, Marxist-tinted orientation, the PDG began to conduct a "debunking" campaign (*campagne de démystification*). It was, in reality, an attempt to gain total control of people's minds. But it also represented a genuine concern to uproot superstitions that were considered incompatible with modern progress and to protect gullible people from unscrupulous practitioners.

Elements of traditional religious systems came under attack first. The beliefs in genies, sorcery, the cult of ancestors, sacrifices, and initiation rites were lumped together under the label fetishism (fetish worship), and the PDG set out to suppress them. The campaign against fetishism was mounted through the radio and the press in the different vernaculars. Each party federation was asked to make public the secrets surrounding initiation rites and to expose sorcerers and fakes. With the help of the militia, fetishes and masks were collected, exhibited in public, and burned at great public autos-da-fé. At section party headquarters plays ridiculing the traditional beliefs were given.

Beginning in early 1960 teams of young people transformed many of the traditionally sacred forests into banana and coffee plantations. Men belonging to the older generation forbade eating anything grown there, but the authority they had formerly commanded was undermined when no disasters befell either the young people who had worked the plantations or the ones who burned the masks. Some leaders of indigenous cults fled to Liberia, where eventually a number of their sacred masks were sold for high prices. Some cult leaders committed suicide; others were poisoned. During the presidential elections of 1961 the inhabitants of three Toma villages protested against low coffee prices and lack of goods in their area by refusing to vote for the single candidate nominated by the party. Malinké officials countered that these mishaps occured because of the remaining belief in fetishes and sent militia to burn what was left of the sacred masks.

No nationwide study was available in early 1975 on the lasting effects of the debunking campaign on indigenous beliefs. A poll conducted by the French sociologist Claude Rivière among his students of history and sociology at the Faculty of Social Sciences of the polytechnical school in Conakry showed that Marxism was regarded as the only doctrine that promised—with some adaptations to African conditions—economic and social development. Generally, educated young people tended to regard the indigenous beliefs as belonging to the elderly and as incompatible with the goal of creating a Guinean nation. They refused to engage in certain traditional rituals or medical practices, which they denounced as ridiculous. But there were indications that Guerzé, Toma, Coniagui, Baga, and others reverted to their old beliefs when they returned home after working or studying elsewhere. The wearing of amulets, talismans, and various charms as protection against evil forces continued to be prevalent in towns as well as in rural areas.

In the years 1959 and 1960 Muslims were stirred by a wave of accusations. A circular of October 16, 1959, addressed to all party sections, explained the official position on Islam. Pan-Islamism was denounced as reactionary, pan-Arabism as racist, and Islam generally as conservative. The circular, however, pointed out that these statements did not signify atheism but only a condemnation of superstitions and an attack on the swindlers among the Muslim teachers, who made and sold charms purported to make the buyer pass an examination, win a lover, or punish an enemy. The circular caused dismay and indignation, especially in the Fouta Djallon, where political and religious power traditionally had been concentrated in the hands of a few ruling families. In the Touba area President Touré's followers, during one nightlong debate on debunking, managed to incite the people against a local leader, Sheikh Sankoun, who was forced to flee to Senegal. His sons remained and continued their teachings, but they no longer played a political role. From then on the party took pains to install as commandant at Touba either a Christian or a Muslim of another brotherhood than the local Qadiriya. In 1961 Koranic schools, along with all private schools, were closed but were reopened shortly afterward.

The debunking campaign was mainly directed against superstitious elements in indigenous and Islamic beliefs, but the Christian churches also came under attack during those years. The suppression in 1958 of all youth organizations other than the party youth wing especially affected Christian organizations. In 1959 the weekly mission radio broadcasts from Conakry were suspended. The nationalization of private schools in the winter of 1960 to 1961 began with the schools operated by the White Fathers in the Nzérékoré region. Eventually about sixty private schools were closed throughout the country, and the teachers—three-quarters of them Guineans—were transferred to public schools. In August 1961 the French archbishop, Monseigneur Gérard de Milleville, was expelled as a first step toward the total africanization of the Christian clergy. Raymond Tchidimbo, whose mother was Guinean and whose father was born in Gabon, was nominated in his place. The Roman Catholic missions were implicated by the government during the disturbances of 1967 over food shortages and distribution difficulties, and all European missionaries were asked to leave, presumably because they had criticized the government's economic policies.

Tchidimbo was accused of involvement in the coup attempt against the regime on November 22, 1970, and was condemned to life in prison. There were indications at the end of 1974, however, that relations between President Touré and the Roman Catholic Church were improving and that Tchidimbo might be released.

CHAPTER 6

LIVING CONDITIONS

Guinean living conditions in the mid-1970s were characterized by widespread rural underemployment, limited urban employment, inflated prices, an extreme shortage of consumer goods, and a black market that flourished despite intensive government efforts to suppress it. The great mass of cultivators had largely locked themselves into a subsistence economy, from which they had never completely emerged despite the introduction of cash crops half a century earlier. As cultivators seemed to be able to provide at least for their most basic needs, they were better off than ordinary wage earners, who depended on the cash economy and who often could not buy even essential goods because they were either too expensive or not available at all.

In comparison with the vast majority of Guineans a small number of high government and party officials lived much more comfortably. It was access to goods rather than income that set them off from others. Many privileges went with a particular position rather than with the individual who held it.

A high official of either the government or the Democratic Party of Guinea (Parti Démocratique de Guinée—PDG) was entitled to a substantial house, often one that had formerly belonged to a French colonial administrator. He had a chauffeured automobile at his disposal. If he lost his job, he also would lose the use of the house and the automobile. His children were the first to be considered for a coveted opening at an institution of higher education as long as he held his position. He and members of his family had first priority in seeing a good doctor, getting a bed in a hospital, or having a prescription filled. Most important, in times of universal shortages, he received priority in obtaining locally produced or imported goods for himself, his friends, and relatives.

President Ahmed Sékou Touré officially and repeatedly acknowledged the emergence of a privileged class. Black-market dealers were periodically punished and their belongings confiscated (see ch. 13). Officials were forbidden to accept gifts and favors and were urged to live in an austere manner; special levies for the party were taken out of their salaries. Scarce essential goods were rationed, but their distribution was entrusted to local party committees so that even at the lowest level a party position or close connection to one who held such a position was the only certain way of getting even basic necessities, such as rice and cooking oil.

By early 1975 a shadowy middle group had emerged. The number of Guineans included was impossible to ascertain, but their economic situation placed them somewhere between the privileged few and the impoverished majority. This class included, among other people, the official who helped himself first to the crops he collected, the minor government employee who received an important item in return for the border-crossing permit he had given a merchant, and the farmer who sold his surplus at steep prices on the black market.

PATTERNS OF LIVING

Cultivators

For the rural population, living patterns and work schedules were governed by the seasons. Every rural family accepted the fact that crop yields depended on the level of rainfall and other factors beyond their control. In good years they harvested and stored enough food to last until the earliest crops of the next harvest began to mature. When the annual rains were light or erratic, when parasites reduced yields, or when illnesses prevented the family from working, the food reserves for the next year were seriously reduced. Then the period of food scarcity that usually preceded the harvest could become disastrous. Even in average years harvests were sometimes inadequate to last through the year, and scanty meals weakened the people just as they were entering their busiest season of planting and cultivating the new crops. In some years in certain areas, after a bad harvest the period of scarcity brought serious illness or death to people, many of whom were already enfeebled by a lifetime of erratic and inadequate diets, malaria, and other illnesses.

The yearly cycle began with the clearing of land that often had not been under cultivation during the previous year. This was done by men and boys during the dry season. Formerly they accomplished this by cutting down trees and large bushes and setting the entire area afire. The French and later the Guinean government forbade this method; yet in the 1970s it continued to be employed in remote areas. Generally, however, tree stumps, branches, stalks, and dry grasses were cut, gathered into a pile, and burned (see ch. 11).

The dry season was also the period for the men to construct and repair the fences that protected fields from cattle and other animals. Goats and sheep generally roamed freely in and around villages, so that nearby fields had to be fenced. Occasionally traps were set to catch smaller wild animals for food. Fields that were farther away were sometimes protected with rudimentary barriers made from thorny branches. Fencing was particularly important among people like the Peul of the Fouta Djallon who combined cultivation with stockraising. Owners were fined if their straying animals damaged someone's crops. In 1974 the government was obliged to repeat its exhortations to the local authorities to build fences for livestock and to enforce official regulations for fencing. Birds and monkeys, too, were a constant threat to crops. Boys, sleeping in makeshift shelters, watched over the fields during the growing season.

Toward the end of the dry season, the head of the household decided which fields to use and what crops to plant. The land was prepared either by plowing when draft animals were available or in most cases with the farmer's ubiquitous tool, the short-handled hoe *(daba)*. Plowing might take from one to two weeks, but hoeing might last up to three months depending on the size of the field. Either job, the plowing or the initial hoeing, was done by male members of the family because the women were busy with their kitchen gardens at this time. Occasionally people who could afford it gave hoeing parties, for which they invited groups of young men to help with the work in return for food and entertainment. The work of clearing and turning over the soil was usually done collectively by male members of an extended family, but subsequent tasks were performed by members of individual households.

The first rains signaled the beginning of a long period of hard work, especially for the women, who played a major role from planting to harvesting. They not only were busy with seeding, weeding, and other tasks connected with the cultivation of the family's main crops—usually rice, millet, or fonio (a variety of millet)—but they also took care of their own gardens. These plots were close to the home and were under intensive, continuous cultivation; they were fertilized by household wastes and, wherever possible, by animal manure. Men built and repaired the fence surrounding these gardens, but all other work connected with the cultivation was done entirely by women. Mothers often worked with babies strapped to their backs, leaving the other children under the supervision of young girls. Gardens became the mainstay of the family when land was scarce, when yields declined, and when men left regularly to work elsewhere for wages.

The women hoed the gardens in the dry season, dug up roots, and turned under remaining plants for the enrichment of the soil. Where taro (cocoa yam) was grown, it was usually the last crop of the growing season and the first to be immediately replanted. When the first rains came, women often planted maize (corn) by making holes in the ground between the taro and dropping three or four kernels into each one. Timing was important; if dry days followed the first rains, the maize might die. If heavy rains followed, the taro leaves might shoot up too fast and block the sunlight for the maize, which ideally should appear first. Wives in polygynous families helped each other during these crucial days.

Then the women might cut cassava stalks into small lengths and plant them in mounds. Cassava needed little care and could be left in the ground until needed. In the Fouta Djallon it might take up to two years to mature; therefore, women planted it in only one-half of their gardens at any one time. Further south in Lower Guinea and in the Forest Region it grew faster. Women also planted groundnuts (peanuts), tomatoes, chilis, pumpkins, sweet potatoes, yams, tobacco, and other crops.

When the maize had grown to a height of twenty inches or more, the soil in the entire garden was covered with leaves to preserve its humidity. The maize was ready to be harvested about three months after it had been planted. It was roasted or boiled for immediate consumption or fire dried for storage.

When the women were not busy with their gardens, they worked in their families' fields. They hoed a second time and, later in the season, a third time to loosen the soil. They did the weeding and later helped with the harvest. Sometimes they took along their chickens in order that they might forage for food in the fields.

People in the Forest Region planted early-yielding rice in fields that were close to the villages and later yielding varieties on deforested hillsides farther away. Only the Kissi, who were expert cultivators, planted rice in the bottom or marshy valleys in April and May when the rainy season was well under way. They counted on the growth of the plant to keep the heads of rice above the water level, which rose slowly with the rains. Harvesting began in October and lasted to about January.

Where oil palms grew, villagers made a thick red oil from the pulp surrounding the kernel. They used this oil in their diet. Either the inner kernels were exported, or women and children cracked them with stones to retrieve an oily substance, which was used to light lamps and as a cosmetic that rendered hair soft and shiny. Kola nuts, either red or white, were harvested during the dry season from the middle of October to the end of December and on a lesser scale in May and June. Rich in caffeine, the nuts were bitter and refreshing to the taste and played an important role at social occasions.

In some areas, especially in those close to cities, some men also had gardens where they grew vegetables strictly for sale. Traditionally, however, certain jobs were performed only by men and others only by women. Men did not cook, and women did not hunt. Men built and repaired houses, granaries, and fences, but women cut and tied the grass needed for thatching roofs and plastered the walls with a mixture of clay and water. Men carved wood, and women made clay pots. Generally men did the heavy and intermittent work, such as clearing and preparing the ground; women performed the tedious and continuous routine tasks, such as weeding and hoeing.

Certain occupations indicated affiliation with an ethnic group or a former caste (see ch. 5). Only the Peul were systematic cattle raisers. Their ancestors had become sedentary after conquering the Fouta Djallon in the eighteenth century, and they depended mainly on the growing of rice and fonio, but the Peul remained attached to their herds, which had traditionally produced an important part of their income. They could sell the animals in times of crop failure; they used them in ceremonies, as a source of milk and meat, as draft animals, and for the fertilization of the fields. Cattle, sheep, and goats were individually owned, but their care might be entrusted to someone else. During the dry season the animals grazed in the valleys on fallow or harvested fields; but in the rainy season young men took them to the mountainsides and plateaus.

Former serfs were the blacksmiths in the Fouta Djallon. Often they specialized; some made only cooking pots and watering cans; others produced only the tools that the cultivators needed, such as the hoes, axes, knives, and adzes. Everywhere in Guinea blacksmiths played an essential role in the rural economy.

Cultivators could live for long periods without spending money. Usually a small holding was sufficient to provide food for the family and an occasional marketable surplus to pay for clothing, taxes, and other needs. After independence, however, official producer prices for agricultural products were too low to provide incentive. In 1961 coffee, for example, brought growers only about half what it did before independence. Consequently farmers began to grow crops less for sale and more for their own subsistence. President Touré at an economic conference at Labé in 1964 publicly chided the cultivators for not trying to improve their living standards. He said that, instead of earning money by growing more cash crops, they seemed content to live in thatched huts without electricity or running water. According to the president, they did not seem to care whether each member of the family had a proper bed to sleep in or whether their children were properly dressed.

The president did not mention, however, that farmers not only were paid little for their crops but also could not find goods to buy with the money they earned. Sixty percent of imported consumer goods, such as transistor radios, bicycles, building materials, watches, flashlights, automotive parts, foodstuffs, and other items, were estimated in the late 1960s to be bought by the people of Conakry alone. Another 20 percent may have gone to the regional capitals; 10 percent, to the main towns of the *arrondissements* (districts); and only 10 percent, to the villages.

Cultivators continued to need at least minimal amounts of cash to buy the things they could not produce, such as kerosene, tools, salt, items of clothing, or medicine. They were obligated to contribute to life-cycle ceremonies of members of their extended families. Among the Peul the elders of major lineages traditionally calculated what and how much was needed and divided the amounts among the minimal lineages, whose elders in turn decided what each household had to give (see ch. 5). Sour milk, kola nuts, and meat were commonly used in such ceremonies, but some families contributed money instead.

The people sold at the market whatever they did not need for themselves. Women especially were active traders. They sold fruits, vegetables, roosters, eggs, palm oil, or whatever else they had. People came on foot, on bicycles, and in trucks if they lived far away. Some bought at small village markets for resale at larger town markets. Since prices at the market were regulated, it was common practice to try to sell at far higher prices on the roads leading to the markets. Sellers were often relatives of the buyers who thus could be relied on for help in times of need. Such black-market dealings were therefore usually not reported to the local officials.

Going to the market, although economically motivated, was a welcome break in the daily routine and was considered practically a holiday by rural people. Another respite was the weekly meeting of the Local Revolutionary Power (Pouvoir Révolutionnaire Local—PRL) (see ch. 8). Local and national political subjects were discussed along with the latest economic directives from Conakry. Personal affairs, including perhaps some villager's marital problems, were also topics of conversation. After the discussion there was usually dancing. Sometimes a reception was given for a visiting official.

For rural youth various sports became an important leisure activity, partly because many of them shuttled back and forth between the countryside and the towns, where sports had been introduced many years ago, and partly because sports were actively encouraged by the political party. Local and regional budgets allocated money to build soccer fields. People eagerly listened to regular radiobroadcasts reporting regional, national, and international matches. They learned about Guineans who excelled in various sports, such as Ping-Pong, which the Chinese Communists had introduced to Guinea, and volleyball, which the Soviets had introduced. Students in secondary schools regularly played basketball and taught the game to their relatives in the countryside. Basketball had been introduced into Guinea by the United States Peace Corps.

Urbanites

Guineans who settled in towns adopted a mode of life that was partly alien to traditional ways. They had to make individual decisions on budgeting their money for rent, food, clothing, and other expenses and had to learn to get along with strangers. City dwellers had to work regular hours instead of adjusting their lives to the irregular demands of an agricultural occupation. They had to accept the fact that various income levels produced different consumption patterns, whereas in the country living styles did not vary much from one household to another.

Urbanization in Guinea was a fairly recent phenomenon. In the early 1970s probably no more than 12 percent of the population lived in agglomerations of more than 10,000 inhabitants (see ch. 3). Yet the population of most cities had doubled within the last decade. People came to escape the rigors and monotony of farming or because they needed to earn cash. They were attracted by the excitement of city life and the prestige attached to wage earning. For some, their original migration to

104

the towns initiated an extended period of seasonal movements. Many returned to their families and villages each year to help with the farmwork during the planting season or to work on plantations and commercial farms. Some eventually became established in the towns, learned salable skills, and settled permanently into an urban living pattern. But even they continued to maintain close ties to their home villages and returned for frequent visits.

The government tried repeatedly to stem the flow of people to the urban centers. The Three Year Development Plan (1960–63) had included the creation of 15,000 jobs in industry and transport; when most of these jobs failed to materialize, party leaders at an economic conference in Mamou in April 1963 decided to take steps to stop the rural exodus. Beginning in 1966 the so-called fake unemployed in urban areas were rounded up by the army during the dry season, which was when most migrants came to town, and were employed for a period of time in enforced labor (see ch. 10). The conference had suggested that the labor stint be for three months for first offenders and twelve months for second offenders and that after each stint they be sent back to the rural areas. It is not clear whether this proposal was observed. After 1966, however, the movement of migrants apparently diminished, and the roundups seem to have continued in this form for only two or three years. One French source surmised that thereafter those who arrived and could not find jobs were recruited into the militia.

A large percentage of urban dwellers were young. A survey made in the mid-1960s by French sociologist Claude Rivière in the Conakry suburb of Dixinn-Port showed that 38 percent of the inhabitants were between fifteen and thirty years old. Only 27 percent had been born in Conakry. Another study conducted in the match and tobacco factory at Wassa-Wassa outside Conakry showed that in 1965 four-fifths of the employees were under the age of thirty. At the canning factory at Mamou in Middle Guinea, 96 percent of the workers were under forty years old.

Among the salaried workers were increasing numbers of women, partly in response to deliberate efforts by the party to afford them equal rights with men. They worked as nurses (a job formerly held only by men), teachers, veterinarians, and telephone operators. They were railroad conductors, directed traffic, and checked luggage at customs inspection points on the borders. At the Wassa-Wassa factory 30 percent of the workers were women.

A great number of urban women worked independently as traders. They bought fish from fishermen for resale. They had small shops or stalls at the market—some fronting for relatives who as government officials were not allowed a trader's license. Others grew vegetables on plots near the towns and sold them at very high prices in urban markets. Some sold baskets that their husbands had woven. Some made and sold raffia bowl covers or clay pots. Others sold food that they had prepared or soap they had made. Women seemed especially attached to these traditional occupations. Typically things were sold piecemeal, such as one aspirin, one peeled orange, one fragment of a bar of soap, or a single cigarette.

Men, too, were merchants, selling glass beads, cheap sunglasses, new and used clothing, matches, pens, kerosene, and flashlights. They sat under lean-tos made of poles and thatch, which shaded them from the sun or rain, or they sat on the ground in the open with their wares displayed on mats. Some worked at traditional jobs as, for example, jewelers and weavers. Leatherworkers sold sandals, sheaths for knives, purses made from snake or crocodile skin, and coverings for passages from the Koran. Woodcarvers sold furniture, and blacksmiths sold tools. The Peul had a near monopoly on embroidering hats and garments. Some of these traditional artisans were itinerant, traveling back and forth between the city and the countryside. Modern occupations included shining shoes, repairing bicycles, cutting hair, and driving cars and trucks.

Rivière's Dixinn-Port study showed that 27 percent of those who made a living in that Conakry suburb were government employees. Twenty-five percent of the active population, however, was unemployed and survived only because of the hospitality of their relatives.

In 1975 no detailed comprehensive study of family budgets had been published. Since 1960 price inflation had been rapid enough to reduce the value of the Guinean currency by about 80 percent (see ch. 10). Wages and salaries in both government and private enterprises had increased only moderately, and purchasing power had therefore been heavily eroded. By 1967 the first attempts were made to ration essential goods and foodstuffs, which by then had become scarce. In the early 1970s rationing had become severe. Distribution of oil, sugar, and rice, the main food consumed at all meals including breakfast, was handled by the local party committees at set prices that were about one-third below those prevailing at the market. On the open market basic foodstuffs were increasingly hard to find, and they cost infinitely more on the flourishing black market. Other foodstuffs such as vegetables were not distributed at party headquarters and brought astronomical prices on the open market.

Hardest hit was the average low-paid urban worker. Almost his entire cash income was spent on food and housing. Many survived probably only because they received gifts of fonio, rice, and other items from their relatives in the countryside. Even people who were able to save money, perhaps because there were several wage earners in a family, could find such items as bicycles, transistor radios, shoes, and other clothing only on the black market.

Privileged among the wage earners were those working at mining complexes, such as Fria. Aside from their salaries they received higher rations, good housing, and free hospital and medical care; and they were able to buy local and imported goods at special prices in company stores. After 1969 some of these privileges had to be reduced in an effort to curtail the flourishing black market that had grown up around the city.

City living, however, had its compensations. People went to see motion pictures, and in Conakry they could see performances of, for example, the world-famous Ballets Africains at the People's Palace built by the Chinese Communists. Urbanites had a greater chance than rural people to watch sports events. The stadium in Conakry, which had been built with Soviet funds in 1964, received substantial allocations in the annual Guinean budget. On Sunday mornings people could watch young men competing on a bicycle-training course that circled the city of Conakry. The best cyclists were rumored to be those Malinké who made a living carrying black-market goods on bicycles across the border from Ivory Coast.

HOUSING

The vast majority of rural Guineans lived in dwellings that they made of locally available—and usually free—material. Such houses were widely found even in the smaller towns and gave them a strictly rural character. The most common house in the countryside was the round, windowless dwelling made of wattle and daub or of sun-dried mud bricks, having a floor of packed earth and a conical roof of thatch. In larger versions of this kind of housing, the overhang of the roof shaded an outer veranda. In some cases the veranda was enclosed by masonry made of mud bricks and subdivided into several small rooms with ornamental window openings. The roof extended nearly to the ground, making it resistant to the violent storms that often preceded the rainy season. The interior framework, which occasionally was decorated with carvings, was often smoke smudged and dark. Some Peul constructed their houses on foundations two to three feet above the ground because of termites that attacked both the wood and the mud bricks. Herders and those Coniagui and Bassari who moved every few years to new fields of cultivation lived in huts made of straw or bamboo mats that could be easily dismantled and set up again. In the Forest Region people constructed a variant of the typical round dwelling by using branches and strong reeds woven into a latticework frame and plastered with mud.

The men placed a stick in the ground and with the aid of a string traced a circle. On this pattern they drove stakes every four inches or so, except where they planned to leave openings for one or sometimes two doors. Double lines of reeds—one inside, one outside—were attached horizontally to the stakes with the help of fibrous vines. This framework was then filled in and covered with a mortar made of clay mud.

To make the roof, a large post, usually the trunk of a straight tree and as tall as the desired peak of the roof, was placed in the middle of the building site. The post was taken out once the roof was finished. For very small dwellings the entire roof was constructed on the ground and then lifted in one piece onto the wall. The roofs were usually covered with straw or, occasionally, the leaves of raffia palms. For storage and temporary houses, the leaves of oil palms were used in some parts of the country. Women cut the leaves, tied them in conical bundles, and carried them on their heads to the building site. After the last bundle was put in place, the edge of the roof was evenly trimmed.

When the house was finished, a fire was lit inside and kept burning for several days and nights until the walls were dry. Then the house was whitewashed with a brush made of raffia fibers attached to a stick. The last task was to set wooden doors into the openings, one facing the road and sometimes a second one in the back. Simpler versions of doors were screens of raffia palm leaves stiffened with cow dung.

Many houses were destroyed by the fires that were kept burning all night. In time white ants ate away the poles, wind and rain eroded the plaster, and the thatched roofs began to leak. Usually rural dwellings lasted for five to ten years. Roofs were repaired every year at the end of the dry season before the onset of heavy rains. Houses that were badly worn usually were not repaired but were allowed to collapse. The poles were used for firewood, the old site was planted to pumpkins or maize, and a new house was built on a new location.

Everywhere in Guinea the square or rectangular dwellings of mud bricks cemented together and covered with tin roofs with signs of progress. They were built by government and party officials, veterans, merchants and, in the Fouta Djallon, not only by Peul but also by those former serfs who had become comparatively prosperous.

Rural dwellings were equipped with rough furniture made by local craftsmen. The main piece of furniture was the bed, which often consisted of an earthen platform beaten smooth by women of the family. The hard platform was covered with a straw mat, and pillows were tossed on top of it.

Enamelware increasingly replaced clay pottery and traditional drinking gourds. Almost everyone used kerosine lamps, either crude ones fashioned from tin cans and wicks or the storm lantern variety that was usually imported from communist countries and was difficult to obtain. Depending on whether the dwelling belonged to a man or a woman, other common items were cooking utensils, working tools, and hunting equipment of various sorts, which were usually hung on the walls. Prayer rugs, seed boxes, and small jars of potions for dispelling evil spirits were also found. Possession of a transistor radio was a sign of affluence. The space under the conical roof was usually used for storage. Foodstuffs were stored in pots and jars on the rafters, in pits dug under the eaves, and in granaries.

A space close to the house was usually enclosed by screens where family members washed after coming home from work in the fields. There were no toilets—latrines were used instead—and rarely were there wells. Women and children fetched water from a spring or small stream close to the village, carrying it on their heads in buckets or calabashes. Only in larger villages were there wells, dug by itinerant welldiggers. Cooking was usually done in a small fenced area behind the house.

Generally there was a separate dwelling for the head of the family, one for the wife and children (or a separate one for each wife in a polygynous household), and another for unmarried young men. Only very poor families lived together in a single house. Because most houses were small and badly ventilated, people tended to stay outside except during the rainy season and at night.

Among the Peul the oldest son inherited the house of his father and the youngest that of his mother. The others had to build their own houses. Family houses were generally grouped together around a small yard serving as a meeting and prayer area, which was often marked by orange trees and stones to sit upon.

In Forest Region villages, too, the houses of a family were arranged around a central place where large stones, either flat or upended, frequently marked the tomb of venerable ancestors, which served as a meetingplace. Ordinarily, however, the dead were buried at the side of the road, grouped by family. Kola nuts were buried with the dead, and sprouting trees would later mark the spot.

In the Fouta Djallon, residential arrangements mirrored social divisions. The descendants of free Peul, serfs, and artisans all lived in different agglomerations. Villages were usually surrounded by orange, mango, and other fruit trees and by fences that had narrow openings high above the ground so that animals could not enter. Goats were kept outside by branches tied around their necks to prevent them from squeezing through the openings.

Although the rural kind of dwelling was often found in towns, urban houses were more commonly rectangular, one-story frame or mud brick buildings thirty to forty feet long with entrances and small verandas in the front and rear. They were generally without electricity. Indoor plumbing was limited to a few relatively luxurious apartment buildings and well-constructed houses occupied by government and party officials and their families. These had often been taken over from departing French people.

Conakry in the 1970s had a serious housing problem. Few families could afford to rent, much less buy, adequate living accommodations. Many resided in shabby, unpainted dwellings with unglazed window openings that let in little light. Consequently people spent much of their leisure time outside on straw mats, which they spread on the stamped earth of the streets.

Living arrangements in towns often were similar to those existing in the country. Houses of nuclear families were grouped in compounds inhabited by an extended family and were presided over by the oldest living male. The average number of people per household was 3.7 but was higher in long-established Soussou or Baga families. Comparatively few urbanites owned their dwellings, and many of those who did had constructed the houses themselves. The great majority paid rent. The monthly rent for a one-room apartment without water and electricity was about one-fourth as much as for one with those facilities. Even so, the government tried to keep rents low. A typical apartment had two to three rooms, each one roughly six feet square, or just big enough for a bed, a small anteroom, and an open veranda. One-half of the Wassa-Wassa workers lived in homes that had electricity, and one-fourth had running water and indoor plumbing. About 93 percent of the workers cooked on tripods over wood fires or with charcoal and a grill made by blacksmiths.

A successful attempt to deal with slum conditions was made at Fria jointly by officials of the Guinean government and of the consortium that operated the bauxite complex. A new town had been created there in 1957 near the bauxite reserves; but within six years the town, which had been planned for a population of 6,000, had grown to 11,300. Nearly 4,500 of the inhabitants, not counting large numbers of additional temporary visitors, lived in slums teeming with rats, flies, and mosquitoes. Streets, which were dusty in the dry season and muddy during the rains, were so narrow that no car, ambulance, police vehicle, or fire truck could pass through.

It was therefore decided to move the entire population to a new location. This was begun in September 1964. People built their own homes according to strict standards with materials that were given to them. No thatched roofs or walls were allowed, except around toilets and cooking areas. At least two trees had to be planted within the first year. Members of the local party committee explained the resettlement scheme, which involved loss of the old homes without indemnity to owners. The transfer of people, which was conducted in three stages, was successfully completed in February 1967.

CLOTHING

The traditional garment worn by men was a simple flowing robe, generally referred to as a *boubou*. Its color and quality provided an indication of the owner's wealth and position; the cheapest were of plain white muslin. More costly ones were of solid or striped colors, often deep blue and white, and often embroidered. With the *boubou* an embroidered skull cap or one of fur or wool was often worn.

Increasingly, Western-style clothing was replacing traditional dress. Government officials rarely wore the *boubou* in public except on ceremonial occasions. Trousers and open shirts, ordinarily white or khaki-colored, were becoming standard for many Guineans. Sometimes shirts were worn with voluminous pants or net undershirts with shorts. In the uplands shorts and thin shirts were insufficient to offset the cool dampness of early morning, and people often wrapped themselves in blankets during these periods. Sandals were standard footwear. Formerly the pointed slipper was common, but many different styles had become available from leatherworkers.

The basic garment for women was a skirt fashioned from a piece of cloth tied around the waist. With this garment they wore a blouse, which in Lower Guinea often had a full peplum and a low-cut neckline. Printed

110

designs were generally preferred to solid colors. Head scarves, dashingly wrapped, completed the costume. Many women, especially in towns, wore Western-style dresses. Often the wearer covered them with a voluminous transparent gauze *boubou*, brilliantly shot through with gold or silver thread. Western-educated women often wore African dress as sign of their respect for African traditions. The party had issued strong edicts against women wearing miniskirts, trousers, and wigs.

Women traditionally wore their hair in innumerable tight braids that were arranged in intricate patterns. They liked to wear gold jewelry, including bracelets, numerous necklaces, and earrings, sometimes a row of them in each earlobe, which had been pierced in several places. Stylish clothing was of great importance among the young.

DIETARY PRACTICES

Rice was the mainstay of the ordinary diet and the preferred staple throughout the country. Fonio, millet, maize, cassava, taro, sweet potatoes, and other tuberous root plants were substituted when rice was unobtainable. The preference for rice was so strong, however, that many felt that a meal without rice was not a meal.

The ordinary diet was based on these starchy staples and lacked essential vitamins, animal protein, calcium, and other nutritive elements. Different ethnic groups ate varying amounts of meat, fish, and dairy products, but none of them consumed a sufficient amount. Somewhat more fish was eaten by people on the coast and in interior villages along rivers than in other areas where it was less readily available. Consumption of meat was limited to special occasions, even among livestock breeders. Eggs were traditionally not eaten by the producers but were used to raise new chickens or were sold at the market. Food habits were conditioned everywhere by religious attitudes. Taboos often limited the consumption of various items.

The basis of the average meal was a porridge made from rice or other starch pounded into meal, mixed with water, and boiled. It was eaten with a hot spicy sauce made of palm or groundnut oil, tomatoes, wild spinach or other vegetables, hot peppers, and various condiments. The housewife's reputation as a cook depended on her ingenuity in varying the ingredients of the sauce. She might add virtually any edible protein available, including beef, mutton, goat meat, fresh and dried fish, or wild game.

Dietary patterns varied with the season. The time before the new harvest was the hungry season if the last year's supplies had been exhausted. During this two- to three-month period people were often forced to search in the bush for wild roots, nuts, and any other available foods.

In the Fouta Djallon November was the month of abundance. Rice was usually still available, and oranges added variety to the diet. By February or sometimes by March or April there was no rice, and fonio was substituted. The hungry season began in April or May and **was** especially severe in June. In July the first new maize and fonio appeared. In October the early rice could be eaten. The Peul preferred sauces made with groundnuts and considered their presence or absence the difference between a rich and poor diet. Along with rice, sour milk and milk products were their basic foods, but these were consumed in smaller quantities or not at all by other groups. The Peul kept cattle more for milk than for meat. They drank it mainly during the rainy season when milk was left over after the calves had fed. They always mixed the milk with water.

For the people of the Forest Region the hungry season was usually in February. By March groundnuts were available, and in June and July cassava and yams were harvested.

Generally people consumed somewhat less than 2,000 calories a day; amounts available were slightly lower in the north and higher in the south. The general nutritional inadequacy of diets led to the prevalence of a number of diseases. Goiter also occurred in the highlands, and nationwide there was a high rate of dental caries.

Townspeople, especially citizens of Conakry, had become accustomed to varying their diet with imported foods. Some of these items became scarce or unobtainable after independence, both because foreign exchange was in short supply and because of difficulties with domestic distribution. Some staples were imported from communist countries. In times of need, however, the government depended heavily on basic foodstuffs that were distributed under United States assistance programs. Food preparation occupied a great deal of a woman's time. Grains had to be crushed between stones or pounded in a mortar before being boiled into a porridge. Men usually did not cook, but among the Coniagui and Bassari men caught and cooked the fish, which women did not want to eat. Men also prepared and ate certain meats that women were forbidden to consume because of taboos. Women prepared tobacco, which they smoked in pipes and which the men chewed.

Each wife usually prepared all meals for herself, her children, and her husband, who took his meals in rotation in a polygynous household. This was less strictly observed among the Soussou, whose women often fed another wife's children when they lived in the same household. Women and their daughters and young boys customarily ate together. The men and older boys did the same. Few dishes or utensils were used at meals. After washing his hands, each person helped himself from the common dish by taking small lumps of porridge with the fingers of the right hand, rolling them into balls, and then dipping them into the sauce. Most Guineans had only two meals a day, and in some parts of the country this was reduced to one meal a day during the hungry season.

Almost everyone, except strict Muslims, drank fermented beverages in significant amounts. Apart from imported wines or spirits, which only the privileged few could afford, people drank home-brewed millet or corn beer. In Lower Guinea and the Forest Region, palm wine was highly appreciated. This beverage was obtained after a few days' fermentation from a milky liquid oozing out of a tapped palm tree.

HEALTH

Severe health problems ranged from malnutrition, lack of adequate sanitation, and insufficient health services to the existence of a host of communicable diseases and widespread lack of understanding regarding the principles of hygiene. These problems were exacerbated in the mid-1970s by a stagnant economy that prevented the maintenance and expansion of the country's medical infrastructure and the importation of needed pharmaceutical products. Political and economical factors, moreover, led doctors to go into exile and medical students to stay abroad after the end of their training.

Prevalent Diseases

Data on disease rates were incomplete and not representative of actual conditions as they were based on fragmentary records, scattered sample surveys, and specialized reports of research institutions. The country was relatively free of certain epidemic diseases. Nationwide annual vaccination campaigns had effectively checked the incidence of smallpox. Yellow fever and plague apparently no longer occurred. Meningitis and pneumonia recurred from time to time. Cholera was reported in 1970 and led the World Health Organization (WHO) to put the country under quarantine. According to Guinean sources, the outbreak lasted only one month and claimed no more than about fifty lives.

Among the chief endemic diseases were malaria, venereal diseases, and tuberculosis. The incidence of malaria was high, but its prevalence varied from place to place. It occurred more often along the coast in swampy areas and in the neighborhood of flooded rice fields. A malaria eradication program had been under way for many years under the auspices of WHO.

Venereal diseases were widespread, particularly in the twenty-to-thirty-year age-group and, together with tuberculosis, were said to account for more than one-third of hospital admissions. Tuberculosis constituted one of the most important medical problems of Guinea, if not the most important. No reliable statistics were available, but it was estimated that 55 percent of all adults and 35 percent of all children under the age of five were infected. The situation was aggravated by a low standard of living, malnutrition, overcrowding, and an unfavorable climate.

WHO reported some 65,000 cases of leprosy on record in early 1965. Of these 2,500 were considered cured, and 3,500 were under observation without treatment. The prevalence of leprosy, however, was conserva-tively estimated at that time at between 2.5 and 3 percent of the population, which could place the actual number of cases at between 75,000 and 100,000. No later figures were available in 1975.

Schistosomiasis (often called bilharziasis) was widespread. Countrywide infection rates were not available, but there were indications that some 28 percent of the population might be infected. In schistosomiasis the disease-producing organism penetrates the skin of the human foot when the victim enters a contaminated body of water. The organisms reproduce in the liver, and some of them are returned to the soil and to water through the victim's urine. One stage in the organism's development is carried out by snails living in swamps and rivers. Hence the disease is popularly referred to as snail fever. Thereafter the organisms live in quiet water until they find another human host. Like malaria, schistosomiasis causes general debility and lassitude and is disabling rather than fatal. It is extremely difficult to counteract the spread of the disease.

Trypanosomiasis (sleeping sickness), which is transmitted by the bite of an infected tsetse fly, had been declining in incidence since the 1920s. All parts of Guinea were affected but no longer to a significant degree. Prevention of the disease was directed toward vector control.

Parasitic worms were common, as in all tropical countries. Filariasis was present throughout the country, but it was hoped that malaria-control measures had some effect on incidence of the disease, which was caused by the bite of an infected mangrove mosquito or a black fly. People, dogs, cats, rodents, and probably other animals were affected. Amoebic dysentery, caused by contaminated water, was responsible for several hundred admissions to hospitals or dispensaries each month.

Skin ulcers were a major cause of incapacity; they occurred during periods of low rainfall and low relative humidity and were thought to be sometimes associated with dietary deficiency. Hookworm and yaws were prevalent in forested areas. Measles (rubeola) was a disease of great severity in Guinea, and fatality rates were reported to have reached as high as 25 percent in local outbreaks in the 1960s. The Ministry of Health noted, however, that the incidence of measles had been strikingly reduced because of vaccination programs and other preventive measures. measures.

Modern Medical Services

Different departments within the Ministry of Health were concerned with such matters as hospital and dispensary organization, epidemic disease control, training of medical personnel, medical research, and mother-and-child care. One of the most important was the Mobile Prophylaxis Service, which supervised mobile health and epidemic preventative units in rural areas. A special department handled collaboration with WHO, the United Nations Children's Fund (UNICEF), the Food and Agriculture Organization (FAO), and other international bodies.

President Touré announced in a radiobroadcast in 1972 that the government budget for public health had increased six times since independence and that a sixth first-class hospital was soon to be erected to add to the five already in existence. Two of these institutions were in Conakry—the five-story Donka Hospital with 400 beds and three operating rooms and the two-story Ballay Hospital with 250 beds. There was one hospital in Siguiri and a 300-bed hospital in Kankan. The Friguia mining complex operated a forty-bed hospital in Kimbo. According to President Touré, there were also thirteen second-class hospitals, sixteen third-class hospitals, and 241 dispensaries, together providing a total number of 6,858 hospital beds. Except for the hospitals in Conakry these facilities were poorly equipped. They lacked even window screens. Patients were cared for and fed by their relatives.

The dispensaries were distributed throughout Guinea. Larger ones had a doctor trained to give general medical care and to perform minor surgery. Smaller ones were under the care of nurses, who provided medicines and first-aid care. Mother-and-child care centers, of which there were thirty-eight in 1966, gave prenatal checkups and vaccinations and examinations of newborn babies.

At independence there had been no more than sixty doctors in the country, forty-four of whom were Africans with degrees from the School of Medicine in Dakar; and there were fifty-six midwives and 344 nurses (usually males). Within ten years these figures—except for the number of doctors—were reported to have tripled. WHO reported seventy-seven physicians and ten dentists to be practicing in Guinea in 1969, but no later figures were available.

Until 1967 there had been no facility to train doctors in Guinea. Students went abroad to complete the equivalent of a four-year medical education. Increasing numbers of these graduates did not come back. President Touré himself admitted in 1972 that over fifty fully trained Guinean doctors had not returned.

In 1967 a medical pharmaceutical faculty was established at the Gamal Abdel Nasser Polytechnic Institute in Conakry, from which the first students were graduated in August 1973. The National Health School (Ecole Nationale de la Santé), established after independence, had by 1972 trained 1,800 medical personnel, including 293 midwives, 447 health assistants, ninety-seven laboratory workers, 353 health technicians, 147 health workers, and 117 social service assistants.

The government newspaper *Horoya* deplored the insufficiency of Guinea's medical infrastructure. In a lengthy article that appeared in the fall of 1969 it detailed the lack of drugs and the lamentable conditions of hospitals and dispensaries.

The critical shortage of medical personnel was somewhat alleviated by foreign doctors who served for limited periods under technical aid programs. In 1975 Guinea and the People's Republic of China (PRC) signed a protocol renewing the term of a PRC medical mission in Guinea. The signing coincided with the arrival of the fourth team of PRC medical specialists.

The emphasis generally was on prevention rather than on curative services. Children in school and mothers in maternity centers were taught the rules of hygiene. Women generally were drawn into a nationwide educational campaign through efforts of political party committees and radiobroadcasts.

Folk Medicine

Guineans often had recourse to traditional methods of diagnosis and treatment. Many ailments were attributed to witchcraft or malevolent spirits and were dealt with by magical acts and sacrifices. People wore amulets or charms as precautionary measures. Muslims carried verses of the Koran written on pieces of paper inside small leather bags that were hung on their arms or around their necks.

Folk medicine constituted a threat to seriously sick people when it prevented them from seeking modern medical care. Many people, however, alternated between traditional and modern medical practices. Although the government in its "debunking campaign" had repeatedly warned people against charlatans, it attempted to preserve whatever seemed worthwhile of traditional methods of healing (see ch. 5). The National Council of the Revolution, meeting in Labé in January 1967, decided to found an institute for traditional medicine. Regional party committees were ordered to collect in their areas the names of conscientious healers, to note their specialities, to tabulate the names of medicinal plants they used, and to record examples of successful healings. The idea was to adapt whatever traditional practices seemed valuable to modern methods. Speed was stressed, as the old men who had such knowledge were dying out. It seemed, however, that researchers found it difficult to separate the psychological from the physiological factors.

Sanitation

Many Guineans lived under unsanitary conditons. Thatched roofs were havens for rodents and insects; homes were poorly ventilated. Livestock was often kept close to human habitations. Water sources were often contaminated. In most areas drinking water was derived from streams, springs, lakes or ponds, and shallow wells. During the rainy season surface water was heavily silted. Well water had a high mineral content during that period and became at times unpalatable.

In 1961 the Ministry of Public Works, Urban Affairs, and Housing allocated to one of its departments, Water Distribution of Guinea, the responsibility for digging wells and for the purification and distribution of water. Only Conakry and a few of the larger towns had water-supply systems. Conakry's water came from a man-made lake created by the Kale Dam on the Samou River. The main elements of this system consisted of the dam, a nearby waterworks, a forty-six-mile-long conduit to Conakry, a treatment station, two reservoirs, and the local distribution system.

Only sections of Conakry had an organized system of waste disposal. Septic tanks were located in the western part of the city, with disposal to the sea serving somewhat less than 200 buildings. Other areas usually had cesspools. Some villages had pit latrines, but they were little used even where they existed.

Conakry had a citywide garbage collection service using obsolete vehicles. Trash and garbage were used to fill a swampy lowland area, but it was inadequately covered with earth and provided breeding ground for rodents.

In villages members of the militia saw to it that women properly disposed of household wastes and that streets and areas around their houses were kept clean. Principles of sanitation were routinely discussed during the weekly PRL meetings.

Even in the capital few precautions were taken to ensure that food sold in markets or served in restaurants was safe for human consumption. Food was often spread on mats on the ground, unprotected from flies. Eating places often had neither running water nor toilet facilities.

WELFARE

Traditionally the primary welfare agent was the family or larger kinship group to which the individual was bound by mutual obligation, to which he could turn for protection or help, and on which he could rely in old age. In 1975 most rural Guineans of any age had no other source of aid. Often the person who gave help was little better off than the one who received it. During periods of food shortage, for example, resources were shared, and everyone's consumption was simply reduced until stocks were replenished by the new harvest.

The system became less adequate in the towns and cities, where the family was no longer a self-sufficient economic unit. But even there it continued to function in providing hospitality for relatives who had come to seek employment and who needed cushioning against the effects of rapid change. Rivière's 1967 study of Dixinn-Port showed that almost one-third of the households took care of unemployed friends and kin, sometimes remotely related ones. In return, urban dwellers often received food from their rural relatives. Beginning in the late 1960s, as staples became scarce or unobtainable, this assistance was often of crucial importance for city dwellers.

A formal system of social security and welfare, patterned after the French system, existed only for the few Guineans who had steady employment with private enterprises. Employers paid contributions into the National Social Security Fund, which was supervised by the Ministry of Labor and Social Legislation. It provided benefits for old age, invalidism, and other medical needs. It also had provisions for family allowances for children and maternity benefits for women ten weeks before and eight weeks after the birth of a child. A special system was in force for civil service employees.

CHAPTER 7

EDUCATION, CULTURAL LIFE, AND MASS COMMUNICATION

The decision by leaders of the Democratic Party of Guinea (Parti Démocratique de Guinée—PDG) in 1958 to set their country on an independent course and to determine its direction from a purely Guinean viewpoint was reflected during the following decade and the early 1970s by reforms in education that changed its French cultural orientation to one that was preeminently Guinean. In the process a new purpose was also given to schools, which were renamed in the late 1960s. From that time called the Center of Revolutionary Education (Centre d'Education Révolutionnaire—CER), the school, in addition to providing education, was also to be a production unit that was expected to contribute materially to national economic development. Resembling in many respects the work-study plan of schools in the People's Republic of China (PRC), the new schools had the additional goal, particularly in rural areas, of turning out cadres for socialist cooperatives.

Since independence education from primary school to the university level has become available to more and more Guineans. The PDG has brooked no opposition to its own educational policies, however, and education is nationalized. In the early 1970s the exception was the Muslim Koranic schools, which were essentially noninstitutional in character and tolerated by the political party presumably because of the overwhelming predominance of Muslims in the society.

According to independent observers, rapid africanization of the teaching staff and the constant need for more teachers for an ever-expanding student body have resulted in a decline of teaching standards. The introduction of national languages—as yet inadequate in grammatical standardization and modern vocabulary—as mediums of instruction has contributed further to this process. Despite the drawbacks, more and more Guineans in the mid-1970s were receiving an education provided free by the state. Attainment of the goal of universal compulsory schooling remained, however, well in the future, as apparently did the goal of making the population literate in the national languages.

Like education, the nation's cultural life and the communication of information to the people were prime interests of the PDG. Information's first function, according to President Ahmed Sékou Touré, was to ensure the cohesion of the popular mass: "The regime controls and defines information in the context of the ideology and philosophy of the government and uses it to bind the people into a single, homogeneous, and strong group capable of collective decisions and common actions." This concept espoused by the PDG has resulted in complete control over the dissemination of information in Guinea through modern mass media channels.

In the mid-1970s such channels were generally underdeveloped. Radio, considered of cardinal importance, provided quick access by the party and the government to perhaps one-third to one-half of the population. Expansion of facilities was delayed by a shortage of funds. Widespread illiteracy prevented extensive use of the printed media. As a result most communication, including both official and everyday news, was by word of mouth.

Cultural activities, particularly those relating to the performing arts, were promoted as a way to national unity. At the same time they offered a vehicle for keeping the party, its leaders, and party principles and goals before the public in a generally inoffensive way. As in education there was great emphasis on the Guinean aspect of cultural life.

Cultural life of an intellectual nature was much more constrained. Few opportunities were found in the country to exercise intellectual talents freely, partly because of the pressures to conform. In the mid-1970s graduates in increasing numbers were emerging from the country's universities. Ideological training was included in their studies, but an ever-present question remained as to whether party lines could long substitute for other largely nonexistent intellectual pursuits for many Guineans.

CULTURAL LIFE

Literature

All of Guinea's ethnic groups had a considerable body of legends, myths, fables, and proverbs, but the oral folk literature of the Malinké, among whom lived a hereditary caste of musician-storytellers known as *griots* (see Glossary), was especially rich and varied. A caste of *griots* was also found among the Peul. Oral traditions differed among groups, stemming from differing origins, history, and environments, but as in other African societies each group had its legends and epics about tribal ancestors and warriors and myths of the origin of families. Stories explained social customs to the young, and moral fables—which often had comic twists and unexpected endings—emphasized such traditional virtues as justice, hospitality, and goodwill.

In many fables animals and insects were given anthropomorphic roles that added to the interest. But no matter how fantastic the events recounted, the fable held closely to real life, and the spirits and specters described behaved in simple human ways. Proverbs, riddles, problems, and puzzles were also part of village lore and were generally used to instruct or entertain children.

The telling of a story was an art in itself. Part narrative, part song, and often accompanied by music, it involved all the teller's dramatic abilities in mimicry, voice, and gesture. Good storytellers had a wide reputation; the most renowned were the *griots* of the Malinké people. Although the *griots* drew on the general tradition of songs and stories, their specialties were the historical Malinké epic, often of war and battle, and the formal eulogy—both of which were chanted in eloquent, ornate language. Their repertoire also included songs of mockery and satire, love songs, and dirges. In Malinké country, each village had its own *griot* who had served a long apprenticeship in order to learn the requisite sagas, historical traditions, and techniques of singing and oratory. Other *griots* traveled far beyond the Malinké area; some lived a wandering life, earning a meager living with their lute-harps as praise singers and entertainers.

Since the late 1950s the government has stimulated a new interest in the country's folklore by calling for musicians and other performing artists to seek inspiration from the nation's cultural heritage. Moreover, competitive performances culminating in a national contest each year have brought troupes from all ethnic groups into contact with one another and presumably have expanded the general public's knowledge of the folklore of groups other than their own.

Islam brought the Arabic language to Guinea and, with it, the Koran as well as other sacred writings, law books, and literature. Arabic never became an everyday language in Guinea, but the Arabic alphabet —with the help of a special system of accent marks—was later used to transcribe the Peul and possibly also the Mandé language, although it was ill suited for the purpose owing to its incapacity to denote the vowels. The Peul used their written language to translate the Koran word for word and to record the elements of Muslim instruction in simple verse. Later they turned to original composition, mostly in verse, which was based on Arabic models. Their poetry was preeminently religious but also touched on social or philosophical subjects or life. A characteristic form was the lyric satire on manners. The language often recalls that of the psalms; there is the same sense of religious longing, and some of the poetry has a simple lyric beauty. It has been stigmatized as derivative, but at least some of it seems to have a value of its own. Much was translated into French by Gilbert Vieillard, a French administrator.

Literary works by modern Guinean authors were first published in the early 1950s. By the early 1970s ten such authors (nine who wrote in French and one in English) had received some international recognition. The political writings of President Touré had also become relatively well known. Among the literary writers, Camara Laye had the widest reputation abroad and was numbered among the most important African novelists who wrote in French. A Malinké, born in Kouroussa, Laye was educated in French schools in Guinea and then went to Paris to train as an automotive technician. In 1953 his first novel, *L'Enfant Noir* (The African Child), was published in Paris. This story of his life from early childhood until his departure for France had overtones of the traditional spirit world that surrounded the goldsmith trade of his father. Acclaimed for its literary merit by critics, the work had appeared in several different English translations through 1969—titled either *The African Child* or *The Dark Child.*

Laye's second novel, *Le Regard du Roi*, appeared in 1954. Set also in Africa and having similar overtones, its success was equal to that of his first novel. An English translation titled the *Radiance of the King* was published in 1956. In that year Laye returned to Guinea where, in the years after independence, he became disillusioned by growing restrictions on intellectual freedom. In 1965 he managed to leave Guinea and had remained in exile through the early 1970s. In 1966 his third novel, *Dramouss* (subsequently published in English as *A Dream of Africa*), which depicted a country under the control of a tyrannical dictator, appeared in France.

Fodéba Kéita, poet, choreographer, and founder of the Ballets Africains, was also publishing in the early 1950s. His first volume, *Poèmes Africains* (African Poems), appeared in France in 1950. The following year Kéita's poetry was banned from French Africa because of its Marxist and anticolonial nature. He subsequently published a combined work, *Le Maître d'Ecole* (The Schoolmaster) and *Minuit* (Midnight), in 1953; *Le Théâtre Africain* (The African Theater), date unknown; and Aube Africaine (African Dawn) in 1965. Kéita held cabinet posts in the postindependence government, but at the end of the 1960s he lost favor with President Touré and was accused of complicity in an attempted coup in 1969. He reportedly was sentenced to death and sometime thereafter was believed to have died.

Another poet and playwright, Condetto Nénékhaly-Camara, had a small volume of poetry published in France in 1956. He also had two plays, *Continent Afrique* (African Continent) and *Amazoulou* (an epic drama of the Zulu king Shaka), published in France in 1970. Other poets included Alpha Sow, Sadan Moussa Touré, and Mamadou Traoré (better known as Ray Autra). Sow's poems have been published in Dakar and Paris and also in *Présence Africaine*, the Paris-based cultural review that has offered encouragement and a place for publication for Guineans and other African authors since the late 1940s.

An author of note was Djibril Tamsir Niane, whose early work *Soundjata ou l'Epopée Mandingue* (Sundiata, or the Manding Epic) was published in Paris in 1960. An account of the founder and legends of the ancient Mali Empire, the story purports to be based on oral history preserved through the centuries by *griots* of Upper Guinea. A Russian edition was published in Moscow in 1963, a Czech edition in Prague the following year, and an English translation appeared, under the title

Sundiata, in 1965. Niane also collaborated with the French writer Jean Suret-Canale in writing the *Histoire de l'Afrique Occidentale* (History of West Africa), published in 1960, and contributed a number of articles to the scholarly journal *Recherches Africaines* in Conakry during the early 1960s. Two plays by Niane, *Sikasso* and *Chaka,* were published in one volume in France in 1971.

Also cited among Guinean writers were Emile Cissé and Modupe Paris. Cissé's known works included one full-length and one short novel. Published in the late 1950s, both were set in the surroundings of the independence struggle and tended to be instructive. Paris lived in the United States for many years and wrote in English. His major work, autobiographical in nature, was satirically titled *I Was a Savage.* It was published in the United States in 1957 and in Great Britain in 1958.

A Guinean author who came to public attention in the mid-1970s was Alioum Fantouré. Fantouré's novel *Le Cercle des Tropiques* (The Tropical Circle) received an award in France in 1973. The book was published by *Présence Africaine.*

Traditional Dance, Music, and Drama

In preindependence Guinea, dancing was the principal means of self-expression and recreation of both men and women, young and old. Guineans danced on all occasions—on a holiday, to welcome an important visitor, at full moon, or often solely from the sheer joy of living. Elaborate ritual dances evolved for recurrent formal occasions. There were dances for the great events in the lives of individuals—birth, initiation, marriage, sickness, death, and burial. Others were developed for communal occasions, such as the seasonal dances of the agricultural cycle, which were performed before sowing or harvest or to ensure the coming of the rains, and the dances performed before hunting or battle and after a successful hunt. These ritual dances were generally controlled by sorcerers, secret societies, or age-groups that also had their own rituals, usually centered around a propitiatory incantation and sacrifice.

Dancing was also frequently connected with everyday work, especially the communal work of the villages: harvesters, for example, danced on their way to the harvest field. Although dancing was primarily a social and communal activity, in later times various professional dancers and entertainers performed for the people.

The style of dancing was expressive rather than formal; its effect came more from the rhythmic activity of the body as a whole and interpretation of a character or mood than from disciplined precision of footwork or line. The accent was on collective rather than individual performance, although there were often short solos in which individuals could show their special skill and versatility. The solo might be performed by the leader in a secret society dance, a mourner in a funeral dance or, on less formal occasions, by each dancer in turn. Sometimes the solo dancer created a character and enacted a simple mime. The overall character of the dance was, however, usually the pattern of a group moving in unison, rhythmically and in uncomplicated fashion—the dancers might move around a circle or in single file with hands on each other's shoulder; they might advance and retire in a circle or in line abreast; or they might leap on the spot.

Dancers wore ceremonial clothes that were made in many colors, patterned with paints, dyes, or embroidery, and covered with ornaments, tassels, and plumes. There were special ritual costumes that included bark, fiber, and raffia skirts, wild animal skins, and elaborate and convincing representations of strange animals and spirits. Headdresses were fantastic, some tall and pointed, others built up on a headband of brilliant white and colored plumes, and others imitative of birds or animals. Masks also were worn, especially by the leaders or initiates in secret societies. Some performers often used tall stilts, on which they were adept and fast moving—there were special stilt dances, such as the Guerzé hunter's dance. Such traditional dancing, which had long served the purposes of animist ritual, was later adapted to serve Muslim ritual.

Traditionally singing and instrument playing were developed primarily as an accompaniment to dancing and so became communal rather than individual activities having significant social and religious roles. Special songs, melodies, and music had special purposes, and there were often strict rules governing when and by whom each musical instrument might be played. Musical education was sometimes a part of the initiation retreat.

Music and singing also accompanied much of the everyday work of the village, especially communal work. Working songs, accompanied by a single drummer or a small orchestra, helped to ward off fatigue, raised morale, and gave rhythm and stimulus to those working at such tasks as hoeing, sowing, harvesting, carrying burdens, paddling canoes, or housebuilding. Such music was usually provided by amateurs, but sometimes the musicians were professionals.

Instrumental music was provided chiefly by percussion instruments, most of all by drums. Common was a wooden drum or tom-tom, consisting simply of a large open wooden cylinder that was usually played while lying on its side. Special slots cut in the body gave some wooden drums variations of pitch or timbre; these were employed in the drum language used to give secret commands to dancers.

Skin-headed drums were a Malinké importation, which in some places superseded the wooden drums. Some had one skin and varied in size from four-foot-high funeral drums to small ones played for dancing. Some of the latter were mounted in batteries of three or more drums to produce a particular rhythmic pattern. Other kinds were played while hung around the neck, and the small hourglass drum, so called from its shape, was played tucked under the arm or between the legs; by varying pressure on the drum's series of tension cords the drummer could vary the pitch produced. During the colonial period, imitations of the conventional bass drum of Western military bands came to be used.

Other percussion instruments included a wooden xylophone, called *balafon* by the Malinké, and sistrums. The Bassari used a notched section of bamboo, over which a stick was rubbed, as a percussive instrument. A variety of rattles, gongs, and bells was also used, and almost any object that could be beaten with a stick to make a loud noise might be improvised on occasion.

Stringed instruments—harps and guitars—were rare and, when found, were usually played by individual performers, such as sorcerers or *griots*. The commonest form of harp had seven fiber strings stretched between opposite ends of a forked or bowed stick mounted in a sounding box. The most common stringed instrument—much used by *griots*—was a lute-harp or guitar, often known as the West African harp, which consisted of half a large calabash used as the soundbox and a long wooden pole that protruded from its rim to form the neck. It usually had three or six metal or fiber strings, but sometimes had more.

The principal wind instrument was a straight or slightly curved horn made of a variety of materials and usually sounding only one note. A small orchestra could be formed using several horns each having a different pitch, which by alternation produced a simple melody. There were also wood or bamboo flutes, often played as individual instruments, and various sorts of whistles.

The music was characterized by its subtle and complex rhythms. Drum beats were always syncopated, and a large number of different kinds of drums could be used together for contrast, producing an intricate series of overlapping rhythms. A dance might be accompanied by combinations of drums, xylophones, and rattles and further assisted by hand clapping, foot stamping, and the rhythm of bells worn by dancers and musicians.

The melodies played by harps, horns, or flutes were generally simple, rhythmic, and repetitive. They ranged from minor melodies of the flute, often heard in Kissidougou, through the strong melodies played by lute-harp and xylophone combinations popular in Kankan and Lower Guinea, to the martial, bell-like rhythms of a fourhorn orchestra, common among the Malinké around Kankan as well as among the Kissi, Guerzé, and other groups living in the Forest Region. A framework of rhythm and melody provided wide scope for the enterprise and virtuosity of the individual musician.

The songs accompanying dances were sung by the dancers, the musicians, or the audience. There were set chants for many ritual dances whose unvarying detail was essential to their validity. These were learned at the time of initiation to adult life or to secret societies and were carefully guarded secrets. There were also special songs, as there were special dances, for the rice harvest, for other field work, for funerals, and for many special occasions.

These chants were often antiphonal. The leader's part, which was largely extemporaneous and often consisted of topical comments, would alternate with that of the chorus, which could be a chanted set of couplets, a repetition of the leader's narrative, or a characteristic humming. Sometimes the chorus hummed in imitation of stringed instruments played pizzicato or imitated bird and animal cries. The individual recital reached its highest form with the *griots*, who sang traditional epics as well as songs of praise or mockery that were of their own composition.

Guinean drama can be said to have existed for as long as the traditional dances, since these included, at least in their ritual forms, all the elements of dramatic presentation. Such dances were often supposed to represent, possibly with some degree of genuine belief, the presence of spirits or heroes of the tribe. In some cases they constituted a rudimentary play having developed characters and a skeleton plot that was transmitted to the audience by mime or by the accompanying song.

The Coniagui dance of the cock was an example of this kind of dance. In it young men wore enormous headdresses portraying a cock's red crest and wattles and white plumes. In the Forest Region "bird men" wore elaborate costumes built up of layer upon layer of colored feathers. Groups of warriors or hunters in full dress also did mimed dances. Among the Bassari a group of women danced an elaborate mime of the life of their menfolk. Appropriately dressed and faithfully mimicking the originals, one age-group society of the Guerzé used to act out a caricature of European administrators—the governor, the regional commandant, his adjutant, the army captain, and the European doctor. A common dramatic aid was the use of masks to make the wearer resemble the person or spirit he represented.

Contemporary Performing Arts

Since independence the government and the PDG, the latter especially through its youth arm, the Youth of the African Democratic Revolution (Jeunesse de la Révolution Démocratique Africaine—JRDA), have attempted to exercise control over all aspects of the performing arts and to develop them along lines that would emphasize Guinean culture and excise French cultural influences. The scheme envisioned active participation of the entire population in these arts for the stated purpose of strengthening national unity and the generally unstated but implied purpose of increasing support for the PDG and the government.

Among early government steps for the promotion of the Guinean performing arts was the establishment in 1959 of a national ballet troupe known usually as the Ballets Africains. The troupe was formed from an earlier group founded in Paris by Fodéba Kéita in the 1950s that had comprised singers, dancers, and instrumentalists from various parts of French West Africa. Since its constitution as a purely Guinean organization, the troupe has given many domestic performances, but the primary thrust of the Ballets Africains has been to display Guinean arts to the outside world. The troupe had performed in numerous countries in both hemispheres, including making several visits to the United States (one of which was in 1973).

In the field of music, the postindependence directive of the PDG to "go back to the sources of African art and culture" was accompanied by a general cessation of broadcasts by Voice of the Revolution radio in Conakry of European music and its replacement by African music and songs. As a result, by 1961 opportunities in Guinea for hearing European classical and other music had largely disappeared. Music of the jazz and Latin American genres continued to be played, however, and the PDG proscription did not apply to Western musical instruments, at least to the kind found in modern dance bands.

During the 1960s promotion of the performing arts brought formation of literally thousands of troupes in villages—where they were trained under the guidance of the *griots*—and in larger towns throughout the country. A pyramidal system of competitions existed that started with selections at the level of the roughly 8,000 local PDG units and then proceeded in stages through the party's some 200 district sections and thirty regional federations to the national Cultural Fortnight (Quinzaine Artistique) contest held annually in Conakry.

In the mid-1970s categories in the Conakry festival included chorus, folk dancing, traditional instrumental ensemble, ballet, theatrical play, and modern dance and concert band. In contrast to the recognized artistic accomplishment of performers in the Ballets Africains, both Guinean and foreign critics have noted the general amateurishness of finalists in various categories. Moreover, the themes of plays and playlets exhibited a preoccupation with party aims and government policies; for instance, performances at the 1973 festival included *Vigilance at the Frontier*, *Defense of the Revolution*, and *Exhortation to Work*. In presentation and the instruments used, the music of the traditional ensemble was authentic, but the songs that accompanied it frequently referred to the party and the merits of PDG leaders.

Especially popular throughout Guinea was modern dance music played in West African versions of jazz and Afro-Cuban styles. Western jazz was received enthusiastically during the French period, and its local African version continued to spread after independence with the support of the PDG—official recognition was given to this genre in the establishment of the National Syli Band in 1959. By the mid-1970s at least half a dozen dance and modern concert bands had been accorded national status, among which was the Gendarmerie Women's Band, and another thirty groups had been officially designated PDG federation-level bands. A number of small combo bands had also been formed, and about forty recognized bands existed throughout the country, each of the larger population centers having one or more.

There was no information on whether the song accompaniment of Western jazz numbers and Latin American music was presented as originally written or whether new words were substituted that had

127

bearing on the Guinean milieu—in line with PDG admonitions to emphasize African culture. The extent to which new Western jazz and Latin American compositions were used was also unknown. In the early 1970s, however, jazz music was being composed and songs written by Guinean musicians using folklore themes, although there was complaint over the lack of originality often displayed, and a 1974 report stated that the JRDA's national committee had opened a training center for modern musicians.

Conakry had several nightclubs where bands played for modern-style dancing. The various bands and combos in other urban centers and towns presumably provided similar dance music at entertainment spots or for special groups. In the rural areas constituting most of the country, however, traditional dancing continued much as in the past. Some diminution of special ritual dancing may have occurred as the result of the PDG's "debunking" campaign of the late 1950s and early 1960s, directed at certain indigenous religious practices, and the associated destruction of ritual masks (see ch. 5). But there was little reason to believe that dancing at family or village events did not go on as before.

Visual Arts

Traditional painting consisted of decorations on pottery, which soon wore off; the designs and colors applied to masks; and the ornamentation of inner and outer walls of dwellings. Some masks were coated with a vegetable resin that was polished to give a brilliant, generally blackish, lacquerlike finish. Other masks, however, were polychrome, the principal colors used being white, red, and black. Various ethnic groups had a range of patterns—some geometric—to represent particular spirits and divinities; the banda mask of the Baga was decorated with such designs.

Wall painting was found among the Kissi, where the outside white kaolin plaster of the house might be decorated with traditional and sometimes stylized representations of village and household scenes in a greyish monochrome. Ceremonial tombs often had simple designs in red and white. Muslims in different parts of the country traditionally used geometric patterns, carved on the plaster and then painted, for inside wall decoration.

There was little information available on Western-style painting or on modern Guinean artists. The Belle Vue National School of Fine Arts (Ecole National des Beaux-Arts de Belle Vue) in Conakry taught painting in the Western styles. Jacob Chaya, a graduate of the school, had received some official recognition in Guinea for his work.

Sculpture in both wood and stone is found in Guinea. That in stone is largely archaeological and consists of statuettes that have been unearthed by the Kissi in large numbers along stream banks and at or near the sites of former villages in the area of Kissidougou and Nzérékoré in the Forest Region. The statuettes are generally of human figures carved from soft materials, such as steatite (soapstone) and schist, and usually range in height from about four to eight inches. Known as *pomdan* (sing., *pomdo*), they remained of uncertain origin in the early 1970s but were thought to date generally from about the sixteenth century. The Kissi people of Guinea believed the figures represented their ancestors who were trying to communicate in this form with their descendants. There is evidence that Kissi artists themselves made similar carvings from stone for ritual purposes, probably into the twentieth century.

Wood sculpture is highly susceptible to decay in Guinea's climate, and few examples of pre-twentieth-century work were extant. Information on present-day carving was scarce. The Kissi were known to have carved wood figures at one time similar to the stone *pomdan*, but whether this art form continues was unknown. The Baga have also produced notable pieces, including carved bases to support drums as well as busts of females used in dances. Masks used by the various ethnic groups presumably are replaced from time to time by local artists. In general, however, contemporary wood carving appeared to consist principally of masks and small human and animal figures made for sale. Carving of ivory figures for the same purpose was also reported.

Handicrafts

For some time after the French conquest the inaccessibility of much of the area and the conservative tastes and relative poverty of Guineans combined to preserve indigenous handicrafts intact. Once imported goods and materials began to reach consumers in quantity, however, they had an important impact on certain handicrafts, notably those in iron and textiles. In such cases the indigenous crafts were not usually modified or improved by contact with the newer industrial processes; they either continued as before or tended to die off. French attempts to foster and improve craftwork through schools, technical courses, and adult classes met with little success, as those reached were more often would-be officials than traditional craftsmen.

The extensiveness and importance of handicrafts were not clear in the early 1970s. The continued agricultural and subsistence nature of the economy and the shortages of imported consumer goods that existed after the mid-1960s probably helped some handicrafts not only to survive but even to expand. In late 1971 Guinean women were reported to practice numerous handicrafts, including basketweaving and the making of various straw products. A remarkable development had apparently occurred in fabric dyeing, which was carried out by local women's cooperatives in various parts of the country.

Among handicrafts actively pursued was the making of jewelry from precious metals. Such jewelry was usually cast or forged, but craftsmen in Kankan and Conakry also did filigree work in gold and silver that exhibited great delicacy. Rings and bracelets were sometimes engraved with geometric designs. Work in leather was a specialty of the pastoral peoples, mainly in the Fouta Djallon, who made both utilitarian and luxury articles that included sandals, belts, and straps; bags and pouches; saddles and harnesses; handles, sheaths, and scabbards for knives and swords; and cases for the Koran. Leather used ornamentally was frequently dyed in colors and incised or engraved with geometric patterns.

Modern cotton textiles have replaced much of the cloth formerly turned out by local weavers. Some weaving by craftsmen continued, however, using the traditional small loom that produced materials in narrow widths of about four to six inches, often in striped color patterns. Embroidery was another continuing craft that had been practiced from early times particularly in Upper Guinea and in the Fouta Djallon, from where it spread to other areas. Other handicrafts presumably of some significance in modern Guinea were pottery making, which might be carried out as a cooperative activity of the women of an entire village, and blacksmithing.

Scholarship and Intellectual Life

In the traditional way of life there was a preoccupation with the actual and concrete and little interest in the abstract. Although the supernatural invaded every part of day-to-day life, it was in realistic terms, and artistic symbolism was employed not to depict an abstract unknown but rather to make the unknown and the supernatural seem more concrete. Any detached intellectual inquiry was thus precluded by the viewpoint from which the physical world was seen.

Islam introduced such innovations as the Arabic language and alphabet; various technical improvements, such as the lunar calendar of weeks, months, and years; more efficient and standardized Arabic systems of measurement; written numbers; and possibly the decimal system of counting. But, above all, Islam introduced for the first time a respect for learning and for the intellect. The Koranic school, which functioned in almost every Muslim village, taught reading, writing, spelling, and grammar to a portion of the population and gave a few students instruction in legal and literary studies. This important new intellectual tradition was not one of original thought, however; it aimed not at genuine intellectual inquiry but rather at inculcating by rote a predetermined body of known facts, mainly religious (see Education, this ch.).

The French in their turn brought a new language and a new and highly developed intellectual discipline and culture that they attempted to transmit to some Guineans through French schools. French education, however, was provided on an inadequate scale and strictly along European lines. The resulting instruction in the three Rs—with a little history, geography, and science—was irrelevant and meaningless to most Guineans; but a few achieved a higher degree of education, and some acquired the elements of the European intellectual tradition. After World War II the small but growing intellectual elite became a recognizable entity possessing a character of its own. At about this time the French administration began to encourage Guinean intellectual initiative by offering prizes for original scientific or literary work and making grants to lecture groups and societies.

In 1938 the French Institute of Black Africa (Institut Français d'Afrique Noire—IFAN) was created in Dakar, Senegal. Its purpose was to sponsor original West African research in physical science, ethnology, and economics and to preserve African culture and native crafts. In 1945 a Guinean territorial branch was founded in Conakry by Georges Balandier, who also founded and edited the branch's journal, *Etudes Guinéennes*, which appeared between 1947 and 1956. Immediately after independence the Guinean unit was transformed into the National Institute of Research and Documentation (Institut National de Recherches et de Documentation—INRD) and was charged with administering the national archives, national library, and national museum as well as a nature reserve at Mount Nimba. In 1959 INRD began publishing the quarterly journal *Recherches Africaines*, as the successor to *Etudes Guinéennes*, which offered a means for the organization's small research staff and the few other Guineans engaged in sociological and scientific studies to publish their work.

The African intellectual community at that time was comparatively small, although the number was swelled somewhat by intellectuals who returned from abroad to assist in building the new republic. By the mid-1960s, however, the politicization of all aspects of Guinean life by the government and the country's one party, the PDG, and growing restrictions on intellectual freedoms, brought disagreement on the part of many intellectuals and their departure into exile. At the same time numbers of students studying in foreign institutions of higher education also avoided or refused to return home for essentially the same reason (see ch. 8).

From about the mid-1960s an increase in the number of intellectuals in the country occurred as students began graduating from new polytechnic institutes established in Conakry in 1962 and in Kankan in 1964. Graduates of programs at higher normal, and certain professional, schools also added to the total. In early 1975, however, the size of the intellectual community could not be determined with any degree of accuracy, nor was there information on the range of intellectual pursuits of its members (see Education, this ch.).

Laboratory facilities existed at various institutions, schools, and national commercial enterprises, but the number of researchers was unknown. Opportunities for research appeared limited at some major facilities because their primary use was for production and production-control purposes. Some experimental work was reportedly conducted, however, and there was the likelihood that staff members carried on individual research projects at those facilities.

Among the principal laboratory facilities were those at the Institute for Research and Applied Biology of Guinea at Kindia. This institute was engaged chiefly in the production of antivenins for treating snakebite, serums, and various animal and human vaccines. Its professional staff included about six researchers and ten technicians in the early 1970s. Another large facility was the National Pharmaceutical Products Enterprise in Conakry, which was reported to carry on some research on local medicinal plants. Agricultural institutions also engaged to an extent in experimental work, as did some national commercial enterprises. Additionally, independent research was reportedly conducted by members of the staffs of the polytechnic institutes.

Control of research was in government hands. Until 1968 INRD was under the general supervision of a cabinet-level state secretary whose office was concerned primarily with the information media; INRD seems to have functioned relatively independently during this time. In 1969 the newly established State Secretariat for Scientific Research apparently took over many of the institute's administrative functions. In 1973 a cabinet reorganization placed scientific research under a ministry in the newly established Education and Culture Domain.

Access by the intellectual community to foreign publications and literature appeared extremely limited. Control of the domestic information media and media content was an established policy of the government and by extension resulted in tight control over the introduction of printed materials for sale or distribution. In the early 1970s the importation and sale of printed matter was in the hands of the national bookstore enterprise, Libraport. The selections available to the public were unknown in general, but the bookstore sponsored an exhibition and sale of Soviet books during April 1974. The only foreign periodical on sale was *Afrique-Asie,* published in Paris by a leftist group favorable to President Touré (see Mass Communication, this ch.).

Foreign governments were not permitted to maintain information or cultural centers as such, and published materials before distribution required Guinean government approval. The United States Information Service (USIS) in Conakry, however, was making accepted books available to Guineans on an individual basis and also to groups in the mid-1970s. Additionally it distributed copies of a weekly bulletin produced by the United States Information Agency (USIA) and also the illustrated magazine *Topic.* The United States mission in Conakry from time to time sponsored art and book exhibits on embassy grounds. Several communist countries, including the Soviet Union and the PRC, had cultural attachés in Guinea. Their missions also sponsored similar exhibits and film festivals and distributed printed materials.

EDUCATION

Government Policy and Objectives

Major educational policies and the principal objectives of education were, in Guinea's one-party political system, ordinarily determined at national meetings of the PDG. Concerned party organs and ad hoc commissions reported their findings and recommendations at such meetings to achieve agreement on the measures to be taken. The measures were then forwarded to the government for adoption and subsequent issuance of any necessary official regulations.

Article 44 of the Constitution of 1958 states that every citizen of the Republic of Guinea has an equal right to education. In line therewith the government early decreed that education was compulsory for all children between the ages of seven and fifteen and free at all levels from primary school through university. The PDG also decided that education was to be secular, a policy that brought a confrontation between the government and the Roman Catholic Church in 1961, the closing of church schools, and the absorption of most non-Koranic private schools into the public system.

During the 1960s the party initiated a series of reforms intended to excise all colonial aspects from the existing educational system. Foremost of these efforts was the elimination of course content and instructional features that led to alienation of the student from his own society; in other words, there was to be africanization of educational materials, principally in the social fields such as history and geography. Another decision was to replace French with various vernaculars as the principal languages of instruction; material progress toward this goal was achieved only in the early 1970s. Replacement of foreign teaching staffs was also undertaken, and this objective had been practically reached through the secondary school level.

The position was taken that education and life were inseparable in all their aspects, whether social, cultural, political, or economic. To effect a fusion of education and life, a new approach was needed that would impart the skills and techniques best suited to Guinean requirements and at the same time instill the positive attitude toward work demanded by the country's socialist system. In the process the student must also reject the individualism introduced by the French and become a part of the popular mass, a concept labeled "communaucratism" by President Touré.

Development of the new school did not have a smooth path, however, and numerous problems continued to exist in the mid-1970s. In 1961 education was changed to a four-year primary school (first cycle) that was followed by two secondary levels—the first of three years (second cycle), which was soon changed to five years, and the second of five years (third cycle), which was changed to three years. Because of extremely limited facilities, however, only a relatively few pupils—selected by examination—were able to go on to secondary school. The large majority, the party decided, would enter proposed postschool brigades where they would learn a trade; such brigades were never formed, however. In 1964 primary school was extended to five years, and the following year it was announced that farm schools would be established to which unsuccessful secondary school candidates would go. Again such schools were never set up as envisioned.

In 1966 a new concept was introduced. President Touré declared that every scholastic establishment must become a center of technical, professional, political, and civic education. About this time an announcement was made that lower secondary education would be divided into two specialized programs—one rural, the other placing greater emphasis on technical and vocational instruction. The rural program secondary schools were to be newly set up in rural areas; each such school was to be called the School of Rural Education (Collège d'Enseignement Rural-—CER). The CER was to be concerned primarily with agricultural practices and land use, but it was also a productive unit that would promote cooperative methods of work and ultimately become the nucleus of an'agricultural cooperative. The second category consisted of existing lower secondary schools at *arrondissement* (district) seats, which were transformed into schools of agricultural techniques or schools of industrial techniques, both in essence vocational schools.

Considerable opposition appears to have arisen in the countryside to the new CER. Numerous rumors circulated about the first few concerning alleged promiscuity, student exploitation, and the purpose of the instruction, which was believed aimed at keeping the children of farmers from going to urban areas. The PDG made strenuous efforts to counteract the rumors, and the school designation was changed—"revolutionary" being substituted for "rural"—thereby implying that it was a new kind of education that was for everyone, not only rural children.

In 1967 the National Council of the Revolution (Conseil National de la Révolution—CNR), the legislative body of the PDG, carried the democratization idea a step further by abolishing the existing distinction between the *collège* and the *lycée*, the former providing three years of lower secondary education only and the latter providing six years of successive lower and higher secondary study. The following year the basic school organization was established at six years of primary school (first cycle), three years of lower secondary school (second cycle), three years of higher secondary school (third cycle)—vocational and technical schools were also at this level, although course length varied somewhat—and four or more years of higher education (fourth cycle).

Also in 1968, which is known in Guinea as the year of the cultural revolution, the CER was redesignated Centre d'Education Révolutionnaire (Center of Revolutionary Education). In theory every school was a CER or potentially one, and subsequently official reports often used the terms *school* and *CER* synonymously. The difference between CER was basically whether or not a given school was actively engaging in productive activities and providing the practical training to prepare students as eventual formative members in the government's scheme to establish socialist cooperatives (see ch. 11).

Actual progress in forming functioning CER institutions was unknown. The only data available indicated that eighty-five active centers existed on the third cycle level in 1972 and that about 8,000 trained students from that level, mostly from rural areas, were theoretically available to man cooperatives beginning in the fall of 1973. A variety of problems was noted in efforts to expand the number of active centers. They included, in addition to difficulties in providing the necessary land and facilities for production purposes, a reported lack of desire by some teachers to introduce productive work into the school program and a lack of conviction concerning the orientation of the CER program. In 1974 the implications were that many urban schools were still operating along pre-CER lines, at least in that they were not engaging in productive work.

The basic school organizational pattern established in 1968 remained in effect in 1975. In apparent anticipation, however, that planned agricultural cooperatives would not be ready to receive students completing the twelfth grade in the third cycle, a new thirteenth grade was established in the 1973–74 school year. (The school year begins in September and ends in July.) The fitness of the individual for a cooperative was to be determined during the added year, and he was also to acquire mastery of needed professional techniques. The thirteenth grade was treated as an educational unit in itself and designated as a separate CER.

Administration and Financing

Top-level administrative responsibility for education was shifted between cabinet posts on several occasions during the period from independence to the early 1970s (see ch. 8). In 1972 overall responsibility was placed in a supercabinet office designated the Education and Culture Domain, and direct responsibility for education was divided between two subordinate ministers, one heading the Ministry of Preuniversity Education and Literacy, the other heading the Ministry of Higher Education and Scientific Research.

There were indications that the numerous reforms in education carried out during the latter 1960s and early 1970s had occasioned some changes in the national administrative structure, and the picture remained unclear in early 1975. Below the national level regional education offices apparently still functioned as before. Such offices, one in each geographic or development region, were headed by a school inspector *(inspecteur d'académie)* who had responsibility for all primary and secondary education in his region. The inspector presumably continued to have individual subordinate officers in charge of first-cycle and second-cycle school programs and supervision. Other subordinates included officers in charge of teaching methods and school production activities. Actual inspection of primary education in the administrative regions was carried out by individuals working out of the regional office, but secondary education inspection was conducted, at least through the 1960s, by individuals from the national education office in Conakry. In the mid-1970s university education was supervised by a director of higher education, and each of the country's two polytechnic institutes had an administrator general and a director of studies. An elected student administrative council, presided over by the administrator general, played an important role in directing and managing school activities.

Current expenditures for education were met principally by the national budget, at least through the 1960s. Local communities participated in the construction of schools on the primary level through contributions of voluntary labor; during the early 1960s numerous primary schools were also built under the human investment program (see ch. 2). Many such schools, however, were essentially nonpermanent structures classified by a United Nations Educational, Scientific and Cultural Organization (UNESCO) consultant as temporary shelters according to international standards. During the decade capital construction concerned with secondary-level schools and higher educational institutions was financed from funds provided by foreign countries.

In the early 1970s expenditure for teaching and other educational staff was provided by the national general budget; funds were also furnished for materials and supplies. Maintenance of institutions of higher education was likewise the responsibility of the national government, but maintenance of schools on the first, second, and third cycles had been assigned to the *arrondissements* and the administrative regions. Problems appeared to have arisen in this connection, and a meeting of the CNR in 1972 stressed the *arrondissement* and administrative region responsibility. The CNR also declared that local budgets would be rejected if they did not provide for school development and equipment.

During the latter 1960s and early 1970s an average of about 19 percent of the national current expenditure budget was allocated to education, an amount higher than in Liberia and Senegal, about the same as in Sierra Leone, and less than in Ivory Coast. There was no information on the amount of expenditure by local jurisdictions.

Primary and Secondary Education

Both primary and secondary education experienced phenomenal growth during the 1960s and early 1970s. Between 1958 and 1972 the number of pupils in the elementary grades increased more than fourfold, from some 42,500 to almost 184,000, while secondary enrollment rose at an even greater rate, from 2,600 to more than 71,000 (see table 4).

Table 4. *Guinea, School Enrollment and Number of Schools and Teachers, Selected School Years, 1958–72*[1]

	1958[2]	1967[3]	1972[3]
Primary			
Enrollment			
Male	33,021	102,986	124,672
Female	9,522	46,541	59,200
Total enrollment	42,543	149,527	183,872
Number of schools	287	1,605	2,008
Number of teachers	505	4,060	5,304
Secondary			
Enrollment			
Male	2,179	27,279	55,524
Female	468	9,100	15,892
Total enrollment	2,647	36,379	71,416
Number of schools	9	252	279
Number of teachers	62	1,086	2,125
Higher Education			
Enrollment			
Male	0	n.a.	2,603
Female	0	n.a.	271
Total enrollment	0	660	2,874
Number of schools	0	2	2
Number of teachers	0	95[4]	122
GRAND TOTALS			
Enrollment	45,190	186,566	258,162
Number of schools	296	1,859	2,289
Number of teachers	567	5,241	5,551

n.a.—not available.

[1] School year beginning in September-October of the preceding year and ending July of the stated year.

[2] Public and private schools.

[3] There were no private schools.

[4] School year ending in July 1966.

Source: Adapted from Claude Rivière, *Mutations Sociales en Guinée*, Paris, 1971, p. 199; "Les Travaux du CNR: Rapport de la Commission de la Culture et de l'Education" (première partie), *Horoya* [Conakry], No. 1925, August 18, 1972, p. 3; United Nations Educational, Scientific and Cultural Organization, *World Survey of Education, V: Educational Policy, Legislation, and Administration*, Paris, 1971, p. 552.

The course of instruction during the six years of primary education covered eleven different subjects. Study was nonspecialized, but an effort was made to instill a feeling for well-done work. Education in civics included cleaning public areas, tree planting, and other activities that helped to give an understanding of the social requirements of the individual. Formal study covered indigenous language, French, history, geography, arithmetic, natural sciences, drawing, music, sewing, and physical education.

The goal of introducing national languages as languages of instruction in primary school appears to have made headway only in the early 1970s, but pupils in fourth grade and above continued to be taught in French during 1973 and 1974. The chief difficulties in the changeover were lack of textbooks, vocabulary deficiences in modern terminology, the need to develop and standardize grammar, and inadequate teacher qualifications in indigenous languages. In 1973, as a means to improve teacher qualifications, the Higher Council of Education recommended that the four existing primary normal schools begin specializing in instruction in the language or languages used in the geographic region in which the school was located.

About 10 percent of the pupils completing primary school went on to second-cycle education in the early 1970s. Approximately one-fourth of this group consisted of girls, and that proportion appeared to hold throughout the second cycle. At the end of the second cycle examinations were taken, and successful candidates were awarded a *brevet* (certificate) that was prerequisite for entry to secondary education at the third cycle; some 12,000 individuals took the examinations in 1974. At the end of third-cycle studies the student could take the examinations for the *baccalauréat* (diploma), possession of which was essential to going on to higher education. There were indications that a requirement was being instituted that holders of this diploma complete an additional year of studies in a thirteenth-year CER before becoming eligible for higher education. Candidates for the *baccalauréat* numbered almost 7,300 in 1974.

General secondary education, in both the second and third cycles, was ideally to consist of about 40 percent of general course work, 20 percent of specialized technical or vocational instruction, and 40 percent of productive activities, according to the basic plan for the CER. To what extent that goal had been achieved by the more than 260 general secondary schools was unknown in early 1975.

The common program of studies of the general second-cycle schools totaled 720 hours of instruction during the school year. The curriculum included philosophy and ideology, the national and French languages, history, geography, mathematics, sciences (physics, chemistry, and biology), administrative accounting, and instruction in the techniques of teaching. The same program was taken by third-cycle students plus statistics and business administration. Third-cycle students received 870 hours of general studies instruction during the school year, and the amount of specialized training was also greater (435 hours compared to 360 hours for second-cycle students).

Vocational-Technical Schools

Technical courses formed a standard part of the curricula in the general secondary schools of both the second and third cycles. In the early 1970s more intensive vocational-technical training was furnished by about ten technical schools *(écoles professionnelles),* half of which were in

Conakry. Institutions in Conakry included the National Arts and Trades School, National Health School (training paramedical personnel), National Telecommunications School, a fine arts school, and a school providing studies in commercial and secretarial subjects.

Vocational training in agriculture was given at two schools, one at Tolo near Mamou (opened originally by the French in 1933), and one at Foulaya near Kindia. At Bordo outside the country's second largest city of Kankan was another arts and trades school; in 1973 plans were announced also for the construction of a second national health school at Kankan.

Entrance to the various vocational-technical schools was by competitive examination. In 1972 enrollment was reported to total 2,311 students, of whom 681 were girls. A substantially higher enrollment figure was announced in 1973, but it was not known whether the increase was because of expansion of facilities or was in part owing to other institutions' having been newly classified in the technical school category.

Two other specialized institutions were the National Institute of Languages and the National Teaching Institute, both located in Conakry. The former was charged with such tasks as developing a method of translating scientific terms into the national languages and standardizing national language grammars. The National Teaching Institute was concerned with improving teaching methods and materials and with the organization and conduct of seminars both to acquaint teachers with new developments and to retrain instructional personnel.

Higher Education

In 1975 the country's higher educational facilities (fourth-cycle education) consisted of the Gamal Abdel Nasser Polytechnic Institute in Conakry and the Julius Nyerere Polytechnic Institute in Kankan. Construction of the former began in the early 1960s with Soviet assistance—the first, limited, enrollment took place in the fall of 1962—but completion of some units did not occur until the latter part of the decade. New facilities have continued to be added by the Soviet Union, including a printing plant and a language laboratory inaugurated in 1974.

In 1974 the institute in Conakry had thirteen schools and faculties, including medicine and pharmacy. An important part of the institute was the Higher School of Administration (Ecole Supérieure d'Administration), which was charged with training and politically indoctrinating individuals for the upper civil service levels. The school was originally established in 1962 as the Preparatory School of Administration (Collège Préparatoire d'Administration) to train middle-level officials but was converted to a center for senior administrators under the name National School of Administration (Ecole Nationale d'Administration) in 1963. In 1964 the name was changed to Higher

139

School of Administration, and the school was integrated into the institute in 1965.

In the early 1970s the course of instruction lasted five years, the fifth year being devoted entirely to the researching and writing of a thesis. There was an emphasis on accounting, finance, and economics, including planning and statistics. The history and ideology of the PDG were standard elements of the curriculum for all students. In line with the CER status of the institute, students of the Higher School of Administration participated in manual labor on the institute's farm and in rural areas under supervision of the Local Revolutionary Power (Pouvoir Révolutionnaire Local—PRL). Together with students returning from advanced study abroad and others successfully completing university work in Guinea, graduates of the Higher School of Administration were required to take a postgraduate seminar in party ideology given, primarily, by senior members of the PDG.

Entrance to the Higher School of Administration was similar to that in other faculties and schools of the institute, requiring a *baccalauréat* and the passing of selective examinations. Upon graduation, however, assignment to a government post was made by the National Political Bureau (Bureau Politique National—BPN) (see ch. 8). In the school year beginning in 1970 the Higher School of Administration had an enrollment of 294, of whom forty-five were women.

The polytechnic institute at Kankan opened as a higher normal school in the fall of 1962 but two years later was raised to university status. In early 1974 the institute had thirteen faculties distributed between a main campus in Kankan and one outside the city at Bordo. In connection with the school's main function of training teachers for secondary schools, and to satisfy the productive activities requirement in the country's educational philosophy of study and work, students in the first and second years engaged in agricultural production and then in the third and fourth years taught part-time in various local urban secondary schools. Owing to the general shortage of teachers in the overall school system, members of the fifth-year class taught full-time.

Until 1964 entrance to university work required only the *baccalauréat*, but in the school year beginning in 1965 selective examinations were additionally introduced. Enrollment in the two institutions has grown dramatically, totaling almost 2,900 (including some 270 women) in 1972 compared with fewer than seventy in 1962. Nothing was known of the quality of instruction in comparison with that of other universities in West Africa in the mid-1970s.

Teacher Training

Despite the great increase in the number of teachers—from under 600 in 1957 to over 7,500 in 1971—the country's expanding school system has experienced continuing shortages. Training of primary school teachers was carried out at four primary normal schools at Koba, Pita, Dabadou,

and Gueckédou—one in each of the country's four geographic regions—
and at more advanced schools at Faranah and Macenta. The primary
normal schools accepted graduates from the ninth grade—recommendations were made in 1973 that the entrance requirement be raised to
completion of eleventh grade—for a two-year program. The other two
schools accepted students completing tenth grade for a three-year
program.

Secondary school teachers were originally trained at the Julius
Nyerere Higher Normal School. Although this school was transformed
into an institution of higher education in the mid-1960s, it continued to be
the principal source of secondary teachers in 1975. Graduates of the
Gamal Abdel Nasser Polytechnic Institute in Conakry also provided
some secondary school teachers. The need for qualified secondary school
teachers remained acute, however, and in 1973 the Higher Council of
Education recommended the construction of two secondary teacher
training institutions to be located at Kindia and Labé.

The teaching staffs of the country's two higher educational institutions
were recruited mainly from among graduates of those schools and from
individuals who had received degrees abroad. During the early 1960s a
substantial number of the teaching staff consisted of Europeans. These
had been gradually replaced by qualified Guineans, but some foreign
teachers were still part of the school faculties in the mid-1970s.

The teacher shortage at primary and secondary levels was accentuated
in part by reported absenteeism and lateness associated with a lack of
interest in teaching. A change in career to other fields considered less
demanding also was occurring; privileges accorded teachers did not
compare with those in some other positions, where the appointee was
given transportation and facilities for easily securing food. Individuals
who had received teacher training were also reported by the government
to have fled Guinea in sufficient numbers to affect the available teaching
staff. Others were turning to teaching in Koranic schools. which
according to government reports were showing a disturbing increase in
number.

Guineans Studying Abroad

Several hundred students at various levels were studying abroad at
independence. According to a government report the number rose to
2,000 by 1962. The total apparently declined during the mid-1960s to
between 1,000 and 1,500 owing in part to the start of university-level
studies in Guinea, the opening of more places in the country's secondary
schools, and introduction of a policy of restricting the length of study
abroad. In 1973, according to President Touré, there were somewhat
under 1,400 holders of Guinean scholarships studying in foreign
countries.

During the 1960s most students who were sent abroad went to the
Soviet Union and the communist countries of Eastern Europe, although

some also went to various Western European countries (mainly France), the United States, Canada, the PRC, and several African countries. In the early 1970s among countries in which Guinean scholarship recipients were studying were Algeria, Egypt, and Tunisia in Africa; Bulgaria, the German Democratic Republic (East Germany), Poland, Romania, the Soviet Union, and Yugoslavia among communist nations in Europe; Belgium; and Cuba.

For a variety of reasons considerable numbers of students who went abroad in the 1960s did not return home. To some extent this was because of opposition to the regime, a loss of belief in the PDG ideology while abroad, or an acquired preference for life in a country that permitted greater freedom of expression than was allowed in Guinea. Other reasons were economic, including the possibility of securing a relatively good job abroad or, where the job opening at home was satisfactory, a dislike of the probability of having to support various relatives from the individual's extended family (see ch. 5). The PDG early established a scholarship committee to review each applicant's reliability.

Literacy and Adult Education

The reduction of illiteracy has been one of the country's main stated goals since independence. In the mid-1970s the importance attached to the problem was apparent from its inclusion in the cabinet-level post of minister of preuniversity education and literacy within the governmental structure. After independence the Three Year Development Plan (1960–63) allocated GF150 million (for value of the Guinean franc—see Glossary) for a literacy campaign, and further unknown amounts were provided during the remainder of the 1960s and in the early 1970s.

The rapid expansion of primary education in the 1960s increased literacy in French to a limited degree. The main intent of the program, however, was to spread literacy in the national languages. Few results appear to have been achieved by the latter 1960s, and in 1968 the PDG initiated a campaign that was intended to bring about general literacy in record time. The success of this and subsequent efforts appeared minimal as President Touré, in a 1972 discourse on the spread of information, indicated that literacy in the national languages was still negligible. At that time also, according to the president, less than 10 percent of the population could read and thoroughly understand articles in French, such as those appearing in the PDG daily newspaper, *Horoya*.

The introduction of the national languages into the primary schools around the beginning of the 1970s will increase literacy in those languages in time. The government and party's immediate interest, however, was the nonschool population, and numerous exhortations and recommendations have been made and directives issued to stimulate action, but with little result. One of the reasons listed by the CNR in 1972 for the lack of success was the general feeling that the promotion of literacy was a job for teachers. In 1973 recognition of this attitude was finally made by the

142

Higher Council of Education in a decision to give priority to the use of teachers in the literacy campaign: "Every classroom, urban or rural, was to be used for a literacy course for adults given by a teacher."

Equally, if not more, hindering than the apparent lack of enthusiasm for active participation in the literacy campaign was the shortage of instructional materials and supplies. In 1972 the CNR enumerated an insufficiency of mimeograph machines, stencils, paper, notebooks, and the like. It also noted delays in making materials in national languages available to the public and cited as an example the failure of the national printing plant to get out a set of traffic laws in Malinké that had been turned over to the plant two years earlier.

MASS COMMUNICATION

The generally low literacy rate and difficulties of radio reception in various parts of the country meant that traditional word-of-mouth communication continued to be important in the transmission of official information. It was the principal method used, through the PRL, to acquaint villagers in many areas with government policies and directives. The absence of a local press and local radiobroadcasts also meant that information on area happenings was spread almost entirely by word of mouth.

Fundamental to the activities of the modern media in Guinea was the government position on the purpose and goals of mass communication. That position was outlined in a statement on the information organs by President Touré at a cabinet meeting in early January 1972. According to the president, in a revolutionary people's regime such as that possessed by Guinea, a basic function of information was to ensure the cohesion of the entire people. This was in essence accomplished through the presentation of information elaborated in a form that was compatible with the morals, goals, principles, and methods accepted by the regime and so designed as to instruct and mold the people continuously. Guinea's modern media functions contrasted in this respect with those in "nonrevolutionary" countries, which according to President Touré were primarily intended to amuse and entertain and only incidentally to inform.

The Printed Media

The Press

Development of the printed media in Guinea was extremely limited during the colonial period, and the literate public was largely dependent on reading materials—mainly in French—that came from outside the colony. In 1958, just before independence, the Guinean press consisted of less than half a dozen newspapers and periodicals. They included *La Presse de Guinée*, a general interest newspaper published in French three times a week in Conakry and circulating between 1,500 and 2,000 copies. The colonial government regularly issued the *Journal Officiel de la Guinée*, in which official decrees and notices of civil service appointments appeared. A scholarly journal, *Etudes Guinéennes*, which was largely devoted to ethnographic writings, was published under the auspices of the Guinean branch of the Dakar-based French Institute of Black Africa (Institut Français d'Afrique Noire—IFAN). A daily news bulletin was also circulated in Conakry by the French Press Agency (Agence France Presse—AFP) to a small list of subscribers.

The printed media have experienced little development since independence. In September 1958 a single small newspaper, *Guinée Matin*, was published. It appeared four times a week in Conakry until February 1959, when publication ceased. The preindependence AFP news bulletin continued somewhat longer; it was discontinued in December 1959. The following month the government-supported Guinean Press Agency (Agence Guinéenne de Presse—AGP) began publishing a daily mimeographed bulletin. An estimated 600 copies were printed, almost all of which were circulated to government officials and the foreign diplomatic corps. The bulletin reportedly still appeared daily in the late 1960s, but there was no later information on its continued existence.

In April 1961 a new daily newspaper, *Horoya* (meaning dignity), began publication. Officially labeled an organ of the PDG, *Horoya* has been issued continuously since then and was the only newspaper known to be published in the country in early 1975. It was of standard newspaper size and consisted of four to eight pages. The language used was French, although on extremely rare occasions some materials were in one or more of the vernacular languages.

The content of *Horoya* consisted mostly of speeches and statements by President Touré, coverage of visits by foreign dignitaries, and information on economic and social development, including reports of various government and party agencies. Important laws and decrees were also carried in full. Guinean sports, principally soccer, were given frequent coverage, and signed articles on cultural topics appeared from time to time. International news, concerned primarily with Africa and the socialist world, was reported occasionally. Miscellaneous items included signed poems, which always had some political import, and an occasional specifically labeled editorial. Pictures were a regular part of each edition; a full page was often devoted to photographs of special events.

The circulation of *Horoya* was unknown but had been estimated by the USIA at about 20,000 in 1973. In 1974 individual copies cost GS5 for the four-page editions and GS10 for the eight-page copies (for value of the syli—see Glossary) at various outlets in Conakry. Subscriptions (cost unknown) were obtained throughout the country through each PRL (see ch. 8).

After independence the official journal of the former colonial administration was continued under the title *Journal Officiel de la République de Guinée*. It has appeared since on a regular basis twice each month, and in early 1975 its contents included laws, decrees, ministerial orders, notices of civil service appointments and changes, and various other official pronouncements.

In early 1961 the National Confederation of Workers of Guinea began publishing *Le Travailleur de Guinée*. This periodical appeared irregularly but was issued until at least the late 1960s, according to available information. In 1969 two new periodicals commenced publication: *La Militante*, a magazine aimed at women, and *Horoya-Hebdo*, a PDG magazine of broader interest. The first issue of the semimonthly *La Militante* appeared in January 1969, but a shortage of funds brought the magazine's demise at the end of that year. *Horoya-Hebdo* (literally, Horoya Weekly), running up to fifty pages or more per issue, carried material similar to that of *Horoya* but in addition included such features as a crossword puzzle and a small selection of jokes.

Outside the country an exile opposition group began publishing the newspaper *La Guinée Libre* in Paris in late 1973. A four-page weekly in French, it presented information on the Guinean political, economic, and social situation from the viewpoint of the exiles. Publication was suspended for unstated reasons in mid-1974 and apparently had not resumed as of early 1975.

Books and Publishing

During the 1960s various works by President Touré were published in Guinea, and additional volumes appeared in the early 1970s. School textbooks were published locally, and a revision of a standard French-language dictionary was reportedly in publication in 1973. Information on the publication of other books was, however, not available.

At independence Guinea had only one or two small printing plants in operation. A large modern printing facility, built and financed by East Germany, was opened in Conakry in the fall of 1961. This plant, named in honor of former Congolese Premier Patrice Lumumba, who had been assassinated early in 1961, functioned as the government printer in the mid-1970s, publishing administrative documents, the government's semimonthly official journal, and an unknown part of the school textbook requirement. It also printed the PDG daily newspaper *Horoya* and was the publisher of President Touré's writings.

Radio

Radiobroadcasting began in Guinea in the 1950s. A French experimental station was constructed in Conakry in 1953, and regular programs were broadcast from 1956. The effects of Guinea's "no" vote, rejecting membership in the French Community in September 1958, were felt as well in the broadcasting field, not only through the departure of the French staff but also in their removal of some equipment (see ch. 2). The new Guinean government was able, however, to renew broadcasting on a limited basis in 1959. In 1961 East Germany donated a 100-kilowatt shortwave transmitter that was installed under the supervision of Soviet,

East German, and Czechoslovak technicians and went into operation late that year. In 1967 modern studio facilities provided through aid from the Federal Republic of Germany (West Germany) went into service. West Germany also furnished technical training for Guinean radio staff in the 1960s.

In 1974 there was a single, government-operated radiobroadcasting system, which was referred to variously as the National Radio Broadcasting Service (Radiodiffusion Nationale) or Radio Broadcasting Service of the Republic of Guinea (Radiodiffusion de la République de Guinée) and which usually identified itself in broadcasts as the Voice of the Revolution. Transmission was from Conakry in both shortwave and mediumwave bands at power outputs ranging between ten and 100 kilowatts. At least one relay station was known to have been built during the early 1960s, and others reportedly had been planned; information on any further construction, however, was unavailable. In early 1972 President Touré stated that regional broadcasting stations should be built at Labé, Kankan, Nzérékoré (or Macenta), and Kakoulima, but what progress, if any, had been made was unreported as of early 1975.

In the early 1970s domestic broadcast time was between twelve and eighteen hours a day; one report stated that it was twenty-four hours daily in 1974. Extensive coverage was given to the activities and speeches of President Touré and to various party and government events. News was broadcast several times a day both in French and in Guinean vernaculars. Program detail for 1974 and early 1975 was unavailable, but presumably much of ordinary programming was designed to be instructional as well as entertaining, in line with President Touré's concept of the function of the mass media expressed at a cabinet meeting in early 1972.

In September 1961 Guinea initiated an international service that broadcast three times daily. In the late 1960s international broadcasts were transmitted for about six hours each evening in French. In 1974 the Guinean international service also had occasional broadcasts in Arabic, English, and Portuguese, and early that year transmission was reportedly newly begun in Wolof to neighboring Senegal. The latter broadcasts included attacks on President Léopold-Sédar Senghor of Senegal, with whom President Touré had strong disagreements (see ch. 9). Beginning about January 1973 a transmitter located in the Conakry area that identified itself as "Liberation Radio of the African Party for the Liberation of Guinea and Cape Verde" started broadcasting programs in Portuguese to Guinea-Bissau (then Portuguese Guinea). Transmission continued at least to early 1974, but information on activities after Guinea-Bissau attained independence in April 1974 was unavailable.

The extent to which domestic broadcasts were heard throughout the country was not known in early 1975. Guinea's varied topography and the location of its radio transmitters at Conakry in the low coastal area apparently created some reception difficulty in many areas. In 1973

146

USIA estimated, however, that perhaps 30 to 50 percent of the population was reached by the broadcasts. Estimates of radio receivers varied considerably, but in 1974 the number appeared to be somewhere between 100,000 and 125,000; this compared with an estimated 12,000 to 50,000 in the early 1960s.

A considerable number of broadcasts in French by foreign countries outside Africa were directed at West Africa. In 1974 they included Voice of America (VOA) programs totaling 5½ hours daily, British Broadcasting Corporation (BBC) transmissions of over four hours, and broadcasts by the Soviet Union consisting of four hours in French and one-half hour in Poular. The Eastern European communist countries aimed French-language programs—ranging from one-half hour to over three hours a day—either toward the continent or specifically toward West Africa. The PRC broadcast in French to North and West Africa about four hours daily.

Few African nations had international programs directed at West Africa. In 1974 they included Algeria, one hour daily in French; Egypt, one-half hour in French and one hour in Poular; Ghana, four hours in French; and Nigeria, two hours in French. The French-speaking countries bordering Guinea had regular domestic programs both in French and in vernacular languages that could be understood in Guinea, and Sierra Leone and The Gambia had similar vernacular programs. These neighboring state programs were often more audible than Guinean broadcasts, and it was reported in the late 1960s that many people listened to them, especially those from Dakar. VOA programs, which were relayed from Monrovia, Liberia, were also reported to be tuned in regularly. There was no information, however, as to how many Guineans were listening to international broadcasts in 1975.

Films

The film production industry was nationalized and under the control of the state enterprise Syli Cinema, which had facilities to process both sixteen-millimeter and thirty-five-millimeter film in either black and white or color and of either long or short footage. Efforts had been made in the 1960s to nationalize fully all aspects of distribution, but a boycott, which lasted over one year, on the delivery of foreign feature films by two French companies that had long operated in French-speaking Africa resulted finally in a compromise permitting continued private distribution and the operating of some private motion picture theaters. In the early 1970s the government theaters showed mainly French, American, and Soviet feature films and documentaries, as well as some produced in the PRC, Eastern Europe, and India.

At the end of the 1960s Guinea had a total of twenty-eight motion picture theaters, of which fourteen were state owned and fourteen remained in private hands. Since then the number has increased, and a total of thirty-five was reported in 1973; at least nine were in Conakry.

The estimated number of seats was 14,000, but attendance records were unavailable.

Guinea had several film producers who were recognized for their abilities by the African cinematographic world. At least two of these producers had received training in communist countries, another two in the United States, and one in West Germany. Through the 1960s, however, only three feature-length films had been produced by Guineans, and their film output consisted largely of short pictures and documentaries. Later information on the production of feature-length films in the early 1970s was lacking. Guinean films have received a number of prizes at international film festivals, including one awarded at Leipzig in 1968 and another given at Ouagadougou, Upper Volta, in February 1973.

SECTION II. POLITICAL

CHAPTER 8

GOVERNMENT AND POLITICS

By early 1975 the country had been under the complete control of the Democratic Party of Guinea (Parti Démocratique de Guinée—PDG) and its leader, President Ahmed Sékou Touré, for more than sixteen years. At that time President Touré had been head-of-state longer than anyone else in Africa. With the assistance of a small group of close supporters, all of whom simultaneously held the most important posts in both the party and the government, President Touré exercised tight control over all reins of authority. Rule was exercised primarily through the PDG. More than in any other African country, the government functioned only as an administrative appendage of the party. PDG officials supervised government administrative activities at all echelons, from top to bottom.

By the late 1960s the PDG was able to exercise total domination over all public structures—social, economic, and religious as well as political —around which any opposition to its rule could conceivably be gathered. It was by such methods, as well as through frequent and often violent purges of the secondary levels of leadership within and without the party, that President Touré and his associates were able to dominate the country effectively.

That major opposition to this domination existed could be judged from several factors, including the departure from the country since the early 1960s of hundreds of thousands of Guineans, the periodic arrests and trials of actual or alleged plotters, several assassination attempts, and a major invasion by external opposition forces in 1970 (see ch. 3; ch. 13). This opposition was fueled primarily by disenchantment with the governing party's economic policies, which had ruined the country's domestic economy, as well as by hatred engendered by the PDG's political actions. Among the intellectual minority, hostility sprang from differing political attitudes—some more conservative than the governing party proclaimed, others more radical than PDG practices implied.

Nevertheless, President Touré's continued rule indicated that considerable personal support existed for him and his party. This support was based in part on a continuation of the aura created by the party during its successful campaigns against the French and the existing social structure during the late 1950s and the early 1960s. Despite the widespread problems of the postindependence economy, the changes wrought then continued to provide a significant portion of the rural population with a better life than they had led under the domination of the traditional system. A final measure of support was provided by the party structure itself. A large number of Guineans found satisfaction in their involvement in party activities and in the access to jobs and power provided thereby.

THE CONSTITUTION

In early 1975 the country was still governed under the Constitution that had been enacted immediately after independence in 1958, making it the second oldest constitutional system on the African continent. Guinea arrived at independence as a self-governing territory of the French Union. Colonial control had gradually decreased after World War II as French interest in holding onto a vast colonial empire declined (see ch. 2). In West Africa most powers had been placed in the hands of local Africans in conformity with the *loi-cadre* (enabling act) passed by the government of France on June 23, 1956. In Guinea during the first half of 1957 the popularly elected Territorial Assembly of sixty members was created as the sole controller of most legislative issues. Its members chose the twelve-member ministerial council called the Council of Government with Sèkou Touré as its head. He was the leader of the PDG, which had already come to dominate the country's political life and which had won fifty-seven of the assembly's sixty seats.

Particularly because the attainment of internal self-government did not bring with it any indication that independence was in the immediate offing, the major activities of the assembly and council were aimed at securing a firmer hold over the country for Guineans and for the PDG. By the end of 1957 some 4,000 elected village councils and twenty-five district councils, largely dominated by PDG supporters, had been created to serve as the nucleus of local government. They replaced the chiefs as the lowest level of legal authority, a move largely motivated by the opposition to the PDG of the tradition-minded chiefs as a whole and their close association with the French. French officials remained in office as the executives in charge of regional units, but their authority was circumvented by the appointment of PDG members as their deputies.

In its efforts to remold relations with its colonies, France sought in 1958 to create a French community linking the African colonies as autonomous self-ruling members of the French Republic. In the referendum on this issue in September 1958, Guinea alone among France's colonies rejected this move. France promptly declared all its ties with Guinea ended, and Guinea became an independent republic on October 2, 1958. Without further election, the existing Territorial Assembly announced that it had become the National Sovereign Constituent Assembly. This constituent assembly adopted the indepen-

150

dence Constitution on November 12, 1958, making itself into the country's National Assembly. Sékou Touré was declared to be the country's first president.

The basic principles on which the new country's Constitution was to rest were set forth by its framers in the document's preamble and first few articles. Article 1 states that Guinea is to be a democratic, secular, and social republic. Sovereignty is vested in the people, to be exercised through elections of deputies to the legislative body and through election of the chief executive. Article 22 provides for the election of presidents of the republic by universal suffrage.

In practice the exercise of popular sovereignty takes place under the vigilant supervision of the PDG. Deputies to the National Assembly are elected on the basis of a single national list and by a majority ballot. This provision makes the election of any opposition candidates in the assembly impossible, as the party polling the largest number of votes automatically wins all assembly seats. In his commentary on the Constitution, President Touré explains the provision for a single national list by saying that deputies should not be influenced by any regional, ethnic, racial, or religious considerations but should serve only national interests as trustees of the nation as a whole.

One provision states that, in the interest of African unity, Guinea could surrender its sovereignty fully or in part to a larger political entity. Although it reflected the government's attitudes at independence, no practical use was being made of this in the early 1970s, despite efforts in Guinea's first years of independence to form a union with Mali and Ghana (see ch. 9).

Legislative powers were vested by the Constitution solely in the National Assembly. Legislative initiative was granted to individual deputies as well as to the president of the republic. In actuality, however, most legislation is created by executive decrees.

Executive powers are entrusted to the president, who is the head-of-state and supreme military commander. He also served as head-of-government until appointment of the country's first prime minister in 1972. In the exercise of his executive powers the president is assisted by the cabinet, the members of which he appoints and dismisses at will. The cabinet is responsible solely to the president, who carries full responsibility for the exercise of the executive function. There is no provision for deposing the president. In view of the common identity of the leadership of the party and the government and their unity of action, there cannot be said to be any separation of executive and legislative powers, a concept that is, however, rejected by the PDG leaders.

The National Assembly, by affirmative vote of two-thirds of its membership, may amend the Constitution or submit a proposed amendment to popular referendum. Initiative in proposing a change in the Constitution belongs to the president and to the assembly.

CENTRAL GOVERNMENT

The Presidency

The president stands at the apex of the whole structure of the government. He is the head-of-state, controls the executive branch and the armed forces, conducts foreign relations, is trustee of the independence of the judiciary and may grant pardons, submits legislation to the National Assembly, and initiates constitutional amendments.

The presidency is endowed with broad powers by the Constitution, and President Touré not only has exercised these to the fullest but has gone well beyond them. He not only has controlled the executive but also has dominated the legislative and the judicial branches of the government. He has done so in his capacity as both head-of-state and leader of the PDG. As secretary general of the party, he has had a decisive voice in the formulation of party policies, and he has directed institutions and activities in all spheres of public life (see Political Dynamics, this ch.).

According to the Constitution, the president is chosen for seven-year terms in direct elections based on universal suffrage by absolute majority on the first ballot or by plurality on the second. The details of this provision were of little actual consequence as no one has ever given serious thought to running against President Touré. The original clause of the Constitution limiting a president to two terms in office was amended in 1974 to allow unlimited reelection. Sékou Touré was selected as president by the National Assembly in 1958. Chosen in January 1961 in the first popular election held since independence, he was reelected in 1968 and in January 1975.

The president forms his own cabinet, appointing its members by decree. Ministers are individually responsible to the president for the performance of their duties and may be dismissed by the president at any time. The president also appoints all officials in the public administration and military service. In practice ministers and higher officials are appointed by presidential decree; minor officials, by orders of the appropriate minister. The president is responsible for the execution of all laws and signs all government acts.

The legislative initiative exercised by the president effectively gives him control over legislation, since most draft laws are submitted by the president—a fact that assures their passage. The proposals of individual deputies, if any, would have to be cleared with the president. The bulk of actual legislation is done by executive decrees, which often are not formally published, and not infrequently by administrative fiat.

Legislative Bodies

In early 1975 the National Assembly consisted of one house composed of deputies selected by the PDG and confirmed by national election; the members did not represent constituencies. The term of office was five years. According to the Constitution, the assembly elected its officers once a year at the beginning of the first session. The chief officer of the assembly, its president, originally ranked in inportance immediately below the president of the republic, but the diminution of the power of the assembly in later years led to a loss of his prestige.

The assembly had the sole right to legislate. It approved budgets, initiated expenditure, and was charged with controlling the nation's finances under the Constitution. The president of the republic was responsible to it for the policies of his cabinet. Legislative drafts and proposals were to be studied by the appropriate committees of the assembly before being submitted to general debate. The domain of legislation was to be unlimited. International treaties and agreements of certain specified kinds were not to be considered valid unless ratified by the assembly. The draft budget was to be submitted annually to the assembly for enactment into law not later than the November 30 preceding the year to which the budget applied.

Article 19 of the Constitution gave the National Assembly the right to scrutinize the activities of the executive through oral or written questions, interpellation, hearings, and investigations by committees. Ministers, as well as designated civil servants, were to be questioned at debates of the assembly or by its committees.

Formally the assembly's legislative supremacy, its fiscal control, and its investigative authority balanced the extensive powers of the executive. Actually there was no opposition between the two branches because both were guided by the policies of the ruling party and both were vehicles of a single leadership. Such clauses as those giving the assembly the right to question the executive and to challenge budgets or treaties decided upon by the executive were virtually inoperative.

A constitutional amendment of 1963 provided for the creation of a body known as the Permanent Commission of the assembly; members were elected by the assembly from its own ranks. The commission was intended to function when the assembly was not in session to pass initial judgment on urgent legislation proposed by the government. Such legislation was then to take immediate effect although the amendment stipulated that the new law must be presented to the next session of the assembly for ratification.

Although the government in early 1975 continued to refer to the Constitution as the country's fundamental charter, it was also generally stated that Guinea had passed beyond the stage created by the document into a more advanced status, a "revolutionary regime" replacing the earlier parliamentary form that the Constitution had created. Without issuing a new constitution or amending the original document, the National Congress of the PDG, a body selected by the national leadership, was regarded as the country's primary legislative authority. Below it the party's National Council of the Revolution was declared to be Guinea's policymaking body. The National Assembly was to function only as the country's third-level legislative body, one charged with writing the laws to implement the policies created by the national council, which in turn followed the general guidelines set by the National Congress. Thus, all decisions on fundamental laws and even on constitutional amendments were effectively decided by the national council.

For example, it was the party's national council, not the elected National Assembly, that modified the Constitution in December 1974 to permit President Touré to run for a third full term in office. In addition the council decided that the size of the National Assembly should be increased from seventy-five to 150 members. Whether the assembly later met to ratify these very important decisions was not considered material.

In late December 1974 the country held national elections for president and for the newly enlarged 150-member National Assembly. More than 99.8 percent of the 2.4 million registered voters were reported as turning out for the polls. Every one of them cast a ballot for President Touré. Having only a single slate of National Assembly condidates, the voters were unanimous in that vote as well.

Deputies did not represent geographical constituencies but were purportedly drawn from the country at large. In fact ninety of the candidates had been selected by the party's regional organs and four each by the women's, youth, and labor organizations. The other forty-eight were selected by the National Political Bureau (Bureau Politique National—BPN). Of this assembly one-third were teachers, one-fifth were women, and nearly one-fifth were technocrats, officials defined as directors of large government offices or state enterprises. Four of the 150 were military officers. Given the fact that the assembly exerted no meaningful power, membership could be regarded as an honor given out by the party to loyal followers.

The Cabinet and Executive Agencies

During the first fourteen years of independence, President Touré directed the work of the executive establishment with the assistance of a cabinet in which other important leaders of the PDG held the posts. Also, he personally held several key ministerial posts or delegated them to junior ministers within the Office of the Presidency. In 1972, after considerable turmoil during 1971 caused by wholesale political purges of party and government officials, including twenty-one former ministers, President Touré appointed a prime minister to direct the work of the cabinet. Nevertheless, the president retained direct control over two or three ministries of particular interest to him and continued to select and appoint cabinet members, all of whom remained directly responsible to him for their actions. The Constitution specifies that, in the event the office of president is vacated, the cabinet will continue to function until a new president is elected. In an emergency or during his absence from the country, the president can delegate his powers to one of the ministers.

The Council of Government, which had been formed under the *loi-cadre* in May 1957 as the preindependence cabinet, was abolished at independence. In its place President Touré selected eleven ministers and seven secretaries of state to serve as his Council of Ministers, or cabinet. Most of the secretaries of state were in charge of units of the various ministries. The cabinet, however, like almost all elements of the country's administration, has been characterized by almost constant changes in form during the 1958–75 period. The cabinet varied between seven and thirty-four ministers, the number of secretaries of state, virtually junior ministers, being in an inverse proportion. At times all the secretaries of state were included as members of the cabinet; at other times only a few of them had cabinet rank. Almost continuous structural reorganization of the various ministries took place throughout the 1960s and into the 1970s. New ministries were formed as certain areas of activity took on added importance, and others were consolidated. New directorates, departments, and bureaus were created within ministries, and some agencies were shifted from one ministry to another. There was much redesignating of functions, especially in the economic sphere.

In 1972, after the appointment of Louis Lansana Béavogui as the country's first prime minister, the basic system was amended to create two distinct levels of ministerial posts. Since then the form of the cabinet has remained largely stable, although its exact composition, regarding both membership and assigned posts, continued to vary with some frequency. In the post-1972 structure the government was divided into seven elements known as domains. Each domain dealt with some broad range of national interests, bringing together all agencies of the administration that dealt with such matters as social affairs or the economy under one minister of domain. One domain was headed by the president, a second by the prime minister, and the other five by other members of the PDG's seven-member BPN. Each minister of domain had under him from three to six ministers heading specific ministries.

In the governmental administrative hierarchy, the chain of command reached directly downward from the president through a chief administrative officer at every level. Each administrative chief was directly responsible for the affairs of his unit to the officer in charge of the echelon above him.

Various executive controls converged in the agencies of public administration. Most important was the control exercised by the party units at each level. There were the controls personally exercised by the president or by representatives of his office. Some executive departments worked under the scrutiny of special inspection units; the police had a general concern with the conduct of all agencies.

Overcentralization and a shortage of adequately trained and experienced officials often made for inefficiency and an air of improvisation in government operations, especially at the middle and lower levels of the bureaucracy. There was much policy but few clear precedents, and rules were subject to change without notice by higher authority. Many routine decisions, avoided or postponed by officials fearful of making mistakes, moved slowly upward to higher authority, coming at last to a minister or frequently to the president himself.

The Constitution states that the cabinet and the national assembly members may not be arrested or prosecuted while in office. In both cases, however, the immunity may be lifted by the president, and numerous members of both bodies have been prosecuted in the government's frequent purges. The Constitution also states that cabinet members may not hold any other position or exercise a profession while in office, but this provision has been totally disregarded, particularly with respect to the holding of key posts within the party.

Attitudes Toward the Constitution and Legal System

The major reason that Guinea's Constitution could remain largely unchanged for such a relatively long period in the face of revolutionary changes taking place in the country and throughout the African continent is to be found in the attitude of the ruling party and its leaders toward constitutions in general. Such documents were regarded only as objects required to strengthen claims to legitimacy. In the debates leading to passage of the Constitution in 1958, in numerous later speeches by President Touré, and in the actual application of the laws, it was continually made plain that the Constitution could be altered, bent, or totally ignored to suit PDG objectives. This attitude applied not only to the Constitution but also to law in general. In the words of the president of the National Assembly, the government is "not and never shall be among those . . . stifled by their own laws." Although only two amendments had been formally added to the Constitution, the document had been effectively altered many times by laws, regulations, and presidential decrees, many of which were in direct and obvious conflict with its provisions.

Article 2 of the Constitution, for example, specifies that the country will be divided into communes and circumscriptions; but only a year after its passage a simple ministerial regulation created an entirely new regional and local structure. As of early 1975 no steps had been taken to rectify this divergence between constitutional provision and actual practice. The variances in more serious matters were just as striking.

The Constitution does not specify how the judiciary is to be organized, leaving its structure to the realm of law. It does, however, make the president the only guarantor of judicial independence. Under his control the judicial authorities have taken as their guiding principle the supremacy of the ruling party's interests. They have brought to the application of justice the sociopolitical attitudes of the PDG that control all governmental practice.

REGIONAL AND LOCAL ADMINISTRATION

Party and state, closely intertwined at the national level, could almost be described as unified at the local level. It was difficult, and in some cases impossible, for the average Guinean citizen to distinguish between the two, particularly in his village. Local and regional government was under the control of the minister of interior and security.

The largest subdivisions within the country's administrative structure were four regions, each corresponding almost exactly with one of the country's major geographic divisions and, slightly less exactly, with one of its major ethnic elements. Few government and no party services existed at the regional level. In the post-1972 cabinet one minister, nominally stationed at the regional capital, was charged with encouraging development in each region. The army, the police, and a few other organizations had major divisions along the lines of these regional designations.

Second in size but first in importance in the country's structure were the twenty-nine administrative regions. It was at this level that most control was exercised and central government services were dispensed. Each administrative region was under the authority of a governor appointed by President Touré. The governor was assisted by three deputies (secretaries general): one for economic affairs, one for social affairs, and one for fiscal control. According to the law each administrative region had a popularly elected forty-member general council. The law limited their duties to approving the regional budget. Below the administrative region was the *arrondissement* (district), of which there were about 220 in 1974. The executive head of the *arrondissement*, called the commandant, was responsible to the administrative region's governor. Although no party organs existed at the level of the four regions, party structures exactly paralleled those of the government at both administrative region and *arrondissement* levels.

At the local level the basic unit of control was a part of the party apparatus. The basic cell of the PDG was the rank-and-file committee, found at village and ward level. Ideally the headquarters of committees in rural areas were sited in central villages not more than six miles from their farthest sectors. The area encompassed had an optimum population of at least 1,500; it was subdivided into several sectors, each having three delegates elected at a general meeting to represent it in rank-and-file committee deliberations. Directing the operations of each committee was a bureau. According to changes announced in 1974, each bureau was to have seven members, including at least one woman. All were elected by a congress of all party members for a three-year term. This bureau was completely enmeshed with and almost indistinguishable from the village-level unit of government.

This basic unit of government was the Local Revolutionary Power (Pouvoir Révolutionnaire Local—PRL), merged with the local rank-and-file committee and under the control of the committee's bureau; its chairman, who headed the PRL, served as mayor. The PRL's governmental functions were performed under the supervision of the mayor, who in turn was responsible to the section's bureau, the commandant of the *arrondissement,* and the regional governor. The mayor was assisted by a deputy, whose major responsibility was finance, and by four departments, each headed by a member of the committee-PRL bureau. The departments were called the Local Economic Development Department, Local Administration Department, Local Social Department, and Local Public Works and Communications Department. Their work was meant to be carried out principally through voluntary labor, a continuation of the PDG's emphasis on human investment.

The local economic development departments were concerned with the growing of agricultural products, their marketing, and the distribution and sale of consumer goods to villagers. PRL funds were obtained from rebates on taxes collected by the central or regional governments and from marketing and housing taxes, forestry permits, and profits from the PRL's own production activities. In addition all of the profits earned from the marketing of local produce and consumer goods in the local PRL store were divided among the members of the committee-PRL bureau.

During the era of French rule, Conakry and several of the other large towns were granted municipal status with mayor-council forms of government. This status was abolished soon after independence. In early 1975 all prominent towns served as seats of regional government and in many cases composed a single *arrondissement,* but no separate municipal forms of administration existed. The government of the capital city, however, was different from that of the rest of the country in several respects. It constituted a separate administrative region, divided for some purposes into Conakry I and Conakry II, each having its own party sections. Administration was controlled by a single government, without reference to a general council. The party unit, or PRL, functioned at the ward level. The Conakry I and II divisions substituted for *arrondissement* or even regional-level organs.

THE LEGAL SYSTEM

Sources of Law

At independence the new country's first legislation provided that all laws then in effect should remain in effect as long as they were compatible with the country's new sovereign status and were "in conformity with the interests of the republic."

This wording, although giving colonial legislation continued applicability, seemed designed to provide a means for the government or courts to disallow laws, as required, on political grounds. As of early 1975, however, this had not happened. Instead, in line with President Touré's frequent directions that the courts not "slavishly" follow the colonial directions, the courts had developed a new Guinean common law, drawn largely but not entirely from French concepts.

To the preexisting French colonial laws have been added the

158

postindependence Guinean laws and regulations. These were hierarchically arranged in order of precedence: the Constitution; proclamations (not defined; the Constitution itself was the only proclamation issued as of 1975); international treaties; laws and ordinances; decrees; ministerial orders and decisions; and regional government orders and decisions.

Laws were defined as those acts passed by the National Assembly or by its Permanent Commission. Ordinances, given equal importance, were acts put into effect by the president without legislative approval. Presidential decrees or ministerial orders were made under the authority of existing laws.

Despite the appearance of a new form of common law, French-style codes provided the basis of court actions. The French Commercial Code remained in effect, almost untouched. The French Civil Code also remained in effect, although in some cases it was substantially modified by postindependence legislation. The new legislation included uniform marriage and divorce laws, which for the first time were applied to Guineans under customary law. In the area of criminal law, the French codes were entirely replaced by a new penal code in 1965 and a companion code of criminal procedure in the following year. Although in several respects they remained modeled on the French example, the new Guinean codes brought changes of considerable legal interest, as they left a great degree of discretion to the judges, to precedent, and to decisions based on reviews by higher courts.

Offenses against the law were divided into three categories, based on the severity of the punishment provided for the offense. *Contraventions*, further divided according to severity into three classes, were minor violations punishable by a limited term of imprisonment or a fine. *Délits* were more serious offenses, punishable by terms of fifteen days to five years and fines over GF36,000 (for value of the Guinean franc—see Glossary). *Crimes*, a class of offenses that would be called felonies under English law, were serious acts punishable by prison terms of more than five years or by the death penalty.

Court Structure

During the colonial era minor legal matters, particularly civil disputes, were most often the responsibility of customary courts presided over by appointed local chiefs. As part of its attack on the institution of the chieftaincy after independence in 1958, the new PDG government abolished these courts and replaced them with elements of the local committees of the ruling party, called at different times people's courts *(tribunaux populaires)* or revolutionary courts. The new bodies functioned as mandatory tribunals of conciliation rather than as petty courts of law. Disputes concerning such matters as marriage, divorce, personal status, and entitlement to land had to be brought initially before these bodies. Only if their conciliatory efforts failed could the matter be brought to a regular court.

159

Above the village-level tribunals were two kinds of justice-of-the-peace courts, one of which had only civil jurisdiction. In addition there were four courts of first instance, one located in each region. A single court of assizes had original jurisdiction in major criminal cases. Ordinary appeals from all lower courts except the court of assizes were heard by a single court of appeal in Conakry. The highest court in the system was the Superior Court of Cassation, whose major function was to clarify the law and to ensure unity in its interpretation. It also served as the court of appeal in decisions rendered by the court of assizes.

A major restructuring of the court system was undertaken by legislation in mid-1973. Primary objectives of the judicial reform were the creation of a collegial court system at all levels to replace the earlier single-judge benches and the provision of wider access to the courts by placing them at lower levels throughout the country. At the three lowest levels the new judicial bodies were all renamed people's courts. Each was to be constituted by a three-judge bench.

At the lowest level in the restructured system were the people's courts of the villages and city wards. The chairman of the party's local unit, the rank-and-file committee, served as president of the court. As mayor of the PRL, this same official also headed the unit of local government. The other two members of each of these courts were to be elected annually by the local party membership. In each body a local civil servant acted as court clerk.

The jurisdiction of the new village-level people's courts was slightly broader than that of their predecessor tribunals. Their primary responsibility still involved attempts to arrive at solutions to family problems and other matters of personal law through conciliation. In addition, however, the new village-level people's courts had jurisdiction over civil matters involving amounts of less than GS7,500 (for value of the syli—see Glossary), a major sum by village standards. Their judgments could be taken on appeal to the next judicial level for complete retrial. Although lacking criminal jurisdiction, the village courts did have police powers, enabling them to order the arrest of suspects for trial before higher courts.

Unlike the village courts, the people's court at the *arrondissement* level had jurisdiction in both civil and penal matters. In its civil competence it heard cases on appeal from village-level courts and served as the court of first instance in matters involving less than GS15,000. Its competence in penal matters was limited to the first two classes of *contraventions*. The president of the court was either the *arrondissement* commandant or a full-time magistrate, if one had been assigned. An officer of the gendarmerie could be appointed to serve as prosecutor, and a court clerk was regularly assigned by the Ministry of Justice.

People's courts at the level of administrative regions served as courts of first instance for any civil matter and for penal offenses involving serious *contraventions* or *délits*. These bodies also heard cases on final appeal from the *arrondissement* courts and served as courts of instruction for cases within the region involving offenses classified as *crimes*. In this role the regional courts supervised the investigation of *crimes;* they reviewed the evidence and determined whether it was sufficient to bring the accused to trial. In their investigations evidence both for and against the accused was to be considered, from witnesses and documents as well as from directed police work. The law stated that such investigations must be completed and charges brought within a period of three months. Regional courts were headed by appointed magistrates; as of mid-1974 only sixteen of these judicial bodies had been created.

At the next higher level were two different kinds of court with an interlocking membership: criminal courts and courts of appeal. These were located in Conakry and at the four regional headquarters. A criminal court had jurisdiction as court of first instance for all serious criminal matters. Its seven members included the president and two judges of the colocated court of appeal. The other four members of a criminal court were called jurors and were chosen from a list of sixty political and administrative officials decreed annually as competent for that jurisidiction. Cases were presented by a prosecutor, or by his assistants, from the Ministry of Justice; the same prosecutor was also assigned to the colocated court of appeal.

Each court of appeal was divided into civil and criminal chambers and could function as a court of first instance if it chose to call up a case in progress before a regional court. It did not hear appeals from cases tried before a criminal court.

At the pinnacle of the reformed court system was the Superior Court of Cassation, which remained unchanged. As before the reform, its only duty was to hear cases on final appeal from lower courts. Appeals could be brought before the court only on procedural grounds, such as questions of jurisdiction or violation of law by the lower courts. If this highest court ruled in the appellant's favor, the case in most instances was sent back to the court of origin for retrial. In cases brought to it from a court of appeal, however, the Superior Court of Cassation made the final judgment. Neither the Superior Court of Cassation nor any other judicial body had the power to advise upon or to judge the constitutionality of Guinean laws.

The bench of the highest court was composed of three magistrates and two people's judges. The latter were chosen from a list like the juror members of the courts of appeal. The prosecuting officer was the country's procurator general, who also served as head of the country's entire judicial service. Appeals could be brought by the convicted parties or at will by the procurator general. No safeguards existed to protect these judges, or those at any other court level, from political interference.

In addition to the standard court structure, Guinea had several courts serving specialized purposes. Until independence complaints of citizens against acts of the government were tried, in line with French practice, by an administrative court. After independence this body was abolished, but in 1965 it was reestablished with a companion court of conflicts. The administrative court was the only body before which a citizen could bring litigation against an act of the government. There were no appeals from its decision, although they were subject to veto by President Touré. The court of conflicts was called into session solely to resolve disputes between the administrative court and the regular courts.

Beginning with legislation creating the High Court of Justice shortly after independence, Guinea has had a number of judicial or quasi-judicial bodies to try those accused of political crimes. Some of these bodies were created by law, but others were the result of presidential directives and arose on the spur of the moment. The High Court of Justice was designed to hear only cases concerning state security. It was composed of the president of the National Assembly, three cabinet ministers, and three members of the National Assembly selected by President Touré.

In the mid-1960s, as part of the government's efforts to crack down on what it regarded as efforts by its enemies to undermine the country's economy, the Special Court was created solely to try crimes involving the country's external commerce. It had four members: three were from the political ranks of the government, and the fourth was the president of the court of appeal. No appeal was allowed from its decisions or from those of the High Court of Justice.

From time to time, according to presidential decision, other bodies were given judicial authority in political matters. Thus after a purported plot to assassinate President Touré in 1969, an executive body of the PDG, called the National Revolutionary Council, was constituted as the country's revolutionary tribunal. Those accused before it were convicted, without personally appearing, on the basis of tape recordings of their purported confessions. Without hearing any defense the tribunal sentenced thirteen of the accused to death and about thirty others to at least twenty years' imprisonment.

After the invasion of November 1970, at least 160 people were tried before the National Assembly, serving under presidential appointment as the Supreme Revolutionary Tribunal (see ch. 13). Again the accused were not given a chance to defend themselves; most were heard by tape-recorded "confessions," and the proceedings were broadcast over Radio Conakry. Ninety-two people were sentenced to death, including several who had already been executed in 1969.

POLITICAL DYNAMICS

Political life in early 1975 centered on the activities of President Touré and the PDG. The key to the party's success in continuing to dominate the country, despite oppositon, lay in its formative years. Even before independence it had won the adherence of the vast majority of the

162

national population, largely by making an appeal to the people on issues with which they were personally involved.

Background

Movements toward racial equality and the inherent rights of people to rule themselves had first been stirred among the limited number of educated Guineans by events in Europe and the statements of Allied leaders in World War II. A certain limited degree of political liberalization was achieved shortly after the war (see ch. 2). At first the politically sensitive members of the elite—civil servants, teachers, labor union leaders, and a few educated chiefs—placed their hopes for further developments in the voices and votes of those few Africans who had been seated in the French legislative bodies to represent African interests. Their African aspirations were generally supported by the left wing of the French political spectrum, the communist and socialist parties.

By 1950, however, the leaders of the interterritorial African Democratic Rally (Rassemblement Démocratique Africain—RDA) had realized that the best hopes for achieving their goals lay in the creation of mass political parties. The leaders of the RDA's Guinean section, the PDG, set out to create such a mass movement. As a first step they undertook to create or encourage the politicization of the trade unions that were becoming active among the urban workers. Such workers constituted only a tiny fraction of the largely rural, agricultural work force; but their regular incomes, existing organization, partial break with traditional culture, and contacts with modern innovations made them the only advanced element of significant size in the society.

At the outset the PDG had to compete with groups organized on ethnic and regional lines around certain members of the African elite, most of which were little more than creatures of the colonial administration. These organizations, clinging to social ideals that in two generations of colonial rule had lost most of their relevance, were no match for a party that promised to redress long-standing popular grievances through mass action. The simple program of the PDG had powerful emotional impact, and the party attracted an ever-increasing following. Its aims were to achieve the end of colonial exploitation, improved living conditions, equality with Europeans, and national self-government within a broader West African entity. Nationalism was to be translated into an assault on the ethnic barriers that the party saw as dividing the people and rendering them incapable of winning their rights.

The party program brought into focus popular discontent, and it turned half-realized yearnings into specific demands. In party activities, people found a means of self-assertion and a vehicle of social prestige. The party slogans and declarations gave a sense of personal and national pride to the many whose forebears had been held as slaves or serfs by their stronger neighbors and who themselves had been classified as subjects in their own land by a white administration (see ch. 5).

The party found a single ready-made issue to serve as the major source of its appeal to the vast rural majority: opposition to the rule of the chiefs. Colonial rule had completely altered the chief's role. It had been that of the ranking local leader, whose limited authority rested on popular acquiescence. After the arrival of the French the local chief became, in effect, a member of the lowest unchallengeable rank of the French administration. No longer dependent upon the popular will, many of the chiefs acted despotically, knowing their actions were protected by the threat of French forces. The French allowed or encouraged their petty despotism by honoring those among the chiefs who were most successful in collecting taxes and organizing labor levies. Those chiefs who insisted upon putting the interests of their followers first were soon replaced.

The PDG based its appeal on a demand for reforming or ending the role of the chiefs, promising a turnover of local authority to elected villagers. This promise was fulfilled by the party as one of its first acts when self-government was obtained in 1957. The people responded enthusiastically to the vigor and charm of the young leadership, particularly Sékou Touré, a brilliant speaker; and they showed themselves accessible to the efficient organizational techniques of his lieutenants.

"Independence" also became a catchword and one of the most powerful symbols of the movement. It meant equality with the French and an end to the indignities of subject status. It also meant liberation from the restraints of the ossified traditional order and, for youth and women, escape from a social order in which parental and male authority was complete. Only in 1958 did it finally come to mean absolute political independence from France. In September 1958 the country by referendum chose national independence, voting overwhelmingly against entering the newly established French Community (see ch. 2).

The fact that Guinea was alone in rejecting the French Community, which was linked with France's subsequent retaliatory steps to cut off all assistance, also reverberated to the advantage of the PDG's image. The PDG's isolated action won the immediate acclaim of groups throughout much of the rest of Africa and the world at large that were demanding an end to colonial rule everywhere. The new government was thus able to portray its president to the Guinean people as an internationally respected leader of progressive forces throughout Africa.

Thus at independence the party, in the form of its leader, President Touré, took on the personality of a hero figure for the vast majority of the people. The scope of their support was reflected in the preponderance of the votes in the referendum: 1.1 million to 57,000. The support came not only from the abolition of the role of the chiefs but also from the steps taken to ensure reform in the roles of women and youth and from the exhilaration of the party's triumph over colonialism. The PDG had thus gathered a great deal of goodwill upon which to base its authority and power in the postindependence era.

The Postindependence Era

The political dynamics of postindependence Guinea may be summed up as a battle by President Touré and the PDG to retain the support obtained before independence despite widespread public disillusionment resulting from the government's political and economic policies. From the beginning President Touré and his colleagues had to struggle with economic and political difficulties that their own policies had created or intensified. As early as 1961 it could be said that food shortages and high prices had begun to dissipate popular enthusiasm for the government and its projects. Although the president still could count on strong support from most of the people, the economic difficulties quickly took on a political complexion.

Evident factors in the strength of the PDG in the late 1950s and early 1960s were the effectiveness of its leaders; the tightly knit party organization and its efficient techniques of communications, propaganda, and control; the absence of any organized political opposition; and the support, often deeply emotional, commanded by the party among the mass of the people. The party regarded itself as the creative instrument of the popular will in the task of making Guinea into a strong, modern nation and bringing about the ultimate emancipation and unification of all Africa.

Party, government, labor unions, the national youth movement, and the women's organization constituted the main components of the structure by which the country was ruled. The people were mobilized behind official policies and programs, and the young leaders and functionaries were recruited and developed. This integrated apparatus not only conveyed party decisions and government directives downward but channeled information about popular grievances and preferences upward. Its components provided the only ladders on which ambitious men and women could climb the organizational pyramid, at the apex of which were the national leadership of the party and the government.

The ascendancy of President Touré was unquestioned, but until the mid-1960s he appeared to function as the head of a collective executive rather than as a personal center of power. The leaders around him also exercised an important voice in the conduct of national affairs. In the formulation of policy there was considerable give-and-take between them and the president. During the late 1960s this give-and-take had gradually been reduced as President Touré assumed an ever-stronger grip over all decisionmaking. With the example of what had happened to colleagues and predecessors in purges, the other leaders placed less importance on their individual opinions. All sought to agree with the president. Earlier alignments within the cabinet and the BPN along ideological or foreign policy lines seemed to disappear.

Policy decisions were placed before the people and repeatedly explained to them through the channels of the government, the party,

165

and the mass organizations. Public discussion was welcomed, but no open disagreement with a settled policy or criticism of the government or its leaders was tolerated.

The party sought to retain the support of the majority through control of all sources of information and education, through total control over all existing social bodies, and through force. It also sought to continue the reform of the social order and to create a state-owned economy based on the Marxist model. After largely nationalizing the economy, in line with the party's socialist ideology and as a part of the efforts at direct control of all organizations, the governing party attempted to implement plans for national economic changes. Many attempts, however, resulted in serious economic failures, particularly in trade matters (see ch. 11; ch. 12).

The PDG's economic programs had negative impacts on popular support for the party in two ways. First, although the seizure of the existing company assets had little direct effect on Guineans because most were foreign owned, the accompanying restrictions on smaller traders did have an impact on the Guineans, who constituted most of this group; but the adverse political impact was relatively easy to control. Such traders were locally influential persons, but they constituted only a small element of the society. Second, and much more serious, was the popular reaction to the virtual collapse of the economy that accompanied these moves, most notably the disappearance of consumer goods, often including even local basic foodstuffs, from the market.

These deprivations led many Guineans to resent first the government's economic policies, then the government, and finally its leadership. This negative impact was followed and reinforced throughout the 1960s and early 1970s by the reaction to other government policies. The imposition of totalitarian controls on the society was particularly resented by elements of the educated minority. They and the ambitious men of the younger generation, educated since independence in party-controlled schools, were also disaffected by the decline of personal opportunities for advancement. The political and economic changes limited opportunities to attain positions under party control that went, often without consideration of qualifications, to those with connections among the party elite or to those who had displayed unquestioning adherence to the PDG and the directives of its leader, President Touré. The government's reaction, even to the most moderate objections to its policies, was forceful and generally violent suppression aimed at anyone who could conceivably be accused of being involved in the disagreement. This reaction to criticism was frequently aimed at remarks from within the ranks of the party's own supporters on the Right and the Left. The violent reaction, in turn, generated new hostility and widespread fear. All of these factors played major roles in the flight into exile of a large portion of the country's population.

Those who remained in the country clearly appeared to include a majority among whom support for the PDG and President Touré remained a strongly felt principle. These people were motivated by several factors. The party's strongest adherents appeared to be those whose loyalty was linked to their own personal advancement or that of relatives in the party, in the party-dominated state bureaucracy, or in state-owned business and industry. Others were reacting to successful propaganda efforts portraying those who opposed the party leadership in any way as traitors in the pay of neocolonialist foreign powers eager to snuff out the country's independence. For many others, particularly among the rural majority, support stemmed from the actual improvements the party's rule had brought to their status through changes in the social order.

Party Structure and Operations

The lowest level units of the party were found in each village and town ward, as well as in military, police, and work organizations. The number and composition of the lowest echelon reflected a major change in party philosophy in 1964. Until then the PDG's leadership had sought to make the party not only mass based but all-encompassing. Already large at independence, by 1960 the party had some 26,000 cells, and its membership included about half of the country's adult population. In 1964, however, a decision was put into effect to make the PDG a cadre party—one to which only the political elite and its militant supporters might belong and encompassing less than 15 percent of the adult population as members. This required the dismissal of 70 percent of the party's members and a huge reduction in the number of units. At first a restriction was also imposed on the size and representation in the party's local and regional executives of the two major auxiliary movements, the Youth of the African Democratic Revolution (Jeunesse de la Révolution Démocratique Africaine—JRDA) and the National Women's Committee (Comité National des Femmes—CNF). This move was short lived, however, and the original policies regarding membership and the mass organizations were restored during the following years. Only the limitation on the number of cells was continued.

The basic units of the PDG were called base committees or rank-and-file committees. These were inseparable from the PRL, the lowest element of local government, at the level of the country's 4,000 villages (see Regional and Local Administration, this ch.). It was through the PRL's open meetings that nonparty members had a voice in the control of the party and country. An additional 3,800 party rank-and-file committees were found in production units, that is, in businesses, factories, farms, government offices, and military and police units, where they formed an amalgam between the party, the workers, and management.

The aims of the basic party organizations were stated as aiding the masses to organize themselves for the struggle to realize the objectives pursued by the party and applying decisions made by higher echelons.

Public meetings were held weekly, at which policies and programs of the PDG were explained and the whole community was encouraged to discuss national and local problems. The committee's major duties were to organize support for the decisions and directives of the central and regional authorities. They controlled the distribution of consumer goods, including foodstuffs, to the local population and were responsible for reporting to the security services of the party and state anyone regarded as hostile to the PDG. Thus the committees possessed considerable power over the lives of the average citizens (see ch. 6).

Above the rank-and-file committee was the party section, corresponding to the *arrondissement* in the governmental structure. In 1974 there were about 200 party sections. Above the sections were thirty party federations. These corresponded to the country's twenty-nine administrative regions, with one extra federation to serve a subdivided Conakry administrative region. There were committees of the JRDA and the CNF alongside the PDG units at each echelon, all the way to the national level. At the federation and national level there were also corresponding labor union bodies.

At each level of the party, leadership was vested in an executive body called a bureau. At the highest level this body was the National Political Bureau (Bureau Politique National—BPN). At the section and federation levels and, at least during much of the 1960s, at the local and national levels, the bureaus were composed of thirteen members. At the local level all of the bureaus' members were elected by the members of the party units. Here, as at all other levels, the heads of the JRDA and CNF filled two of the posts by right. The section and federation bureaus were similar except that at the section level only ten of the thirteen members were elected, the commandant of the *arrondissement* filling the chairman's position. At the federation level only nine bureau members were elected, the regional governor and the head of the regional committee of the labor unions also serving as members by right.

Bureaus of the rank-and-file committee were elected for one-year terms, those of the sections for two years, and those of the federation for three. This structure was much less democratic than it appeared to be, as in each instance the single slate of candidates for bureau offices was selected by the higher echelons of the party. In addition at each of these levels an executive was chosen by the party's central leadership from among the bureau's elected members. In the village the mayor automatically served as chairman of the bureau. At the section level he was called the committee director, and the head of the federation bureau was labeled the federal secretary.

In order to provide a broader voice in decisionmaking at the higher levels, the Section Conference, composed of leaders of its various elements, met twice a year; and the Section Congress, which included all the leaders of the constituent units as well, met every two years. The Federation Conference and the Federation Congress filled similar roles, and this congress also met every three years.

The highest governing body of the party was its National Congress, which met at least every four years to review the results of past policies, decide major policy directions for the future, and elect the secretary general and the members of the Central Committee. At least once a year another key body, the National Council of the Revolution, was convened. It was composed of the most important political leaders, called together to develop shorter term policies and to ensure the party executives' adherence to the latest National Congress directives. These were the real legislative bodies in the Guinean party-state.

The highest party organ in early 1975 was the small Central Committee, within which the real nucleus, the seven-member BPN, formed the key part. Until party reforms in early 1972, the Central Committee had been considerably larger but lacking in authority, serving only a loosely defined role as the standing committee of the National Congress. The reforms formally transferred the party's executive authority from the BPN to the Central Committee. The Central Committee's role was redefined to make it the daily policymaking and guidance body of the PDG, responsible for proper implementation of the decisions of the National Congress and the National Council of the Revolution. Its statement of duties made it responsible for directing and controlling all of the country's political, economic, social, cultural, and administrative affairs.

Initially the new Central Committee had four working committees to deal with economic, social, educational, and organizational affairs. A fifth body, a party planning committee, was added, apparently in 1973. In addition the 1972 changes included creation of an investigative agency to assist the Central Committee in its political and administrative control measures. It was headed by a former BPN member, who was given the title of permanent secretary-inspector general of the party. In addition to these committee duties, each member was assigned responsibility for watching over developments in a particular area.

Despite the broadening of power seemingly indicated by the strengthening of the hand of the Central Committee, the continued concentration of authority in the BPN could be judged from its official designation as the Central Committee's executive agent and from the provision allowing it to take any action deemed necessary in the intervals between Central Committee meetings. Moreover, in early 1975 President Touré served as head of the Central Committee, and each of its four working committees was chaired by a BPN member. In addition to the president, the prime minister, and the five other BPN members, the Central Committee included twelve other cabinet ministers and the party's permanent secretary. Only four of its members were drawn from other positions. Two of the members were women, including the only female cabinet minister.

The party's Central Committee exercised direct supervision over the actions of the lowest party units. When the bureau of a federation or a section, for example, was felt to be weak in its support for party directions or was thought to have antagonized major portions of the local population, the Central Committee was free to suspend the offending unit. It could then appoint a public safety committee to function as its replacement.

Each member of the Central Committee was given responsibility for overseeing the party's organization in particular administrative regions. Either they or BPN members headed inspection teams that visited the party sections. The teams were charged with checking the political authority of the party and the respect given the administrative agencies in each area; the capacity for political mobilization as evidenced in congresses, parades, sports, arts fetes, and voluntary development programs; the fulfillment of fiscal and other civil duties by party members; and the general administrative efficiency of the sections. On such an inspection the Central Committee member held a public conference, after which he conferred privately with the section executive committee and inspected the headquarters. Afterward he conducted criticism meetings with the section committee, the governmental administrative services, the unions, and other organizations. President Touré himself frequently went on inspection trips. On such occasions he often had private discussions with local leaders and gave them personal directives, seeking to win agreement as well as obedience.

Public meetings, conferences and discussions, party-organized fairs, festivals, dances, sports and cultural events, and parades were important techniques for ensuring mass participation. All were important media for generating interest and support for PDG policies in a people with a love for pageantry, a propensity to act in communal ways, an appreciation for oratory, and a tradition of public discussion and consensus. Symbolism and the repetition of slogans were employed to attract and hold the popular imagination.

Leadership

In early 1975 the core of the national leadership consisted of the seven members of the party's BPN and a few others. The BPN members held the key ministerial posts in the cabinet. This handful of national leaders was led by President Touré, head of the party and government. Few of the members of this top ruling group had received any higher education, but all had attended local primary and secondary schools under the French. A few of them were graduates of the William Ponty School at Dakar in Senegal. Most of them, like President Touré, had been employed in the colonial administration and had entered politics through the labor movement. Most had been members of the original PDG when it was still part of the RDA, and many of them had belonged to it from the time of its establishment. A large number of Guineans graduated from European or American universities and technical schools in the 1960s and early 1970s. Few of them, however, were in key posts. Many had either failed to return to Guinea or, having returned, had fled the country.

Within the BPN there was a division of labor: each member was in charge of a particular section of activity under the overall supervision of President Touré as party secretary general. A rigorous party discipline bound the members of the BPN and the larger Central Committee to accept and to work loyally for the decisions that had been formally made. Long association and an apparent basic unity of outlook have helped them to do so. During much of the 1960s they reportedly enjoyed wide freedom of expression in their deliberations, as long as these remained within their own ranks. Differences of opinion usually were resolved by discussion and compromise.

The Ninth Congress of the PDG in early 1972 took actions that seemed aimed at reversing the growth of the absolute power of President Touré, notably the creation of the new Central Committee and the appointment of a prime minister. The latter move was announced as being intended to relieve the president from the duties of supervising the government in order to leave him free to deal with what were described as ideological tasks.

In reality, however, the changes, while perhaps relieving both the president and the BPN of some administrative tasks in the government and the party, did little or nothing to reallocate political power. In part the appointment of a prime minister may have reflected the president's desire to be able to send someone with full authority to negotiate in foreign countries, as President Touré rarely left the country.

The party militants constituted the elite group that interested itself in all aspects of government and community life. In implementing party decisions, party militants were expected to supervise the general fulfillment of tasks allotted to various sectors of the community and to bring to the party's attention transgressions or deviations.

An interesting comparison could be made between the ethnic composition of the power structure's officeholders and the country's population. In the early 1970s it was believed that the Peul and the Malinké ethnic groups each constituted about 30 percent of the population (see ch. 4). The remainder was composed almost equally of persons associated with the Soussou and the Forest Region groups. At the broader level of the middle and upper elite, one outside observer has identified the ethnic origins of the holders of the several hundred highest posts in the government, party, civil service, and state-controlled corporations. Here Peul, Malinké, and Soussou were found in fairly representative proportion. The peoples of the Forest Region were not fairly represented, probably reflecting economic and educational factors in the country's least developed region rather than any political discrimination.

By contrast, ethnic distribution in the topmost ranks was clearly skewed. In both the thirty-four-member cabinet and the twenty-four-member Central Committee, over 60 percent appeared in 1973 to be Malinké and about 25 percent Peul, a clear indicator of Malinké political domination.

The nine most important officeholders included seven Malinké (among them President Touré, whose mother was actually Peul but who was raised in Malinké country). The other two were Peul. According to some observers, a voice in the BPN was given to each of the four regions, as one of the Malinké was from Lower Guinea and another was from the Forest Region. Among the five Malinké cabinet ministers in the BPN, three were related in some way to President Touré's family.

Perhaps more interesting than their ethnic backgrounds were the tenure and control demonstrated by this key group's composition. At the very top, the seven members of the BPN also held seven of the eight most important posts in the government: president, prime minister, and five of the six senior ministerial (minister of domain) posts. The sixth minister of domain was a close associate and former BPN member. Only one person near the pinnacle of power in the PDG, Lansana Diane, the party's permanent secretary, held no government post in 1974, having lost face in the crisis of November 1970.

Seven of these nine holders of key positions were already numbered among the thirteen BPN members in 1961. Actual continuity was even stronger. Of the other postindependence BPN members, two still held other important cabinet posts, and one was in ill health. Only three had fallen from power, despite the almost constant turnover of lesser officials and several bloody attempted coups and purges.

Mass Organizations

The PDG regarded mass organizations not merely as auxiliaries but as components of the party, completely subject to its political direction and committed to the service of its goals. The principal mass organizations were the labor unions and the women's and youth groups. The labor movement, which predated the establishment of the PDG-RDA, provided the initial base of organized support for the party and the hard core of its leadership. The women's and youth groups—the CNF and JRDA—were formed by the party as vehicles for mobilizing these previously unorganized segments of the population. There were some other less important organizations, but these were also party dominated.

Women's committees, while having their own hierarchical organizations, were also an integral part of the PDG and, through them and their membership in the executive committees, women participated on all levels in the direction of party affairs. The youth organization, the JRDA, was a separate entity, but it proceeded "in perfect harmony with the political orientation of the party." It was governed by the same general regulations that applied to the PDG, on which it depended for funds, and "should never be considered anything else than a specialized section of the party." The basically political character of labor unions and the unity of labor and the party were emphatically stressed.

Domestically the mass organizations were charged with mobilizing the support of labor, women, and youth for official policies and programs. Through informal contacts and cooperative relations with similar organizations in other African countries, they were also unofficial instruments of Guinean foreign policy.

The party early attracted women to its ranks through the promise it held out to them of liberation from their traditional subordination to men. They took an aggressive part in the political battles that preceded the party's advent to power. With legal equality and educational opportunity, women entered into positions of public responsibility in significant numbers. Delegations of Guinean women attended numerous international women's conferences and received visiting delegations from national and international women's organizations. Their closest ties were with both African and communist groups.

The JRDA was established by the PDG on March 26, 1959. Like the CNF, its structure mirrored that of the PDG from top to bottom. It was concerned with all questions "of interest to youth." It conducted political and social education courses and was active in sports, theater, folklore, dancing, and singing. Its members—seven to twenty-one years of age—were subject to the same rules of discipline as party members. The JRDA played a key role in organizing voluntary labor for the "human investment" program. By giving officially approved focus to the recreational activities of young people and involving them in political work, it served as a training ground for future party leaders.

The labor unions, relatively powerful before independence, have been completely made over into elements of the party. The structure of the National Confederation of Workers of Guinea (Confédération Nationale des Travailleurs de Guinée—CNTG) differed from that of the other three national organizations. The CNTG existed only at the top, serving to link together separate national craft unions and professional organizations. At the regional level there were supposed to be associations loosely linking all the local unions, modeled on the CNTG at the national level. At the local level labor units in different enterprises were associated with these national unions rather than with the CNTG. Within any single enterprise employing more than fifty people, however, there was a committee tied closely to the party's local elements. This committee served not only to ensure the party's political control over the management of the enterprise and the political and professional education of the workers but also to ensure the smooth functioning of the one or more unions represented in the enterprise. The party's close control of the unions was assured at both bottom and top. In addition to having party militants hold all key posts at all levels, the CNTG itself was headed by one of the seven members of the BPN.

Political Philosophy

President Touré has devoted much effort to attempting to define the governing party's ideology and his own political theory. The alleged reason for the creation of the post of prime minister in 1972 was to permit the president to spend more time on ideological matters; so directly under the Office of the Presidency he had installed a minister of ideology. More than ten volumes of his collected speeches and writings were published between 1958 and 1972, and many of these appeared in more than one edition. Heavy emphasis was placed on ideological indoctrination in all Guinean schools, and a special school had been created solely to reindoctrinate students completing higher level training programs abroad. The governing party's radio network, daily newspaper, and weekly magazine devoted great portions of their coverage to ideological matters (see ch. 7).

President Touré's philosophy has generally been labeled a variation of African socialism, although it owed a greater debt to the Marxist-Leninist ideology than did most of the other ideologies usually associated with African socialism. President Touré's major departure from Marxism lay in his strong rejection of the concept of the inevitability of class struggle. Like other African socialist thinkers, he felt that Africa was largely free of the capitalist class and could therefore progress directly from the traditional communalism of the village to the modern socialist state. For him a philosophical concern with class warfare could only tend to blur the really vital issue—the need for a national unity that would bind together ethnically diverse peoples.

To avoid the growth of capitalism as the modern economy developed and as the need to accumulate capital became vital, both the means of production and large-scale trade were to be held exclusively in state hands. Foreign investment would be restricted to projects the government found it could not develop by itself and, in any case, would be tightly controlled by the state.

In ideology, if not in practice, the official attitude toward foreign investment reflected not only the attitude toward capitalism but also the insistence upon total independence from foreign control. This insistence upon nonalignment and a vocal dedication to African unity played the key theoretical roles in the Guinean foreign policy (see ch. 9).

Without a feudal or capitalist class to serve as an enemy, the PDG relied upon other issues—underdevelopment and neocolonialism—to mobilize its supporters. After 1971, however, President Touré's opposition to the Marxist concept of class struggle apparently lessened. The cause of this reappraisal was the development of a belief that a fifth column (agents of foreign interests) was at work inside Guinea and that it represented the greatest threat to the country. He had begun to voice a belief that the fight of the people against this purported "silent invasion" was analogous to this Marxist concept.

President Touré's philosophy placed a high value on what he called democracy, but his use of the word bore little resemblance to the concept in the West. It was predicated neither on constitutions nor on parliamentary rule. Instead the will of the people, and therefore democracy, was expressed through the party, the central element in the country's political structure and society. That a dictatorship existed was openly admitted. Dictatorship and democracy were not regarded as conflicting terms as long as the dictatorship claimed to embody the will of the people.

The concept and form of the party and state clearly stemmed from the lessons learned by the party leaders in the first political organization with which they were familiar, the French Communist Party. The PDG was thus Leninist in form without being Marxist in philosophy. Membership was generally open to everyone willing to purchase a membership card, but leadership posts in the PDG were restricted to the so-called party militants—those who were willing to spend considerable effort on its behalf and to follow its lead unhesitatingly. It was a party organized along the lines of democratic centralism; that is, all members could express their opinions on new issues through party channels but, once a decision was reached by the party's central leadership on any issue, all disagreements would cease, and the center's directive would be unchallengeably obeyed. The only remaining discussion allowed was to be devoted to the question of how best to implement the directive and to self-criticism sessions concerning failures to achieve the assigned objectives. Further, obedience was expected not only from party members but also from the population as a whole, as the party and its members served as the voice of the people. Force could be used as a necessary component to ensure this obedience.

Individualism had no role in this ideology, and thus civil rights were of little importance. Recognition of the importance of the individual not only was in conflict with democratic centralism but also was contrary to President Touré's concept of African tradition. He viewed traditional society as being based on the collective good of the village, not on the good of the individual. Accordingly a man conceived of himself only as a part of the social whole, not as an entity distinct unto himself. Individualism was regarded as a French concept that had infected the Guinean intellectual elite and was, therefore, a challenge to the party.

Elements of Opposition

Political disaffection in Guinea in early 1975 must be related to the strain caused by the effort to develop and transform the country. The industrialization program had incurred a heavy foreign debt without creating effective means of repaying it. Efforts to exploit the country's mineral wealth promised to be self-liquidating and to provide increased tax and foreign exchange resources, but there was as yet no assurance that these benefits would trickle down to the average Guinean instead of creating isolated islands of prosperity (see ch. 6). The government's attempts to regulate trade had at times brought the movement of goods almost to a standstill. Shortages of food and other consumer goods created by wage and price controls, the reduction of imports, and the effect on agricultural production of inadequate spending and neglect were inflicted on a population already living at the subsistence level (see ch. 11).

At the same time that the people have been asked to bear these hardships, they have been pressed to increase their efforts and to welcome profound changes in their personal and social lives. Human investment programs of obligatory volunteer work have demanded unremunerated labor on public projects from every able-bodied adult. Farmers have been urged to adopt new, and for them unproved, methods and to combine in cooperatives. In the absence of capital, equipment, and technical knowledge, the cry for increased production has emphasized the need for people to work harder, and PDG plans have required the setting of work norms in agriculture as well as in other fields. Lack of continuity has also been a major problem, spurred by frequent, almost constant changes in personnel and objectives.

The effort to remake the society and to reconstitute its values has relied not only upon education but also upon law and fiat. The decrees granting women legal equality with men and prohibiting child marriage or marriage without the consent of the principals have been enthusiastically received by women and young people, but they have profoundly affected long-established relationships within the family and the kin-structured local community (see ch. 5). The shock has been felt most deeply by the older generation but, in suddenly being propelled into new roles in relation to each other and to their elders, the young people themselves have paid a penalty of uncertainty and emotional conflict.

The national development plans were designed to lay the economic and social foundations of Guinea as a modern nation within a short span (see ch. 10). A major premise was that a maximum effort could be sustained and would be justified by its rewards. Although notable progress has been made with respect to education and some areas of industrial infrastructure, living standards have generally worsened. Even though signs of popular restiveness have called for relaxation of the pressure on the people, some elements of the PDG have demanded even stronger measures.

The widespread resentment toward the governing party engendered by its economic and political actions has been balanced by the executive controls the PDG has been able to exercise over the great majority of the population. Most of those who did not support the party withdrew into political indifference rather than exert overt opposition.

Although many of those who had been suppressed in the succession of purges since independence were only attempting to bring about peaceful changes in policy, the actual enemies of the ruling group were real, numerous, and varied. Those who had actively opposed the government in its early years, generally supporters of the old order who were disappointed by the loss of power of the chiefs and the ethnic interest groups, were out of touch with their potential opponents within the younger generation. The new youth, on the other hand, also constituted a potential political problem. Organized in the JRDA and groomed in the schools as the "shock force of the revolution," they have tended to outrun the adult leadership and to present it with the task of keeping youthful impatience from changing into left-wing opposition.

In much of Africa coups by the military have become commonplace and almost invariably successful. Although this could not be ruled out in Guinea, the government had spent more than eight years attempting to ensure that the army was led by loyal party supporters on the one hand and did not have control over all the elements of force necessary to ensure a successful coup on the other (see ch. 13). By 1972 it seemed clear that all opposition leaders had been eliminated, had fled the country, or lived under constant police surveillance.

As a result, in early 1975, with one broad exception, no organized opposition to the PDG's continued rule could be openly perceived. The one exception was not to be found within Guinea but rather within the Guinean exile community.

The Guineans who had left their country probably numbered at least 600,000, and the number may have exceeded 1 million. The exiles themselves claimed they numbered over 2 million. The largest single group of exiles was in Senegal, and Ivory Coast apparently provided haven for the next largest number. According to President Léopold-Sédar Senghor of Senegal, there were 800,000 non-Senegalese in his country in 1973, and the majority of these were generally agreed to be Guineans. Ivory Coast statistics of 1969 indicated that 150,000 Guineans were residents there. Other significant groups were found in Sierra Leone, Liberia, Mali, and The Gambia as well as France.

It was not possible to judge the motivation of this large, varied exile group. For example, the Guinean government alleged that large numbers of these exiles remained supporters of the PDG, but in early 1975 there was no independent information to indicate this. The government claimed that 75,000 Guineans among those resident in Sierra Leone had come to the Guinean embassy to cast ballots for President Touré in 1974. Even during the colonial era a number of Guineans had left the country to go to other French colonies where economic or educational opportunities were better. In the 1955 census, for example, slightly under 70,000 Guineans were listed as having been out of the country for one month or more. Thus a precedent had long been established, one that would incline Guineans faced with hardship in their own country to emigrate.

During the colonial era Guineans had freedom of movement across the borders with other French-speaking states. After independence this movement became highly restricted as the Guinean government made such flight illegal and attempted to block the flow with border patrols, although with little apparent effect. Those Guineans who left without permission were subject to arrest upon their return. By the 1970s laws had been passed holding parents legally responsible if their children fled the country, and the property of those who left was subject to seizure. Despite these stringent laws large numbers of Guineans continued to flee the country.

Without doubt, almost constant deterioration in the economy was the primary motivation in the flight into exile of most Guineans. Even among those for whom objection to the governing party's policies was the major cause of flight, many were not interested in actively opposing the government.

In early 1975 active opposition abroad was concentrated generally among former soldiers who had served in French military units before Guinean independence and among the intellectual elite. The large group included a sizable proportion of the country's university graduates, a number of former cabinet ministers, and at least seven ambassadors. These people led the two political organizations that were active among the exiles: the Guinean National Liberation Front (Front pour la Libération Nationale de Guinée—FLNG) and the Association of Guineans in France (Association de Guinéens en France—AGF). These groups received financial support from the large number of Guinean merchants who were forced into exile by the government's trade policies. The prime source of potential insurgents according to most observers was the large number of Guinean veterans of the French army who were not allowed by President Touré to return to their homeland after independence and for this reason remained implacable foes of the current government. This group provided the experienced troops for the invasion effort in November 1970 (see ch. 13).

These active opponents in exile included both those who opposed the purportedly radical philosophy of the government and those who felt that the government had failed to adopt truly socialist policies. Neither group could be said to be clearly predominant, and the distinctions themselves were often blurred by personal ties and animosities. Virtually all the leaders of the exiles have been condemned to death in absentia, as traitors, by President Touré's government.

The external opposition had been so weakened by dissension, notably over the best method of overthrowing President Touré and by the question of who would be allowed to succeed him, that in early 1975 the external threat appeared more theoretical than real. Whatever hopes the exiles had of forcefully overthrowing the government had been lessened by the loss of their potential sanctuary when the Portuguese withdrew in

1974 from Guinea-Bissau, which had served as their base for the 1970 assault.

CHAPTER 9

FOREIGN RELATIONS

Most public information regarding major events in the country's foreign relations has resulted from the impassioned verbal confrontation of its leaders with France, other European states, and nearby African countries. This began with France's sharp rejection of Guinea when it achieved independence in 1958. Spurred by the accompanying loss of French development assistance and rapid offers of recognition and aid from the Soviet Union and Eastern Europe, Guinea established close relations with the communist countries. Later it opened and maintained friendly relations with the United States and several other Western states despite apparently irreconcilable ideological differences. This divergence has reflected the fact that, despite the verbal displays, the major lines of Guinean foreign policy have most often been determined by largely pragmatic considerations.

In the early 1970s communist, Western, and wealthy Arab states were all cultivated in order to encourage much-needed development assistance. Guinea's ideological conscience was salved by maintaining a careful balance to ensure that no single foreign interest predominated.

FOREIGN POLICY AND MANAGEMENT
OF FOREIGN AFFAIRS

In the realm of foreign affairs as in most other matters, all major decisions were made by President Ahmed Sékou Touré. The post of minister of foreign affairs was always assigned to one of several trusted associates within the top leadership of the governing party, the Democratic Party of Guinea (Parti Démocratique de Guinée—PDG). Louis Lansana Béavogui, the prime minister in 1975, had served earlier as minister of foreign affairs for several years.

The ruling party's ideology, expounded by its theoretician, President Touré, played a role in foreign policy formation, but its application was not allowed to interfere with or override more practical considerations except on a limited number of issues. Pan-Africanism and anti-imperialism were heavily stressed in this ideology and at times had played an important role in policymaking, most notably in regard to Portuguese colonial rule in adjacent Guinea-Bissau (see Regional and Intra-African Relations, this ch.). Although a Guinean diplomat long served as the administrative head of the Organization of African Unity (OAU), the government showed little interest in continental and regional bodies working to achieve the unity that an ideological adherence to pan-Africanism would demand.

Denunciations of "imperialism," defined in the sense used by the most radical states, did not make Guinea hesitant to maintain close relations with some of the Western countries most often so labeled. The real consideration in deciding upon friendship was whether the countries would provide the assistance that the Guinean government felt it needed for national development. Particular sensitivity, both to racism and to interference of any kind, and equal treatment without regard to size or strength were also of considerable importance. As with pan-Africanism, little real attention was paid to international organizations. A major effort was devoted to ensuring that the country would not be, or appear to be, aligned with one of the world power blocs, a policy that explained the emphasis on mixing aid from East and West (see Relations with Communist Countries; Relations with the United States, this ch.).

Because of his awareness of the number of coups d'etat in other African countries that had occurred while their heads-of-state were away, President Touré rarely left the country after 1966. In the 1967–74 period, for example, he had departed Guinea only once, aside from two one-day trips to the nearby capital of Liberia. This reluctance to travel abroad often left the country at a marked disadvantage in international meetings.

In 1972 Béavogui was elevated to the newly created post of prime minister while retaining supervisory control over the Ministry of Foreign Affairs. This new rank gave him sufficient status to deal with foreign leaders on a more nearly equal level, and some observers have suggested that the need to strengthen his hand in international negotiations was the major reason for the creation of the post.

In the 1960s, in addition to direct presidential involvement, the responsibility for Guinean foreign affairs had been split between the Ministry of Foreign Affairs and the Ministry of Foreign Trade. Although this second ministry had disappeared by 1972, a somewhat similar division of duties was instituted in 1974 with the creation of the Central Division for International Technical Cooperation to handle foreign assistance programs. This unit, like the Office of Protocol, was assigned directly to the Office of the Presidency.

In 1974 Guinea maintained embassies in twelve African countries, the United Kingdom, Japan, the United States, the Soviet Union, Romania, the German Democratic Republic (East Germany), Cuba, and the People's Republic of China (PRC). Several of the Guinean ambassadors to these countries were also accredited to a number of other states. The United States, seven African, three Western European, four Middle Eastern, and three Asian states, as well as the entire roster of communist countries except Albania, had embassies or missions in Conakry. Many of these embassies, however, were very small establishments.

REGIONAL AND INTRA-AFRICAN RELATIONS

Despite the heavy ideological attention to pan-Africanism since independence, Guinea's ties with other African states have been generally weak and sometimes even hostile, and it has played only a minor role in the continent's interstate organizations. Several practical considerations have been involved. More divisive—and fewer unifying —forces had appeared to slow or prevent the unification with other states that had been expected at independence. Guinea's economy, because it was similar to that of many neighboring states, had little to offer them, and therefore few economic connections had been established. The nationalism of the individual states proved a greater force than the widely subscribed to, but little worked for, African unity. Linguistic and political differences proved less surmountable than had been anticipated. Guinea's role as the first French-speaking state in sub-Saharan Africa to achieve independence and as the prime challenger of French colonialism in the region no longer automatically gave it a leading role in intra-African affairs, as time had reduced the significance of these factors.

In the main, however, Guinea's declining role in intra-African affairs could be attributed to President Touré's own frequent policy reversals and his unfriendly attitudes toward the leaders of a number of other countries. Within the region and the continent, his expressed preferences have been for regimes that espouse an ideology compatible with his own. Yet even governments that voiced a similar ideology or agreed with Guinea's views on major international questions often have been subjected to sudden virulent attacks by President Touré in speeches broadcast over Guinea's radio station, Voice of the Revolution. Such actions, as well as the flight of large numbers of refugees, led other African leaders—far and near, radical and conservative—to be extremely cautious in their relations with Guinea. Neighboring states were particularly concerned with Guinea's actions.

The Sénégal River Basin States

Considerable effort was exerted during the 1960s for the creation of a regional grouping bringing together the Sénégal River basin states: Senegal, Mauritania, Mali, and Guinea. The long river and its major tributaries arise in northern Guinea, flow through Mali, and form the boundary between Senegal and Mauritania. The river is an actual or potential transportation route and a source of electric power, irrigation, and groundwater for a large, arid, and generally poor region. A unified approach by the states involved is required because of the international nature of the waterway and the scale of foreign aid needed to complete the desirable projects (see ch. 11).

Senegal

Senegalese President Léopold-Sédar Senghor's line of reasoning about the river had met no opposition from the other three governments involved, but for a long time he was the only active proponent of such a regional body. Guinea, the least dependent upon development of the river, was separated from Senegal by major ideological differences. In addition its internal difficulties significantly affected its relations with Senegal. The two states were at opposite ends of the spectrum in regard to economic policies and relations with their common former colonizer, France. The Guinean government has often claimed that Senegal, along with France and Ivory Coast, was supporting efforts by the exile opposition to overthrow the Guinean government. A majority of the hundreds of thousands of Guineans who had left their country because of economic and political problems had settled in Senegal, a fact that strongly affronted the Guinean government, which felt that Senegal provided refuge and support for those plotting its overthrow. During many periods the Guinean government radiobroadcasts were designed to be as hostile to the Senegalese leaders as possible.

The frequently temperamental relations between Guinea and Senegal have led on several occasions to the closing of their respective embassies. Despite the affronts, however, President Senghor has made major efforts to reconcile the differences between the two countries and generally has ignored the hostile statements coming from Guinea.

The four states of the region had formed the joint Sénégal River Basin Development Commission in 1964, but this agency had never had a chance to function, in large part because of Guinean intransigence. In March 1968, after a summit meeting between the four heads-of-state, a new body called the Organization of Sénégal River States (Organisation des Etats Riverains du Sénégal—OERS) was formed with an elaborate administrative structure and considerable hopes.

The government of Mali was overthrown by a military coup later that year. Although the new Malian government strongly supported the OERS, Guinea refused to recognize the new government and for this reason withdrew from the joint body, again bringing plans to a standstill.

A restoration of friendly relations between Guinea and Senegal in 1970 brought a brief resurgence of OERS negotiations, but renewed disagreements led once again to a decline. By 1972 the other three states were ready to go ahead without the participation of Guinea. They formed the Sénégal River Development Organization (Organisation pour la Mise en Valeur du Fleuve Sénégal—OMVS) on March 11, 1972, but left room for the later admittance of Guinea.

Mali

While President Modibo Keita was in power in Mali, Guinea's relations with that country were friendlier than those with any of its other neighbors. The presidents and ruling parties of the two countries maintained similar attitudes toward most internal and external affairs, although Mali was somewhat more cordial to France. In the early 1960s

184

and again in 1968 President Touré had gone so far as to propose a formal union between Guinea and Mali, and President Keita had spoken favorably of the idea.

In November 1968, however, President Keita was overthrown by a military coup. The new leaders adopted policies that were at first considerably less aligned with those of Guinea. In February 1969 a plot allegedly occurred in the Guinean army, and several of those implicated attempted to flee to Mali. The two events brought Guinea's relations with Mali to a low point. But by the end of 1969, spurred by conciliatory gestures by the Malian government, President Touré's opposition had lessened. By 1974 relations had returned to normal, although the two countries were not as close as they once had been.

Relations with Ivory Coast

Guinea's relations with Ivory Coast, its neighbor to the southeast, have been plagued by the same problems as those with Senegal, and the basis of the conflict has been ideological. Both Senegal's President Senghor and Ivory Coast's President Félix Houphouët-Boigny have remained closely associated with France on the international scene. Both countries, but particularly Ivory Coast, have adopted moderate pro-Western foreign policies and have rejected President Touré's ideas of socialist internal development.

Ivory Coast has been second only to Senegal as a refuge for Guineans fleeing their country and for the operations of exile groups opposing President Touré. Relations between Guinea and Ivory Coast generally have been strained as a result of the Guinean government's verbal assaults radiobroadcast against Ivory Coast. On at least one occasion, in fact, Guinean troops were mobilized close to the Ivory Coast frontier. At one brief point in 1972, however, relations became almost cordial when the Ivory Coast president, who had worked closely with Sékou Touré in the African Democratic Rally (Rassemblement Démocratique Africain—RDA) between 1946 and 1957, paid a state visit to Guinea in the hope of permanently ending the hostility. This seesawing relationship continued in early 1975 and appeared likely to continue for at least as long as Ivory Coast allowed the Guinean exiles to remain active within its borders.

Other Neighboring States

Beginning in the mid-1960s Guinea emphasized the establishment of close relations with its two English-speaking neighbors, Sierra Leone and Liberia. Friendly relations were also maintained with The Gambia. In the first half of the 1970s, however, Guinea's closest ties among the nearby states were with Sierra Leone.

Sierra Leone

Although divided from Guinea by a different colonial heritage, Sierra Leone and its larger neighbor share a number of geographic and population interests. Two-thirds of Sierra Leone's land frontiers are with Guinea, and a number of ethnic groups straddle national borders that are generally defined only by vague watershed lines. In addition the two countries' natural economies are similar. Although their economies are not linked in any formal way, Sierra Leone has served as the major source of scarce consumer goods for most of Guinea. These commodities are carried into the country along traditional routes across the frontier, often by Guinean merchants who have succeeded in purchasing import licenses from the PDG despite the purportedly rigid exchange controls (see ch. 12).

In addition to these connections, President Touré has regarded relations with Sierra Leone as his bellwether for pan-African relations between French- and English-speaking Africa. The two capitals are only 100 miles apart, whereas Nigeria, the most powerful English-speaking West African state, although of interest to Guinean foreign policy, is over 1,000 miles away.

At an early date the Guinean president had established ties with Siaka Stevens, the leader of Sierra Leone's legal opposition party, the African Peoples Congress (APC). In March 1967 new national elections brought Stevens to the fore. He was appointed prime minister but was immediately overthrown by a military coup d'etat. He and other APC leaders went into exile in Guinea. A subsequent military coup in 1968 returned the country to civilian rule, and Stevens was invited to take the role of prime minister.

Prime Minister Stevens had become close to President Touré during his exile in Guinea and, like several other APC leaders, he admired the operation of the PDG. In June 1970 President Touré proposed the unification of the two countries. After the November 1970 invasion of Guinea, Sierra Leone promptly offered its support, and suggestions that the invaders had come from staging bases in Sierra Leone were quickly rejected (see ch. 13). In December 1970 the two governments announced a mutual defense treaty. The primary intention of the treaty was to lend Guinea added support in the face of what President Touré alleged were continuing threats of intervention from Portuguese forces in Guinea-Bissau.

In early 1971, after the treaty was agreed upon but before it was signed, another military coup d'etat was staged in Sierra Leone. The country's army was strongly divided, and the pro-Stevens forces captured the coup's leaders. Fearful of another attempt, however, Prime Minister Stevens flew to Guinea and signed the mutual defense treaty. The next day a Guinean force, composed of about 200 men, three jet fighter aircraft, and one helicopter, arrived in the Sierra Leone capital and assumed the duty of guarding Prime Minister Stevens. Portions of this Guinean force remained until 1974. Close relations between the ruling parties and the presidents continued into 1975.

Liberia and The Gambia

Liberia played a role that was similar to but less significant than that of Sierra Leone in Guinean foreign policy. Geographic and population links also existed. Although the governments of the two countries were often at opposite ends of the political spectrum, their direct interests were not in conflict. As a result, relations between President Touré and Liberian presidents during the 1960s and first half of the 1970s were particularly cordial.

Relations with The Gambia also have been notably friendly. This has resulted generally from the fact that The Gambia is almost entirely surrounded geographically by Senegal, Guinea's rival. By maintaining friendly connections with Guinea, The Gambia thus could demonstrate its independence of Senegal. Guinea's particular warmth for the small country stemmed from an incident in September 1970 in which Gambian security forces captured an insurgent group from the Guinean exile opposition as it was preparing for an invasion of Conakry. The insurgents were turned over to the Guinean government. Although this did not prevent the November 1970 invasion, it did impress the Guineans with The Gambia's friendship.

Guinea-Bissau

Guinea very actively supported the nationalist forces attempting to end Portuguese colonial rule in adjacent Guinea-Bissau, from their first appearance in the early 1960s until their ultimate success in 1974. The only significant nationalist organization, the African Party for the Independence of Guinea-Bissau and the Cape Verde Islands (Partido Africano da Independência da Guiné e do Cabo-Verde—PAIGC), had maintained its headquarters in Conakry and its rear area bases in Guinea close to the border with the Portuguese colony. Portuguese forces, including large numbers of locally recruited African troops, sought to crush the nationalists from 1962 through early 1974. By then the nationalists clearly controlled major portions of the colony's interior and had set up a rudimentary administration. The PAIGC leadership declared itself to be the national government in 1973 and was promptly recognized by Guinea and then gradually by a large number of other states. Success, however, resulted from events in Portugal. In April 1974 the conservative government was overthrown by liberal forces who were either tired of or opposed to the colonial wars in Portugal's African colonies. The last Portuguese forces withdrew from Guinea-Bissau in late 1974, after the PAIGC had already assumed control of the newly independent country.

The leader and major force of the PAIGC until 1972 was Amilcar Cabral. Cabral's residence in Conakry was close to that of President Touré, and the two leaders espoused a similar ideology on domestic and international affairs. Cabral was assassinated in Conakry in early 1972 by a dissident member of the PAIGC. The PAIGC leadership that succeeded him also remained in debt to Guinea, and the two countries remained very close in 1975. The nature of their relationship was changing, however, as the Guinea-Bissau government gradually moved from Conakry to establish itself in the newly independent state.

Guinea's support of the PAIGC was entirely in consonance with its anticolonialist ideology and was carried out despite significant risk. Raids into Guinea by Portuguese forces and aircraft had been frequent, although generally confined to the border areas. Even so, the cost to Guinea of its support for the PAIGC had been high even before the havoc caused by the attack on Conakry in November 1970. Guinean support for the PAIGC continued, nevertheless, reflecting the insistence of the country's leaders on putting some political and ideological objectives before economic considerations.

Relations with Ghana

After Guinean independence the first country to respond to the new republic's search for relations with other countries and for aid was Ghana, which had only obtained its own independence from British rule in 1957. Ghana's first president, Kwame Nkrumah, had an ideological commitment in both internal and external affairs that closely paralleled the philosophy espoused by President Touré. On November 23, 1958, President Touré signed an agreement with President Nkrumah in Accra, forming a Ghana-Guinea union, which they described as the foundation stone for a "United States of West Africa."

Three years later Mali, then led by President Keita, a long-time associate of President Touré, joined in the formation of a Guinea-Ghana-Mali union. In the interim the concept of the union had changed from a close federation to a loose association of states. A charter for the union, to be called the Union of African States, was agreed upon by the three countries. According to the charter, the activities of the projected union would be concerned mainly with coordinated approaches to domestic problems, close cooperation in foreign affairs, a joint defense system, and coordinated exploitation of the economic resources of each state.

Interest in the union flagged, however, as the leaders of the three states came into conflict on a number of points and as practical problems intervened. By 1963 their interests had switched to emphasize a much looser but larger association formed that year, the Organization of African Unity (OAU), which grouped all the states of independent Africa.

In February 1966 Nkrumah was overthrown by a popularly acclaimed military coup d'etat while he was on a state visit to Peking. Upon returning to Africa, he was given refuge in Conakry, along with about 100 of his entourage. President Touré took a major symbolic step by proclaiming Nkrumah "co-president" of Guinea. He announced that Guinea considered itself in a state of war with Ghana and intended to have its military and militia forces march on Ghana to reinstate Nkrumah by force. This threat was more alarming to Ivory Coast, through which the Guineans were presumed to be planning to march, than to distant Ghana.

Guinea had demonstrated its enmity for Nkrumah's successors in a number of other ways, including seizing and detaining the Ghanaian embassy staff after the overthrow, seizing Ghanaian fishermen in Guinean waters, and turning over to Nkrumah Ghanaian assets in Guinea. The Ghanaians believed that the funds used to support Nkrumah in Guinea were drawn from payments owed by the Guinean government on a loan made in 1958 by Ghana. President Touré allowed Nkrumah to use the Guinean radio in attempts to stir up resistance to the military rulers within Ghana. Conakry thus served as the center for whatever efforts Nkrumah planned for a return to power.

In October 1966 the military government of Ghana retaliated by seizing then-foreign minister Béavogui and three other senior Guinean diplomats, as well as fifteen students, aboard a Pan American World Airways flight carrying them from Conakry to an OAU foreign ministers' meeting in Ethiopia. The Ghanaian government admitted that its actions appeared to be in direct violation of the norms of international law. It justified its actions by pointing out that Guinea had declared itself to be at war with Ghana and declared that the aim of the action was to obtain the release of Ghanaians held against their will in Conakry. After two weeks of pressure by the leaders of the OAU, the Guinean travelers were released when their country agreed to allow OAU observers to interview the Ghanaians in Conakry and to guarantee the safe departure of those wishing to leave.

Gradually Nkrumah's freedom of movement and his access to communications became restricted either voluntarily or under Guinean governmental pressure. After 1967 he had little free contact with foreign visitors. Many of the followers who came with him in 1966 voluntarily returned to Ghana during 1968. By early 1971 he appeared to be confined in his activities and kept within the villa given to him by President Touré. It was unclear whether he was under a form of house arrest or stayed there because of the security threat heightened by the large reward for his capture posted by the government of Ghana.

The hostility generated between the two states in 1966 continued into the early 1970s. Guinea slowed but did not stop its stream of propaganda attacks against Ghana both in its radiobroadcasts and at meetings of intra-African organizations. The ill will continued in 1972 but gradually lessened as the Ghanaian military leadership relinquished power to an elected civilian government. This government, however, was composed of strong opponents of Nkrumah. After its subsequent overthrow in January 1972 by a military group slightly more sympathetic to Nkrumah and particularly after Nkrumah's death in April 1972, relations between the two states returned to a normal diplomatic level.

FRANCO-GUINEAN RELATIONS

The conditions under which Guinea broke its colonial ties with France in 1958 had played the major role in Franco-Guinean relations during the early 1960s. Although the break with France had been peaceful, the Guinean leaders, in the course of their campaign for independence, had aroused a strong anti-French sentiment among the people. This was reinforced by a wave of resentment caused by the abrupt departure of the French, who were accused of taking with them material needed by the Guineans, including telephones, office equipment, general supplies, and anything else that was movable. The French were blamed for the inefficiency of administrative agencies that attempted to carry on with inexperienced supervisors directing untrained subordinates. Intense bitterness against the French continued to be manifested during the early months of Guinean independence.

Denunciation of France, a popular theme among all ethnic elements, seemed, in fact, to be exploited to promote national unity. After the first year's struggle with the problems of establishing a new state, however, anti-French feeling gradually moderated.

A modest degree of French assistance was offered in 1963, the first small break with France's policy of refusing any aid or other support to Guinea. This policy had resulted from Guinea's refusal to join the French Community in 1958. Trade with France had declined sharply after independence largely as a result of the opening of new markets and sources of supply in the communist countries.

Some facets of French involvement, however, have remained important to Guinea. Despite the campaigns to africanize cultural affairs, French influences have remained dominant in education and important in administration, law, and several other fields. French remained the language of the government and of the elite. A number of French citizens remained in the country into the early 1970s, some as small planters and businessmen and others of more radical political bent as advisers to the government. They were estimated at more than 1,000 in 1970. The bauxite works at Fria, the country's most important industrial enterprise until the 1970s, continued under French management, although most smaller foreign companies, almost all French, had been nationalized.

In late 1965 the government described as a plot what was actually an open attempt to form a legal opposition party. President Touré accused France of being involved, and charges against French diplomats resulted in a break in diplomatic relations, a situation that persisted in early 1975. During the second half of the 1960s contacts between the two countries were minimal, and the Italian embassy in Conakry looked after French interests.

The National Congress of the PDG attempted to encourage a move toward reconciliation in 1967 if France would offer economic terms favorable to Guinea. But French President Charles de Gaulle remained opposed to the granting of such assistance as incompatible with the events of 1958 and unfair to those other French-speaking West African countries that had remained on friendly terms with France.

A rapprochement seemed to be possible in 1970 as President Touré sought to establish warm contacts with President de Gaulle's successor, Georges Pompidou. A cultural festival led to the first visit of French officials to Guinea since 1965 and to speeches by President Touré supporting Franco-Guinean relations. Little progress was made on the diplomatic front, however, as President Touré continued to accuse high French officials, particularly the secretary of state for African affairs, Jacques Foccart, of involvement in plots against him. Those accusations began even before the 1970 invasion and the purges that followed, in which about thirty French citizens were arrested.

After Foccart's retirement in 1974 active efforts to renew relations, begun in 1973, were pursued with considerable interest on both the French and Guinean sides. These negotiations were continuing in early 1975. The major impediments were conflicting financial claims. Guinea has demanded that France restore the funds lost to Guinea by the suspension of pension payments due Guinean veterans of the French army. These funds have been withheld by France since the 1965 diplomatic break because of Guinea's refusal to agree on compensation for French business interests in Guinea that had been nationalized. Guinea also has refused to repay French aid loans made before independence. The question of the release of the twenty French citizens who remained in Guinean jails as a result of the 1971 treason trials was also a major snag.

RELATIONS WITH COMMUNIST COUNTRIES

Guinea's break with France deprived the country of its only existing source of financial and technical assistance. Western countries, including the United States, hesitated before offering to fill this gap for fear of offending French President de Gaulle. The Soviet Union perceived that Guinea's move gave the country popular appeal with many independence movements elsewhere. The Soviets stepped in with offers of considerable aid to fill the void. Diplomatic relations were established with the Soviet Union almost immediately, and Soviet and Eastern European trade delegations were at work shortly thereafter.

Because their foreign trade was conducted by state agencies, the communist countries, unlike Western countries, were able to offer Guinea bilateral barter agreements fixing the level of trade in advance. Under these clearing agreements they offered swing credits permitting Guinea's imports of noncapital goods to exceed its exports by a considerable margin. In addition to these short-term trade credits, they provided medium-term and long-term loans to finance imports of capital equipment and construction of development projects (see ch. 10). Within six months of Guinean independence, the Soviet Union and five Eastern

European countries had signed trade agreements guaranteeing the purchase of Guinea's agricultural exports. By 1961 their trade probably constituted nearly one-third of Guinea's foreign trade (see ch. 12).

The agreements for longer term capital aid and technical assistance were signed soon after the trade agreements. The first Soviet aid was provided by an August 1959 credit for the equivalent of US$35 million (see ch. 10). This was used in the construction of a stadium and a hotel in Conakry, as well as a refrigeration plant, a sawmill, and a cannery, and to improve railroad tracks and expand the Conakry-Gbessia airport. Several of the Soviet-sponsored projects turned out to be unremunerative, however, and Guineans were angered by the poor quality or inappropriateness of much of the equipment the Soviets delivered. These included tractors designed for use in Siberian winters and the construction of a radio transmitter for Conakry-Gbessia airport atop a mountain rich in iron ore, whose magnetic field blocked transmissions.

The major Soviet project was the construction of a large polytechnic institute. For both financial and political reasons, however, its opening was delayed, and its image as a Soviet showcase had all but disappeared by the time it opened. In the interim the Soviet Union and the other Eastern European states had provided a large number of teachers and medical personnel to Guinea and had provided many Guineans with scholarships to Soviet-bloc schools (see ch. 7). The propaganda effect of this Soviet effort was considerably lessened by the firsthand insights gained by the Guinean students regarding Soviet society and by frequent incidences of racial discrimination.

A further brake on the growth of Soviet influence was imposed in mid-1961 by the beginning of increasing aid from the West, particularly from the United States and the Federal Republic of Germany (West Germany). It was capped by the announcement by the Guinean government in December 1961 of the involvement of Soviet embassy personnel in what President Touré described as a plot against his government by left-wing intellectual elements within the PDG. The Soviet ambassador was forced to leave Guinea. At about the same time the Soviet government came to realize that, despite its revolutionary and socialist rhetoric and considerable Soviet effort, Guinea was not about to make an economic leap forward to set the example for more conservatively governed African states or to provide the political leadership in Africa that would turn those other states leftward. Therefore, the priority of attention the Soviet Union had sought to shower on Guinea declined. It took a steep dive in 1962 when Guinea declined to serve as a staging point for Soviet aircraft en route to Cuba during the Cuban missile crisis and blockade.

The major revisions that followed the November 1964 reform of the Guinean political party led the new Soviet leadership to believe that Guinea was once again moving in a socialist direction, and therefore they made efforts to reestablish warm relations. This was aided by the removal from power in 1964 of Soviet leader Nikita Khrushchev. President Touré had regarded Khrushchev as responsible for the purported Soviet interference in 1961. It was also aided by a general harmony between Soviet and Guinean policy on most major international questions: Vietnam, Rhodesia and South Africa, the civil war in the Congo, and the desire for a general disarmament agreement. Guinea's inability to repay the substantial short-term trade debt to the Soviet Union accumulated under the bilateral agreements had led to a reduction in trade toward the mid-1960s. In 1965, however, it was rescheduled and converted to long-term debt, permitting the resumption of increased trade.

Soviet and Eastern European interest in Guinea continued in the 1970s, although at a lower level. Trade increased, and new capital commitments were made. Of the first Soviet capital commitment, the equivalent of US$35 million had been disbursed in the early years, a total of US$60 million by 1965, and US$76 million by 1967. In 1969 a long-term loan equivalent to US$92 million was granted for the construction of a bauxite mining project (see ch. 12). The project was completed in 1975, but a portion of the credit remained to be disbursed. Capital commitments from Eastern Europe had totaled US$25 million in the early 1960s, and until 1974 no significant additional long-term or medium-term aid had been received from them. In that year negotiations were under way with Romania, reportedly for significant aid.

At Guinean independence in 1958 Soviet and Chinese communist competition for leadership of the communist parties and revolutionary movements throughout the world had come to the fore. Each sought to align Guinea on its side, as each regarded the new republic as the African state with the greatest dedication to revolutionary change. The Chinese Communists made a major attempt at winning Guinean support in 1960 with their initial aid program to Africa, an interest-free loan equivalent to US$25 million. It was presented to President Touré while he was being enthusiastically received on a state visit to Peking. Nevertheless, the Guinean government did not align itself with Chinese communist policies. After the events of December 1961 made plain the decline of Soviet prestige in Guinea, President Touré did extend limited support to the Chinese Communists in their ideological conflict with the Soviet Union but only on issues in which Guinean and Chinese positions happened to coincide. Even this apparent move toward the PRC was soon ended, however, as the Chinese Communists rejected the pragmatic Guinean position of welcoming economic assistance from any quarter.

Chinese communist aid and contacts, which had been curtailed during the Cultural Revolution in the PRC (1966–68), continued on a reduced level until after the PRC had begun to reassert its foreign policy in 1969. Seven new projects were begun in that year. By 1970 the PRC had risen in the trade ranks to become Guinea's third largest source of imports, aided by Guinea's dependence on rice from the PRC after the United

States food shipments declined. The project for Chinese communist assistance in building a Kankan-to-Mali railroad had been discarded because of events in Mali. A proposal for assistance in rebuilding the Conakry-to-Kankan railroad was then discussed but by 1975 had apparently been dropped as too costly.

The November 1970 invasion gave the communist states a chance to improve relations with Guinea. All of these countries rapidly and strongly condemned the attack, attempting to link it to Portugal's membership in the North Atlantic Treaty Organization (NATO). Support was not limited to words, however, as the PRC announced a grant or loan equivalent to US$10 million, and the Soviet Union established a naval patrol off the Guinean coast to prevent a repetition of the attacks. The naval patrol continued in early 1975, as did other significant Soviet, Chinese communist, and Cuban military and civil assistance projects (see ch. 13). In return the Soviet air force was granted the use of Guinean airport facilities for reconnaissance flights over the Atlantic Ocean, and Soviet naval vessels received bunkering rights in the port of Conakry. Thus in early 1975 both the Soviet Union and the PRC clearly held significant positions in Guinea. The extent of their real influence over the sensitive Guinean government, however, was difficult to measure as President Touré continued to make a considerable point of balancing the communist states' position with Western involvement.

RELATIONS WITH THE UNITED STATES

After some initial hesitancy the United States established diplomatic relations with Guinea in 1959, a move followed by a state visit to Washington by President Touré later that year. During that trip President Dwight D. Eisenhower approved a small aid program, providing scholarships for more than 150 Guinean students at American schools. Of much greater significance to United States-Guinean relations, however, was the interest of American aluminum producers in the development of Guinea's remaining untapped bauxite deposits (see ch. 12). President Touré was apparently favorably impressed by the potentialities of this investment, which could provide the country with a firm economic base for the first time.

Guinean attitudes toward the United States also improved in early 1961 because of President John F. Kennedy's expressions of interest in African development and his announced opposition to colonial rule. A significant American aid program was negotiated in May 1961, including the supply of food grains under the Public Law 480 (later Food for Peace) program and a small Peace Corps program. Over the next ten years significant aid followed, totaling US$103 million by 1971.

The American food grains provided a vital cushion for Guinea's governing party during a time when problems encountered with their own production and distribution systems would otherwise have caused grave internal concern. Nonetheless, American private investment proved to be a greater determinant of United States-Guinean relations than any governmental factors. Although these private investments included several other endeavors, it was the large-scale mineral developments with American assistance that mattered, primarily the development under American management of the sizable bauxite deposits near Boké.

This development was led initially by Harvey Aluminum and later by the international mining consortium called Halco, consisting primarily of one Canadian and two American companies with lesser inputs from West German, French, and Italian interests. The Boké operation was under a mixed enterprise with 49-percent government participation. The Boké project required major development of the region's infrastructure (a railroad, port, and mining town) as well as the mining operations themselves. The development required foreign capital amounting to over US$339 million, mostly arranged in the United States (see ch. 12). Another American interest, Olin Mathieson Chemical Corporation, had a major share in the older bauxite and alumina complex at Fria until it sold its interest to a Canadian firm at the end of 1974. The bauxite and alumina exports, as they came on line, would provide the underpinning for the entire Guinean economy and most of its foreign exchange.

Several problems arose in United States-Guinean relations at different times, particularly in 1966 with the expulsion of the Peace Corps and an attack on the American embassy. These occurred after Guinean government allegations of United States involvement in the seizure of Guinean diplomats by the unfriendly government of Ghana. Despite such incidents and the severe differences in ideology and conflicting views on many major international issues, Guinea preferred to remain on good terms with the United States, a preference motivated both by the profitable joint mining arrangements and by the need to balance the influence on Guinea of the communist states. This friendly attitude continued unabated in early 1975, even after most American aid and technical assistance had been suspended in 1971 as part of the general reduction in American aid programs.

RELATIONS WITH OTHER STATES

Guinea attached an importance to its relations with a number of other states, all on the basis of their serving as alternate sources of significant aid. During the 1960s West Germany provided considerable assistance to Guinea in a variety of fields. Its aid to the Guinean army's engineer battalion, for example, was the only Western source of any military or police training after independence. In part this aid was intended to compete with that offered by East Germany in an effort to keep Guinea from granting recognition to East Germany. Nonetheless, changing policies brought about such recognition in 1970. By that time Guinea had incurred a considerable financial debt to West Germany. West Germany was accused of deep involvement in the November 1970 invasion of

Conakry (see ch. 13). The resident West German diplomats and aid officials were expelled in early 1971, several West German business figures were arrested, diplomatic relations were broken off, and the debt payments were stopped. Formal relations had not been restored by early 1975, although Guinea, favorably impressed by the West German government's efforts in 1974 to remove the political obstacles to such a restoration, had released the remaining German prisoners.

In the 1970s Guinea's search for development assistance broadened to include less traditional sources, such as Romania and the wealthy Arab oil-producing states (see ch. 10). Guinea began to emphasize the connections of its Muslim majority with the Islamic world. Announcements by the Guinean government that aid had been offered by a foreign country had on many occasions turned out to be incorrect. Nevertheless, in 1974 it did sound as if Guinean efforts to gain the financial backing of the Arab countries had met with some success.

Prime Minister Béavogui, upon returning from a tour of the Middle East, announced that assistance had been offered to ease both short-term and long-term burdens. Libya, Egypt, Kuwait, Bahrain, Abu Dhabi, and Qatar had offered loans to ease the pressing balance-of-payments deficits. It was announced that the same group of states, along with Romania, had offered to participate in financing various new industrial facilities, most notably the long-promised key project for construction of facilities to convert the country's bauxite exports into alumina and aluminum products before export. Such a move would greatly improve Guinea's export picture but would require careful cost calculations, some assurance of markets, and a great deal of foreign development assistance (see ch. 12).

MEMBERSHIP IN INTERNATIONAL ORGANIZATIONS

Although it no longer appeared to seek a major role in them, Guinea remained a member of many international bodies. A Guinean, Diallo Telli, served as secretary general of the OAU from its inception until 1972. Guinea had been admitted to the United Nations (UN) in December 1958 and in early 1975 belonged to nearly all of the UN's specialized agencies. One exception, clearly in line with its economic policies, was its voluntary exclusion from the General Agreement on Tariffs and Trade (GATT). In 1974 it became a charter member of the International Bauxite Association (see ch. 12). It is a member of the International Bank for Reconstruction and Development (IBRD, commonly known as the World Bank) and the International Development Association (IDA). Guinea was also linked to the European Economic Community (EEC, known as the Common Market) by the so-called Lomé Convention of February 1975 (see ch. 12).

SECTION III. ECONOMIC

CHAPTER 10

CHARACTER AND STRUCTURE OF THE ECONOMY

Long regarded as the most favorably endowed of the French-speaking countries of West Africa in agricultural, mineral, and hydroelectric potential, Guinea nonetheless found itself fourteen years after independence on the United Nations (UN) list of the world's twenty-five least developed countries. Favored by a climate less arid than in most of West Africa, Guinea was disadvantaged by predominantly poor soils, a low level of literacy, and a transportation system that was already obsolete at independence.

In 1972 the rate of economic growth since independence was thought to have barely kept pace with the growth of population. Despite its determination to assume virtually complete management of the economy to develop the social and productive structure along noncapitalist lines, the government had experienced enormous difficulties in asserting this control because of its inability to curb inflation and maintain the value of the currency. A flourishing black market and smuggling trade diverted a large proportion of available goods, earnings, productive energies, and resources from legal channels. The average Guinean who lived outside the self-contained subsistence economy was hard pressed to supplement the meager official food ration with black market goods that were largely beyond his means. Agricultural production for the official market had stagnated, and the processing industries installed by foreign aid were mostly operating far below capacity.

In the interim a favorable trend in world demand for crude bauxite had permitted the conclusion of a series of agreements with foreign investors for the exploitation of Guinea's rich bauxite resources, sometimes estimated as surpassing in size and purity all but those of Australia and perhaps Brazil. Despite the high-risk political climate and restrictions on convertible currency, the government had also succeeded by 1974 in negotiating the first of the investment agreements it was seeking to finance exploitation of large untapped iron ore deposits in the far southeast. Exports of bauxite and alumina (aluminum oxide powder) had already been furnishing three-fourths of the country's foreign exchange, but their contribution to national income had been largely confined to wages and dwindling royalty payments, as is characteristic of the foreign-owned enclave kind of mining development. As its bargaining position improved, the Guinean government in concluding its new agreements and revising the old had taken over 49 to 51 percent ownership of all mining enterprises, had insisted on an increasing share in mining earnings and decisions, and had joined with other bauxite-producing nations in formulating new export tax measures and demands for increased export prices and more processing capacity (see ch. 12).

After a ten-year gestation period, the first and largest of the new bauxite mining projects came into production in 1973, and a second, smaller one followed in 1974. Three more bauxite projects and two iron ore projects were still in the planning stage as of early 1975. A report of the UN Economic Commission for Africa (ECA) concluded that the stage of real growth in Guinea's national income seemed likely to have started in 1973. It would at least be an unparalleled opportunity for real growth, although there remained a possibility that the opportunity could be neglected and the new foreign exchange resources used in ways that might fail to generate the overall increase in economic and social investment needed to improve the welfare of the average Guinean. Unless some degree of monetary and fiscal stabilization could be achieved, prosperity generated by the mineral projects might continue to be confined to isolated pockets where a few thousand Guinean workers enjoyed a privileged living standard considerably higher than that of most of their compatriots (see ch. 6).

PROBLEMS OF INFLATION AND LAGGING GROWTH

The UN list of the world's twenty-five least developed countries was established by the UN General Assembly in November 1971, with Guinea as one of fifteen sub-Saharan African countries listed. The basic criteria used for selection were that a country have a per capita income of less than US$100; that incomes generated in manufacturing constitute less than 10 percent of gross domestic product (GDP—see Glossary); and that less than 20 percent of the adult population be literate. Guinea's per capita income was usually estimated at the equivalent of US$80 or US$90 at the official rate of exchange, which does not reflect actual purchasing power; manufacturing was thought to generate about 5 percent of GDP; and the UN source estimated that in 1968 about 5 percent of the population over fifteen was literate (see ch. 7).

Guinea also met the definition of a least developed country in certain other respects. More than 50 percent of agricultural production was for subsistence consumption; rice yields per acre were below the world average; and Guinea had a demonstrated weakness in export performance and foreign exchange earnings. Manufactures furnished only 0.03 percent of exports; and two primary products—bauxite and alumina—accounted for 75 percent of export value, alumina being classified as a primary product rather than a manufacture.

In important features of development potential, however, Guinea differed from the typical least developed country. Most of them were landlocked, lacked a railroad, and their mineral and hydroelectric resources, if any, had been inadequately surveyed. Thus they not only had insufficient foreign exchange earnings or fiscal resources of their own but also lacked the capacity to attract sizable private foreign investment, so that the gap would have to be filled by foreign aid on concessional terms. Especially in Africa, most least developed countries had more or less critical problems of rainfall and groundwater supply, and a sizable share of their population derived its traditional livelihood from nomadic herding, which was not practiced in less arid Guinea. Most bordered the desert, and their best arable land was in the semiarid Sahelian region. Guinea not only possessed potential advantages in all these respects, but it had already attracted sizable private foreign investment, and its foreign aid receipts were estimated to have averaged the equivalent of US$40 million a year from 1960 through 1971. The resultant foreign debt, however, had been incurred on terms more onerous than those considered suitable for least developed countries (see Public Finance and Development, this ch.).

Although Guinea's economy had started from such a low base as one of the world's least developed, it did not attain much real growth during the 1960s. According to the *World Bank Atlas of 1974*, during the twelve-year period from 1960 through 1972 Guinea's estimated annual rate of real growth in GDP fluctuated around an average of 2.8 percent. The target set by the UN for its second development decade was 6 percent a year. Guinea's population was assumed to have grown at the same rate as GDP, so that the average annual rate of growth in per capita product (at constant prices) was assessed at zero.

On the basis of per capita growth rate, Guinea had thus appeared in 1972 near the bottom of the list of fifty-four developing countries: on a par with Ghana—whose economy had also suffered from unproductive spending and onerous debt terms—and ranking above five countries afflicted by the 1972 drought. Moreover, Guinea's limited growth had taken place during the first five years of the period. In the seven years from 1965 through 1972, its per capita growth rate was thought to have been negative, at about −0.3 percent a year. In the first five years the growth of production had been dominated by the foreign-owned Fria company's output of bauxite, alumina, and electric power, so that the rate of growth in the rest of the economy may be surmised to have been considerably lower. The only readily available comparison was in official estimates that in the period 1959 through 1962 total GDP grew at 8.2 percent a year and gross national product (GNP), excluding Fria, grew at 4 percent a year. It was not clear whether these rates were at current prices or were deflated by the official price index.

As is sometimes the case for developing countries, reliable statistics on which to base assessments of comparative growth were largely lacking.

Since 1964 no data had been available on national income or GDP, and price indexes were unreliable. Moreover, the estimated rate of per capita growth was based upon the assumption that population had grown throughout the 1960–72 period at a rate of 2.8 percent a year. Both higher and lower estimates for population growth have been arrived at by usually reliable sources (see ch. 3).

Information about Guinea's economy published abroad is often politically motivated. Some such accounts, remarkably objective in their reporting of detail, have been published by writers initially attracted by the country as a long-awaited example of noncapitalist decolonialization, who therefore may be thought to have an emotional stake in the experiment's success. The government's critics abroad sometimes interpret economic trends in ways designed to reflect maximum discredit on government policy. Few series of reported facts, therefore, can be accepted without reservation and analysis by the reader, but it is not possible to spell out the probable bias of every source used.

Within the country the highest Guinean leadership has sometimes engaged in penetrating criticism of the country's economic progress. President Ahmed Sékou Touré has frequently denounced government officials, for example, for corruption or incompetence. At times cabinet ministers and less influential overt critics of government agencies or policies have been arrested and sentenced as fifth column agitators (see ch. 13). As most authorized economic transactions involve some government agency or policy, this has reduced the flow of economic information to an uncertain trickle. There is also a Guinean law against divulging statistical information.

Because of this dearth of information, estimates of the distribution of the labor force by sector of activity and of the origin and utilization of domestic product and other resources must be based upon insufficient data. Most sources estimate that if subsistence activities are included, the rural sector—cultivation, livestock husbandry, forestry, and fishing—occupies about 83 percent of the active population; but other estimates have ranged as low as 65 percent. Most of these people are engaged in the subsistence sector on small family holdings of a few acres. Another 11 percent may be engaged in full-time traditional trading or handicraft activities on an artisan scale, employing no paid workers. Because of big new construction projects, the number of wage and salary earners employed in the monetary (modern) sector of the economy is thought to have increased considerably since the mid-1960s, at a more rapid rate than production. From around 100,000 in 1968, their number increased to 136,000 in 1971 and may have grown by 1974 to around 150,000 or some 6 percent of the labor force.

Government self-criticism indicated that numbers of unqualified personnel had been employed in the railroad and state-owned industries as well as in the government-managed trade and banking sector, where militant membership in the ruling Democratic Party of Guinea (Parti

Démocratique de Guinée—PDG) or having the right connections was sometimes alleged to be the chief prerequisite for a responsible position. By the early 1970s, however, the situation was said to have improved considerably as increasing numbers of qualified graduated of institutions of higher education became available (see ch. 7). Labor productivity remained generally low except in mining, where the ratio of capital to labor was very high.

Because of low productivity, incomes generated in agriculture, forestry, and fishing probably constituted only about one-half of total GDP, including the returns in kind to subsistence producers, and a much smaller proportion of monetary GDP, which excludes subsistence. Most estimates placed the share of manufacturing at only abount 5 percent of total GDP, despite fourteen years of priority investment in the creation of manufacturing capacity. An acute shortage of raw materials, high production costs, and stagnant rural consumer incomes had limited manufacturing output to a fraction of capacity. Before the first of the new mineral projects came into production, mining was thought to be generating only about 6 percent of domestic incomes. Its contribution should be materially improved, not only by increased production but also by the improved share of earnings to be retained within the country under a revised agreement with the earlier mine operators. An unduly high share of GDP was thought to be accruing to nonproductive tertiary activity—trade, transport, and services, Incomes generated in government administration (excluding trade, transport, banking, and productive public enterprise) may have exceeded 15 percent of GDP.

Even less is reliably known about the utilization of resources than about their origin. In principle, centralized planning was intended to assure the strict ordering and enforcement of priorities in the allocation of scarce domestic or imported goods and services to capital formation in preference to public or private consumption. A ministry of planning had been established soon after independence, and in the sixteen ensuing years three successive development plans were launched: the Three Year Development Plan (1960–63), the Seven Year Plan (1964–71), and the Five Year Development Plan (1973–78) (see Public Finance and Development, this ch.). The three-year plan was financed largely by aid from the communist countries and carried out with the help of technicians and equipment sent by them. The two subsequent plans made greater use of financing from other official sources and from foreign private investors. Imports under the plan (that is, successive development plans) were in principle kept quite separate from the general import program and were not included in statistics on foreign trade. They were intended to have high priority and to consist entirely of capital equipment or construction materials for development projects.

Some speeches by President Touré suggested that, despite the official commitment to strict enforcement of priorities, the actual allocation of resources had been highly disorganized. The existence of a parallel illicit market offering prices many times higher than those enforced on the legal market diverted a substantial proportion of imports as well as domestic products, and both officials and private traders were said to engage in large-scale illegal transactions.

Early self-criticism within the party had alleged that even within official channels imports were sometimes diverted from priority objectives. One such scandal dealt with the alleged use of medium-term or long-term foreign aid credits earmarked for development projects to finance imports of consumer goods and the subsequent waste of the consumer goods thus financed because of oversized orders and bottlenecks in transport and distribution.

In the five years from 1965 through 1969 inclusive, the latest years for which data were available, imports authorized by the ministry of planning averaged about 18.7 percent of total imports (see ch. 12). Imports for the foreign-owned bauxite and alumina complex at Fria averaged another 11 percent of total imports and may have included some capital equipment for renewal or expansion, as well as fuel oil for the thermal power plant and chemicals or other processing inputs. Otherwise, however, very little capital formation is thought to have taken place outside the framework of successive development plans.

External critics of the government alleged that the composition of the imports authorized under the plan actually differed very little from those under the general import program and that in fact most of them were destined for public or private consumption rather than for capital formation. In the absence of more comprehensive data, such allegations could not be verified or disproved. Some members of foreign aid missions reported that since 1970 the government had taken measures to see that priorities were more respected, at least in the spending under its immediate control.

Moreover, whereas capital formation under the early three-year plan had been concentrated on unproductive infrastructure or on manufacturing plants (some oversized) for which no raw material base had been provided, a major share of the capital formation actually realized under the ensuing Seven Year Plan had been by profit-conscious foreign investors. Much of the investment under the three-year plan had produced a sizable foreign debt without producing the means of repaying it, but the new mining investment was designed to be self-liquidating.

Because of the long gestation period characteristic of mining projects, much of the investment accomplished under the Seven Year Plan did not begin to pay off in production until late 1973. Although the rate of productive capital formation had thus been substantially improved during the second half of the decade, throughout the 1960s the allocation of resources had reportedly been seriously distorted by the virtual breakdown of the regular distribution system and the rapid growth of the parallel market—that is, the smuggling trade and the internal black market (see ch. 12). The problems of distribution could be ascribed in part to transportation bottlenecks and to the cumbersome and inexpert attributes of bureaucratic intervention in the matching of supply to demand. They were soon magnified by the acute shortage of imports and domestically produced goods, which was both effect and partial cause of inflation and the rapid depreciation of the currency.

Until March 1960 Guinea had been a member of the franc area (see Glossary). Under the arrangements in effect at the time, France supported the stability and guaranteed the convertibility of the common currency of the African franc area countries on condition of a measure of French control over monetary discipline. This control was exercised through France's dominant voice on the governing boards of the regional central banks—in this case the bank of the West African Monetary Union. As a member of the union, Guinea had been obliged to permit free transfers within the franc area, and there had been a serious flight of capital out of the country just before and after independence. In March 1960, therefore, Guinea opted for monetary autarky, establishing its own central bank and its own currency, the Guinean franc. Strict foreign exchange controls were imposed and the currency made unconvertible, like those of the Eastern European countries.

Unsupported by the backing of franc area foreign exchange reserves, the new currency had quickly succumbed to the same speculative forces and lack of confidence that had generated the flight of capital. The Guinean franc was not accepted on any foreign exchange markets except those of neighboring countries, where in the course of the 1960s it lost four-fifths of its value. The government refused officially to devalue the currency, which was kept at par with the common currency of the African franc area. In an attempt to offset the effects on foreign trade of the overvalued currency, the government restricted and taxed imports and subsidized transport costs and trading profits on crop exports.

By the end of 1972 the disadvantages of an unconvertible currency had become abundantly evident, and President Touré announced that in another five years he hoped to be able to make the currency convertible, if its value could be bolstered by successful development of the nation's mineral wealth. In the meantime the generally cautious monetary policy followed by African franc area institutions had brought them under increasing attack by members in the early 1970s. The Malagasy Republic and Mauritania had withdrawn from membership and established their own currencies, and some other member countries had attained revised agreements with France that gave them a greater voice in the formulation of a more expansionary policy while providing automatic safeguards against too consistent a drain on French exchange reserves. Although it had succeeded in eliminating French dominance of its trade and banking much earlier than most of the countries that had remained within the franc area, Guinea also appeared to have prospered less than most in the interim, and its example had reportedly deterred some other African franc area countries from prematurely abandoning the relative stability of their common currency.

Guinea's experience had been one of stagnation in most sectors of activity, accompanied by rapid inflation. The people's vote in September 1958 against entering the French Community without concessions had indicated their apparent agreement with Sékou Touré's proclaimed conviction that true autonomy, even if accompanied by poverty, was to be preferred to prosperity accompanied by neocolonial foreign domination. According to the French Africanist Jean Suret-Canale, the Guineans at independence had expected a grave economic crisis to follow the break with France and had been prepared by their leadership to endure the most rigorous austerity as a result. When the immediate hardships failed to materialize and many found themselves better off than before, this initial resolve was succeeded, in 1959 and 1960, by a euphoria that was to have unfortunate consequences for economic stability.

According to other sources, the government's own vigilance in observing development priorities, although it continued to be stressed in official statements, was relaxed in practice. Moreover, there was little mention of the need to tailor development spending to available physical resources or to the economy's capacity to absorb foreign aid. Expansionary spending and limited resources created a situation that undermined solidarity by fostering the development of profiteering, graft, and corruption. The austerity later endured by large elements of the Guinean population is often assessed by foreign observers as the consequence of overspending and waste, rather than of the careful husbanding of resources that the people had been led to expect.

After the break with France, Guinea's commitment to state trading, and later its lack of a convertible currency, had made it heavily reliant on bilateral barter agreements with the centrally planned economies of the Soviet Union, Eastern Europe, and the People's Republic of China (PRC), later supplemented by smaller amounts in Food for Peace shipments and other commodity assistance from the United States. In the preoccupation with industrial development in the early years, agriculture was relatively neglected, and the producer prices set for cash crops were lower than before independence. Declining production and increased smuggling of export crops made it increasingly difficult to balance a significant portion of the heavy imports under the bilateral agreements with corresponding exports, and a heavy debit balance was accumulated. The usual difficulties in securing replacement parts and repairs reportedly soon rendered useless much of the early investment in tractors and heavy equipment. The acute shortage of foreign exchange for imports of needed fertilizers, fungicides, and industrial raw materials hampered any increase in production, and the shortage of consumer goods further reduced the incentive for cash crop production.

Inflation had already become so evident by 1963 that the government decreed an exchange of old banknotes for new, hoping to sterilize some of the illicitly acquired funds in circulation. This measure was ineffective in stemming the expansion of demand, and in 1964 the government decreed a 10-percent decrease in prices. Goods immediately disappeared from authorized markets. After 1965 the stagnation of production became more evident, and foodstuffs became increasingly scarce. The first official rationing measures in urban areas were introduced in 1967 and thereafter became progressively more restrictive (see ch. 6).

Because of the lack of reliable accounts, the sources of the expansionary pressures against available resources could not be documented, but some observers surmised that during the 1960s the government relied increasingly on the central bank for expansionary money creation to finance its budget deficits. They found strong evidence that the central bank was used for financing current consumption expenditure as well as capital formation. Deficit financing of public enterprises was said to be encouraged. For example, in an effort to offset the overvaluation of the currency, the state trading enterprise incurred heavy losses in subsidizing crop exports. Little of this subsidy, however, was allowed to trickle down to the producer, where it might have served as an incentive to increase production. The high cost of exports (in Guinean currency) resulted only in part from the low average yields in African agriculture. An element of final cost resulted from waste owing to long loading delays at Conakry port. The port possessed modern facilities but, according to one foreign press report in the mid-1960s, only two of its thirty modern forklift trucks were in operating condition. Another large element of cost derived from the increasingly inefficient operation of the obsolete meter-gauge railroad (see ch. 12).

In 1968 the state trading agency's export subsidies were equivalent to 31 percent of total export costs for bananas, 57 percent for coffee, 143 percent for palm kernels, and 147 percent for pineapples. To the extent possible, these subsidies were met from the import equalization tax, but the agency's losses in 1968 were, thought to have reached GF3.7 billion (for value of the Guinean franc—see Glossary). These were not met out of the central government budget but were carried forward or financed by borrowing, further fueling expansionary pressures.

Rapid monetary expansion and a declining volume of domestically produced goods and services created an inflationary gap between domestic demand and supply that, because of the foreign exchange shortage, could not be filled by net imports of goods and services. Instead the remaining inflationary gap between total demand and aggregate resources, estimated by one source at about 10 percent of GDP, was filled by a steady upward pressure on the price level.

A French study published in late 1972 concluded that the purchasing power in foodstuffs of the minimum daily wage in Conakry, after a definite rise between 1951 and 1958, was slightly lower in 1963 than in 1951. Between 1963 and 1972 it was said to have declined drastically. Virtually all of a worker's wage was absorbed by rent and by food, consisting of rice and tomato sauce at every meal, when obtainable. Few urban dwellers were able to afford meat or green vegetables (see ch. 6). Even at the official rate of exchange, wages in Guinea were said to average less than in Dakar, Senegal, or Abidjan, Ivory Coast, and prices were many times higher when goods could be obtained at all. In 1974, for example, when Dakar was known as one of the highest priced cities in Africa, one source reported that the price of a pound of rice at Labé, in Middle Guinea, was more than seven times higher than in Dakar, a pound of sugar seven to ten times higher, a yard of cotton cloth ten times higher, a quart of peanut oil ten to twelve times higher, and a pack of cigarettes twelve times higher.

Beginning in early 1967 the improved prospects for mineral development had seemed likely to slow the depreciation of the currency, but the slide resumed because of expectations of a possible coup d'etat. The rate offered for Guinean currency in neighboring countries and on the black market in Conakry reflected the political apprehensions stimulated by the abortive invasion of late 1970 and continually refueled by the government's allegations of extensive fifth column activity and the arrests of actual or alleged plotters (see ch. 8; ch. 13).

Monetary expansion was accelerated when foreign operators reaped a quick profit by introducing expertly counterfeited Guinean franc bank notes to an estimated volume of GF8 billion. To stop circulation of these notes and the embezzled and illegal funds thought to be fueling the dizzying rise of prices on the black market, a reform was decreed in October 1972 by introducing a new currency, the Guinean syli. President Touré placed part of the blame for inflation on the counterfeiters. He also dismissed the governor and deputy governor of the central bank and attached the bank to the presidency with himself as governor. A number of outside observers believed that this change was more apparent than real and that the bank had always been under strong executive control. In most countries credit and currency expansion by the central bank is limited, it enjoys considerable autonomy, and one of its functions is to counteract overexpansionary spending by the executive and the legislature. In Guinea, however, the president sought to place the blame for monetary overexpansion on the bank.

A little more than 12½ years had elapsed since the introduction of the Guinean franc. In a series of public speeches in October 1972, President Touré reviewed some of the trends of the intervening period. The surrender of old bank notes for new, he said, indicated that since March 1960 the volume of money in circulation had increased by at least eight times (not counting the illicitly held notes not surrendered). This rate of expansion had not been justified by the rate of economic growth. Production, instead of increasing, had been dropping steadily year by year. The imbalance between supply and demand had resulted in exorbitant prices, especially for foodstuffs. A large proportion of the national product had been smuggled out of the country to be sold across the borders, particularly in Sierra Leone.

The president acknowledged that the previous currency's value had been destroyed by too much money chasing too few goods. He ascribed the inflation in part, however, to the activities of Lebanese traders, as well as to the economic behavior of the people. In a characteristic attribution he declared that the rapid increase in money supply had been a form of deliberate sabotage against the state:

> New currency notes were constantly issued, in violation of the currency issue regulations of the government. Since the governor and the deputy governor of the central bank were members of the Fifth Column, all the inspectors and managers of the bank's branches had been recruited into the Fifth Column to help sabotage the country's economy and ruin the nation.

The president also denounced the inadequacies of government officials, some of whom took advantage of their position to cheat the peasants. He attributed this to the fact that some of those given responsibility were uneducated (see ch. 8). He added that after fourteen years of independence such a state of affairs could no longer be tolerated. In the future, he said, all those having any claim to a position of responsibility will have to be educated. In another address to a mass rally in Conakry, he said that the people had been greatly scandalized by the embezzlements and financial malpractices discovered in the past. The government would take measures to end such malpractices, he said, and would not hesitate to arrest or to execute anyone who worked against the country's progress. Currency smugglers were also to be shot on sight.

A number of high-ranking economic officials had already been among the twenty-one former cabinet officers purged during the mass arrests of 1971 (see ch. 8). They included the former minister of financial control, two former ministers of foreign trade, the former minister of the rural economy, and the former minister of planning. No direct explanation was given for the arrest for alleged fifth column activities of so many long-standing supporters of President Touré, but the president shortly afterward said that any official whose work failed to give positive results would be not only dismissed but also arrested. He accused those responsible for carrying out past agricultural policies of systematically organized sabotage to prevent the Guinean peasantry from becoming developed.

After a series of fairly large budget deficits in the late 1960s, a stabilization effort had been inaugurated in late 1969 that succeeded for a time in balancing the government's current operating expenditure by increased tax collections (see Public Finance and Development, this ch.). At the time of the October 1972 currency reform, an effort was also initiated to make sure that more transactions took place through regular banking channels and that credit was more selectively extended. The policymakers were convinced, however, that the primary solution to the inflation problem could be found only in increasing production rather than in possibly futile efforts to reduce the overall backlog of demand. In addressing a mass rally, President Touré commented:

> The foreign ambassadors in the country appreciate the Guinean people's capacity for mobilization and resistance, and they cannot understand therefore why work is not yet seriously organized. Active measures will therefore be taken to organize production.

Some external critics were skeptical of the party's resolve as having been repeated too often in the past, with little visible result. This time, however, President Touré could also refer to the prospects of rapidly growing future earnings from bauxite exports. In an August 1971 article the French writer Claude Rivière, a specialist in Guinean affairs, had passed in review the series of expedients for economic survival taken up in succession by the Guinean government. First had come the light processing industries installed by foreign aid, which had thus far proved a failure. Next there had been a period of reliance on United States grants. Then there had been an attempt at revival through a cultural revolution on the Chinese communist model, with its local revolutionary powers and production brigades (see ch. 11). To reorganize agriculture, which Rivière described as in catastrophic, dizzying decline, would, however, take too much time for too uncertain a result. Therefore, even as it continued to relaunch the rural revolution at annual intervals, the government was relying in the last analysis on one of the most common and least socialist, but also least burdensome, of expedients—collection of royalties on exports of crude minerals.

Unfortunately the efforts undertaken to bolster the new Guinean syli were not sufficient to offset the immediate pressures upon it from within and without, and it quickly succumbed to the same forces that had beset the Guinean franc. The pressure from within was usually ascribed to the government's monetary policy, and the external pressure was caused by the deteriorating balance of payments. Like many other developing countries in 1974 and 1975, Guinea was caught in the worldwide inflation that caused a sharp decline in its terms of trade (the ratio of export prices to import prices). Imports of petroleum products and of rice, on which it was heavily dependent, tripled in cost.

The crisis affecting many developing countries was recognized by an emergency conference of the UN General Assembly in April and May 1974. The conference was convened by Algeria in an effort to preserve solidarity between the oil-exporting countries, which were growing richer, and the countries dependent on exports of agricultural raw materials, which were being progressively impoverished by the trend in the terms of trade. Among other resolutions approved by the conference was a special UN emergency program to mobilize aid for thirty-three nations most seriously affected by the crisis, including Guinea and many other sub-Saharan African countries. Guinea subsequently received promises of aid from most of the oil-exporting countries (see Public Finance and Development, this ch.).

At the same UN emergency conference, the third world countries had joined in approving a declaration of the establishment of a new world economic order calling for the formation of raw material producers' associations, for the linking of export prices to import prices, and for nationalization of foreign-owned industries with compensation to be fixed by domestic instead of international law. By joining the International Bauxite Association and by subsequently linking its new bauxite export tax to the price of finished aluminum, Guinea was thus becoming part of a worldwide effort by developing countries to improve their terms of trade through more active pressure in international forums.

Partly as a result of these efforts but mainly because of increasing mineral production, Guinea's current balance of merchandise trade was expected to show marked improvement after 1974, permitting a better rate of repayment of outstanding foreign debt. Although capital inflow was expected to diminish for a time, some sources predicted that efforts to bolster the syli should be greatly assisted by the increase in bauxite exports, alumina prices, and export taxes, which could increase fiscal resources and perhaps the supply of imports. Even should unproductive spending be restrained and the price level brought more into line with those of neighboring countries, however, it might be difficult to achieve a stable currency and to encourage investment of capital and effort in the improvement of productive resources if people at home and abroad were led to perceive the country as under perpetual threat from external enemies and internal fifth column elements.

STATE PARTICIPATION IN ECONOMIC ACTIVITY

In principle almost every aspect of economic activity was under nearly total central or local government control. Not only were the usual sectors nationalized, including radio, posts and telecommunications, railroad and air transport, electric power, and matches and tobacco; but the government also had a complete monopoly of authorized domestic and foreign trade, banking, and insurance. Manufacturing plants were for the most part run by public enterprises. Diamond mining, forestry, and trawling were preserves of the government, and it controlled the authorized marketing and processing of the products of such traditional rural activities as cultivating, herding, and canoe or line fishing. Regional authorities were assigned crop and livestock production targets by the central government, and village committees were supposed in theory to see that they were attained (see ch. 11).

It may be surmised, however, that at least as late as 1972 a predominant share of the actual domestic product eluded government control. Much of it consisted of the food produced by traditional cultivating and herding families for their own consumption. A substantial share of crop and livestock production was probably smuggled out or sold on the black market. Trading profits and markups on crop exports, which in principle were supposed to accrue to the government budget, were inflated by the participation of a growing swarm of middlemen and part-time traders. Three-fourths of export value, and probably a major share of value added in industry, consisted of bauxite and alumina produced by the Fria complex, which until February 1973 was wholly owned by a consortium of private foreign firms.

Fria's private power plant and railroad also accounted for much of the growth in their respective sectors during the 1960s. The government greatly increased its share in electric power production after 1971 and its share of railroad and mining activity beginning in 1973, when it took over 49 to 51 percent ownership of all bauxite mining and alumina enterprises. At the same time, however, total foreign private investment in mining had begun what promised to be a steady increase, so that in absolute terms the private sector might become more important than formerly.

In the trading sector, dissatisfaction with the results of nationalization had led to decentralization of the state foreign and domestic trade operations in 1961 and to a brief and disastrous experiment with permitting private trading in 1963 and 1964 (see ch. 12). The state monopoly of trade was then resumed in its decentralized form, involving a number of separate trading agencies for individual commodities or classes of commodity. The government maintained regional and local shops at which peasants were, in principle, to be encouraged to exchange their crops for consumer goods, but the prevailing shortage of consumer goods precluded their effective operation.

Persisting dissatisfaction with the results or lack of results obtained by the government agencies and public enterprises, particularly in the economic field, led to almost continuous changes in their nomenclature and organization throughout the 1960s and into the 1970s. New ministries were formed or new directorates, departments, and bureaus created within ministries or shifted from one ministry to another, and their functions were constantly being redesignated (see ch. 8). In consequence, lists of acronyms and organizational charts became obsolete almost as soon as they were published.

The changes tended also to multiply the number of bureaus and public enterprises involved in attempting to control or influence economic activity. The number of public enterprises, for example, was said to have increased from about twenty in 1960 to more than seventy in 1973. One well-informed source reported that government enterprises and societies (not further defined) had increased from around fifty to more than 125.

In mid-1974 President Touré announced the creation of a new National Economic Council and six committees of state for cooperation. The National Economic Council was to be headed by the president and to consist of members appointed by decree from among the ranks of government and ruling party functionaries. It was to review almost every aspect of the economy, and all economic programs were to be submitted to it, including the development plans, the annual allocations for the plans, the fiscal budgets, and the annual import and export programs. No agreement for foreign aid, trade, or investment would be valid without the council's approval. It was also to carry out a periodic check on the efficient use of the various public budgets and to review the evolution of prices, wages, production, and other variables influencing the level of activity. The six committees of state were to be presided over by designated cabinet ministers and were to deal with economic negotiations involving foreign countries or their nationals or international organizations.

LABOR

Data on the country's labor force were variously reported. According to the 1972 census, about 2.6 million people were between the ages of fifteen and sixty-four. Of these about 6 percent were thought to be wage or salary earners in the modern monetary economy. Of the wage and salary earners, some 22 percent were reported to be in public administration, and of the remainder a high proportion were probably employed by public enterprises or other government-sponsored activity. An analysis published by Alain Cournanel in a French periodical in September 1972 concluded that the data released since independence on wage employment in Guinea were of variable value but that the only complete study without obvious errors, though probably inflated, was one carried out by the office of labor in 1966.

The same French source suggested that construction was probably one of the major employers of wage labor. Later statistics released by the government, however, appear to include workers employed on mine construction projects, for example, under employment in mining rather than in construction. It was reportedly characteristic for employment on the preliminary phases of a major project greatly to exceed the employment offered by the completed installation. For example, after the Fria mining complex came into full operation around 1962, it employed only about 1,000 Guinean workers (the africanization program had increased the number to around 1,500 in 1972). Building the project, however, had mobilized more than 10,000 wage earners. This may help to account for the fact that the total number of wage and salary earners in employment apparently declined after independence.

The 1972 French source reported that the total number of wage and salary earners had declined from 109,440 in 1957 to 88,940 in 1966. A major decline in employment had been in construction and mining, from 18,190 in 1957 to 8,600 in 1966. Wage employment in rural activities had declined from 32,000 to 25,000, largely as a result of the departure of a number of French planters and the decline of export crop production. The 1957 data had also shown 19,000 people employed in domestic service. The 1966 report showed only 6,800 ordinary workers and 2,200 skilled workers employed in services of all kinds. It is possible that domestic service was not included as a modern sector activity.

It is probable that the estimate of around 150,000 wage and salary earners in 1973 included some 10,000 workers reportedly employed in completing the bauxite mine, railroad, and port project in Boké Administrative Region. Employment in "mining" had increased by 23 percent in 1973 alone, to around 18,000 people; but the two mines then in operation, at Fria and Sangarédi, did not employ more than 3,000 Guinean workers, so that this increased employment must actually have been in construction and could be expected to come to an end unless new projects then in the planning stage could take up the slack.

Most employment estimates also suggested that in 1973 more than 20 percent of wage and salary earners were in the rural sector, including increased employment in trawling and shrimping projects sponsored by foreign aid (see ch. 11). This suggests that the number of wage and salary earners in agriculture and forestry had not increased significantly since 1966, when it was given as 25,000, of whom 9,000 were in banana production and 3,000 in pineapple production. The French article of September 1972 concluded that, since independence, some 15,000 former plantation workers in export production had abandoned the agricultural wage-earner class to swell the ranks of the unemployed. There is no statistical evidence, however, that they did not go into production for themselves. Some may have found employment on government rural projects or on the large-scale rice projects undertaken for a few years by the so-called private tractor entrepreneurs, as the total number of rural wage earners had declined by only 7,000. The reduction in export production of bananas was attributable in part to the greatly reduced yields on African plantations. The same article reported, however, that the overall decline in agriculture was reflected in a mounting exodus from the rural areas to the towns.

In 1963 a PDG economic conference had recommended that the government conduct periodic roundups of idle migrants to the towns, referred to as "fake unemployed," and use them in work on collective fields for a period of time, after which they would be deported to their respective rural homelands. This recommendation was apparently not put into practice until 1966 and thereafter was continued for two or three years. During the worst of the dry season, when overpopulation reached a peak in the garrison towns of Conakry, Kindia, Labé, Kankan, and Nzérékoré, the army conducted roundups of surplus able-bodied men, who were put to work on projects where they did not compete with existing wage earners. It is not entirely clear whether this practice effectively discouraged migration to the towns, but after 1966 rural inhabitants reportedly were increasingly retreating into subsistence production or leaving the country. The 1972 article suggests that idle urban workers may have been increasingly integrated into productive units of militia or production brigades dispatched to the rural areas. It remained unclear to what extent such productive units consisted of volunteers and to what extent such service was made a prerequisite for subsequent employment or other privileges.

Before independence the labor union movement under the leadership of Sékou Touré was an important political force for independence and also an important force in improving the welfare of African workers. Since independence political party pronouncements consistently have paid tribute to the interests of wage-earning workers before those of any other element of the population, but the unions have been brought under total control of the governing party (see ch. 8). The assumption seems to be that what is good for the PDG is good for the workers, and strikes are apparently unknown.

The newspaper *Horoya*, sponsored by the government party, sometimes found the Guinean worker unappreciative of the employment opportunities provided by the big new construction projects. In mid-1973, for example, when official plans for increasing production were focused on a Chinese communist-inspired cultural revolution, the Chinese communist engineers on the Tinkisso dam project were reportedly having difficulty with Guinean workers, who had failed to adapt readily to the kind of work norms expected of Chinese workers. *Horoya* accordingly denounced the Guinean workers concerned as saboteurs and counterrevolutionaries.

The government has effectively enforced africanization programs in the few remaining firms under foreign management, which are chiefly in the mining sector. The improvement has been most notable in the nationwide increase in African staff at technical and management levels and in the overstaffed civil service. Unfortunately in the early years not all of those newly hired at these levels had appropriate qualifications. The lot of the few thousand African workers in the mining operations and the single alumina processing plant has also been materially improved.

Except for the civil service, however, and for the minority employed in private enterprise, such fringe benefits as health care, training, and social security are usually not provided (see ch. 6). Except at the mines, where provision in kind includes housing, food, and access to imported goods through commissary privileges, the gains made by wage earners since independence have been eroded by inflation and its consequences. Successive upward adjustments in the minimum wage have failed to keep pace with unofficial price increases.

BALANCE OF PAYMENTS

Guinea does not publish a consistent series of balance-of-payments accounts. When a thoroughgoing system of reporting of foreign exchange transactions is maintained, the balance of payments provides a reasonably accurate picture of economic relations with foreign countries from year to year. In the few estimates of Guinea's balance of payments occasionally published by foreign sources, however, the pattern tends to be obscured by the country's continuing heavy reliance on bilateral clearing agreements with centrally planned economies, under which the indebtedness resulting from a consistent excess of imports over exports has been repeatedly deferred. Moreover, such balance-of-payments estimates do not reflect the volume of smuggled trade and illicit foreign exchange transactions.

There have been conflicting accounts of how heavily the servicing and repayment of outstanding debt would burden future foreign exchange earnings (see Public Finance and Development, this ch.). Guinea's debt is relatively high in relation to past per capita GNP, but much of it has been specifically incurred against repayment in future mineral exports. These exports, and repayment of the debt, are expected to reverse the pattern of Guinea's balance of payments. In the past there has been a deficit on the current balance of goods and services, partially concealed by barter agreements and by deferral of a portion of dividend or interest payments owing under services. This deficit has been more than balanced by a substantial net inflow on capital account.

At latest report, in mid-1974, it was generally assumed that, when 1974 data were assembled a year or two later, there would prove to have been a substantial improvement in exports resulting largely from bauxite exports and perhaps in part from increasing world market prices for crop exports. World market prices for such essential imports as rice and petroleum products, however, had been rising more steeply, so that their cost in Guinean currency had more than tripled in three years. One French source predicted that export earnings would double from 1973 to 1974 but that the amortization and interest payments due in 1974 on the outstanding foreign debt would absorb about 90 percent of this anticipated increase, so that if debt servicing obligations were fully met, the net surplus on goods and services might be only about 10 percent higher in 1974 than in 1973.

After 1974, however, increased export earnings might result in a somewhat larger surplus on current account. Production at the Sangarédi bauxite mine would advance toward full capacity and would be supplemented by exports from the Kindia mine and some years later from the other new bauxite mines. Moreover, the calculations cited did not take into account the new and higher export tax imposed in January 1975 (see ch. 12). The movement of world market prices for minerals and for such agricultural exports as pineapple in various forms, palm kernels, and coffee was on the uptrend in 1974 and thereafter could not be predicted.

In 1974, and probably in 1975 and 1976, the improving balance on current account was expected to be offset by a sharp drop in the net inflow of foreign investment and official lending as the financing of the largest bauxite projects under the five-year plan was completed. The outflow of capital should increase if the government meets an increasing share of its debt repayment obligations. Once the feasibility studies for the Tougué and Dabola bauxite projects have been completed, however, a new inflow of investment from Yugoslavia and Switzerland can be expected; and if financing is found for the proposed US$550 million Trans-Guinean Railroad, there will be a substantial new inflow of lending in the 1980s (see ch. 12).

PUBLIC FINANCE AND DEVELOPMENT

Separate budget operations are sustained for the central government, for the twenty-nine administrative regions, and for the 220 *arrondissements* (districts). Only the central government budget must be approved by the National Assembly. The financial operations of the administrative regions and *arrondissements* are reviewed by the Ministry of Finance and may be approved by presidential decree. The many public agencies, such as the equalization fund that operates to support agricultural exports, and the more than seventy public enterprises engaged in trade and manufacturing activity also have independent budgets, and their financial operations are reviewed by a separate body, the Ministry of Financial Control. No consolidated account of treasury operations is published, so that it is not possible to obtain accurate information on overall receipts and expenditures.

For the central government's operations, only the draft budgets as voted by the National Assembly are published. They do not give an accurate picture of actual receipts and expenditures but set forth anticipated revenues and the government's intentions concerning expenditure for the coming fiscal year. Guinea's fiscal year is the same year used for reporting agricultural and industrial production, foreign trade, and all other data, from October 1 through September 30. Central government transactions are divided into an ordinary budget for current operating expenditure and a capital budget comprising the public investment program of the Ministry of Planning.

Until fiscal year 1970 the planning year extended from May 1 to April 30, but beginning October 1, 1969, it was changed to coincide with the fiscal year; thereafter annual appropriations were voted for investment in the same manner as for current expenditure. Expenditures under the current budget correspond roughly to the usual definition of public consumption, comprising wages and salaries of government employees, goods and services required for current use and maintenance, and servicing of public debt. Expenditures under the investment (planning) budget correspond to the usual definition of public capital formation. It may be that, if financing provided under the plan was used for imports under the general import program, as sometimes alleged, there could have been some confusion between capital formation and consumption.

Some sources have concluded that both anticipated tax receipts and estimated expenditures in the budgets voted by the National Assembly have considerably exceeded the receipts and expenditures actually realized. In the early 1970s some improvement was reportedly effected in forecasting tax yields. The government's financial difficulties, however, meant that some of the investment expenditure forecast in the annual budgets was never carried out, either because of unanticipated delays or because the projected foreign lending did not materialize.

The figures published for the budgets voted by the National Assembly reveal that from the mid-1960s the government consistently sought to achieve a small surplus of current revenue over current expenditure that could be used to defray a portion of needed investment (see table 5). There is reason to believe, however, that because tax receipts had been overestimated and current operating expenditure had consistently exceeded expectations, there was actually a series of fairly heavy deficits on the current budget in the late 1960s. This meant that the capital budget, and a portion of the current budget as well, had to be financed by domestic and foreign borrowing, so that the scope for investment expenditure was significantly reduced. In consequence, spending under the Seven Year Plan fell short of target, and completion of a number of projects had to be deferred. In late 1969, however, new import and excise taxes were introduced, and more stringent tax collection efforts were initiated. Fairly large arrears of taxes were subsequently collected, helping to produce a small surplus on the current budget in fiscal years 1970 through 1972.

There is little available information on the tax system. Indirect taxes, particularly those on imports and exports, appear to furnish the major share of revenues. In addition to the regular import tax, there is a special equalization tax on imports designed to finance the export crop equalization fund. In 1969 an additional import surtax, equivalent to 100 percent of the regular import tax, and a special excise tax on domestic products were imposed. In the interior, taxes were imposed on crops and livestock. Goods sold at local open-air markets were heavily taxed. In 1972 certain of these taxes were suspended in an effort to relieve the food shortage.

Other taxes include payroll taxes and social security taxes on employers, a company tax, a progressive income tax, a tax on wages and salaries, and a head tax imposed on all citizens, both men and women. The rate of the head tax reportedly progressed from the equivalent of GF500 per capita in 1957 to the equivalent of GF2,800 in December 1973. Old people and children under the age of fourteen were formerly exempted from the head tax, as were students, war veterans, and women with more than four children. Since 1969, however, all citizens are subject to the tax. One source reported that in the early 1970s proof of having paid the head tax was required in order to receive food rations. It claimed that, whereas families formerly would seek to underreport the number of adults in order to pay fewer head taxes, families anxious to receive the maximum food ration were now paying the tax for nonexistent family members or people who had died, thereby causing an apparent increase in the population.

Some obscurity surrounds the sources of the budget's nontax revenues and the financial operations of the state enterprises. In nationalizing trade and other sectors of the economy, the ruling party stressed the prospect that the profits would thus accrue to the state and could be channeled into capital formation for development under successive plans. There is some suggestion that the appearance of this process may have been maintained despite the fact that almost all government enterprises have been operating at a loss. Not only were the public enterprises inadequately capitalized in the first place, but the government has apparently failed to cover their losses, which are met instead by borrowing or are simply carried forward against future earnings. Public enterprise gross profits are heavily taxed, and a large share of profits remaining after taxes is also supposed to be transferred to the government budget. Even their depreciation allowances must be paid over to the state, so that when they need to renew their equipment they must apply to the plan for financing. Thus despite the reported heavy losses of state enterprises, they have apparently furnished, or at least have been expected to furnish, a major share of the nontax revenues anticipated under the draft budgets as voted.

The government's external critics alleged that the system legally created for approval of the central government budget by the National Assembly and for periodic review of financial operations by separate institutions established for the purpose was honored more in principle than in practice. They claimed that the pattern of expenditure both at the central government level and in the individual geographic or administrative regions was actually determined by the highest echelon of the governing political party.

The Ministry of Financial Control was created in 1967 to examine the accounts of the regions and of the public enterprises and other government agencies. There were unconfirmed rumors that the ministry had discovered misappropriations and waste. Its reports were submitted to the presidency. The minister, Baldet Ousmane, and a number of ministry inspectors were reportedly arrested and executed during the purges of 1971 (see ch. 8; ch. 13). A number of others were sentenced to long terms of imprisonment as alleged fifth columnists. The ministry was still in existence, however, in 1974.

Development Planning

At independence in 1958 Guinea was relatively underdeveloped in view of its potential. Under the French, Dakar in Senegal had been promoted as the area's major port and trading center. Most of the French export crop plantations—except for a limited number of banana plantations—and most of the processing capacity created by French firms had been located elsewhere and the consumer goods they produced exported to Guinea. At independence the French were just beginning to realize plans

Table 5. Guinea, Budgets Voted for Central Government, 1965–73[1]
(in million Guinean francs)[2]

	Annual Average 1965–67	1968	1969	1970	1971	1972	1973
Current Revenue							
Domestic Revenue							
Direct taxes	3,046	3,500	3,260	3,490	3,520	3,610	3,700
Indirect taxes	6,620	6,700	6,800	6,990	7,170	7,260	7,530
Other tax revenue	1,320	1,230	1,410	1,640	1,270	1,480	1,520
Nontax revenue	4,366	5,100	5,806	5,460	5,396	6,080	5,750
Errors and omissions	358	70	...	...	...	...	...
Subtotal	15,710	16,600	17,276	17,580	17,356	18,430	18,500
Foreign grants	873	150	400	300	4,020	2,300	2,300
Total[3]	16,583	16,750	17,676	17,880	21,376	20,730	20,800
Current (Ordinary Budget) Expenditure							
Defense	3,070	3,500	3,630	3,720	6,480	7,210	7,470
Agriculture	113	120	105	110	90	120	130
Education	3,534	3,850	4,320	4,570	2,080	2,210	2,300
Health	1,453	1,650	1,735	1,680	1,490	1,670	1,820
Other	5,990	6,380	6,810	7,070	7,120	6,690	6,480
Total	14,160	15,500	16,600	17,150	17,260	17,900	18,200

Current surplus (+) or deficit (−)	+2,423	+1,250	+1,076	+730	+4,116	+2,830	+2,600
Capital Investment (Plan) Expenditure							
Agriculture	853	550	410	350	380	960	2,900
Mining, Industry, and power	4,350	7,180	2,920	2,860	2,150	3,070	8,800
Transport and communications	4,710	6,320	1,460	2,680	1,990	3,190	7,600
Education and housing	1,080	780	270	720	540	630	3,500
Health	150	110	56	170	320	780	1,200
Other	460	1,660	1,760	1,950	216	1,300	2,800
Total	11,603	16,600	6,876	8,730	5,596	9,930	26,800
Overall deficit (−)	−9,180	−15,350	−5,800	−8,000	−1,480	−7,100	−24,200
Financing of the Deficit							
Foreign borrowing	5,860	6,850	5,200	6,500	1,200	4,400	20,000
Domestic borrowing	3,320	8,500	600	1,500	280	2,700	4,200
Foreign grants and loans, total	6,733	7,000	5,600	6,800	5,220	6,700	22,300
Foreign grants and loans, as percent of investment spending	58.02	42.17	81.44	77.89	93.28	67.47	74.63

. . . means none.

[1] Guinea's reporting year ends September 30.

[2] For value of the Guinean franc—see Glossary.

[3] In 1971, probably more than 90 percent of this anticipated revenue was actually received. In other years, however, both revenue and expenditure voted probably substantially exceeded actual sums realized.

designed eventually to make Guinea the rice-exporting granary of French West Africa.

Until World War II most French investments, such as that in the Conakry-to-Kankan railroad, were designed to facilitate French administration or enterprise (see ch. 2). After World War II the emphasis shifted somewhat. A ten-year plan to be applied to all the French overseas territories was formulated in 1946, but because of the acute shortage of foreign exchange in France it remained largely inactive. It was later superseded by a four-year plan for the period 1949 through 1952—generally known as the Monnet Plan—and a subsequent four-year plan for the years 1953 to 1957. These plans, however, did not involve comprehensive planning for the economy but only outlined the priorities for public capital spending. Expenditure in Guinea under the two plans totaled the equivalent of GF10.4 million, of which GF300,000 was for public buildings and schools, GF5.4 million for the improvement of Conakry port, GF2.7 million for roads and other transportation infrastructure, GF1.3 million for controlled inundation of potential ricefields, and GF700,000 for other rural improvements.

The three successive development plans since independence, unlike the previous French plans, were intended in principle to permit centralized planning of investment by both the public and the private sectors to determine the development of both the traditional and the modern economies, from village level to national level. The first plan in particular, however, was criticized by both external sources and government leaders as having turned out to be a simple shopping list of desirable projects, without adequate coordination or economic planning. A statistical basis had apparently been lacking on which to assess the probable physical resources available and the limitations on the economy's capacity to absorb foreign aid spending.

The first development plan was formulated amid the difficulties attendant upon independence and Guinea's vote against participation in the French Community, which resulted in the abrupt departure of most French technicians and other qualified personnel (see ch. 2). It had been drawn up in some haste and under intense pressure of events at the Ministry of Planning, with the assistance of a French team consisting of the socialist professor Charles Bettelheim and his colleagues Jacques Charrière and Jean Benard. This draft was then adopted by the Fifth Congress of the ruling party in 1959 as the Three Year Development Plan (1960–63), which in fact had later to be extended into 1964.

The plan text consisted of two parts: general policy directives and the proposed plan for allocation of investment expenditure by sector of activity and by project. The general policy directives placed primary emphasis on achieving decolonization of every aspect of economic life. Contrary to later disclaimers by some sources, they stated that this was to be accomplished by the creation of a totally noncapitalist economic system involving state ownership of industry, a government monopoly of trade and banking, and the reorganization of agricultural production on the basis of cooperatives.

The plan itself placed primary emphasis on the development of industry. It sought to increase the share in total production of manufacturing, public works, trade, and services. This would automatically reduce the relative importance of agriculture.

In actual practice the neglect of agriculture during the period of the three-year plan was greater than had been intended by the planners. By May 1967 about 83 percent of the investments listed under the plan had been completed. The cost, however, had been GF43 billion, instead of the GF39 billion foreseen. Moreover, of this total some 57.4 percent had been spent on administration and transport, which had been slated to absorb only 36.4 percent. Investment in productive capacity in mining, power, manufacturing, and agriculture had received only 29.1 percent of the total, instead of the 47.6 percent planned. Only 11.2 percent, or some GF5 billion, had been spent on agriculture, and part of this spending did not create any permanent capital improvements but went for such imports as tractors unsuited to tropical conditions. Spending on education, health, and other social investment had taken 13.3 percent of the total, fairly close to the plan target of 15.9 percent.

Plan projects actually completed by 1964 or soon thereafter had included such unremunerative showcase projects as the Soviet-built 25,000-seat sports stadium and polytechnic institute; the Chinese communist-built People's Palace; and an impressive highway that ended just outside Conakry. Tractors, earthmoving and roadbuilding equipment, rolling stock for the railroad, and Soviet aircraft for the new Guinean airline had been imported at heavy cost on credit, but before the debt had been repaid many of the items had become inoperative for lack of maintenance and replacement parts.

Some GF2.1 billion was spent for improving the runways at Conakry-Gbessia airport and GF2.6 billion for a water-supply conduit from the dam at Grandes Chutes to Conakry. Investment in productive capacity included a printing plant, a slaughterhouse and refrigeration plant, a match and tobacco factory, a cannery, a furniture factory, a sawmill, and a particleboard factory. Five years after completion most of these plants were not producing enough to repay the debt incurred for their construction (see ch. 12).

In a statement accompanying the subsequent Seven Year Plan, the Guinean leadership acknowledged some of the setbacks of the three-year plan, which were ascribed to external pressures from French trade and banking interests and to a number of internal problems. These included the lack of statistical data on which to base plan estimates, the haste and pressure under which the plan had to be drawn up, and the lack of coordination and ordering of priorities among those responsible for carrying out individual projects. Costs had also exceeded expectations on most projects, notably on regional public works projects that cost more than GF1.2 billion although they had been scheduled for completion without cost by the use of volunteer labor under the human investment program (see ch. 11).

It had been intended, moreover, to finance 25 percent of the plan from such domestic resources as trading profits of government agencies. The decline of agricultural exports had eroded profits, however, and the profits actually accumulated were not transferred to the plan on schedule. The statement ascribed this delay to growing pains in the government trade monopoly, such as red tape, corruption, and administrative anarchy.

The overall target of the three-year plan had been a growth rate of 15 percent a year. According to the official statement, the actual rate of growth had been 8.2 percent a year in domestic product, including the output of the foreign-owned Fria enclave, and 4 percent a year in national product, excluding the value added by Fria. The statement nevertheless declared the plan a success, in that it had accomplished its primary objective of disengagement from the colonial trading system.

The ensuing Seven Year Plan extended officially from May 1964 to September 1971, but most capital expenditure in the two succeeding years ending in September 1973 was devoted to the completion of mining and manufacturing projects that were to have been finished during the plan period. This meant that the subsequent five-year plan could not be started until October 1973. According to preliminary reports, about two-thirds of the spending called for under the Seven Year Plan had been completed by the end of 1971. It is said to have amounted to some GF90 billion, or more than twice the amount spent under the extended three-year plan. It is not clear how much of the total spending was actually financed from domestic resources, which were supposed to have furnished nearly 50 percent of the financing. During the entire period through September 1973, spending on agriculture came to only about one-half of the level proposed under the plan; spending on mining and manufacturing, however, was about 2½ times that projected under the plan.

It appears that much of the investment actually realized was in the Boké mining project and in power projects and highways, all financed by foreign investors. Some sources, however, reported that this same foreign investment was being entered again as financing under the subsequent five-year plan.

The five-year plan was approved by the party congress in September 1973 and came into effect in October 1973, but by early 1975 it was not yet clear what the sources of financing were to be. Total expenditure for the five-year period was set at the equivalent of GF586.6 billion, which if realized would entail an annual average expenditure five times higher than that under the previous two plans. Self-sufficiency in food grain production and increased production of export crops were said to be priority goals of the plan, but the share of proposed spending allocated to rural development was only 5.3 percent, proportionately lower than the share proposed under the previous plans although somewhat higher than the share actually spent on agriculture under the Seven Year Plan. The targets set for crop production were in several instances lower than the targets originally set for 1963 under the three-year plan.

The largest shares of proposed spending were allocated for mining, electric power, and roadbuilding. More than 50 percent of projected investment was to be semipublic investment in mining, apparently involving the mixed enterprises formed to exploit the new bauxite deposits and possibly the iron ore deposits as well. About 13 percent would be in electric power development. Among the projects listed were several that had been on the shopping list for the previous two plans, including the first phase of the large-scale Konkouré hydroelectric project, regarded as providing the basis for future development of an aluminum-processing industry. The third high-priority objective was highways and bridges, for which credit contracts had been concluded with French, Italian, and Spanish engineering firms.

The 3 percent of proposed investment allocated for manufacturing was reported to include construction of a pulp and paper complex, which had also been on previous shopping lists but which it was now claimed that the Chinese Communists had offered to finance. A petroleum refinery was to be financed by Algeria. The plan also mentioned a new cement plant with a capacity of 200,000 tons.

In mid-1974 President Touré announced that Guinea was assured of foreign aid worth about the equivalent of US$180 million to $200 million to finance the five-year plan. Commitments had been received from the People's Republic of China (PRC), the Soviet Union, Yugoslavia, Romania, and a number of the oil-producing Arab countries, in addition to the financing already committed earlier for the semipublic mining enterprise.

At the same time the Guinean leadership was speaking in terms of a "target 1980" program more ambitious than that included under the five-year plan. Besides agricultural development the program would include completion of the bauxite projects of Tougué and Dabola and the iron ore projects at Nimba and Simandou (see ch. 12). The Tougué and Simandou projects would require construction of the proposed 745-mile Trans-Guinean Railroad and an associated deepwater ore port at Conakry at a cost variously estimated at from US$550 million to more than US$1 billion.

The goal of 1980 had been set for iron ore production because new Japanese steel mills would then be ready to import the ore; but it was not clear whether the target dates of 1980 and 1982 were realistic for so extensive a project. Plans for a steel mill had also been mentioned in connection with the five-year plan and the "target 1980" program.

Foreign Aid Resources

Published information on Guinea's foreign aid receipts since independence was uncoordinated and fragmentary. An American business publication estimated that Guinea had received the equivalent of at least US$800 million in foreign aid by 1972 (apparently including foreign private investment) and that in 1972 and 1973 it was able to obtain commitments of an additional US$300 million to US$400 million in foreign exchange or equipment in connection with bauxite mining projects. A United States government source reported in December 1972 that Guinea's foreign aid receipts had averaged the equivalent of US$40 million a year since 1960.

Financial flows from abroad can be compared only if the terms on which they were received are taken into consideration. These range from outright grants to loans received on terms ranging from soft (concessionary, with low rates of interest and long terms of payment) to hard. Usually loans from multilateral organizations are extended on relatively soft terms. Official bilateral loans may be somewhat harder, export credits harder still, and private supplier credits hardest of all. Except for petroleum investment, private foreign direct investment in developing countries usually expects a return of about 10 percent. A 1973 report of Western Europe's Organization for Economic Cooperation and Development (OECD), calling for softer terms in official lending to nations on the UN least developed country list, singled out Guinea as a glaring example of poor treatment in official lending. The report did not specify which official loans were meant. The early capital commitments received from the Soviet Union and Eastern European countries were at low rates of interest, around 2.5 percent, whereas the average interest on official loans to developing countries was 4.4 percent. The export credits received under the bilateral agreements, however, may perhaps have been on harder terms; and Guinea has also received suppliers' credit from Western countries. Interest rates on direct credits from the Export-Import Bank, for example, could range from 7 to 8.5 percent.

A 1972 OECD report had stressed that the consensus of all concerned was that the developing countries themselves bear the fundamental responsibility for their debt management. This position had generally been maintained by creditor countries in the case of Ghana, the most notorious instance of some unscrupulous foreign private suppliers taking advantage of poor debt management by a recipient government. The succeeding Ghanaian government had finally denounced a large portion of this debt in 1971. Some press sources dubbed Guinea " a mini-Ghana" because it had also incurred some debt for unproductive purposes, although on a smaller scale than in Ghana.

Africa Contemporary Record had reported Guinea's external debt outstanding at the end of 1969 as totaling the equivalent of US$308.6 million, of which US$64.5 million was multilateral—a loan for the Boké project from the World Bank Group (see Glossary)—US$216.3 million was bilateral official lending, and US$27.7 million was private suppliers' credits. These were loan funds committed but not necessarily disbursed. Loans disbursed amounted in total to US$249.6 million. Two years later, at the end of 1971, total loans disbursed amounted to US$291 million, of which US$54 million was export credits, official or private. By this date Guinea had also received the equivalent of US$95 million in outright grants and US$150 million in the estimated book value of private foreign direct investment.

In order to compare the relative debt burden incurred by the developing countries, the 1972 OECD report adjusted the total liabilities of each country arising from foreign financial flows to reflect the differing interest rates and repayment periods of the different components included. This was done by calculating the 1971 value of the future debt service payments due, that is, the amount through the immediate payment of which the debtor country could hypothetically eliminate its debt in one stroke. This sum was then expressed as a percentage of 1970 GNP. According to this formula Guinea's adjusted official and private foreign debt in 1971 was equivalent to 84 percent of 1970 GNP, one of the highest ratios reported. This formula may perhaps be inappropriate in Guinea's case, however, as much of the debt outstanding at the end of 1971 may have been slated for repayment out of the proceeds of future bauxite exports that did not enter into the 1970 GNP.

The same objection may perhaps be made to another formula expressing the debt service payments due for the next fifteen years as a percentage of fifteen years' exports. On this scale Guinea's debt service ratio was 53 percent, one of the highest on the list; but the fifteen years' exports were based on exports in 1968 through 1970, instead of on the greatly increased bauxite exports anticipated.

At the end of 1970 Ghana's total debt outstanding had been twice as large as that of Guinea. After a portion of the debt was denounced in 1971, however, Ghana's adjusted debt was only 34 percent of 1970 GNP, compared to 84 percent for Guinea.

Some unofficial publications were expressing misgivings in 1973 and 1974 over the burden of the debt incurred thus far on Guinea's future national income and foreign exchange earnings. In view of the customary caution of the multilateral lending institutions, however, it may perhaps be surmised that they would not have approved new loans without some assurance that the country's outstanding debt obligations did not exceed its ability to repay.

External critics of the government alleged that in 1974 it was experiencing some difficulty in securing new short-term trade credits because of the backlog of deferred repayment obligations on the credits already received. In addition to substantial debit balances owing under bilateral agreements with the Soviet Union, the PRC, the Eastern European countries, and Yugoslavia, Guinea had also accumulated such debits under bilateral agreements with Morocco, Algeria, Egypt, Mali, and Senegal. The last two countries had been important sources of supply for meat, peanut oil, and other foodstuffs, but because of the debt these imports had been cut off, contributing to the chronic problem of food supply.

The largest amounts of bilateral official debt are reportedly owed to the Soviets and the Chinese Communists. Since 1965 about US$50 million of short-term bilateral debt had been converted into long-term debt. The entire long-term debt to the Soviet Union, including this element accumulated under the clearing agreements, is to be repaid out of bauxite deliveries from the Kindia mine over a period of thirty years (see ch. 12). When combined with the debt incurred for the construction of the Kindia project, it will absorb 90 percent of the mine's production. This has led some sources to conclude that Guinea's mineral earnings for the next thirty years are mortgaged for repayment of its debt. There is no evidence, however, that the output of the other, larger, mines will be used to repay any debt except that incurred for their construction.

As a recipient of foreign financial flows the Guinean government has remained steadfastly nondiscriminatory. President Touré has declared on numerous occasions that aid will be accepted from any source without regard to political alignments or power blocs as long as it comes without political strings and does not compromise his country's neutrality or independence of action. Such objections have sometimes been raised, however, in the course of the sixteen years since independence. Some sources have seen evidence that the resulting frequent twists and turns in foreign relations have had the effect of retarding economic development. Published sources also contain obscure references to specific aid projects suddenly abandoned because of psychological difficulties or unexplained disagreements (see ch. 9; ch. 12).

Guinea's vote against joining the French Community had taken place in September 1958, and independence was proclaimed in October 1958. Relations with France deteriorated very rapidly thereafter (see ch. 2). French personnel departing from Guinea were accused of adopting a scorched earth policy, removing construction and telecommunications equipment, for example, failing to train Guinean replacements, and taking accounts and instruction manuals with them. Some French projects were abandoned uncompleted, and valuable installations that had been completed were allowed by the Guineans to deteriorate from neglect in the early years of independence (see ch. 11).

There was thus an immediate emergency need for foreign assistance to fill the gap left by the French. The first country to respond with a loan was Ghana in November 1958. Trade missions from the communist countries arrived a few weeks after independence, prepared to conclude bilateral barter agreements. The first trade agreement was signed in February 1959 and the first aid agreement with the Soviet Union in August 1959. Western countries promptly recognized Guinea's independence but were slower in offering aid, reportedly influenced by French President Charles de Gaulle.

In 1959 the United States furnished 5,000 tons of rice and 3,000 tons of wheat flour, and in 1960 it made available another US$1 million worth of surplus agricultural commodities. An agreement with the United States in 1959, signed in 1960, provided for the training of English language teachers in Guinea and for 150 Guinean students to be sent to the United States for further training. An aid agreement was also signed with the Federal Republic of Germany (West Germany). Aid had also been furnished by Morocco and the Arab Republic of Egypt.

At the beginning of 1959 the first shipments of goods from the Soviet Union and countries of Eastern Europe had arrived. Commitments of capital by these countries had been made early and by the end of 1962 amounted to the equivalent of US$127 million (see table 6). This consisted of long-term or medium-term loans at low rates of interest, repayable over periods of up to twelve years. Of the US$14.4 million committed by the United States through 1962, US$8.4 million was grant aid. The remainder was in surplus agricultural commodities, later known as Food for Peace. This food was sold to the people of Conakry. Of the proceeds in Guinean currency, a portion was set aside for the local currency needs of United States government staff in Guinea. Most was to be spent by the Guinean government for development purposes. According to reports at the time, however, it was not so spent because of a fear of fueling inflation. For fear of propaganda, the Americans were not allowed to label their rice shipments. They were nevertheless known to come from the United States, and early shipments were dubbed "cement" by Guineans because they were unsuitable for the preparation of Guinean dishes.

The fragmentary and sometimes conflicting nature of data published in official sources on Guinea's foreign aid receipts through 1973 makes comparison of receipts from different sources chancy at best. The United States aid authorities gave a fairly comprehensive and detailed accounting of their grants and loans to Guinea. Data published by the UN on aid to Guinea from the centrally planned economies, however, include only capital commitments. Information on bilateral official aid from other sources is incomplete, and data on private suppliers' credits and direct investment by year are entirely lacking. Guinea was reported to have accumulated a sizable debt to West Germany by 1971, and a large portion of this may have consisted of private suppliers' credits.

Little new capital was committed by communist countries between the end of 1962 and the end of 1968. For a time the Soviet Union had paused to reexamine its aid policies, meanwhile suspending aid to all foreign countries. In the case of aid to Guinea there was also some mutual dissatisfaction with the progress of existing projects (see ch. 12). Economic relations had not been interrupted by the expulsion of the Soviet ambassador at the end of 1961 (see ch. 9). In early 1962, however,

Table 6. Guinea, Incomplete Estimates of Foreign Aid Receipts, 1953–73
(in million US dollars)

Source of Aid	1953-62	1963-66	1967-68	1969	1970-71	Total 1953-71	1972-73
International Organizations							
World Bank Group[1]	..	..	..	64.5	9.0	73.5	..
UN Development Program (UNDP)	0.4	7.3	3.4	2.6	3.1	16.8	1.1
Other UN sources	0.2	0.5	0.4	0.1	0.8	2.0	0.1
Total	0.6	7.8	3.8	67.2	12.9	92.3	1.2
Bilateral Official Sources							
Commitments of Capital by Communist Countries							
Soviet Union	76.0	..	..	92.0	..	168.0	..
Eastern Europe[2]	25.0	..	..	..	..	25.0	..
People's Republic of China (PRC)	26.0	30.0	..	..	10.0	66.0	..
Total[3]	127.0	30.0	..	92.0	10.0	259.0	..
Soviet military aid	n.a.	n.a.	n.a.	n.a.	n.a.	25.0	n.a.
United States[4]							
Official loans	..	10.4	..	..	..	10.4	..
Supporting assistance grants	3.5	20.5	..	..	..	24.0	..
Other grants	4.9	9.8	2.2	0.8	0.2	17.9	..
Food for Peace	6.0	17.1	3.4	7.5	12.1	46.1	5.5
Peace Corps	..	3.0	0.2	0.2	0.4	3.8	..
Total	14.4	60.8	5.8	8.5	12.7	102.2	5.5

United States military aid	...	0.9	...	...	...	0.9	...
Federal Republic of Germany (West Germany)							
Economic	5.0	12.7	2.6	0.3	n.a.	n.a.	n.a.
Military	n.a.	n.a.	n.a.	n.a.	n.a.	7.0	n.a.
Italy	0.01	1.3	0.3	...	n.a.	n.a.	n.a.
Belgium	...	...	0.03	...	n.a.	n.a.	n.a.
United Kingdom	...	0.06	...	...	n.a.	n.a.	n.a.
Switzerland	0.01	0.1	0.01	...	n.a.	n.a.	n.a.
Canada	...	0.6	0.3	...	n.a.	n.a.	n.a.
Other	n.a.	n.a.	n.a.	n.a.	n.a.	n.a.	n.a.
Export-Import Bank	...	...	...	22.8	0.4	23.2	...
Other suppliers' credits	n.a.	n.a.	n.a.	n.a.	n.a.	n.a.	n.a.
Private Overseas Direct Investment (PODI)	na.a	n.a.	n.a.	n.a.	n.a.	150.0	n.a.
TOTAL	n.a.	n.a.	n.a.	n.a.	n.a.	n.a.	n.a.

... means none; n.a. means not available.

[1] Includes International Bank for Reconstruction and Development (IBRD, commonly known as the World Bank); International Development Association (IDA); and International Finance Corporation (IFC).

[2] Excludes Yugoslavia, an important aid partner.

[3] Apparently includes only medium-term and long-term capital commitments; excludes sizable short-term credits under bilateral clearing agreements.

[4] United States figures, like communist figures, are for authorizations or commitments, not all of which are necessarily disbursed in the period in question.

the United States had somewhat increased its aid effort, so that Guinea was never again quite so exclusively reliant on communist aid sources.

The American scholar Marshall Goldman pointed out in 1967 that, whereas in most areas of the world the Soviets had begun their foreign aid program only after the Americans had had the opportunity to make the first mistakes, in Guinea the sequence was reversed, and the latecoming Americans had a chance to learn from Soviet blunders. In the cold war atmosphere of the early 1960s, American press reports found more tales of Soviet aid mismanagement to report from Guinea than from any other recipient country in the history of Soviet aid. The Guineans were reportedly inclined to hold the Soviet technicians responsible for the introduction of oversized factories or heated tractors. The Soviets said that they had been misled into overhasty expenditure by the urgency of Guinea's need after the withdrawal of the French.

The communist countries had been scheduled to provide as much as 80 percent of the medium-term and long-term capital used for investment under the three-year plan. There were no subsequent reports of how much actually had been contributed by different sources to this plan or to the subsequent two plans. The sources of financing appear to have been more diverse, however, under the seven-year and five-year plans, and there was greater reliance on private direct investment, which had played little part in the three-year plan. Yugoslavia continued to play an important part in sponsoring power projects, and reliance on projects sponsored by the Chinese Communists appeared to have increased (see ch. 12). The capital commitment by the Soviet Union in 1969, equivalent to US$92 million, was to finance the Kindia bauxite project.

Under the terms of the UN Emergency Operation, launched by the UN General Assembly on May 1, 1974, special financial assistance was to be mobilized, through either multilateral or bilateral channels, for the thirty-two developing countries deemed to have been hardest hit by the economic trends of the preceding year. Guinea was one of those designated to receive such special assistance. The mobilization effort was focused upon the oil-exporting countries. The ultimate objective was a three-way flow in which a growing proportion of surplus financial resources generated by oil sales would be channeled to developing countries in the form of direct investment or low-cost loans. Recipient countries would then be able to import from the industrial nations the capital goods and other products and services needed for development.

After the Guinean prime minister made a tour of a number of Arab states in mid-1974, President Touré announced that offers of assistance had been received from almost all of the oil-exporting countries, including Algeria, Libya, Saudi Arabia, Kuwait, Bahrain, Abu Dhabi, and Romania. Algeria was to finance much of the proposed oil refinery and to take future iron ore exports. Libya, Egypt, Kuwait, and Saudi Arabia were to participate in a new bauxite mining enterprise. Kuwait sponsored a fishing enterprise. Guinea also hoped to enlist the aid of some of these countries in longer range plans for aluminum- or steel-producing facilities.

In January 1975 the United Nations Development Program (UNDP) approved country programs for ten developing countries. The program for Guinea for the years 1974 through 1978 would receive some US$23.4 million, more than it had received from the UNDP in the entire period since independence. Of the total program, US$8.5 million was to be allocated to the development of human resources, US$7.1 million to rural development, US$5 million to infrastructure, and US$2.7 million to mining and industry. In addition the UNDP had already granted to Guinea a portion of the US$3 million in special resources earmarked for helping the twenty-five least developed countries.

BANKING AND CURRENCY

The Banking System

The Central Bank of the Republic of Guinea (Banque Centrale de la République de Guinée—BCRG) was established on March 1, 1960. In 1972 it was attached directly to the presidency, and President Touré took over as its governor. Before that, it had in principle operated as a semiautonomous institution, although some sources questioned its degree of freedom from executive control. The BCRG possessed the usual functions of a central bank: issuing currency, regulating the volume of credit, acting as banker for the government, and participating in the formulation of monetary and fiscal policies. Upon its founding, President Touré had stated that its fundamental role was to keep the volume of money in circulation constantly adjusted to the value of products on the domestic market—that is, to the aggregate supply of domestic and imported resources available. Taking over as governor of the bank in 1972, President Touré had denounced the previous governor for conspicuously failing in this assignment.

Four of the five French private commercial banks that had once operated in Guinea had their licenses revoked in August 1960; the fifth bank lost its license in January 1962, completing the nationalization of the banking system. The function of the commercial banks was exercised at first by the central bank through branches taken over from the private banks in the main towns of seventeen administrative regions. In 1961, however, three specialized banks for credit extension were created, and at latest report they were said to be performing the commercial bank function.

The banking system also includes a postal checking system and the National Savings Bank (Caisse Nationale d'Epargne—CNE). Credit expansion, however, has been the function of the central bank and the three specialized banks. The stabilization program of 1969 succeeded in limiting further expansion of credit. The increase in the overall money supply was also reduced to some extent, and such increase in money supply as did take place was in the volume of money in circulation outside the banking system. After the currency reform of 1972, therefore, regulations were introduced making it compulsory for government agencies and state enterprises to make more frequent deposits with the banking system and limiting withdrawals by individuals.

The specialized banks established in 1961 were the National Credit Institution for Trade, Industry, and Housing (Crédit National pour le Commerce, l'Industrie et l'Habitat), the National Bank for Agricultural Development (Banque Nationale de Développement Agricole), and the Guinean Bank for Foreign Trade (Banque Guinéenne du Commerce Extérieur). They based their credit expansion partly upon deposits made with them and partly upon borrowing from the central bank. The stabilization program caused deposits to level off after 1969, and thereafter the banks' lending was increasingly derived from drawing upon their balances at the central bank. Agricultural credit had made possible the acquisition of tractors on easy terms by private entrepreneurs; but credit to smallholders, which was extended by the cooperative system, had been severely limited since 1964. In general, credit to the private sector was relatively insignificant, reportedly constituting less than 5 percent of total credit. Credit to the government and state enterprises accounted for most credit expansion.

Currency

Until March 1, 1960, Guinea used the African Financial Community franc (Communauté Financière Africaine franc—CFAF), which was tied to the French franc at the rate of CFAF50 to one French franc, so that the exchange rate in United States dollars followed successive devaluations of the French franc. On March 1, 1960, the new Guinean franc was introduced. It was not tied to the French franc. In practice, however, its official value was kept at par with that of the CFAF, which was tied to the French franc. Thus on August 23, 1971, when the United States dollar was floated, the Guinean franc retained its value in terms of the French franc but was devalued in terms of the dollar. After the devaluation of the dollar in December 1971, however, Guinea realigned the dollar value of its currency so that it was devalued in terms of other currencies. On October 2, 1972, a new currency, the Guinean syli, was introduced, and ten Guinean francs were exchanged for one syli. The word *syli* means elephant in the Soussou language, and the qualities traditionally associated with the word were expected to convey an image of strength and solidarity to the new currency. One syli was divided into 100 cauris, named after the cowrie shells that were the main African medium of exchange in precolonial times.

Neither the Guinean franc nor the syli was usually accepted on foreign exchange markets. Within a few weeks after the introduction of the Guinean franc in March 1960, however, a parallel exchange market had developed in Conakry and in neighboring Freetown, Sierra Leone, and

Monrovia, Liberia, where foreign banknotes were traded at rates 60 percent above the official rate.

As it became increasingly impossible for Guineans to obtain foreign exchange at the official rate, or imported goods at corresponding prices, the smuggling of products out of the country had increased. They could either buy consumer goods in neighboring countries at prices much lower than at home or could convert the foreign exchange proceeds into Guinean currency on the parallel exchange market, giving earnings averaging ten times what they could have obtained for their produce at home. In this way Guinean currency was smuggled back into the country. The Conakry foreign exchange black market in the mid-1960s had an average daily volume of transactions of about GF2 million to GF3 million. After severe penalties for currency smugglers were introduced and border guards given orders that they could be summarily shot, the volume of transactions on the currency black market reportedly declined. Volume was also very low at times when the unofficial rate for foreign currency reached a peak.

An American source reported that, although the Guinean franc was officially at par with the CFAF in 1971, it was selling on the parallel market at a discount of 75 to 80 percent. This meant that the price of one United States dollar was averaging four or five times the 1960 rate, which was equivalent to a price rise of about 20 percent a year. Although the basic disparity between official and black-market exchange rates reflected disparities in price levels and purchasing power, fluctuations in the black-market rate sometimes took place primarily in response to political events or expectations.

Thus according to *Pick's Currency Yearbook*, the black-market rate of the United States dollar in 1965 averaged about six times the official rate. The black-market rate expressed as a multiple of the official rate then rose to 7.3 or more in March 1966 after the arrival of deposed Ghanaian leader Kwame Nkrumah in Conakry. Improved expectations for mining development brought it down to 5.5 by the end of March 1967 but, after fears of a possible coup d'etat had increased the hoarding of gold coins and foreign currency, it reached a new high of 8.0 to 12.0 in March 1969. It then declined steadily to about 7.0 to 7.5 in Conakry in March 1970. In the fall of 1970 it began to increase again under the impact of mounting shortages, rising prices for smuggled goods on the internal market, increasing corruption on all levels, and higher rates for bribing officials. In Conakry the black-market rate rose to ten times the official rate, but at that price there were few buyers and few transactions. This was also true when the rate rose to a similar level during the purges of 1971. Severe penalties had also reduced the volume of trading.

Despite increased enforcement of monetary controls, the value of the currency did not improve very much after the introduction of the syli in October 1972. By November 1972 the black-market rate was 8.7 times the official rate, but turnover was low. During 1973 there were very limited dealings, seldom exceeding US$1,000 to US$1,500 a day. Black-market rates fluctuated between wide extremes.

CHAPTER 11

AGRICULTURE

Despite Guinea's fifteen years of emphasis on industrialization or collective effort, it remains a predominantly agricultural economy of small independent family cultivators. About 83 percent of the active population is thought to be engaged in rural activities: cultivation, herding, forestry, or fishing. Production of most food and export crops declined after independence and by 1968 had not regained the 1958 level. Despite its agricultural base and favorable natural conditions giving it the potential capacity to be more than self-sufficient in food and agricultural raw materials, the country was unable to feed its growing urban population, which had become largely dependent on rice imports. In 1974 the problem of urban food supply had become increasingly critical.

The year 1974 was one of widespread famine in Africa; but the worst that most published reports had to say of Guinea's rural cultivators was that many had returned to a subsistence scale of existence because of the lack of incentive to produce a surplus for cash sale or exchange. In fact, as in other African countries, most of the cultivators had probably never departed from a subsistence way of life. Travelers returning from Guinea in 1974 reported localized famine in the arid northeast, where droughts alternated with destructive floods in the Upper Niger plains. Despite roughly three years of poor rainfall, however, the nationwide effects of the drought had been mild compared to conditions in some other West African countries.

Since independence the country had changed from a net exporter to a net importer of food. This trend was not uncommon in African countries since independence, as the number of Africans in government service and other urban activities had increased. Neighboring Senegal, for example, had also been unable to produce a rice surplus to feed its urban population and even in years of favorable climate had been obliged to spend the equivalent of US$25 million for rice imports. In Guinea's case, however, the problem had been compounded by stagnating production of both food crops and foreign-exchange-earning export crops, by the disruption of the distribution system, and by rapid inflation and loss of confidence in the currency (see ch. 10). Much of the food produced was smuggled out of the country or sold at exorbitant prices on the black market. In Conakry food and certain other supplies were rationed. In 1974 the majority of low-income Conakry families were said to be getting rice, their usual staple food, only once every two or three days and meat only once every three months.

A study by the Food and Agriculture Organization (FAO) of the United Nations (UN) concluded that in the twenty years from 1952 through 1972 Guinea's food production had grown at an average rate of 2 percent a year while its demand was growing at 3.4 percent a year. Average dietary energy supply for the country as a whole was consequently thought to be only about 88 percent of that required in 1972 (see ch. 6).

At the third national economic conference in December 1973, President Ahmed Sékou Touré declared that, despite excellent climatic conditions, the country's agriculture was lagging badly, necessitating annual food grain imports of around 60,000 tons, at a cost in foreign exchange equivalent to US$14 million. The subsequent rise in world market prices for rice increased the cost in Guinean currency of the same quantity of rice in 1974 and was expected to double or triple its cost in the reporting year ending September 30, 1975.

The president said that, although since independence the government had imported some 2,500 tractors and tens of thousands of oxplows, there was a shortage of food in most of the country's administrative regions, including those formerly regarded as the great rice granaries of West Africa. The owners of the tractors, he said, were currently using them to tow wagonloads of passengers rather than for agriculture. The shortages obliged many workers to leave their work to search for food, and the workers were obliged to pay exorbitant prices because, as the saying goes, to an empty stomach all commodities are beyond price.

The president promised that under the new Five Year Development Plan (1973–78) there would be renewed efforts to increase domestic food production, particularly of rice. Each owner of a tractor should be required to use it for production and to deliver to the government some twenty tons of white rice a year. Twenty tons multiplied by 2,500 tractors should supply 50,000 tons of rice to replace imports. The wording of this formula suggested increased reliance on the so-called tractor bourgeoisie of private entrepreneurs, denounced by official ruling party ideology, in place of the reliance on collectivization attested by party resolutions.

In subsequent speeches, however, the president suggested that many of the nation's tractors would be owned, or at least used, by the local production brigades that were a prominent feature of party policy statements. The president also promised continuing emphasis on improving production by turning out more graduate farmers from secondary schools.

In his December 1973 speech the president had blamed the food shortage largely on private traders, alleging that more was actually being produced than formerly but that it was being smuggled out of the country. He declared that in future the traders would be circumvented by organizing direct links between producer and consumer. In mid-1974 thousands of passports were nonetheless issued to private traders to buy food in neighboring countries to relieve the critical shortage in Conakry. Then in early 1975 President Touré announced that henceforth all private trade would be abolished and farmers would be obliged to pay their taxes in produce rather than in money. In this way he hoped that the government would be able effectively to carry out its proclaimed role as direct link between producer and consumer.

TRADITIONAL TENURE AND CULTIVATION PRACTICES

Because of the prevailing dearth of economic information emanating from Guinea, the evolution of traditional tenure and cultivation practices since independence has been reported in a rather detailed anthropological or sociological context rather than in terms of its effect in retarding economic development (see ch. 4; ch. 5; ch. 6). Guinea shares many of the problems that have arisen from resistance to change in other African countries with somewhat similar traditions. In some instances the severity of such problems has been mitigated by Guinea's less arid climate. The Peul herders of Guinea, for example, no longer have a nomadic tradition like their counterparts in countries with less rainfall and surface water. Cultivators and stockraisers are the same individuals or families, whereas elsewhere there is often fierce hostility between them.

In Guinea, as in much of Africa, many groups at the beginning of the colonial era practiced shifting cultivation, in which villages might be moved from time to time to a new area of uncleared land. This practice soon gave way to bush fallow, in which fields within reach of the permanent village were rotated. Without manuring, much of the land could be cultivated for five years at most before being exhausted and then required a longer period under fallow. The average cultivating family thus required from five to six times as much land as was kept under actual cultivation.

By independence most land was under secondary vegetation cover (see ch. 3). Bush fallow, with its long years of fallow and consequent high land requirement, has progressively given way to more continuous cultivation of the plots nearest the village. In a few areas of population pressure on the land, fallow has been progressively reduced, and the outlying fields may be largely devoted to monoculture of a single dryland (rain-fed) food grain, resulting in rapid exhaustion of the soils. It appears, however, that problems of population pressure and monoculture have been less severe in Guinea than in many countries of Africa. The progressive exhaustion of the country's soils must thus be attributed primarily to other causes, notably to neglect of conservation practices (see ch. 3).

Some Guinean peoples practice cultivation techniques that are relatively advanced by African standards. Peoples along the coast and in the Forest Region, for example, grow inundated swamp rice by transplanting seedlings from nursery seedbeds. Elsewhere, however, dryland rice is grown by destructive burning of brush or grassland and

237

wasteful broadcast sowing, and yields are low. At independence animal traction was being used in some areas where grazing was available but, for the most part, time-honored cultivation methods employing such rudimentary implements as the short-handled hoe were apparently still used by the overwhelming majority of cultivating families in the late 1960s. These methods permitted the cultivation of only about one acre for each active family member, not counting land devoted to fallow or to such semicultivated products as coffee and oil palm. Compounds worked by the extended family had given way to holdings cultivated by the nuclear family, often polygynous (see ch. 5).

With the short-handled hoe, soils could be cultivated to a depth of only a few inches. Where animal or green manure was available, it would usually be used on the plots nearest the village, which were kept in most continuous cultivation. Since 1964 credit or advances against the harvest from the village cooperatives had been severely limited, and foreign exchange had been lacking for the import of fertilizers to be distributed to village producers. Some pesticides had been distributed at intervals but had been used primarily on commercial crops. There was little published evidence that traditional methods had been altered since independence by the distribution of improved seed or other supplies. There was no mention of any introduction of crop rotation sequences or other soil-improvement measures.

It appeared that in a number of regions cultivating families were still employing the traditional slash-and-burn system of clearing and cultivating, in which wood ash was used temporarily to enrich the soil but in which burning impacted and impoverished the soils over the long term. There were many variations of slash-and-burn techniques, but all required careful timing to clear and burn the brush at the end of the dry season, just before the rains arrived. The secondary regrowth of brush was cleared with a long machete. Any trees remaining might be felled, but the stumps were usually left standing. The brush was assembled into piles and burned to create ash gardens for planting. This technique was more intricate than the simple firing of brush or grassland that was still practiced in defiance of restrictions in some localities.

Most of the routine tasks of cultivation were performed by the women and children (see ch. 6). Men did the heavy clearing of new fields and usually had charge of cash crops, most of which were products of semicultivation absorbing only a few days of labor each year. The kitchen gardens surrounding the village dwellings usually contained a variety of intermingled crops for home use, including chilies, other spices, tomatoes, beans, and other vegetables, and often tobacco, sugarcane, and cotton. Groundnuts (peanuts), maize (corn), and such tubers as taro and sweet potatoes might be grown in the kitchen garden or in the outlying fields. Mangoes, citrus fruits, bananas, pineapples, and a variety of other fruits were grown. Most outlying fields were devoted to the country's major staple food crops: rice, cassava, maize, millet or sorghum, and fonio (a species of North African crabgrass with seeds that are used as a kind of tasty but nutritionally inferior millet). A number of these staple crops were grown in most of the country's administrative regions, although their relative importance might vary (see Crop Production, this ch.). In the 1970s one source indicated that maize was being grown predominantly in Lower Guinea and on the savannas of Upper Guinea and that millets were grown predominantly on the Fouta Djallon.

The principal modification in customary land tenure practices since independence has been that the power of reallocating vacated land resides with the local political party committees rather than with the traditional lineage heads or chiefs. Families retain their customary land use rights, however, and the proportion of collectivized land is not much greater than in previous times. Where land is in ample supply, the introduction of the tractor has permitted the clearing and cultivation of much larger holdings than formerly, but these are largely exploited by the new tractor bourgeoisie and have not modified the customary pattern of tenure in the average village.

Legal title to all land belongs to the state. The government is thus entitled to take over neglected land. The government does not suffer from a shortage of land, however, but from the lack of means to attain adequate yields on the land that it inherited from the French administration at independence. Consequently the law has been allowed to remain unenforced throughout much of the country.

At the beginning of the colonial era, the French had proclaimed that vacant and ownerless lands were state property. In fact, however, no land was without a claimant group. It might appear to be vacant because under the practice of bush fallowing a few years' cultivation might be followed by years of fallow in which the land reverted to bush. In temporarily leaving a clearing, however, a lineage did not relinquish its claim to it.

Most of the village fields allocated to the chiefs or commandants under the French administration were collectivized at independence, and the large units reverted to the region or the nation. The Guinean government also reasserted state ownership of neglected land, regarded not as vacant but as insufficiently improved. The criterion was to be that any land not cultivated or otherwise improved over a period of three years either must be improved within a further period of six months or could revert to the state. In practice the law has been used to acquire land already subject to modern tenure rather than to interfere with traditional tenure practices.

Traditional land tenure systems in the country vary in detail from group to group. All were founded upon the communal usufructuary principle, by which rights to use land pertained to the individual family but disposal rights were held by the group (originally the lineage, now the local party committee) and exercised by lineage elders or by other traditional authorities, chiefs, or community leaders. Tenure practices among the Peul of the Fouta Djallon were formerly more hierarchical than in the rest of the country (see ch. 5). Former serf peoples derived their cultivation rights from their masters. Although these conditions were changed at independence, full recognition of the change has taken time.

Elsewhere a family first clearing a piece of land was presumed to have acquired land use rights for itself and its descendants. The rights might descend in a family in a manner resembling inheritance, except that it did not convey the right to sell or otherwise dispose of the land (see ch. 5). If a field were not used or retained for fallow, the rights would lapse and could be reassigned by the elder or chief. Kin absent for long periods would retain their rights.

Where land was abundant, chiefs or other local notables with access to labor could afford to clear and cultivate more land and thus maintain larger holdings, although before independence it was reportedly uncommon for a traditional holding to exceed twenty acres. With a tractor an entrepreneur of the 1960s not only was able to clear and plow more land but must have a holding in excess of twenty acres if use of the tractor were to be economically justified. Because unused land held by the government was subject to the same usufructuary principle as land held by a traditional group, some large holdings were thus acquired.

Where population pressure on available land was greater, tenure would usually be more egalitarian because tradition imposed a moral obligation to provide each family with the use of enough land for subsistence. This meant that in most areas of the country in 1975 landholdings still conformed to the customary pattern of small-scale family tenure.

AGRICULTURAL DEVELOPMENT POLICIES

Under successive national development plans agriculture had been given high priority in principle but received a relatively low share of actual spending: 11 percent under the Three Year Development Plan (1960–63), 7 percent under the Seven Year Plan (1964–71), and a proposed 5 percent under the Five Year Development Plan (1973–78). This dearth of funds was only one of the many setbacks encountered by the government's proclaimed rural development policies.

The agricultural policy formulated at independence advocated a gradual transformation of rural society to permit eventual collectivization of crop and livestock production in community collective farms on the Soviet model. The transitional phase of transformation was to take place through the creation of cooperative structures at the level of the village and the administrative region, supplemented by state farms and other national institutions.

The initial effort to perfect these cooperative structures under the three-year plan had more or less foundered by 1964. In addition to the usual problems of indifference or resistance among traditional village cultivators, it had encountered serious difficulties resulting from lack of funds. In December 1965 a new campaign to promote cooperatives was launched, but it suffered the same drawbacks. By 1968 a number of administrative regions no longer had any rural cooperatives, and those cooperative structures that had been achieved were seldom fulfilling the government's original intentions. Since the late 1960s the policymakers have accordingly put less emphasis upon the village cooperative as the prime mover in the process of gradual collectivization. Nevertheless, the organization of rural producers into cooperatives remains an intermediate objective of government policy that is frequently mentioned in public statements.

The aspect of agricultural policy statements being stressed in 1974 was that affirmed at the eighth ruling party congress in 1967. It had declared 1968 the year of the cultural revolution—a revolution apparently modeled on that of the People's Republic of China (PRC). It placed primary emphasis on the production brigades of peasants and militia to be organized by the Local Revolutionary Power (Pouvoir Révolutionnaire Local—PRL), consisting of a village or group of villages, and on the role of future graduates of the local Center of Revolutionary Education (Centre d'Education Révolutionnaire—CER). The concept of the CER had been introduced in 1966 (see ch. 7). Perhaps coincidentally, the centers appeared to incorporate some of the ideas of the renowned French specialist on agricultural development René Dumont, who had reportedly served as a consultant to the Guinean government until 1962. They were intended to teach modern agricultural methods but also to promote the transformation of rural social attitudes that the cooperatives had failed to achieve. Their graduates were to form the nucleus of future village cooperatives.

In principle every school, rural or urban, soon became a CER or a potential one, and the terms *CER* and *school* were sometimes used interchangeably. Some of these revolutionary education centers were actively engaged in production in order to provide practical as well as theoretical training to their students. In 1972 it was officially reported that some 8,000 trained students from revolutionary education centers were available to form cooperatives. An unofficial report claimed that the schools had a total of 13,343 students engaged in farming 2,564 acres.

The formation of production brigades modeled on those of the PRC had also been called for by the eighth party congress of 1967. The production brigade was officially described as "a kind of embryo cooperative." Two kinds of brigade were called for: one to be formed at the local level by the PRL for the production of food crops; and the other to be formed by the government at the national level, recruiting party militants to work on state farms or collective fields in the production of export or industrial crops. In 1974 the government daily newspaper, *Horoya*, contained glowing accounts of the operations of some production brigades of the latter type on collective fields near Conakry.

These brigades were, in theory, to be entrusted with the achievement of prescribed Soviet-style production norms. Since 1963, during the period of village cooperative programs, each administrative region had been assigned certain norms to be attained: so many tons of rice, so many acres to be cultivated by tractor, so many by oxplow, and so many by hoe. Most reports indicated that, if these goals were ever fulfilled, it was not by the means prescribed.

In early 1975 President Touré announced that the goal was to form local production brigades in every locality and to equip them with tractors. Each would eventually have an agronomist and an equipment operator. Such brigades would be created to produce rice, groundnuts, and cassava. Simultaneously, he announced the creation of a new government economic institution to be known as the Regional Council of the Revolution (Conseil Régional de la Révolution), which would be responsible for studying agricultural problems at the regional level.

It was not clear to what extent participation in the production brigades was voluntary (see ch. 10). In the early years of independence, from 1959 through 1961, the national appeal for voluntary labor, known as "human investment," had been fairly successful. The total value of the human investment contributed on such projects in the years 1959 through 1963 was estimated by one observer at the equivalent of GF3 billion (for value of the Guinean franc—see Glossary). After 1961, however, there had been a progressive diminution of interest and participation in human investment projects. For ideological reasons and because of a critical lack of public revenues for development purposes, human investment remained, in official theory, a major resource of agricultural development policy. In the inflationary conditions prevailing, market incentives to the production of cash crops were ineffective. There was consequently considerable pressure on the local or regional authorities responsible for meeting production norms and a continuing danger that overzealous functionaries might make the human investment program in some localities resemble the forced labor conscription that was one of the worst memories of the early colonial period (see ch. 2).

One authoritative source reported that, where such abuses of the human investment program did occur in the early years of independence, they met with popular resistance and brought prompt intervention by the highest government authorities to correct abuses. This source was the prominent French communist leader Jean Suret-Canale, renowned for his history of French colonial policy. His book on Guinea gives the most comprehensive discussion of agricultural policy to 1968.

Contributions of voluntary labor had come up to expectations primarily in local public works projects of evident immediate benefit to the village population, as in the construction of roads, schools, dispensaries, or mosques. Local projects whose benefits were less apparent, such as conservation works and reforestation, inspired little enthusiasm. There was also only marginal interest in projects at the regional level.

Voluntary labor for the cultivation of collective fields also failed to meet expectations.

At last report, in 1968, there were numerous collective fields that had been established since independence at the level of the village, the *arrondissement* (district), and the administrative region. At the village level, however, small individual family holdings under traditional forms of land tenure remained the rule and received almost all of the available labor. In comparison to individual or family holdings, collective fields were of marginal significance in area and, above all, in yield. Yields tended to be exceptionally low on the collective fields because they received only such marginal attention as the peasants could spare from the family holdings that were their primary concern.

The village collective fields were for the most part the same acres previously set apart for the benefit of the local chief or the French commandant. At independence these had usually been spontaneously confiscated by the villagers, to be cultivated in future for the benefit of the community or nation. The proceeds of the crop accrued to the local committee. As had been their custom in the past, the villagers were willing to contribute a few days of labor each season to cultivating the collective village fields; but they expected the proceeds to be used for such customary purposes as ceremonial feasts or the entertainment of visitors. Ruling party directives, on the contrary, favored using the collective fields for the production of cash crops to meet the official norms for export or for delivery to the processing industries, which were critically short of raw materials. When cultivation of such crops was involved, the villagers were inclined to lose interest in contributing their labor. The need for such crops was not immediately apparent to them, and incentives for earning cash were lacking. The disincentive was even greater where the functionaries in charge were distrusted and suspected of diverting the proceeds to their own profit or that of their kin.

At the regional or national level, collective fields had been created primarily by nationalizing the research stations or demonstration farms established by the French or by taking over the former cantonal plantations. In the Forest Region such plantations were primarily devoted to coffee growing. In Upper Guinea they were used for experiments in cotton growing, around Koundara for groundnuts, and around Mamou for tomatoes and later for other vegetables. The human investment program was used to recruit labor.

Problems of Market Incentive

Despite repeated government campaigns to stimulate the production of various cash crops, agricultural production for the market apparently still constitutes a relatively minor share of activity in most rural areas. To some extent this problem is one shared by many emerging African countries. Like Guinea, most African governments have an official monopoly of the collection of crops for urban markets, for export, or for delivery to the processing industries. Almost all, like Guinea, set official producer prices for all marketed crops and skim off a sizable share of export earnings for the government coffers in the form of export taxes or stabilization fund reserves, usually both. When export production costs are higher than world market prices, as has often been the case in Guinea, the stabilization fund must cover transport and other intermediate costs or subsidize the producer. The Guinean government, however, had collected taxes on crops and livestock for local market or for export until they were suspended in 1974 in an effort to alleviate the food shortage.

One foreign observer concluded in early 1975 that Africa's potential for producing food had been seriously underestimated and that at the root of many African countries' food shortages were lack of storage capacity, poor transport facilities, inadequate producer price incentives, and disorganized marketing. This may be particularly true of Guinea, where the poor condition of rural roads was a noteworthy bottleneck in food supply and the marketing system was exceptionally disorganized. Some press reports also indicated in 1974 that few berths were available in Conakry port and that loading equipment had been allowed to deteriorate. As a result fewer ships were making regular calls, and bananas and other export crops sometimes rotted on the docks. Food imports were also arriving less regularly.

Most emerging African governments have had occasional or chronic difficulties whenever the official producer price failed to offer adequate incentive for cash crop production to cultivators who share a traditional bias in favor of subsistence crop production. Senegal, for example, experienced a "groundnut crisis" in the late 1960s when the official producer price was set too low, and disgruntled peasants retreated to growing food grains for their own subsistence, severely reducing industrial oil mill activity and export earnings. There have been many parallels to this experience in Guinea.

The dominant factor distinguishing Guinea's problems in degree or in kind from the similar setbacks encountered by other African countries has been the virtual destruction of price and market incentives owing to its exceptionally rapid rate of inflation. There appears to be little public confidence in the country's currency, which has been unconvertible since Guinea cut adrift in 1960 from the monetary discipline and support of the franc area (see Glossary). Guinea's approach to economic policy has also had a more Marxist orientation than that of most African countries, so that the operation of profit incentives is in any case viewed with some ideological disfavor. Moreover, as Suret-Canale has pointed out, the prevailing inflationary conditions have made successful reliance on voluntary smallholder production for the official market virtually impossible.

In Guinea incentives to cash production by smallholders have been destroyed not only by the gap, much greater than in other countries, between agricultural producer prices and the prices of imports and other consumer goods but also by the frequent total lack of consumer goods for which the cash earned might be spent. The lack of a convertible currency and the dearth of foreign exchange earnings restricted official imports. Available consumer goods were drawn to the black market at prices too high for any but the elite to afford (see ch. 6). In order to buy a piece of soap or a length of cloth, a cultivator might have to smuggle his produce across the border for exchange in Sierra Leone or Senegal.

Smuggling and other forms of traditional trade that evade official channels have long been endemic throughout Africa, where the frontiers arbitrarily determined by the former colonial powers remain meaningless to many rural inhabitants. There are few African countries that have failed to encounter some degree of resistance to the official collection of crops or livestock. Inadequate deliveries of raw material to the textile or food-processing industries have also been a common problem almost everywhere, particularly for livestock deliveries. Herders are accustomed to crossing borders freely and share the traditional attitudes that place a high value on continuing ownership of cattle as a source of status and ceremonial exchange and as the ultimate safeguard against famine. The size of herds, rather than productivity, is valued. Such animals as the herders are willing to sell will be sold where the price is best or when the animals are most short of grazing and therefore in poorest condition.

Distrust of the officials charged with the collection of crops or livestock is also fairly common among African peasants. Such suspicions are likely to be a particularly strong disincentive to cash production, however, where a flourishing black market exists as it does in Guinea. President Touré has publicly denounced some regional authorities for fostering a large-scale smuggling trade in requisitioned crops and livestock across the borders in full view of helpless peasants. The impact of political disaffection on agricultural production in Guinea might be difficult to quantify, but it is thought to be appreciable. Large numbers of herders and cultivators and their families have left the country. The total number of Guineans in exile is estimated at between 600,000 and 1 million (see ch. 8). Cultivating families abandon their holdings; herders take their livestock with them, depleting the national herd. According to one source, emigration of herders from Guinea has been responsible for the creation of the stockraising industry of neighboring Sierra Leone.

Policy Measures of the 1960s

Details of the problems encountered by the government's initial agricultural campaign, which ran out of funds and enthusiasm toward the mid-1960s, have been fairly well documented in published sources, most notably by Suret-Canale. Little information is available, however, on the details or on the progress of subsequent initiatives in the agricultural sector. The fact that very similar initiatives have had to be relaunched at frequent intervals suggests that by the mid-1970s little progress had been made in getting under way even on the transitional stage of cooperative organization, much less on the ultimate goal of collectivization of agriculture. The few reports available also suggested that the years since 1964 had witnessed a repetition or acceleration of the trends already observed in the years immediately after independence. An understanding of these trends may consequently not be without relevance to interpretation of developments in Guinean agriculture in the 1970s.

In the three successive development plans launched since independence, spending on agriculture has always been accorded high priority in principle, but in practice the limited funds available have for the most part been absorbed by other sectors of activity. The 1960-63 plan had theoretically allocated for agricultural development some GF10 billion, but GF4.4 billion was actually absorbed by agriculture during the plan period. Guinea's planners, like those of many other African countries at the same period, had probably calculated the money equivalent of "human investment" in local projects as an important share of anticipated contributions to the plan in the sector of agriculture.

The thrust of the plan was for an intensified national reorientation of the agricultural institutions created by the French colonial administration at three geographic levels: national, regional, and local. Its target for 1963 was to have established seven state farms and sixteen other national production centers at the level of the French experimental centers and research stations; rural modernization centers in each of twenty-eight of the administrative regions from the somewhat similar bodies previously established by the French; and 500 village producers' cooperatives to replace the rather cumbersome French rural development societies.

The GF3.1 billion allocated under the plan for the Soviet-sponsored state farm in the Fié Valley (Siguiri Administrative Region) proved inadequate, and the project was abandoned while barely beyond the planning stage. Apparently funds have since been lacking for the revival of state farms. Even the national experimental and demonstration centers maintained by the French before independence for research in plant breeding and plant diseases have largely run down for lack of financing, although a few are maintained as production collectives.

The rural modernization centers in each administrative region had been established in August 1960. They received funds from the central government to provide services, supplies, and rental tractors to the village cooperatives. They also maintained collective fields at the regional level and collected the proceeds. In the general decentralization of government enterprises at the end of 1961, the rural modernization centers were turned over to the regional administrations, and without central government financing they had collapsed by the end of 1962.

The village cooperatives, most of which had been formally created in order to qualify for the credits and services supplied by the modernization centers, lost their principal advantage in the eyes of the cultivators when the centers were dissolved. The cooperatives had numbered some 472 in

1962 but reportedly involved only about 4 percent of the country's cultivators. By 1964 their number had been reduced to 268, many of them probably inactive.

The decentralization move of 1962 had been followed by a short-lived relaxation of government control over trading in 1963 and 1964 (see ch. 12). During this period a large number of African entrepreneurs acquired trading licenses that were subsequently revoked when the *loi-cadre* (enabling act) of November 1964 put an end to the brief experiment with private trading. This period saw the growth of a new class that has been dubbed the tractor bourgeoisie. Salaried officials and veterans with cash from pensions, among others, were able to take advantage of the dissolution of the rural modernization centers at the end of 1962 to acquire tractors that were beyond the reach of the average cultivator. Tractors were an important advantage in preparing large areas of plain for inundated ricegrowing (see Crop Production, this ch.). The move to cultivation of large holdings with tractors and hired labor was swelled by traders who lost their licenses after November 1964 and was further stimulated after 1966 when the government launched a new rice campaign and removed the price control on rice, making large-scale cultivation a profitable undertaking on the coastal plains and on the savanna lands of Upper Guinea.

The tractor bourgeoisie may have been able to make a profit despite inflation by acting as traders on the side and because they were better situated than smallholders to evade the official collecting and marketing system. The failure of the price improvements after 1966 to elicit market production from smallholders suggests, however, that the rate of inflation had canceled out any improvement that might have been effected in the unproductive cultivation methods of the average smallholder, who was consequently unable to realize a cash surplus at the official producer prices. The system may thus be to some extent self-defeating in that it succeeded in providing an incentive only to the capitalist, that is, to anyone with the advantage of a moderate cash surplus to invest in larger landholdings and a down payment on a tractor or in other improvements that could enable him to realize a return either at the official price or on the black market.

By 1967 this class of farmers, weekend or seasonal farmers, and absentee entrepreneurs had grown enough to inspire a resolution by the eighth ruling party congress at Kankan to adopt any means to prevent the growth of a class of agricultural exploiters in the rural areas. The curious wording of President Touré's speech at the third national economic conference in December 1973, however, suggested that the government had come to accept the fact of private ownership of tractors and to rely upon this class of producers to furnish the surplus for cash sale that could not be elicited from the smallholders or village collectives.

Rural traditions common to most African peoples may also have operated to make the average village producer less interested in the prospect of cash or profit. There were exceptions among some villagers who took advantage of the cooperatives to increase their holdings or otherwise to improve their position. Moreover, trading traditions, which imply familiarity with profit motives and cash transactions, are long established among most of the country's ethnic groups (see ch. 4). The conditions of the 1960s had also caused part-time traders to proliferate among all elements of the population (see ch. 12). In many cases, however, the only resource available for investment by the average smallholding family was additional effort. Most clearly found it advantageous to invest their effort first in their own food crops and thereafter in the numerous other subsistence activities, ranging from fishing to fetching water, that rural life requires and to the social, ceremonial, or apparent leisure activities that rank high on the traditional scale of values.

The 1960–63 three-year plan in fact had to be extended over four years, from July 1960 to April 1964. The subsequent Seven Year Plan (1964–71) was launched in May 1964. The setbacks experienced under the three-year plan and the agricultural policies to be pursued under the Seven Year Plan had been discussed at the sixth ruling party congress in December 1962. The party acknowledged that the operation of the village cooperatives had not succeeded in providing the rural cultivator with a return corresponding to his labor. It resolved that under the Seven Year Plan the villages should proceed directly to the collective stage of production. By the end of the plan 500 village units were to be created and to be known as autonomous units of agricultural production. It was not clear in what way, if any, these units would differ from the 500 village cooperatives that had been the target of the previous plan.

A subsequent economic conference at Kindia in December 1965 relaunched the campaign for cooperatives, which were to unite the previously separate concepts of producer and consumer cooperatives, enabling the cultivators to exchange their crop surplus for consumer goods at advantageous prices. A few experimental units were successful, but they were later succeeded by the production brigades. The barter system was theoretically still in effect in 1974, but few units were functioning as intended. Consumer goods were difficult to obtain at all through official channels, much less at advantageous prices. The official producer prices offered for the crops collected were generally inadequate.

The transitional stage of organization into cooperatives had been intended not only as a step in the direction of socialization but perhaps more immediately as a means of preventing the emergence of a capitalist element in rural society. In this it was conspicuously unsuccessful at the regional level. Even before the dissolution of the regional modernization centers in 1962—which in some cases may have been hastened by local notables anxious to take over their assets—some of those in authority had used the tractors received to clear large areas of land for themselves or for a few notables of the district.

At the village level the cooperatives also inspired in some peasants a desire to take advantage of the supplies and credits offered to expand their own family holdings or to exploit borrowed or rented land. This apparent florescence of economic individualism may often have been fostered by the pressure of traditional obligations to the family or kinship group. Suret-Canale, for example, suggests that even the most honest party functionary or local government official may remain vulnerable to the traditional value structure requiring that he put the interests of his kin before the scrupulous observance of new and unfamiliar regulations or ideological imperatives.

Like Guinea, many other newly independent African governments had also proclaimed that an agricultural structure based upon village cooperatives was in the common African tradition of mutual aid and cooperative effort at the village level. As the cooperative movement in Africa has suffered repeated setbacks in the years since independence, however, many observers have pointed out that traditional cooperatives and mutual assistance followed the network of kinship ties (see ch. 5). As village settlements have expanded beyond the bounds of kinship, this tradition may often come into direct conflict with the new demands for community solidarity and thus may tend to undermine rather than to support the effective functioning of village cooperatives.

Food imports from the United States had been particularly high from 1963 through 1966, when the United States was supplying substantial aid in the form of rice, wheat, and edible oils. Perhaps coincidentally, official pronouncements concerning agriculture during these years tended to emphasize the ideological concern for the transformation of village social structure and the dangers of excessive dependence on food imports from a foreign power. Although later resumed in the 1970s, Food for Peace shipments had been reduced when the United States Congress sharply cut back the United States fiscal year (FY) 1967 program of bilateral aid to foreign countries. In Guinea the year ending September 30, 1969, was officially proclaimed the year of agriculture, and President Touré declared that agriculture must henceforth be the cornerstone of the nation's development strategy. This proved largely to translate, however, into new calls for cultivators and party militants to increase their contribution and effort. There is little evidence that government spending on agriculture was materially increased.

The eighth party congress had been preceded by a call for public discussion, in the course of which a cabinet minister published in the government-sponsored newspaper *Horoya* a series of criticisms of the functioning of government economic institutions. The editions were seized, and the minister was subsequently arrested and hanged. He had alleged, among other things, that tremendous waste and inefficient distribution had accompanied government expenditure on **agriculture**. He cited tons of fertilizer left to deteriorate on the docks, seeds and tractors routinely distributed to regions where they could not be grown or used, and mountains of agricultural equipment rusting in the suburbs of Conakry or lying useless in the rural areas for lack of parts, fuel, and maintenance. According to the minister, tractors imported in the early years of independence had been unsuitable for the climate and terrain.

In addition he declared that the politicians and administrators responsible for organizing cooperative production had taken the greatest pains in improving their own personal holdings, often with equipment and material furnished by the government and labor paid for by the government. The minister charged that, far from encouraging the small-scale producers who were their official responsibility, however, these officials more often discouraged the producers and thus allowed the nation's agriculture to go under. With regard to the production norms assigned by the government to each administrative region, he asserted that many regional authorities announced in radiobroadcasts that they had developed thousands of acres of the designated crops and then two or three months after the harvest sent the government an appeal for emergency supplies of those same crops to feed the local population.

Funds for agricultural development proved even scarcer during the period of the 1964–71 plan than under the preceding plan. High theoretical priority was again assigned to agriculture, and a series of crop campaigns was launched for production of rice, bananas, and other crops. There was an unsuccessful cotton campaign and a coffee campaign that did muster financing for an effective fight against disease and for the distribution of new plants. In 1967 progress on the plan had to be suspended for six months because the treasury was exhausted. The plan period concluded amid a profound silence on the subject, and it was not until October 1973 that the new Five Year Development Plan (1973–78) could be launched.

Under the five-year plan only 5 percent of planned expenditure was to go for agriculture, compared to 11 percent under the three-year plan and 7 percent under the Seven Year Plan. Absolute expenditure should be greater under the five-year plan, however, as far more financing was expected to be available than for previous plans. In agriculture the chief emphasis was to be on rice production to replace imports. Teams of agronomists sent by the Chinese Communists were being brought in to supervise projects for the growing of rice and other food crops and were also running a sugar complex at Koba on the Boffa plain. For the most part, however, it appeared that the targets set for agriculture were to be achieved largely by the voluntary effort of the producers. It is significant that a number of these crop targets for 1978—including those for rice, maize, millet, bananas, pineapples, and livestock—were lower than the targets initially set for 1963 under the three-year plan.

CROP PRODUCTION

In Guinea, as in much of Africa, the level of subsistence production is unknown and can only be estimated. Presumably some record was kept of actual crop exports, but published estimates of agricultural production nonetheless varied widely. Such estimates were published abroad; the Guinean government did not publish regular agricultural statistics. Several published indexes of total agricultural production or food production showed a steady upward progression that suggested routine extrapolation.

Published estimates of production for specific crops generally did not reflect the setbacks in crop production and livestock numbers that were reported by many foreign observers and periodically deplored by Guinean government spokesmen or ruling party congresses. For example, a 1971 work presenting Guinea as an example of progressive development stated that in scarcely any area of agricultural production had it been possible to regain the 1957 level of output. A ruling party economic conference in May 1966 confirmed that rice production had declined steadily since 1957 while the population had been increasing.

Intermittent press reports based upon official Guinean estimates indicated that the government had succeeded in increasing production substantially in 1965 but that poor weather had again reduced the harvest in 1966 and that it had not recovered until 1969. Rice output was then reported to have risen between 1969 and 1971, partly because of a number of foreign aid projects for the reclamation of polder land in the coastal swamps. In 1972, however, production was affected by the drought.

According to the official interpretation the growing food shortage resulted from the fact that population had been increasing more rapidly than production rather than from declining production. This favorable view was reflected in production estimates for Guinea published by the UN Economic Commission for Africa (ECA) and by the United States Department of Agriculture (USDA), which indicated that production of rice and of a number of other crops had been maintained or increased since the mid-1960s.

In an October 1972 speech President Touré reportedly declared that production had been dropping steadily year by year. Reports of the president's speeches published abroad, however, are not always reliable. Neither are some of the statistics of agricultural production to be found in foreign publications. It may be safest, in view of the almost universal reports of declining production, to base calculations upon the series showing the lowest production levels. These data may be regarded as showing the maximum decline in production between 1964 and 1972 (see table 7).

The range of statistical disagreement can readily be measured by comparing these data with the higher ECA figures giving production of paddy (unpolished) rice as 300,000 tons in 1965 and 420,000 tons in 1972.

USDA estimates showed an average production of 308,000 tons of paddy between 1957 and 1959, 355,000 tons in 1964, and 400,000 tons in 1970. Similarly, one set of figures released by Guinean government sources estimated the country's livestock herd in 1973 at about 1.35 million cattle, 589,000 sheep, and 200,000 pigs. Annual consumption was estimated at 10 percent of the herd.

No definitions were given in any of the statistical series on Guinean crops or livestock, but presumably they excluded the large volume of smuggled exports of such crops as coffee, and no doubt they were intended to include an estimate of the unknown volume of subsistence production. The reduction shown in numbers of livestock remaining was attributed primarily to smuggling or to the emigration of herders with their stock as well as to slaughter quotas imposed by government collectors.

Rice and Other Food Crops

Although the people were periodically exhorted to increase their consumption of staple food crops other than rice, the government's efforts to improve domestic food supply were concentrated upon ricegrowing. After a period of neglect in the early 1960s, when attention was concentrated on industrial crops and installations in the ricefields were allowed to fall into disrepair, the rice campaign of 1966 and 1967 was launched under the slogan Produire pour Se Suffire, referring not to production for subsistence but to production for national self-sufficiency.

After United States aid was cut back in United States FY 1967, the price of rice was allowed to rise, and production responded moderately. Suret-Canale reported that in 1968 most of the towns of the interior were being adequately supplied with local rice, although the supply was deficient in Conakry. In his December 1973 speech, however, President Touré declared a shortage of food grains in most of the administrative regions, including those regarded as rice-producing areas. He cited the paradox that such rice-producing administrative regions as Kouroussa, Siguiri, Boké, Boffa, Forécariah, and Dubréka never ceased demanding that the government supply imported rice to feed the local militia, students, and government employees: in short, all the important local elements who were not producing for their own families' subsistence. The problem was said to have become more acute in 1974 and early 1975.

This was paradoxical in that the rice campaign of the late 1960s had focused on reanimating the development of large plains where tractors or oxplows could be employed. Such plains were very limited in the Forest Region and lacking on the plateau of the Fouta Djallon but extensive in coastal Guinea and along the Upper Niger River, where they had been developed before independence but were later neglected. These were the large granary areas cited by the president as requiring imports of rice. They included, among others, parts of Boké and Boffa administrative regions on the coastal plains and Siguiri and Kouroussa administrative

	1964	1965	1968	1969	1970	1971	1972
Food Crops (thousand metric tons)							
Rice (paddy)	360	300	250	270	240	220	200
Cassava	420	390	370	350	270	250	220
Millets, sorghum, fonio	146	150	150	150	130	120	90
Sweet potatoes	85	73	80	82	70	50	30
Maize (corn)	70	73	68	68	52	50	48
Export Crops (thousand metric tons)							
Bananas	40	37	35	27	30	25	31
Pineapples	16	13	15	25	27	30	33
Palm kernels	23	25	25	28	30	30	30
Coffee (robusta)	13	7	15	17	10	9	7
Groundnuts (peanuts)	18	15	19	18	20	22	25
Citrus fruit	10	6	7	9	4	3	4
Livestock Herd Remaining (thousands)							
Cattle	1,500	1,340	1,160	1,120	1,100	980	950
Sheep	343	276	220	200	170	150	150
Goats	491	450	460	445	432	410	398
Pigs	10	19	22	23	24	22	20
Indexes of Production (1961–65 average = 100)							
Total agricultural production	112	92	119	120	120	123	104
Food production	112	92	119	120	121	123	104
Per capita agricultural production	110	89	107	105	104	103	86
Per capita food production	110	88	107	105	104	103	86

regions on the Upper Niger. Sizable plains were also exploited in Gaoual and Koundara administrative regions at the foot of the Fouta Djallon in Middle Guinea, where they had previously been used only for groundnuts.

These plains and bottomland in the Forest Region and elsewhere were inundated during the rainy season, permitting the growing of swamp rice, sometimes referred to in other countries as irrigated rice or wet rice. Dryland rice, also known as rain-fed or mountain rice, was extensively grown where inundation did not occur, notably on the slopes and hillsides of the Forest Region and the drier areas of Upper Guinea. It gave lower yields, however, and involved the destructive firing of brush cover followed by wasteful broadcast sowing. The authorities consequently tried to encourage the fullest possible exploitation of available bottomlands. Firing for mountain rice was forbidden, but the prohibition was not effectively enforced.

The authorities also sought to discourage the growing of fonio where alternative crops could be grown. Fonio is low in nutrition and tends to deplete the soil. It is grown for preference on soils that are already impoverished, as in overpopulated areas of the Forest Region. Some say that it is the only crop grown on the sandy plateau of the Fouta Djallon, but it is also grown extensively in the other major geographic regions. The yield of fonio is so low in many areas that it barely suffices to provide the seed for the next year's harvest. In Guinea such drought-resistant food grains as sorghum and pennisetum millet are grown in the humid regions as well as in the more arid areas. Sorghum, millet, and fonio are usually lumped together in data, and the term *millet* sometimes is used to cover all three.

Estimates on the acreage under individual crops have not been published since the mid-1950s. At that time it was only on the plateau and in the foothills that rice did not rank first in percentage of area cultivated. Fonio came first in those areas and second in most other administrative regions. Millet and (or) sorghum were particularly important around Gaoual and Koundara; maize was particularly important around Mamou, Siguiri, Koundara, and Labé; cassava, yams, and sweet potatoes were grown almost everywhere but were most important in the Forest Region.

Regional Pattern of Crop Potential

Guinea has a fairly broad spectrum of climate and topography that is characteristic of several of the countries extending far inland from the coast of West Africa and that permits considerable diversity in the range of tropical crop and livestock production (see ch. 3). Guinea has an advantage over some of its neighbors, however, in superior resources of water and rainfall. The generally monsoonal climate, bringing heavy summer rains and dry winters, has fostered reliance on rice as the staple of diet, along with maize, sweet potatoes, and more drought-resistant crops, such as millet, sorghum, and cassava. The arrival and duration of the rains are not always reliable. Both droughts and floods are continuing hazards but have generally been less severe than elsewhere in West Africa, despite consistent neglect of water conservation practices.

Soils are generally quite poor, except on the fertile alluvial plains of the coastal regions and the river basins (see ch. 3). Heavy rains, deforestation, and methods of cultivation have combined to create a severe erosion problem. Where seasonal dryness permits, the savanna and the forested areas have been damaged for centuries by the practice of clearing by fire for cultivation or of grass firing for new grazing. Successive fires and the downpour during the rainy season destroy the shallow layer of humus. Erosion damage has been particularly heavy in the Fouta Djallon, in the savannas of Upper Guinea, and in the Forest Region, around Beyla, Kissidougou, and Guéckédou, where population pressure has destroyed the forest cover and has progressively reduced the length of fallow.

Official attempts to prohibit the traditional practice of clearing by fire for dryland rice cultivation, slash-and-burn agriculture, or grazing were universally resisted under the colonial regime and have also failed repeatedly since independence. The authorities are obliged to recognize that the smallholder equipped only with a hoe and a machete and lacking sufficient inundated bottomland has little alternative if he is to feed his family. The dilemma is a common one throughout Africa, where the slash-and-burn tradition is widespread. The relatively well-financed and intensively administered rice program of the Malagasy Republic, for example, has also been unable to eliminate the practice of firing for hillside rice cultivation.

Largely because of the poor soils and erosion, 60 to 70 percent of the country is thought to be unsuitable for cultivation. Some 15 percent of the total land area was actually under cultivation (including fallow) in the mid-1960s, when crop exports were declining and the urban population was heavily dependent upon food imports. Nevertheless, experts seem to agree that sizable areas of the country offer good natural potential for increases in production that would permit the country to supply its own food and textile needs and to increase crop exports.

Although some minor flood control installations have been built along the Upper Niger and coastal plains, riverflow regulation has largely been neglected and land reclamation projects repeatedly abandoned as a result of the periodically strained relations with neighbors and foreign aid donors that have characterized the nation's foreign policy (see ch. 9). Because the principal rivers of French-speaking West Africa originate on Guinea's Fouta Djallon plateau, the nonparticipation of President Touré's government in the Liptako-N'Gourma organization to regulate the Niger River and the difficulties culminating in its withdrawal from the Organization of Sénégal River States in 1972 are sometimes said to have critically impeded the already dilatory progress of those bodies. The drainage pattern of the river basins determines the water table of the entire Sahelian region of West Africa and cannot be effectively controlled without an active degree of cooperation among all the riverain states. Discussion had been under way for decades on the best site for a main regulating dam and subsidiary dams on the Sénégal River and, if action had been taken in time, some observers believe that the disastrous impact of the 1966–72 drought cycle on the Sahelian peoples might have been greatly reduced if not averted altogether.

A French report in 1954 had stressed that the destruction of the soils of Guinea's Fouta-Djallon plateau created a danger the consequences of which would be felt not only by Guinea itself but by all the West African projects based on the use of the rivers that originate there. Some critics later charged that the Guinean government's failure to protect the soils and regulate the flow of the upper reaches of the Bafing (Sénégal) River was likely to frustrate UN-sponsored plans for a dam at Manantali in Mali that would permit the development of several hundred thousand acres along the entire middle and lower course of the river and benefit some 15 million inhabitants of the riverain nations. They claimed that failure to enforce restrictions on deforestation and the destruction of bush or grass cover by fire had accelerated the degradation of soils on the plateau in recent years and that Guinea's best alluvial soils were washing down the rivers. The government radio had announced that the flow of Guinea's rivers had been reduced for the first time in 1974 because of the preceding three years of drought, but some outside critics alleged that the drought had been felt for as long as ten years.

The country's twisted configuration is said to help account for its diversity of climate and crop production. The natural regions determined by climate and topography correspond closely to the four major geographic regions recognized in official terminology (see ch. 3). Thus the coastal areas of swamp, plains, and foothills are in the region of Lower Guinea; the Fouta Djallon plateau or highlands make up most of the region of Middle Guinea; the savanna lands correspond with the region of Upper Guinea; and southern Guinea is officially designated as the Forest Region (see fig. 7).

Detailed variations in topography bring some local variations in rainfall; but the broad zones of rainfall progress diagonally from the west and south to the northeast, which along with the northern tip of Middle Guinea has the lowest average precipitation. The heaviest annual rainfall occurs in the consistently hot coastal areas, where the rainy season lasts an average of six months, usually from April or May to October or November. Average rainfall is somewhat lower in the Forest Region but is more evenly distributed over a nine-month period. In the far south the rains often start in February or March. In the Fouta Djallon average rainfall decreases from west to east, and the rainy season usually lasts about four months; but there is some rain during the other months. The savanna lands have the lowest average rainfall and a long, hot dry season influenced by the harmattan, a trade wind that originates in the Sahara. The water table of the savannas benefits, however, from the drainage system of the river basins, which have plains suitable for productive large-scale dryland cultivation.

The hot and humid climate of the areas along the coast and their expanse of good alluvial soils combine to given them the country's largest area under cultivation. Proximity to the railroad, the port, and the urban market also encouraged production of a variety of crops. Mangrove swamps and marshes, cut here and there by tidal inlets, extend inland for varying distances to a flat, sandy plain that floods heavily in the rainy season. The gravest drawback is recurrent invasion of the coastal areas by seawater, which sweeps up the estuaries and regularly destroys the small dikes and drainage outlets needed to keep saline water out of the ricefields. The regular inundation of the ricefields by rains in summer is beneficial, but the ricefields can be endangered when tidal floods occur during the dry season.

French authorities had visualized the region as a vast rice granary that could feed the growing urban populations of all French West Africa. Its development, however, requires some fairly modern and large-scale

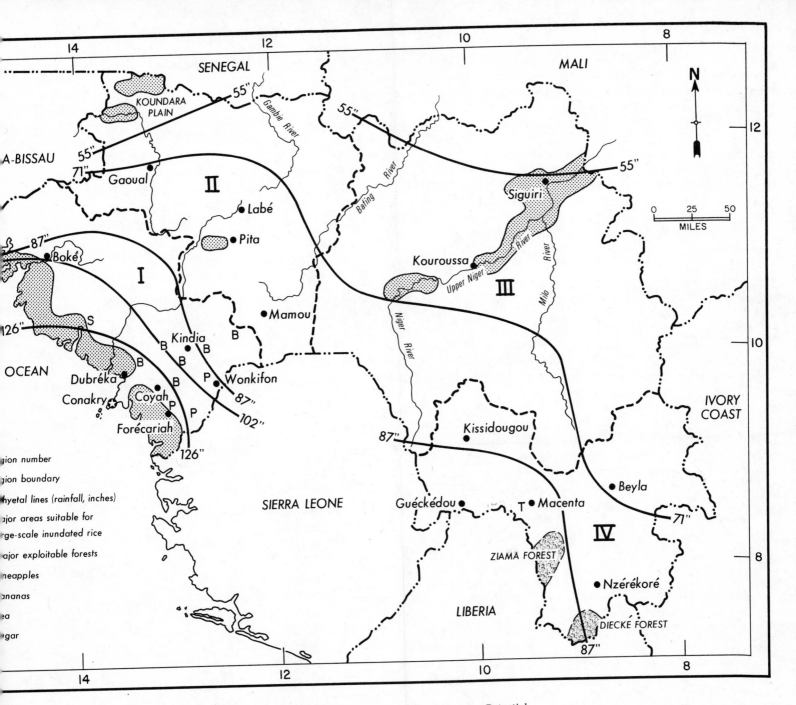

Figure 7. Guinea, Geographic Pattern of Agricultural and Forestry Potential

Map labels:

SENEGAL
MALI
A-BISSAU
KOUNDARA PLAIN
55"
Gambie River
Bafing River
55"
Gaoual
71"
55"
II
Labé
Siguiri
Pita
87"
Boké
Kouroussa
Upper Niger River
Milo River
I
III
126"
S
OCEAN
Kindia
B
B
B
B
B
Mamou
Niger River
Dubréka
B
P
Wonkifon
Conakry
Coyah
P
87"
Forécariah
P
P
102"
87"
126"
71"
Kissidougou
IVORY COAST
SIERRA LEONE
Beyla
Guéckédou
T
Macenta
IV
ZIAMA FOREST
Nzérékoré
LIBERIA
DIECKÉ FOREST
87"

Legend:
gion number
gion boundary
hyetal lines (rainfall, inches)
ajor areas suitable for
rge-scale inundated rice
ajor exploitable forests
neapples
ananas
ea
gar

N

0   25   50
MILES

257

I COASTAL SWAMPS, PLAINS, AND HILLS

Oil Palm
Bananas
Pineapples
Swamp rice
All subsistence food crops

II FOUTA DJALLON PLATEAU AND ADJACENT PLAINS

Stockraising
Fonio
Other dryland food grains
Groundnuts

III SAVANNA LANDS

Swamp rice
Dryland rice
Other dryland food grains
Stockraising
Cotton

IV FOREST REGION

Coffee
Oil Palm
Tobacco
Tea
Timber
Dryland rice
Fonio
Swamp rice
Other subsistence food crops

12

GU

102"

10

ATLANT

II

55"

8

P
B
T
S

installations or operations, such as high embankments, clearing by heavy equipment, desalinization of cleared areas, and construction of a network of drainage canals. Clearing for rice often involves destruction of mangroves, an essential forestry resource. In 1955 some 42,000 acres of swamp rice were under cultivation by traditional methods. Clearing and cultivation were entirely by hand: oxplows and tractors were then unknown in the region's ricefields; but by the mid-1960s entrepreneurs were sending tractors out by ferry from Conakry to work the ricefields of Kabak Island. Guinean agricultural authorities estimated in 1966 that a further 100,000 acres for swamp rice could be reclaimed or developed in the region with the aid of modern protective installations.

Oil palms grow wild along the coast. They are spared during clearing and may be helped to multiply, but semicultivation consists mostly of gathering the nuts. Climbing the trees is hazardous enough to have been increasingly neglected in the mid-1960s when incentives to supply the domestic palm-oil market were lacking. The oil derived from the pulp of the nut was consequently used almost entirely in local subsistence, but kernels were still being exported.

The coastal plains and adjacent foothills have also been the prime source of bananas and pineapples for export. At independence the banana plantations were scattered in the areas around Conakry, Dubréka, and Forécariah and along both sides of the old meter-gauge railroad as far inland as Kindia and Mamou. By 1954 the aggregate acreage of African banana plantations was approaching that of the local French and Lebanese plantations, but the African holdings were smaller and far more numerous. By 1958 the number and extent of French and Lebanese plantations had increased, but their acreage was surpassed by that of African plantations. After 1958 and during the 1960s many of the French and Lebanese left the country, contributing to a decline in production. Some Lebanese forced out of trade in 1964 later bought plantations. In the 1960s banana groves were disappearing rapidly in the administrative regions of Mamou and Kindia, the most distant from port. The pineapple crop was becoming successful on the coastal plains. The fruit plantations and the vegetable truck farms (market gardens) around Conakry were said to be the country's only agricultural undertakings devoted primarily to production for the market in 1968. Attempts to promote truck farming and fruit growing around the cannery at Mamou in Middle Guinea had been less successful.

The equatorial climate of the Forest Region of southern Guinea, with its relatively brief dry season, favors cultivation. One French expert estimated that the region possesses nine-tenths of the country's agricultural potential. Transportation development to link the region to the capital had high priority for the period 1973 through 1982, but in the early 1970s it was fairly isolated from the rest of Guinea and was linked to Sierra Leone and Liberia, favoring smuggling rather than supply of the capital. Moreover, population pressure on the land, particularly among the Kissi people of Guéckédou and Kissidougou administrative regions, has reduced the length of fallow periods between crops and exhausted the soils. The Kissi share with the Baga of the coastal swamps the distinction of being the country's best cultivators of swamp rice, which they grow largely on the bottomlands under natural inundation. The Kissi also grow dryland rice and a great deal of fonio. In Guéckédou Administrative Region in the 1960s repeated crops of swamp rice, dryland rice, and fonio formed a continuous carpet over valleys, plains, plateaus, and hillsides, almost eliminating the natural forest cover. Dryland rice was still cultivated more extensively than fonio. In Kissidougou Administrative Region, however, where soils were more exhausted, the slopes and hillsides were devoted almost exclusively to fonio.

In the late 1960s Kissidougou was the only administrative region in the Forest Region to produce rice surplus to the needs of its population. Conditions for inundated rice culture were equally favorable, however, in the administrative regions of Macenta, Nzérékoré, and Yomou, where little had been done to exploit the available bottomlands. One plain had been developed in Yomou Administrative Region after World War II, but the neglected drainage canals had become obstructed, and the project would have to be completely redone. With few exceptions, the bottomlands of the Forest Region were too fragmented for mechanized cultivation but could potentially be cultivated with the use of animal traction.

Groundnuts, which in most of West Africa are a mainstay of the fairly arid areas, are grown in all the natural regions of Guinea, including large areas of the Forest Region. They are grown in both outlying fields and subsistence gardens. Surplus harvests are marketed but are not an important source of cash income, as they are in much of West Africa.

The traditional mainstay of the Forest Region economy was semicultivation of oil palms, kola nuts, and most notably of coffee. The government had stressed development of the sawmill industry as an important economic resource of the region, inspiring somewhat contradictory reports abroad that the region's forestry resources were being devastated by cutting for the sawmills and that the sawmills were operating far below capacity because transportation and other problems had interfered with the supply of timber.

Official efforts to introduce true cultivation of coffee had not succeeded by 1968. At independence Kissidougou Administrative Region had been the foremost coffee producer, but the area of maximum production extended from Beyla south beyond Nzérékoré and Yomou. The varieties grown were all robustas, which are in surplus world production. Some arabicas, more fragile but in greater market demand, had been grown before World War II, but plans to reintroduce them in the 1960s were not realized. The protected, price-supported French market had been lost, neglect of cultivation had affected crop quality, and recurrent onslaughts of crop disease had reduced the number of trees in production from some

70 million in 1958 to an estimated 40 million or 45 million in 1964. Moreover, domestic prices were too low, and an estimated 50 percent of the crop was being smuggled out.

A new coffee campaign was launched under the Seven Year Plan, but funds to realize many of its targets were lacking. Progress was made in the mid-1960s in curbing disease and in massive distribution of new plants, and prices were increased; but these measures applied primarily to collective fields and apparently did not effectively enlist the participation of the region's many small-scale coffee growers. Most coffee stands were on small family holdings, but more land planted to coffee proved to be available for collective use than land under other crops. When coffee growing was originally promoted by the colonial authorities using forced labor, it was under the supervision of the village or cantonal chiefs, who regarded the coffee land as their own. Consequently many of these stands were nationalized or spontaneously collectivized by the villagers at independence. The tradition of devoting little attention or labor to the collective fields has no doubt adversely affected yields.

Some coffee is grown in those areas of Upper Guinea adjacent to the Forest Region. The dry season in the savanna lands is relatively severe, however, and most of the area's traditional cultivation and stockraising are confined to meeting the subsistence needs of the population. On the river bottomlands, swamp rice is grown by traditional methods using unregulated inundation, but the undependable flow of the rivers, notably the Niger, makes it a chancy undertaking. The vast extent of the adjacent plains, however, and the area's heavy soils lend themselves to cultivation by tractor or oxplow, though unfortunately not to the use of mechanical harvesters. In 1966, 300 tractors were in use to cultivate some 54,000 acres. Another 23,000 acres were being cultivated with animal traction and 33,600 acres with the hoe alone.

Use of both the oxplow and the tractor had undergone many fluctuations and vicissitudes, however, and there were potential problems facing future development of the area. Effective use of tractors required fields of at least 270 acres each. In the mid-1960s most were exploited by entrepreneurs of the tractor bourgeoisie. Collectivization had made little progress in the area after the proposed 17,000-acre Fié Valley state farm had to be abandoned in 1961. Use of tractors was impeded by recurrent floods as well as by poor maintenance and lack of parts and fuel. Soils were not suitable for use of mechanical harvesters, and labor for manual harvesting was in short supply.

The area's relatively low annual rainfall is partly offset by the seasonal rise of the rivers. Beneficial in some years, in other years the river floods have destroyed villages and large areas of crop—notably in 1962 and 1967. Even modern embankments and drainage canals provide no insurance against floods of this magnitude, and these improvements had been provided for only about 25,000 acres of the Niger plains in 1958, primarily in Siguiri Administrative Region and to a lesser extent in

Kouroussa Administrative Region. By 1959, moreover, half of this area already required total renewal of the improvements.

The area's plains extend over some 350,000 acres, of which between 125,000 and 200,000 acres are thought suitable for development with modern protective installations. Thus the Upper Niger plains could rival or even outstrip the ricegrowing potential of the coastal plains and polders. By 1968, however, little had been done along the Upper Niger to add to the flood control improvements abandoned by the French in 1958. Until 1966 low rice prices had resulted in lack of interest in cash production. After the rice campaign of 1966, the revived exploitation of the plains was not accompanied by new flood-regulating installations. At most, some of the old abandoned works were repaired.

The traditional subsistence cultivators of the savanna lands are primarily dependent upon rain-fed crops, including dryland rice, millet, sorghum, fonio, cassava, and groundnuts. In the village plots maize, sweet potatoes, taro, and tobacco are grown. The area's ethnically predominant Malinké herders are sedentary or semisedentary. They may be obliged to drive their cattle in search of water in the dry season, but they do not have a traditional nomadic cycle that involves leaving their permanent settlements.

The Peul of the Fouta Djallon are cultivators as well as being the country's foremost stockraisers (see ch. 4). They graze their herds in the river valleys near their permanent villages in the dry season and move them on to the plateau during the rainy season. Destructive burning of grassland to promote tender new growth for grazing is practiced both here and on the savanna lands. Except in the river bottoms, most of the area's soils are uncultivable and the pastures overgrazed (see ch. 3). Only fonio is planted on the plateau; other crops, of which rice is the most important, are grown in the lowlands. As in the Forest Region, the potential for mechanized cultivation in the Fouta Djallon is very limited. On the plateau itself there are thought to be only some 10,000 acres of plains suitable for rice cultivation, of which 7,000 acres are in Tougué Administrative Region. Gaoual and Koundara administrative regions at the foot of the plateau, however, lie within the confines of Middle Guinea and have fertile plains that could be developed into the third largest area of rice production after the coastal areas and the Upper Niger.

Before independence these Koundara plains furnished groundnuts that were exported by way of adjacent Senegal. The three-year plan had initially contained an ambitious program for the cultivation of groundnuts on a larger scale for an oil mill at Koundara. The oil mill was never built, however, as the government could not afford to furnish the seed and tools for the project. It was to have employed the surplus Peul laborers from the neighboring Pita and Labé administrative regions, who preferred to migrate to Senegal where their wages could buy more (see ch. 6; ch. 5).

An experiment with mechanized collective farming of rice near Koundara in 1961 failed because deep plowing had brought sterile subsoil to the surface. In 1967, however, 55,000 acres of rice were cultivated on the Koundara plains. The cultivators were largely Peul from overpopulated Labé and Pita who had the means to become tractor entrepreneurs. They came for the plowing and sowing in June and July, returned to the towns when the plains were inundated, then returned for the harvest between mid-October and the end of February. Labé Administrative Region alone sent a dozen tractors to the plains each year. The area's disadvantages were the absence of drinking water and the need for labor-intensive manual harvesting. An advantage was the absence of the birds that in other areas required constant watching of the ricefields.

Industrial Crops

A prime goal of successive development plans has been to achieve self-sufficiency in raw materials for the agricultural processing industries: tobacco, cotton textiles, sugar, edible oils, and canned, chilled, or frozen fish, meat, and vegetables. Repeated setbacks were encountered in the effort to develop production of these crops, and most of the raw material requirements had to be filled by imports. In the early 1970s most of the processing plants were reportedly operating at a fraction of capacity. Early programs relied on appeals to party militants to promote the growing of industrial crops on collective fields or by village smallholders. This line of development had failed almost everywhere. There had reportedly been greater success with supervised plantations developed with aid and technical supervision from abroad. A modern pineapple plantation run by a foreign commercial firm supplied a processing plant. Technicians from the People's Republic of China (PRC) were running a tea plantation at Macenta and a sugar complex near Koba on the fertile Boffa plain.

The earliest food-processing projects initiated under the Three Year Development Plan (1960–63) included a Soviet-built cannery at Mamou, completed in 1963. The plan had called for development of crops, supervised by the Guinean government, to take place in coordination with the industrial projects supervised by Soviet technicians. Because the agricultural portion of the plan was largely neglected in favor of other sectors, however, the oversized Soviet installations were ready for operation before much had been done to assure their raw material supply.

The Mamou plant had been intended to replace costly imports of tomato concentrate, heavily used in food preparation by Guinean women. It could process from twenty-five to forty tons of fresh tomatoes a day, but the initial target was set at only 2,000 tons a year. In 1966 deliveries of fresh tomatoes to the plant reached an annual high of 308 tons. Reliance on voluntary production proved impossible, as fresh tomatoes could be sold on the local market for ten times—and in Conakry for seventeen times—the price that the cannery could afford to pay. An old banana plantation nearby was converted to a collective tomato farm employing army conscripts, but this plan reportedly did not succeed. Collective fields using the human investment program were also established around Pita and at Dalaba, where the French hill station had formerly supported a local truck farming industry. In 1974, however, it was alleged that tomato concentrate supplies were being imported from Romania, Italy, and Spain. Although the Mamou cannery had been planned to produce 70,000 cans of concentrate a year, it was said to be producing only 300 in 1974.

The cannery had meanwhile been partially converted to process fruit juices. There were also two other fruit juice canneries. One was successfully operated by the commercial pineapple firm. The other had been built by an Italian firm at Kankan under the Seven Year Plan and opened in 1966. The country has an abundant supply of citrus fruit, but the population prefers its juice fresh, and the product proved not to measure up to export market standards.

Plans to produce canned meats at Mamou also failed because of inadequate planning of both livestock supply and market outlets. The numerically predominant Muslim population feared that canned meats might contain pork or that the slaughter of other animals might not have been performed in the ritual manner.

A quinine plant at Sérédou had been operated by the French agricultural service before independence. Renewal of the plantations was subsequently neglected for lack of funds and labor. The plant had to be closed, but it was reported that the acreage planted in 1963 could be ready for production in 1975.

The tobacco and match factory built by the PRC at Wassa-Wassa, fifteen miles from Conakry, was initiated under the Three Year Development Plan but completed in 1966. Because the firm inherited the high protected cigarette prices introduced by the previous French monopoly, it is the only state-owned manufacturing enterprise that has consistently operated at a profit. Prices were high enough to absorb the cost of importing leaf tobacco supplies and were thought to be high enough to provide an adequate incentive to domestic tobacco production.

Tobacco is grown in subsistence gardens wherever rainfall is adequate, but before independence it was grown commercially only in the relatively moist Forest Region of southern Guinea. There was a private French tobacco estate near Nzérékoré. Near Beyla the French tobacco monopoly had an estate where Maryland and burley leaf were successfully grown by African tenants with seed and support provided by the firm. The leaf was exported to the French plants at Dakar and Algiers. At independence the government planned to grow one-half of the domestic tobacco supply on the estate and get the other one-half from independent African growers in the Beyla Administrative Region.

Instead, the plant was obliged to rely on imports of leaf from the sponsoring PRC, from Malawi, and—allegedly until quite recently—from Southern Rhodesia. The Beyla growers had reportedly not received enough encouragement and had abandoned production. Some 2,500 acres were earmarked for tobacco growing in the administrative regions of Kindia, Dubréka and Forécariah, but the plans could not be realized, reportedly because repeated brush fires had impoverished the soils.

Tea estates five miles outside Macenta, launched under the Seven Year Plan with technical assistance from the Chinese Communists, were reportedly more successful because they were better supported and supervised. Nevertheless, the party newspaper *Horoya* reported in 1970 that the factory, completed in 1968, was operating at only 10 percent of capacity.

After plans for a groundnut-oil mill and associated groundnut production at Koundara had to be abandoned during the three-year plan, an oil mill was built by an Italian firm on Kassa Island in 1968 to employ workers from the exhausted bauxite mine. The mill was equipped to extract oil from both groundnuts and palm-nut pulp. Another oil mill completed by the Chinese Communists at Dabola at about the same time was to process groundnut oil. A palm-oil mill begun earlier by a United States aid project at Dubréka was abandoned before completion. Dabola was less isolated from the port at Conakry than Koundara, but the surrounding region, with its sparse population and impoverished soils, was less suited to production of groundnuts. It is alleged that in 1967 the region produced only 300 tons, whereas the mill was equipped to process 8,000 tons. Imports of groundnuts from Senegal for the Kassa oil mill ceased for lack of foreign exchange, and palm-nut gatherers preferred to use the oil-nut pulp for subsistence or smuggle it to Sierra Leone. It was alleged by one source that in 1974 the country's edible oil supply was confined to subsistence production in the countryside and in Conakry to strictly rationed imports of soybean oil from the United States.

The country's annual consumption of cotton fabric was some 65 million yards in 1966. To reduce the high foreign exchange cost of imports, a national cotton textile complex was established under the Seven Year Plan at Sanouya, twenty-five miles from Conakry. It was an old plant from India, disassembled and reestablished in Guinea with technical assistance from a British textile firm and a loan from a British bank. It had the capacity to replace 48 million of the 65 million yards imported. At full capacity it would consume 3,700 tons of cotton fiber, which was to be grown domestically. In the early 1970s, however, it was still obliged to rely on imported fiber. Because of the dearth of foreign exchange for cotton imports, it was allegedly producing only about 4.4 million yards of fabric, that is, 10 percent of capacity and 7 percent of domestic requirements.

Natural conditions do not favor cotton growing in the area around Sanouya or in most of Guinea's other regions. The government's initial cotton campaign nevertheless distributed seed to committees throughout the country and issued a general appeal that each party militant should sow a plot to cotton. This initiative culminated in the production of a few dozen tons of inferior fiber. The subsequent cotton campaign of the mid-1960s focused on encouraging production along the Upper Niger, where natural conditions were more propitious and rudimentary river irrigation available but where insufficient support and supervision were provided for learning the rather demanding methods of cotton cultivation and harvesting. Moreover, the price offered by the government was well below the price obtainable on the local market. Labor could not be found to work the collective fields assigned to cotton by the local or regional committees, and production was mediocre.

The country's first sugar refinery entered into production in November 1973, but its capacity was reportedly well below domestic requirements. The climate is suited to the production of sugarcane, which is widely grown in subsistence gardens. A project for sugar production was first launched under the Seven Year Plan with aid from the Chinese Communists. It was originally established on a plain along the Kolenté River in Kindia Administrative Region in 1968, the plantations being supervised by the Guinean government and the plant by PRC technicians. The project ran into difficulties, however, resulting from lack of funds. The plant was later reestablished at Koba on the Boffa plain and completed in 1973. At that time only 520 acres of cane had been planted of the 6,200 planned.

Export Crops

Of the export crops, only pineapples had made important gains since independence. Bananas and coffee, which together had furnished 60 percent of total export earnings in 1958, had both been ravaged by disease, and half of the coffee exported was thought to be smuggled out. Products of gathering, such as palm kernels, or of small-scale production, such as groundnuts, continued to be exported on the same scale as before independence but were not thought to have much growth potential unless organized effort were made to improve cultivation practices.

Assistance for pineapple growing had been provided by the World Bank Group (see Glossary). Production of pineapples had nearly doubled since independence. Most of the smaller scale plantations in the coastal plains, however, lacked the foreign exchange for the needed fertilizers and other supplies. A notable exception was a 500-acre plantation run by a Geneva-based multinational trading firm. Guinea had incurred a sizable debt to this firm and had consequently granted it a concession of thousands of acres between Conakry, Forécariah, and Wonkifon. Not being subject to the kind of foreign exchange shortages that plagued the small planters and inhibited government programs, the firm was able to develop its plantation with the aid of imported fertilizers and equipment and to provide whatever technical supervision and organization were needed to operate at a profit. Pineapple production accordingly increased steadily. As a relatively high-priced delicacy on the Western European market pineapple, in various forms, could be shipped by air and thus avoid packing and spoilage problems. Apparently a portion of the crop was shipped by sea, however, for there were reports in 1975 that some pineapple shipments had spoiled while awaiting loading on the docks at Conakry. Moreover, an article in an American periodical in 1972 stated that pineapple exports were receiving a higher proportionate subsidy than bananas. This subsidy may perhaps have applied only to the pineapple exports grown by small-scale African planters.

This 1972 source reported that, in an effort to offset the effects on foreign trade of the overvaluation of the currency, the state trading agency was paying subsidies that in 1968 were equivalent to 31 percent of the export price on bananas, 57 percent on coffee, 92 percent on groundnuts, 143 percent on palm kernels, and 147 percent on pineapples. These subsidies were probably somewhat higher than those paid in previous years. Until 1969 they were designed primarily to cover the high costs of transportation, packing, and spoilage. Most of the subsidy accrued to the government enterprises or agencies involved, and very little trickled down to the producer. Because price incentives to production were inadequate, the price to the producer was increased beginning in reporting year 1969, and the share of the state enterprises was sharply reduced. Even the increased producer price, however, remained far below the price obtainable on the black market or by smuggling, so that a substantial share of exports continued to elude official channels. In 1972 the subsidy was removed from bananas, as it was considered too costly to continue to export them.

Citrus fruits, particularly oranges, are grown in abundance in Fouta Djallon and in the coastal areas. Most are consumed locally or allowed to rot. The canneries, because of high costs for packing and shipping, could not offer a high enough price to divert oranges from the local market, and they do not appeal to Western European consumers because of their spotty skins. Some oranges and lemons were still exported, however, probably to Eastern Europe.

Production of bananas had already declined somewhat before independence because of the effort of conversion to a new and less fragile variety. The new variety, however, proved more susceptible to disease and more easily uprooted by periodic tornadoes. Moreover, the departure of many French planters had reduced average yields.

Export earnings from bananas before independence had accrued primarily to French and Lebanese plantation owners. Although the acreage of African growers had increased substantially in the 1950s, they had not been given the official quality mark used by the whites and had been obliged to subcontract their crop to the French growers at substandard prices. Their average yields were only about one-fourth of those on the large plantations. After independence the French trading regime was abolished, and the growers were organized in regional cooperatives by the government export agency. It did not provide the kind of effective organization and supplies, however, that had formerly been provided to the French growers. Banana production requires a very high level of expenditure on fertilizers, fungicides, irrigation, and packing. Since independence it was estimated that about 50 percent of banana acreage has been destroyed by disease. Lack of supplies and poor transportation have also hindered exports.

Moreover, bananas remain a delicate product requiring costly packing and shipping and subject to spoilage en route. President Touré complained in December 1973 that, for every 100 pounds of bananas shipped to the Soviet Union, only forty-five to fifty-five pounds arrived in good condition. He also asserted that, for every 10,000 tons of bananas exported, the stabilization fund was losing GS72 million (for value of the syli—see Glossary). This would amply explain the government's decision to terminate the subsidy for bananas. Because of Guinea's relatively heavy imports from the Soviet Union, the decline in exports of tropical products after independence had resulted in a mounting debt under bilateral clearing agreements with the Soviets, and continuing exports of bananas had been one way of attempting to retard further accumulation of the debt.

STOCKRAISING

Before independence, Guinea had been a net exporter of livestock. In the early 1960s it had been obliged to import livestock from neighboring countries. These imports ceased, however, when Guinea was unable to pay its debt under trade agreements with these countries. Consequently meat had reportedly become rare in the diet of urban Guineans. Large numbers of Guinean herders had emigrated to Ivory Coast, Liberia, and Sierra Leone, thus reducing the numbers of livestock remaining in Guinea.

Chickens are kept throughout the country, although most are scrawny and subject to disease. Pigs are kept chiefly in the Forest Region, where there are fewer Muslims than in the rest of the country. Cattle in the Forest Region are reportedly allowed to wander and graze at will, so that they become quite wild.

The chief stockraising peoples are the Peul and the Malinké of the Fouta Djallon and the savanna lands. Two-thirds of the country's livestock herd is probably found on the Fouta Djallon. Most of the cattle are of the ancient N'dama strain—small, agile, and strong, with lyre-shaped horns. Because of their resistance to the tsetse fly and to disease they were once in great demand in other parts of Africa. In the 1960s, however, their numbers were allegedly reduced by disease. The small short-haired sheep and goats were also regarded as relatively disease resistant. During the rainy season the grasslands of the Fouta Djallon and Upper Guinea provide ample grazing, and the livestock are in good condition. In the dry season they become worn down by being kept on the move in search of water and grazing. They become more susceptible to disease and less productive of milk or meat.

As in most African countries, stock are valued for their numbers rather than their productivity, and the customary rate of offtake for slaughter is extremely low. When the government decided to insist on taking one animal a year for every ten animals in a given herd, this 10-percent rate of offtake was greeted by the herders and by some of the government's critics in terms appropriate for cruel and unusual punishment. To add to their distress, the price offered by the government for the requisitioned animals was only about one-fifth of what they could fetch on the black market. Moreover, some sources reported that the regional authorities, reviving a practice dating from colonial times, often surreptitiously increased the livestock collection quota and kept the difference to expand their own herds. Some reports alleged that the stock remaining after these raids was not enough even for the customary unselective breeding, much less for any improvement in productive characteristics.

The government, however, was operating two experimental cattle farms supported by assistance from the Soviet Union. One farm at Beyla was experimenting with methods of increasing yields of milk and of meat. The other, at Dabola, was interbreeding the disease-resistant native N'Dama strain with higher yielding breeds imported from Europe.

FISHING

Fish in abundant supply and great variety are found along the coast and in the rivers (see ch. 3). Both the maritime and the riverain peoples fish for subsistence, and dried and smoked fish have traditionally been an important source of cash income for them. Inland fishing is most intensively carried on during the first weeks of the rainy and dry seasons. Baskets, traps, poisons, and hooks and lines are traditionally used. Regulations against the use of dynamite have been difficult to enforce.

Suret-Canale estimated in 1968 that there were some 10,000 traditional fishermen. Many were found among the Baga and the Soussou peoples of the coastal plains, who fished the coastal waters in some 2,000 to 3,000 rudimentary dugout canoes or in 4,250 barks of a type called *kabak* (a boat first introduced from Sierra Leone in the early nineteenth century). About 4,000 of these barks were equipped with motors and 250 only with sails. They were used for coastal goods transport as well as for fishing.

Since independence nothing has been done to increase the fish stocks of the inland waters, which have considerable unexploited potential for development. There is little published information about marine resources off the coast. There have been no reports of inroads on offshore fish stocks or of interference with Guinean fishing by foreign trawlers.

A government effort in 1959 and 1960 to organize the small-scale traditional fishermen into cooperatives failed because the participants used the organization to hold down production and drive up prices.

Trawler fishing on an industrial basis had been introduced by the French in 1954, but the trawlers departed after independence, and a new plan had to be launched. In 1961 a joint Polish-Guinean enterprise was created for industrial fishing, but in 1963 Guinea bought up the Polish share, and it became a government agency known as the Maritime Fishing Office.

Suret-Canale reported in 1968 that the government enterprise maintained eleven of the thirteen trawlers operating out of Conakry and that landings had increased from around 500 tons fresh in 1956 to 2,000 tons fresh and 435 tons frozen in 1967. In the years 1970 through 1972 the catch reportedly averaged nearly 8,000 tons a year. In 1973 it increased to more than 9,000 tons as two new fishing enterprises came into operation and a third was established.

All three new fishing ventures were mixed enterprises in which the Guinean government received 49 percent ownership and 65 percent of the profits in return for its coastal fishery resources. One was named the Japanese-Guinean Fishing Company (Société Nippo-Guinéenne de Pêche—Sonigue). In 1975 it was operating two prospecting boats, two fishing boats, and a refrigerator ship. The Guinea-Kuwait Fishing Company (Société Guinéo-Koweitienne de Pêche—Soguikop) had two trawlers. Another firm was formed by Guinea with KLM, the Dutch airline, which delegated its management to a United States fishing firm. It was called the African Maritime Fishing Company (Société Africaine des Pêches Maritimes—Afrimar).

FORESTRY

The most important species in the country's woodland were mangrove, acacia, rubber, quinine, teak, and ebony. The valuable species, however, were rapidly disappearing. In 1960 there were an estimated 2.6 million acres of classified forests belonging to the state, constituting about 4 percent of total land area. It was not clear whether this estimate included the uncleared areas of mangrove in the coastal swamps, vestigial bits of woodland in the savanna lands or around Mamou, and secondary regrowth in the Forest Region (see ch. 3). Much of the forest cover of the Forest Region had been destroyed or was kept in some localities as a canopy for coffee growing. Primary forest was confined largely to the reserved forests of Diecké near Nzérékoré and Ziama near Sérédou. These forests are reserved for exploitation, not from exploitation. They are meant to be protected from clearing for cultivation or other unauthorized inroads by the local population.

The sawmill installed by Soviet assistance at Nzérékoré in 1964 consisted of used French equipment that had been operating in the Soviet Union, where it was disassembled and shipped to Guinea. It was not designed to withstand equatorial conditions, and breakdowns were frequent. In view of the need for careful exploitation and reforestation of the Diecké Forest, the plant's capacity of 1.75 million cubic feet a year was excessive. The initial production target was set at 1.2 million cubic feet, of which 40 percent was to have gone to supply the furniture factory at Sonfonya. The remainder was destined partly for export to Liberia but largely for repayment in kind to the Soviet Union. By 1967, however, only 560,000 cubic feet were being produced.

At Sérédou, near Macenta, a forestry school had been founded by the United Nations Special Fund, and a particle board factory had been built by a Belgian firm, both completed in 1967. The forestry training center was also supposed to exploit a concession of some 250,000 acres in the nearby Ziama Forest. It was supposed to ship its timber to the sawmill at Nzérékoré, more than sixty-five miles away by poorly maintained mountain roads. The particle board factory was supposed to rely partly on lumber from the sawmill at Nzérékoré and partly on bark-stripped trees left from the quinine operation at Sérédou; the latter plantation, however, had fallen into neglect. This rather complicated program did not work out, largely because of transport difficulties. In 1967 the Guinean government became involved in a dispute with the Belgian firm that had built the particle board operation and that had also nearly completed a soft drink factory at Foulaya. The soft drink plant was never completed.

CHAPTER 12

INDUSTRY, TRADE, AND TRANSPORTATION

In the 1960s the trend in industry and trade had been one of dwindling domestic supply of food and raw materials for industry, declining crop exports, and the growing domination of industrial activity and export earnings by the foreign-owned Fria mining and processing enclave. Because of the low level of industrial demand, the country's abundant hydroelectric potential had as yet scarcely been tapped. Manufacturing capacity installed since independence stagnated for lack of raw materials to process, but the country's rich deposits of bauxite and iron ore were being developed for export in crude or lightly processed form to generate manufacturing income for other countries. The government's ambitions for the mid-1980s and beyond, therefore, focused on the hope of developing its own heavy metal semimanufacturing industries to process at least a portion of its mounting mineral production. Even if markets and capital could eventually be found for such development, however, it appeared that the intervening 1970s would be a decade of growing reliance on exports of crude mineral ores.

The government sought to exert strong control of trade and of much of manufacturing, in consonance with its generally Marxist economic philosophy (see ch. 8). Since 1960 it had exercised a monopoly of wholesale trade and foreign trade (except for the exports and imports of Fria), but there was a large volume of smuggling and illicit domestic trade both inside and outside official channels. Most manufacturing plants were state owned and operated at a loss. In 1973 the government had also begun to increase substantially its share in decisions and earnings in the mining sector. The planners hoped that these earnings would turn the chronic trade deficit of the 1960s into a surplus in the 1970s and permit gradual repayment of the formidable foreign debt.

The transportation system was reportedly in poor condition in 1974. Traffic on the old meter-gauge railroad from Conakry to Kankan was reportedly severely reduced, and most of the roads and motor vehicles had been poorly maintained. Three new mining railroads had been built since independence, and another costly new railroad was proposed from the southeastern border to Conakry, to permit exploitation of the iron ore deposits of the Forest Region.

MINING

For some years mineral exports had been the country's principal source of foreign exchange earnings; but in the estimate of its planners, it had barely begun to realize the ultimate potential of its rich mineral resources. Guinean government sources in 1974 were speaking in terms of eventual annual production of as much as 25 million tons of bauxite and 40 million tons of iron ore. These estimates were considered somewhat ambitious by trade sources. Moreover, they were predicated upon heavy foreign investment or loans for mining and railroad infrastructure, less than half of which had been firmly committed as of 1974. Their availability would depend upon demand and supply conditions in world metal industries, and investment plans could be imperiled by recession in the industrial countries or by continuing development of more readily accessible ore supplies in competing supplier countries.

In any event it was clear that, as a result of the investment already completed or committed in 1974, future mineral production would be many times higher than that recorded in past statistics. During the years 1964 through 1972 the one former iron ore mine had been closed down, and two of the three former bauxite mines had been exhausted, leaving only the mine and alumina (aluminum oxide) plant at Fria (Mount Kimbo) as the country's leading foreign exchange earner in 1972 (see table 8). Thereafter two new bauxite mines came into production in 1973 and 1974; one was far richer than any exploited in the past. Exploitation of three more bauxite deposits and the two rich iron ore deposits in the Forest Region was still in the planning stage in 1974.

Past mining operations had been characteristic enclave developments, employing more than 1,500 Guinean laborers but with few other linkages to the national economy. Equipment and materials were largely imported, and the railroads built from mine to port were reserved for the mine's inputs and output. Salaries paid to foreign employees and profits were largely remitted abroad. Wages and, after independence, the government's royalties on its mineral rights were the only sizable elements of mine earnings entering the national income.

At independence the government's Marxist advisers recommended that it follow the example of Morocco by immediate 60-percent nationalization of all mining enterprises, to be increased to 80 percent after two years and eventually to total nationalization. The government recognized, however, that this timetable was unrealistic in view of the need to attract massive new foreign capital to develop as yet unexploited deposits. Outright confiscation befell only some already established firms that refused to meet government demands, including two diamond mining firms that refused to sell through the government sales monopoly and a French bauxite mining company that proved unable to build a promised alumina plant. In negotiating with new foreign investors the government escalated its demands more flexibly as its bargaining position improved in the late 1960s and early 1970s along with the improving ratio of demand to supply in bauxite markets.

In the six mining agreements with foreign investors in effect in 1974,

Table 8. Guinea, Estimated Mineral Production, 1960 and 1965-72

| Year[1] | Bauxite | Alumina[2] | Iron Ore | Diamonds[3] |
	(in thousands of metric tons)			(in carats)
1960	1,678	484	1,362	1,117,000
1965	1,870	520	1,133	72,000
1966	1,608	525	2,400	72,000
1967	1,639	530	1,050	51,000
1968	2,117	531	...	70,000
1969	2,459	572	...	72,000
1970	2,600	599	...	74,000
1971	2,800	700	...	74,000
1972	3,000	800	...	80,000

... means none.
[1] Guinea's reporting year ends September 30.
[2] Aluminum oxide powder.
[3] United Nations estimate, supplied by the United States Bureau of Mines, includes both gem and industrial diamonds.

the government had increased its participation to 49, 50, or 51 percent and its tax on nominal net profits to at least 65 percent. Above all, it had increased its share in the foreign exchange equivalent of gross receipts. Until 1973 the foreign managers of Fria, for example, had retained two-thirds of the foreign exchange received from sales. Only one-third was deposited to the account of the government in a Swiss bank, the equivalent sum in Guinean currency being deposited to the firm's account in Guinea. In 1974 the government was receiving two-thirds of the foreign exchange equivalent of gross receipts and planned eventually to control the use of 100 percent of the total.

There was no information on the extent to which nominal increases achieved in share participation, ore sales prices, tax on profits, and foreign exchange control have actually augmented the nation's real share of income generated in mining. There was much confusion in published sources between net profits and foreign exchange receipts. Some French sources charged that as of 1970 the operation at Fria had not yet registered any net taxable profit after depreciation and debt amortization and that the new bauxite mine at Sangarédi (Boké Administrative Region) would not show a profit for many years. They claimed that the foreign investors determined the price at which ore was shipped to parent firms abroad and that these prices permitted no recorded profit. Guinean sources, however, announced price increases and tax rates as government decisions to which the foreign companies assented.

The government's share participation is received in return for its mineral rights, most of the capital being supplied by the foreign investors or lenders. The debt incurred is to be repaid out of ore shipments over a period of up to thirty years. In the past, repayment of some foreign debts has had to be deferred, and some of the government's harsher critics charge that in mining the ultimate outcome may be nationalization rather than repayment of the debt. Others claim that the government's share of mine earnings is mortgaged for debt repayment for many years into the future and that the nation is living on advances from the foreign companies against future mine earnings. Some international financial experts, however, reported that the government's policy in the late 1960s and early 1970s had succeeded in substantially improving its real share of mine earnings.

As more trained Guineans became available, the mining enterprises were complying with the government's timetable for africanization of management and technical staff. On the evidence visible in 1974, least progress had been made in satisfaction of the government's demands for more advanced mineral processing capacity within the country. The only processing more advanced than simple ore treatment was at the alumina plant at Fria, in operation since 1960. Frequently reported commitments for other processing plants had not yet materialized in the form of firm construction schedules.

In its effort to improve its bargaining position vis-á-vis the industrial countries that control world markets for metal and ores, Guinea joined with other bauxite-producing countries led by Jamaica and Guyana in forming the International Bauxite Association (IBA), with headquarters at Kingston, Jamaica. The agreement, reached at a conference in Conakry in March 1974, was subsequently signed by seven founding members, who produced some 42.6 million tons of the total world bauxite production of 65.8 million tons in 1972. They were Australia (13.7 million tons); Jamaica (13.0 million); Surinam (6.8 million); Guyana (3.7 million); Guinea (2.6 million); Yugoslavia (2.2 million); and Sierra Leone (600,000 tons in 1971). Two new members and several observer nations had been admitted by the end of 1974.

At the Conakry conference Guinea's President Ahmed Sékou Touré stressed that the goals of the IBA should be to obtain a review of bauxite prices and to increase the pressure for more alumina and aluminum plants near the bauxite deposits. As demand and prices for aluminum increased, the aim should be to achieve a marketing system that would be fair to both producers and consumers of bauxite. He pointed out that much of the value added in aluminum accrued at the smelting stage. Aluminum itself was an intermediate material, and the ratio between its price and the price of finished aluminum manufactures ranged between one to fifty and one to 100. If these conditions persisted, he said, it could take a long time for the Guinean people to develop their country, despite their rich mineral resources.

The Australians realistically pointed out, however, that bauxite, unlike crude petroleum, is produced in many countries of the world, so that the IBA's members could not hope to exert the kind of pressure on prices exercised by the Organization of Petroleum Exporting Countries (OPEC). Moreover, several aluminum companies had developed means of extracting alumina from clays other than bauxite that would become economically exploitable if the price of bauxite should rise beyond a certain point. Such substitutes were already widely used in Eastern Europe, where there is less emphasis on profitability. Rather than one world bauxite market, there are a number of separate markets: specific bauxite sources are tied through their investors to specific alumina and aluminum plants adapted to the use of specific qualities of bauxite, and the aluminum producers control the outlets available. This makes a common price policy very difficult to formulate, as profitability differs widely according to individual circumstances.

In 1974 both Jamaica and Guyana had imposed new levies on exports from their bauxite mines that were calculated on the price of aluminum rather than on the price of bauxite. In January 1975 Guinea followed suit. Guinea's new export tax was not only tied to the price of aluminum but was also applied to exports of crude bauxite at a higher rate than was applied to exports of alumina. This was to encourage the processing of bauxite into alumina within the country. In announcing the new tax, President Touré said that it was expected to yield the equivalent of US$25 million in 1975.

The president also made it clear that Guinea was taking steps to have a greater voice in such mining enterprise decisions as export prices and the destination of exports. Several new national enterprises were going to be formed to hold the Guinean government's half of the shares in the mixed mining enterprises that had been formed with foreign partners. As an equal participant, each of these national enterprises would exercise a vote equal to that of the foreign partners holding the other half of the shares.

The Guinean government's demands that investors provide for more advanced processing capacity have been pressed repeatedly since independence, but it was not clear whether the government's bargaining position had improved enough to turn these demands into reality. In 1972 mineral production had been chiefly in the form of alumina exports to such markets as Norway and Cameroon, where plentiful and cheap hydroelectric power had already been harnessed for aluminum production. Norway had no alumina production of its own, and Cameroon's bauxite resources had not yet been exploited.

Guinea had a rich unexploited hydroelectric power potential that could be harnessed for aluminum production, but it does not have the coke needed for steel production. Moreover, any development of heavy industry of the kind regularly announced as imminent by Guinea's planners would require some assurance of an export market. The small domestic market would not permit adequate economies of scale through mass production. There are also very distinct advantages in the location of metal-processing industries near their most sophisticated markets, as demand tends to be highly specialized.

Foreign loans and direct equity investment of the magnitude needed for mineral development have thus far proved to be forthcoming only from investors in search of a fresh supply of raw material for their own processing plants elsewhere. This was as true of Yugoslavia and the Soviet Union as of the giant private corporations. Investment in the mining of bauxite, for example, directly reflects activity in the aluminum industry, although there is an average lag of ten years between the discovery of a promising bauxite deposit and its coming into full production. Discovery of a rich ore reserve is not in itself enough to make exploitation of the deposit worthwhile. It must first coincide with the expectations of leading aluminum or steel producers regarding supply and demand conditions ten years in the future.

Bauxite

Of the country's five or six exploitable bauxite deposits, only those at Fria, Sangarédi, and Kindia were being mined by the end of 1974 (see fig. 8). The mine and alumina plant at Fria had been in operation since 1960. The first load of bauxite from the new mine at Sangarédi left the new ore port at Kamsar in August 1973. The Soviet-built open pit mine at Kindia (Débelé) was completed in 1975 but had already made its first token ore shipment to the Soviet Union in October 1974. Agreements had been concluded for mixed enterprises to exploit the deposits at Tougué and Dabola, but construction had not yet begun, and the government had not yet lined up enough foreign loan funds to build the required transport facilities. By 1972 the deposits on the Iles de Los off Conakry had been exhausted. The mine on Tamara Island had been closed down in 1972 and that on Kassa Island in 1966.

Government sources in 1974 had estimated the country's total bauxite resources at as much as 8 billion tons, or two-thirds of world resources. The United States Bureau of Mines, however, estimated world resources at 25 or 30 billion tons. Known reserves, which are more thoroughly assessed, were estimated by the Bureau of Mines at 3.5 billion tons for Guinea and 15.7 billion tons for the world. At either estimate Guinea might become a leading world exporter of bauxite by the mid-1980s.

Finance minister Ismail Touré asserted in early 1974 that bauxite production was expected to reach 25 million tons a year by the early 1980s. This estimate was apparently based on expectations that at full capacity the rich deposit at Sangarédi could yield 9 million tons a year; Tougué, 8 million tons; Dabola, 5 million tons; and Kindia, from 1 million to as much as 2.5 million tons. Plans for expanded capacity at Fria were never cited in terms of bauxite tonnage, but there had been agreement in 1972 to increase its capacity for alumina production to 1.1 million tons.

Each of the five deposits was to be exploited by an enterprise in which the Guinean government held approximately half the shares. The other half, and most of the financing, engineering, and technical advice, was being furnished by the Soviet Union at Kindia, by Yugoslavia at Dabola,

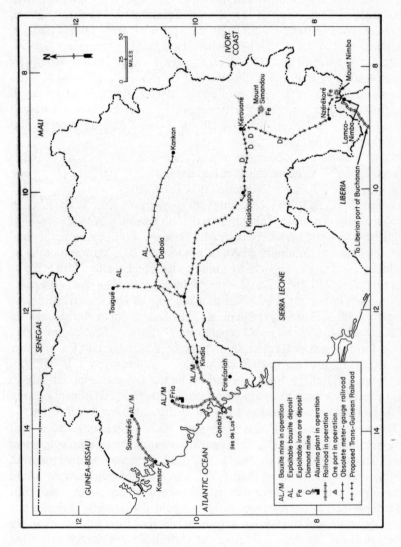

Figure 8. Guinea, Actual and Potential Mineral Activity, 1974

279

by a Swiss firm at Tougué, and by international consortia of aluminum firms at Fria and at Sangarédi.

Friguia

In February 1973 the government arrived at a new agreement with the consortium of private firms that had hitherto wholly owned and operated the Fria complex. A new mixed enterprise called Friguia was created, in which the government held 49 percent and the consortium, now known as Frialco, held 51 percent of the shares. Frialco comprised the French chemical firm Péchiney-Ugine-Kuhlmann (26.5 percent); Olin Mathieson Chemical Corporation of the United States (48.5 percent); British Aluminium Corporation (10 percent); Swiss Aluminium Company (Alusuisse), 10 percent; and the Vereinigte Aluminium Werke (United Aluminum Works) of the Federal Republic of Germany (West Germany), 5 percent. Péchiney had a majority vote on Frialco's board and managed the operation. In November 1974 Olin Mathieson sold its share to the Canadian firm Noranda Mines.

There was no announcement of any change in the disposal of Fria's exports, possibly because the debt had not been fully paid off. Under the 1958 agreement Guinea was entitled to only 8 to 10 percent of production for export to its Eastern European trading partners. Each of the firms in Frialco received a quota of alumina exports. A sizable share (22 percent in 1966) went to Norway, where both Alusuisse and British Aluminium had part interest in aluminum plants. In the late 1960s three-fourths of Péchiney's quota was reportedly going to its Alucam aluminum plant at Cameroon's Edéa dam. Large exports of alumina also went to Spain, where Péchiney and the Aluminium Company of Canada (Alcan) have interests. After Zaire's President Mobutu Sese Seko visited Guinea in 1972, several conflicting press reports suggested that Guinea and Zaire would form a joint enterprise to manufacture aluminum at Zaire's new Inga dam using alumina from Fria; that Kaiser Aluminum was building an aluminum plant at the Inga dam and would use bauxite from Sangarédi; and that future bauxite production from an unspecified Guinean source would be used for a government-operated aluminum smelter in Zaire.

The announcement of the February 1973 agreement stated that between 1962 and 1972 the Fria operation had reduced employment of non-Africans from 387 to thirty and had increased employment of Africans from 855 to more than 1,500. The Guinean government would henceforth take, in the form of taxes, 65 percent of any net taxable profit after depreciation and debt servicing. It would also henceforth decide the use of two-thirds of the foreign exchange received from sales abroad. Its previous foreign exchange share of one-third had been yielded only after difficult negotiations in 1961. The foreign management had subsequently complained that only 27 percent of Fria's receipts were needed for its expenditure in Guinean currency, and the surplus was accumulating in a currency rapidly depreciating in value. This consideration has continued to operate as a strong disincentive to private foreign investment in

Guinea. Frialco had also complained that in consequence its production costs in Guinea were too high to permit it to compete with the price of Australian bauxite.

The company's argument was disputed by the pro-Guinean French communist writer Jean Suret-Canale, whose book on Guinea, written in 1968, gives the most comprehensive account of the economy. He pointed out that the world aluminum industry is highly integrated vertically, in that each of the giant companies owns an interest in subsidiaries producing its raw material and chemical inputs and controls many of its outlets down to the final stage of manufacture. Thus the world market tends to be compartmentalized into vertical segments with separate price structures, and the companies tend to cooperate rather than compete. Thus higher production costs at one stage can often be absorbed in a noncompetitive market where the company is selling to itself.

Boké Project

The Boké bauxite project, completed in 1973, included an ore port and ore treatment plant at Kamsar, a mine and new mining town at the Sangarédi bauxite deposit, and an eighty-five-mile railroad connecting the two. None of the projects's installations was at the town of Boké. Failure to construct a promised alumina plant had resulted in revocation of an earlier investment agreement for the Boké project concluded before independence by Bauxites du Midi (Bauxites of Southern France), a French subsidiary of Alcan. The company had lined up several large aluminum firms in a consortium to provide financing, but they later backed out, and the French subsidiary alone could not finance the alumina plant. In retaliation the government in 1961 confiscated the company's bauxite mine on Kassa Island, in operation since 1952, and its equipment and matériel in Boké region, where preliminary construction of the railroad had begun in 1958. The Kassa mine was operated by the government from 1962 until it was exhausted in 1966.

In 1962 a relatively small American producer, Harvey Aluminum, was in search of bauxite to supply its plant in the Virgin Islands. In October 1963 it concluded an agreement with the Guinean government to undertake the Boké project. Pending the development of the project, it arranged to exploit the rather limited and low-grade deposit on Tamara Island, which was exhausted in 1972. It also built a plant in Guinea to manufacture housewares from imported aluminum.

The Sangarédi deposit was assessed by the Guineans at as much as 200 million tons with an aluminum content averaging more than 60 percent and a very low silica content, making it one of the highest grade deposits in the world. As supply tightened in world bauxite markets, this proved inviting enough to outweigh potential drawbacks to investment, and Harvey Aluminum was able to form a consortium known as Halco to finance the mining and processing installations. Harvey Aluminum was subsequently absorbed by the American firm Martin Marietta, so that when the mine came into operation in mid-1973 Halco consisted of Alcan,

27 percent; Aluminum Company of America (Alcoa), 27 percent; Martin Marietta, 20 percent; Péchiney-Ugine-Kuhlmann, 10 percent; the Vereinigte Aluminium Werke, 10 percent and Montecatini-Edison of Italy, 6 percent.

The mine was operated by a mixed enterprise, the Bauxite Company of Guinea (Compagnie des Bauxites de Guinée—CBG), in which the government had 49 percent of the shares and was to take 65 percent of any net profits in taxes. A government agency, the Boké Improvement Office (Office d'Aménagement de Boké—OFAB), would operate the railroad and the ore port at Kamsar, construction of which was financed by official foreign loans. The agreement specified that the railroad would not be reserved exclusively for the mine inputs and output but could be used to promote development of the surrounding region subject to priority right of use by the mine. By mid-1973 the Boké project had absorbed more than US$339 million in direct investment and loans, including initial loans of US$73.5 million from the International Bank for Reconstruction and Development (IBRD, commonly known as the World Bank); US$20 million in United States aid; and US$25 million from the Export-Import Bank for the purchase of equipment in the United States.

Other Projects

The smallest of the deposits was that on the Débelé near Kindia, estimated at 43 million tons with an average aluminum content of 48 percent. The April 1972 contract with the Soviet Union provided for deliveries of 90 percent of mine production a year for thirty years. Part would be applied against the debt for Kindia and the remainder to retire earlier debts still outstanding. The open pit mine was operated by a government authority, the Kindia Bauxite Office (Office des Bauxites de Kindia—OBK or Obeka). Because the old meter-gauge railroad was unsuitable for ore transport, Soviet engineers built a parallel seventy-mile standard-gauge railroad from Kindia to Conakry and reconstructed two abandoned ore docks in the center of Conakry port to accommodate Soviet ore carriers. The line was officially inaugurated in April 1974, and a first small token shipment of bauxite was made in October.

The Dabola deposit, also exploitable by open pit mining, was assessed at about 300 million or 400 million tons. The April 1971 agreement with the Yugoslav enterprise Energoprojekt created a joint enterprise, the Dabola Bauxite Company, in which the Guinean government held 51 percent of the shares. It will take either 65 or 75 percent of any net profits; reports differ. Dabola is some 210 miles from Conakry. Yugoslavia was committed to build a 152-mile road to the village of Dogome, which is not shown on available maps but may be surmised to be at a junction with the main highway from Mamou to Conakry. For both Dabola and Tougué, Guinea had undertaken to provide rail transport. In 1974 its planners were still seeking financing for the US$550 million

Trans-Guinean Railroad, to have spurs to Dabola and Tougué (see Transportation, this ch.).

The Tougué deposit was one of the richest but was the most remote from major transport arteries. The official estimate was more than 2 billion tons, with an aluminum content of 65 percent. The February 1971 agreement with Alusuisse created a mixed enterprise, the Swiss-Guinean Mining Company (Compagnie des Mines Guinée-Alusuisse—Somiga), to operate the mine and a trading company called Intersomiga, based in Zurich, to handle the exports. Guinea was to take 65 percent of net profit in taxes.

At the urging of Guinea, representatives of Alusuisse met in Algiers in May 1974 with representatives of Energoprojekt to agree on a merger of the Tougué and Dabola operations. Algerian officials also attended and reportedly promised to import finished aluminum from Guinea if the Swiss and the Yugoslavs could agree to build a joint aluminum plant. Guinea also sought to attract official foreign loans from other countries for construction of the proposed aluminum complex. Radio Conakry continued to announce at intervals, as it had ever since independence, that the required commitment had been received from one country or another, notably Romania, Algeria, Egypt, and several other Arab countries. It also reported that the Dabola agreement had provided for two plants to produce annually 300,000 tons of alumina and 150,000 tons of aluminum.

A French business weekly reported in January 1975 that a sixth bauxite deposit was to be exploited in partnership with Libya, Egypt, Kuwait, and Saudi Arabia. It was called Ayekoé and was located in the Boké concession area northwest of Sangarédi.

Iron Ore

In 1974 final arrangments had not yet been concluded for eventual exploitation of the rich iron ore deposits of the Forest Region. Mining of the lower grade Kaloum deposit near Conakry, begun in 1952, ceased in 1966. In 1974 the government had not yet been able to find financing to replace the abandoned equipment and mine the reserves left in the deposit, which had a high content of impurities. The Forest Region deposits, at Mount Nimba in the Nimba Mountains near the Liberian border and in the Simandou Mountains sixty miles to the north, were far more promising. They were of high grade, with about 65 percent iron content. Preliminary press reports variously estimated their size at from 300 million to 600 million tons at Nimba and from 450 million to 1 billion tons at Simandou. There were glowing official predictions that they would eventually make Guinea a leading exporter of iron ore if capital could be raised for construction either of the costly Trans-Guinean Railroad or of other means of evacuating the ore.

The Nimba deposit is not far from the Liberian iron-mining town of

Lamco-Nimba, and it was hoped that by April 1975 agreement could be reached between the Guinean government and the Liberian American Swedish Mining Company (Lamco) on the use of Lamco's railroad to carry the Guinean ore to the port of Buchanan. The line's capacity might have to be expanded. Negotiations with foreign steel companies in 1971 for development of the Forest Region ore had reportedly foundered because the foreign companies favored use of the Liberian line for the ore from both Nimba and Simandou, but the Guineans insisted on eventual construction of the Trans-Guinean Railroad.

Although the world steel industry was booming in 1972, a relatively accessible and abundant supply of high-grade ore in such supplier countries as Australia and Brazil reduced incentives to investment in Simandou or Nimba. Recurrent press reports originating with Radio Conakry alleged agreement with such firms as United States Steel and British Steel, but apparently nothing came of these negotiations. After 1972 reports placed increasing stress on potential sales to Japanese steelmakers, whose production had been expanding most rapidly. In 1974 some Japanese firms were predicting a worldwide shortage of steel by 1980 and urging increased investment.

In 1969 Guinea created the Iron Mining Company of Guinea (Société des Mines de Fer de Guinée—Mifergui), in which the government would have 50 percent of the shares. This was later divided into two corporate entities, Mifergui-Nimba and Mifergui-Simandou, to permit separate share subscription by foreign investors. The governments of Nigeria, Liberia, Algeria, and Zaire were reported to be subscribing to both. The other participants in Mifergui-Simandou had not yet been lined up in late 1974. An agreement on Mifergui-Nimba was signed in Tokyo in April 1973. A Japanese business periodical reported that the participants were Nigeria (10 percent); Liberia (5 percent); Algeria (state steel enterprise, 14 percent); Energoprojekt of Yugoslavia (22 percent); Rudis of Yugoslavia (5 percent); Nichimen of Japan (14 percent); Mitsubishi of Japan (3 percent); Intermaritime Bank of Switzerland (14 percent); the Fiduciary Investment Company (Compania Fiduziara de Investimiento—Cofei), Spanish financiers (5 percent); and the National Industrial Institute (Instituto Nacional de Industria—INI) of Spain (8 percent).

Later reports that other investors, notably Romania, had become associated with Mifergui had not been confirmed by the end of 1974. Finance minister Ismail Touré had explained in 1973 that the Mifergui project would have two phases. Phase I would focus on development of the Nimba deposit, which would yield from 7 million to an eventual 15 million tons of iron ore a year, to be evacuated at first by the Lamco railroad. Phase II would involve development of Simandou, which would yield an additional 25 million tons a year. By 1980, when new steel mills will be completed in Japan, Simandou should be brought into production.

Construction of the Trans-Guinean Railroad should be under way during Phase II and completed by 1982.

Diamonds

Because no reliable data were published on diamond production, some critics of the government could claim that production had declined since independence, and others could charge that production had increased but that the diamonds were being misappropriated. Data available did not include smuggled stones, which were thought to constitute much of production. Before 1959 two-thirds of all diamonds produced were industrial. One estimate reported production of 21,000 carats of gemstones and 51,000 carats of industrial diamonds in 1967, but there is substantial unexplained divergence among different sources.

Production began in 1936 and increased after the 1959 discovery of new alluvial fields with more stones of gem quality. Output in 1959 was 643,000 carats. Alluvial deposits are located between Kissidougou, Beyla, and Kérouané. A Soviet survey in 1963 and 1964 located eight new pipes of kimberlite in Forécariah Administrative Region that might contain some 200 million carats of diamonds, in contrast to previous alluvial reserves of 1.5 million carats.

These new deposits would require complicated and costly drilling equipment. The older alluvial deposits could be exploited by dredging or hand panning. At independence two foreign firms had been operating diamond concessions and washing plants. There were also more than 40,000 individuals engaged in independent placer mining in small hand-dug pits. About 4,000 of these were small-scale entrepreneurs employing two or three others. Independents probably accounted for more than half of production between 1936 and 1960, but they were banned after 1960 because they were regarded by party ideologues as socially undesirable and because they allegedly smuggled out most of their diamonds and would not work in the rainy season. Inefficient panning techniques also caused losses of up to 50 percent and stripped off the top layers in a way that made later mining of the deeper layers uneconomic. For a brief period in late 1963 and 1964 independent placer mining under license was again permitted, but virtually all of the resulting production was smuggled out and, like the concurrent experiment with private trading, this policy was declared a failure and terminated in November 1964.

Before independence legal sales went through the international diamond cartel, but most diamonds were said to have been smuggled into Mali, Liberia, Sierra Leone, or Ghana for sale. Shortly after independence the government broke with the cartel and set up its own office with a monopoly of all diamond purchases and exports. After the December 1958 currency devaluation stones were smuggled in from Sierra Leone for sale, but after the introduction of the Guinean franc in March 1960 the flow was again reversed. All diamond mining was nationalized in March 1961. A state enterprise, the Guinean Diamond Exploitation Enterprise (Entreprise Guinéenne d'Exploitation du Diamant—EGED), was created to run the two operations confiscated from foreign firms. Technical assistance was provided by the Soviet Union.

Suret-Canale reported that in 1968 three deposits were being mined, at Banankoro, Ouroukoro, and Gbinigko, all located between Kissidougou and Kérouané. Modern washing plants had been built at Banankoro and Bounoudou. He also asserted that the planners had not realized that the Soviet aid allocated for geological prospecting in the early 1960s would not be adequate to cover diamond mining development as well. As a result of this miscalculation and of the continued growth of smuggling, he said, diamond production had fallen off sharply by 1966 but began to revive in 1968 after Belgian technical advisers were brought in. This report was echoed by other sources; but Suret-Canale's estimate of only 20,000 carats of diamonds produced in 1966 conflicts with the later official estimates, which show production sustained at 72,000 carats in 1966.

Petroleum Exploration

In June 1974 the Guinean government entered into an agreement with an American oil company, Buttes Resources International, to prospect for oil in a 17,000-square-mile area of the offshore continental shelf. A joint enterprise was created and named Guinean Petroleum Company (Société Guinéenne de Pétrole—Soguip), 49 percent of the shares being owned by the government and 51 percent by the American firm. Guinea was to take 63 percent of eventual profits if oil should be found and exploited at a profit. After a preliminary survey the American company was to select an area of 1,850 to 3,700 square miles for further development. Soguip would have the sole rights to prospect, extract, and market any oil or natural gas found on the offshore shelf. A representative of Buttes Resources International said that the company estimated its chances of finding oil at 80 percent.

MANUFACTURING

Manufacturing activity in 1974 was dominated by the alumina plant at Fria, the only operation in the sector to have contributed appreciably to growth. Other manufacturing plants had mostly been installed before 1965, when in the early rush to industrialize there had been inadequate planning of such matters as markets, production costs, and raw material supply. The resulting problems had been intensified by the disarray of agricultural production and the stagnation of peasant consumer incomes, by the depreciation of the currency, and by the chronic shortage of foreign exchange for imports of materials and parts needed for industry. By the 1970s most plants were thought to be operating well below capacity and in many cases at a loss.

In 1965 a number of small private French-owned plants dating from before independence were still in operation, including a brewery and soft drink plant and plants producing soap, chemicals, and fruit juice. These employed an average of only fifty people, and there were also a large number of small artisan-scale operations. State-owned and -operated public enterprises accounted for the equivalent of US$5.2 million of the total manufacturing output of US$6.5 million in 1965, presumably excluding Fria. The role of some mixed state-private enterprises may have been somewhat enhanced thereafter. Information on capacity completed since 1965 was fragmentary. In many cases the reappearance of a manufacturing project in a later development plan is the first indication that it was not actually realized under an earlier plan, as confidently reported in the foreign press.

A number of the public enterprises had been initiated with communist foreign aid under the Three Year Development Plan (1960—63). These included the Soviet-built cannery at Mamou (completed in 1963); the tobacco and match factory built by the People's Republic of China (PRC) at Conakry (completed in 1966); a furniture factory at Sonfonya; three slaughterhouses; two printing plants; a brickworks; and a fish-processing plant. Beginning in 1963 with the agreements with Harvey Aluminum, a policy of encouraging mixed enterprises was initiated. In 1963 a contract was signed with a British firm for a textile spinning and weaving complex at Sanouya (completed in 1966). It was eventually to use domestic cotton, but the usual problems of supply were encountered. Subsequent contracts provided for enterprises to produce concrete reinforcement bars (Austria); shoes (West Germany); glass (Hungary); and Mack trucks (United States).

In 1964 a program was launched to increase domestic supply of, and capacity for processing, such rural products as groundnut (peanut) oil, rice, sugar, milk, and forest products. A few such projects were realized under the Seven Year Plan (1964—71), including two fruit juice canneries, a Soviet-built sawmill at Nzérékoré; a particle board factory at Sérédou; and a tea sorting and drying plant at Macenta with adjoining plantations built by the Chinese Communists. In 1968 the first groundnut oil mill was completed at Kassa to employ workers from the closed bauxite mine, and a second mill was started at Dabola. One brickworks had been built by the Yugoslavs at Kobeya in 1963, and a second by the Chinese Communists at Kankan in 1973. There was also a tire retreading plant built with United States aid and one or two cement works.

By 1968 most of these operations were functioning poorly, and Suret-Canale has described some of their individual problems in detail. The foremost difficulties were inadequacies in raw material supply, market outlets, and replacement parts. Poor transportation and inadequately trained personnel also burdened production costs and inhibited smooth operation. The cannery at Mamou was the most frequently cited example of failure in both raw material base and market planning (see ch. 11). By 1972 the cannery was reportedly operating at 20 percent of capacity, the Kobeya brickworks at 30 percent, the furniture plant at 35 percent, and the Nzérékore sawmill at 40 percent The tobacco and match monopoly was thought to be the only public enterprise operating at a profit, because of the high protected prices inherited from the French colonial regime. It had brought both a significant saving in foreign exchange and a contribution to government revenues—thus far, the only important manufacturing project except Fria to fulfill these original objectives.

ELECTRIC POWER POTENTIAL

Guinea is sometimes called the watershed of West Africa. Lying across the path of the rain-bearing southwest winds, its mountains receive a heavy rainfall. Many fast-flowing streams descend from the plateaus through deep and narrow valleys, providing an excellent potential for hydroelectric development. A survey of hydroelectric potential started by the French in 1948 was completed by Bulgarian experts in 1961. Total potential was estimated at 63.2 billion kilowatt-hours, of which one-third was on the upper reaches of the Niger River, 16 percent on the Bafing (Sénégal River), and 19 percent on the Konkouré River. Sources that could be immediately harnessed to yield some 13.6 billion kilowatt-hours included the Konkouré (6 billion), the Tominé (2 billion), the Bafing (3 billion), and the Upper Niger (1 billion), By 1974, however, only a small fraction of this potential had been harnessed, and the power system still relied heavily on thermal stations using imported fuel oil.

The electric power system had been nationalized in 1961 and brought under the aegis of the National Electricity Company (Société Nationale d'Electricité). During the 1960s most of the increase in electric power production had taken place at the independently operated thermal power plant at Fria, but after some new public power capacity came into operation, Fria was producing only about one-third of the 470 million kilowatt-hours generated in 1972.

The number of power consumers increased from 7,700 in 1958 to some 20,000 in 1967. At independence only eight of the principal towns had access to electric power for lighting and domestic use, but by 1974 it was claimed that the chief towns of all the administrative regions were electrified. Small diesel generators were used in most of the smaller towns that were not yet connected to the national grid, and for the most part use of electricity in such towns was confined to the home of the local party functionary and to certain hours of the day.

Installed capacity had remained unchanged from 1958 to 1962 at 16,300 kilowatts. Between 1962 and 1967 it had increased to 91,500 kilowatts. A credit from the United States had been used to install supplementary generators at Kankan, Siguiri, Gaoual, and Boké and for a new thermal plant at Conakry. Another thermal plant had been built at Conakry with aid from West Germany. Total installed capacity was still reported as 91,500 kilowatts in 1972, By 1975 it had probably increased to 114,000 kilowatts (see table 9). The Boké project had brought new thermal stations at Sangarédi and Kamsar, and hydroelectric projects on the Donké and on the Tinkisso below Dabola were under way in 1973 and possibly completed in 1974 (see fig. 9).

The dam and power station at Grandes Chutes had been inherited from the French at independence, but its capacity was increased in 1963 with assistance from Yugoslavia. An earth dam was built at nearby Kaléa on the Samou River, creating a reservoir that furnished the water supply for Conakry and regulated the flow to the power station at Grandes Chutes. Capacity at Grandes Chutes was increased from 10,000 to 20,000 kilowatts. By 1974 the Yugoslavs had reportedly completed the second phase of expansion at Kaléa-Grandes Chutes. This comprised a second earth dam at Banéa, five miles upstream from Kaléa, to feed a 15,000-kilowatt power station on the Donké downstream from Kaléa.

The dam and power station at the Kinkon gorge on the Kokuolo below Pita were completed by the Chinese Communists in 1966 and have been used to light the towns of Pita, Labé, Dalaba, and Mamou. In January 1972 the PRC started construction of a mixed earth and concrete dam on the Tinkisso, five miles below Dabola. On completion of the second phase in 1974 Tinkisso was to have installed capacity of 1,500 kilowatts and permit electrification of Dinguiraye and other towns in the region and the development of industry at Dabola.

Hydroelectric projects were assigned high priority under the Five Year Development Plan (1973–78). A dam and hydroelectric station were to be built with Yugoslav aid on the Koukoutamba, which enters the Tinkisso south of Dinguiraye. The project was supposed to be completed by 1980 and to furnish power for processing the bauxite of Tougué and Dabola as well as lighting for the towns of Dinguiraye, Siguiri, Labé, Kouroussa, and Faranah. The five-year plan also revived plans for a hydroelectric project on the Konkouré that had been an unrealized feature of previous development plans. It had first been proposed by the French and the World Bank in 1958 and revived by Soviet technical advisers in 1965. They may have lost enthusiasm when the project was later associated with power for the Western-financed Boké project. More probably, the Konkouré project may have been deferred because the industry developed thus far was operating below capacity and could not economically use such a large volume of energy. The project has usually been associated with ambitious plans for future production of aluminum, iron, and steel. As outlined in the previous Seven Year Plan, the Konkouré project would involve two phases. The first dam would be built at Souapiti, with a 480,000-kilowatt power station. The second dam, with a power station of 720,000-kilowatt capacity, would be constructed at Amaria. A third location farther upstream was shown on some maps.

DOMESTIC TRADE

Despite a series of reforms and reorganizations, the internal

Table 9. Guinea, Installed Electric Power Capacity, 1975
(in kilowatts)

	Thermal[1]	Hydroelectric
Fria	41,214	...
Conakry	12,800	...
Grandes Chutes-Kaléa	32	20,000
Donké[2]	...	15,000
Kipé	1,760	...
Kankan	2,940	...
Mamou	828	...
Kinkon	...	3,200
Labé	35	180
Boké	390	...
Macenta	160	160
Siguiri	250	...
Gaoual	250	...
Nzérékoré	1,050	...
Sérédou	500	640
Kamsar	4,000	...
Sangarédi	2,000	...
Tinkisso[2]	...	1,500
Other	1,500	...
Errors and omissions[1]	3,611	...
TOTAL	73,320	40,680

... means none.

[1] Total thermal power capacity installed was usually reported as 67,320 kilowatts in 1967 and 1972, but thermal stations listed by Voss for 1967 totaled only 63,709 kilowatts. The difference of 3,611 kilowatts may have represented an increase in capacity at Fria or elsewhere.

[2] The installations at Donké and Tinkisso were scheduled for completion during 1974, but the latest reports on their progress were dated 1973; so their completion had not yet been confirmed.

Source: Adapted from Joachim Voss, *Guinea*, Bonn, 1968, p. 209; Jean Suret-Canale, *La République de Guinée*, Paris, 1970.

distribution system was still in chaotic condition in 1974. The critical shortage of foodstuffs and other consumer goods in licit channels of trade arose only partly from deficiencies in production and restrictions on imports. A major problem was that farm produce and imported goods were smuggled to neighboring countries for more favorable exchange or were sold on the black market. Rationing of food and other necessities sent consumers into the black market to pay three or four times the legal price for such items as soap, sugar, rice, and vegetable oil. Production was further curtailed because, in conditions of runaway inflation and lack of confidence in the currency, time spent away from work in search of food or goods for trading was often of more value than wages. Claude Riviére, an authoritative French observer, reported in mid-1971 that the wages and salaries of workers and petty officials had increased by only 10 percent since 1960 while at the same time prices had gone up by between 100 and 120 percent.

Most reports dated from before the introduction of the syli in October

1972, which was designed to correct some of these conditions by restoring confidence in the currency (see ch. 10). Smuggling and black-marketeering apparently flourished unabated in 1974, however, despite draconian penalties. In the early days of nationalized trade many government officials, high and low, had carried on private trading operations on the side through their wives or other agents. Although a law was enacted against the practice, it was said to persist in 1974.

President Touré said in November 1968 that the peasant must helplessly witness the incessant coming and going of heavy trucks across the frontiers, engaging in illicit trade organized by those in authority. An article by Siradiou Diallo in *Jeune Afrique* charged in November 1972 that one regional governor was smuggling to Liberia the coffee officially collected from the growers, another was smuggling requisitioned beef cattle to Senegal, and still another was selling diamonds in Sierra Leone. The peasants were producing less and, even when price subsidies were high, they often preferred to sell through illicit channels. When they got the chance, they sold a good proportion of their products beyond the borders, where they could afford to buy a piece of cloth, a bar of soap, or other manufactures that were beyond their reach at domestic black-market prices.

At independence or shortly thereafter the policymakers had sought to eliminate the middleman and the foreign colonial trading interests at one blow by nationalizing both foreign and domestic trade. According to Suret-Canale, this was not a previous ideological commitment but rather a policy forced upon the government by the uncooperative hostility of the great French colonial trading firms. Complete nationalization of trade and banking had been recommended, however, by a group of French economic advisers headed by the Marxist professor Charles Bettleheim. During 1959 and 1960 a government agency called a *comptoir* had been established for domestic trade and another to handle foreign trade under bilateral agreements with the communist countries and all foreign trade in certain import and export products.

The ensuing chaos was such that in November 1960 the *comptoirs* were given a complete monopoly of foreign and wholesale trade. The foreign-owned trading firms were not confiscated but had lost their chief fields of activity, and most firms departed. The government hoped to siphon trade profits into a fund for development expenditure. By late 1960 the distribution system was said to be near the point of breakdown. Its problems were attributed in part to a boycott by the overseas connections of the French banks and trading firms and in part to inexperience, inefficiency, and spreading corruption. Thousands of tons of imports piled up on the docks, and only a small percentage moved inland. Delays and uncoordinated or inappropriate import authorizations caused a heavy rate of loss from spoilage, and imported equipment rusted or deteriorated from disuse because of lack of parts. Shortages led to sharp price increases, and unrealistic price controls drove imports and some domestic products off the legitimate market.

Far from eliminating the middleman, the state trading system proved so profitable to those with the right connections that would-be middlemen proliferated on all sides. The president commented that "everyone is a trader or wants to become one: the official is a trader, the driver is a trader, the clerk is a trader." Imports exceeded planned levels by 40 percent, with no visible benefit to the economy or the consumer. Experienced retail traders were meanwhile being discouraged by arbitrary denial of import licenses. After the introduction of the Guinean franc in 1960, the disruption of the distribution and price system had been further accelerated by loss of confidence in the currency.

The first solution adopted was to decentralize the state trading operations. In August 1961 the two *comptoirs* were replaced by a number of separate offices to deal with different categories of commodity. In each administrative region a regional wholesale office distributed goods to the government-operated stores and to private retailers. This system still prevailed in 1974, but there had been a brief interval of more permissive policy in 1963 and 1964, when the government monopoly of import and wholesale trade was temporarily relaxed. In the early 1970s the foreign press reported that the government had again become dissatisfied with certain aspects of state trading. On October 31, 1971, it was announced that private traders would henceforth be allowed to trade in agricultural products, hitherto a government monopoly (see ch. 11). There was a later report that hotels, theaters, and nightclubs were to be turned over to private operation. In mid-1974 thousands of passports were given to traditional traders so that they could buy food in neighboring countries to relieve the critical shortage in Conakry.

The 1963–64 experiment with private trading had not lasted long. It was brought about because the regional trading authorities had run up a large debt and because it was hoped that trading could once again be confined to a more limited class, stemming the tendency for everyone to become a trader on the side and thus, by ideological definition, a bourgeois. In 1963 the regional government stores had been temporarily abolished and turned over to cooperatives or to private traders. A regulation decreed that employment as a government official or as a wage or salary earner in either a public or a private establishment was incompatible with activity as a trader.

After a year the experiment with partial private trade was declared a disastrous failure, and state monopoly of foreign and wholesale trade was reintroduced under an article of the *loi-cadre* (enabling act) of November 8, 1964. To enter trade, a retailer was required to have a minimum capital of GF10 million (for value of the Guinean franc—see Glossary). The regional stores were returned to government operation, and the number of private retail trading licenses were drastically reduced—by four-fifths in Conakry alone. In a town the size of Guéckédou, for example, the *loi-cadre* left only three licensed private traders.

Because suppressed demand continued greatly to outpace supply, people in all walks of life had seen their opportunity to profit by becoming traders, and the artificially maintained low prices meant that goods could be smuggled to neighboring countries and sold at a substantial markup. The increasing number of middlemen engaged in each transaction operated to drive up black-market prices and, as the cost of living increased, more and more people were obliged to participate in illicit transactions. It became more impossible than ever for the government to exercise effective control over price manipulation, currency fraud, and other illegal exchanges. Cultivators left their fields to set up as small traders, further affecting production. The effect of the *loi-cadre* was to revoke the licensed status of many of the small traders, but it did not succeed in stemming the tide of illicit activity.

While repeatedly denouncing negligence and corruption among government officials engaging in trade, the ruling party also declared that probably 70 percent of all retail traders must be regarded as enemies of the state. The fact that licensed private retailers could be most easily reached by penalties for profiteering may have contributed to the preference for illegal channels of trade. Before independence the import trade and most wholesaling of imported goods had been controlled by major French colonial trading firms. After nationalization most of the French who engaged in wholesale or retail enterprise were obliged to depart, and the need to fill the vacuum thus created was responsible for part of the initial chaos in the distribution system. Many shopkeepers of Lebanese origin, most of whom had operated on a smaller scale, have remained. Their retail activity was curtailed by the cutback in licenses after 1964 and the government's desire to africanize the trading sector. They have been admonished to enter other forms of activity, such as plantation agriculture, and some have done so. Despite occasional official disclaimers of any antagonism toward the Lebanese as such, those who remain in trade have been among the many convenient targets for denunciation when things go wrong.

Traditionally the larger part of domestic trade took the form of barter within the village or between neighboring villages, but there was also a flow of produce from the villages to the towns in which women played a major role. Little information is available about the extent to which this customary trade has been disrupted by legislation or by shortages and the resulting price distortions.

Food rationing was progressively introduced after 1967, and distribution was placed in the hands of local committees of the sole political party (see ch. 6). A party economic conference in Kindia in December 1965 had launched the idea of boosting incentives to crop production by opening local shops for barter where peasants could exchange their produce for consumer goods at advantageous prices. In theory this system was still in effect at the local people's stores in 1974 but, in practice, few consumer goods were available for distribution at any price.

FOREIGN TRADE

After the country cut adrift in 1960 from the monetary discipline and support of the franc area (see Glossary), the currency depreciated at an estimated 20 percent a year (see ch. 10). The assessment on free foreign exchange markets in 1972 was that the currency was about three or four times overvalued. As the authorities refused to devalue, exports stagnated, and despite drastic curtailment of imports the foreign debt mounted. Most exports did not go to very competitive markets. Some 70 percent of the total in 1972 was alumina and bauxite. Two-thirds of crop exports went to communist countries at above world market prices, and much of this trade was under barter agreements. Yet exports of tropical products had not avoided some of the setbacks encountered by those producers who failed to adapt to mounting competition on the Western European market and compared unfavorably to those of such successful adapters as Ivory Coast.

Only summary trade data have been published since 1965. No definitions are given, and time series may not be consistent. The recurrence of identical figures suggests that some may be government estimates, or they may derive from actual records of goods cleared through customs. In any case export totals are referred to as recorded exports as a reminder that they exclude the large volume of smuggled exports, estimated by Suret-Canale in the mid-1960s at about GF2 billion a year. Imports are referred to as unplanned imports because they exclude not only smuggled imports but also imports authorized under successive development plans. Data on these are available only for the years 1965 through 1969, when they fluctuated between GF2.4 billion and GF4.7 billion.

Inclusion of planned imports would thus add appreciably to the import deficit. If the assumption is made, however, that all major imports under the plan are excluded and that most such imports are financed by some form of foreign loan, then the unplanned imports given in the published statistics would correspond more or less to the value of merchandise imports to be paid for out of current foreign exchange earnings or commercial credits. The planners hoped to reverse the unfavorable balance on merchandise trade once the Sangarédi bauxite mine came into full production. They estimated that Sangarédi exports alone would add the equivalent of some US$35 million to export earnings, or 58 percent of recorded 1972 export value. This would permit a badly needed increase in essential imports and reduction of the foreign debt.

Direction of Trade

The volume of trade with a given country reported in Guinea's data may differ from the figure reported by the country concerned. West Germany's statistical office found that only 5 percent of its imports from Guinea in 1965 had been purchased directly from Guinea; the rest were bought from third countries. The assumption is, however, that the countries listed in the statistics are those of ultimate origin or destination.

The orientation of Guinea's foreign trade has shown variations over the period since independence, partly reflecting its changing commodity composition and partly in response to shifts in official policy. Further and perhaps more substantial shifts of direction were expected after 1973.

The direction of exports had been increasingly determined by the location of aluminum plants connected with the private companies that had invested in Guinean bauxite projects. This explained large exports to Norway, Spain, and Cameroon and perhaps also the reduction in exports to the United States after 1967 (see table 10). For the same reason the orientation of exports might have shifted beginning in 1973 as new bauxite mines came into production. Because production at Sangarédi and Tougué will be higher than that financed by the Soviet Union at Kindia and by Yugoslavia at Dabola, the relative share of communist countries might decline as the relative importance of crop exports continues to dwindle. Among the future destinations mentioned for Sangarédi bauxite exports were the United States, Canada, West Germany, France, and Italy; Tougué was to be exploited by a Swiss firm. The outlook for the longer term, when markets must be found for iron ore and perhaps for semimanufactured metals, was more uncertain. Moreover, after 1972 Guinea had secured much greater control over the use of foreign exchange earnings from mining, and in January 1975 President Touré announced that the country would assume more control over the destination of its crude ore exports.

An internally consistent trade series was available only for the years 1964 through 1972. Comparisons with earlier years, therefore, may not be entirely valid: for example, earlier import figures may have included imports under the development plan.

In the years 1960 through 1962 trade with the communist countries, excluding Yugoslavia, had averaged about 23 percent of recorded exports and 35 percent of recorded imports. Their share of trade then declined radically, reaching an exceptional low of 11 percent of exports and imports in 1966. Beginning in 1967 they again accounted for a mounting share of trade. After the severance of relations with West Germany in 1971, they were taking 23.8 percent of recorded exports in 1972, surpassing the share (21.8 percent) going to the United Kingdom and the six founding members of the European Economic Community (EEC— also known as the Common Market). If exports to Norway are added, the Western European countries listed were taking 37.9 percent of exports. Some 37.6 percent of 1972 unplanned imports came from the communist countries and 27.5 percent from the United Kingdom and the

Table 10. *Guinea, Direction of Trade, Selected Years, 1964–72*[1]
(in millions of Guinean francs)[2]

	1964	1965	1966	1967	1969	1971	1972
Unplanned Imports[3]							
EEC[4]	4,070	5,280	5,280	4,700	3,800	4,500	4,700
United Kingdom..........	1,360	910	670	250	180	150	120
Yugoslavia..........	70	350	760	550	590	590	530
Soviet Union	530	610	950	1,330	1,740	3,800	3,950
Other Eastern Europe	1,275	720	770	840	750	1,350	840
People's Republic of China (PRC)	40	70	220	480	830	1,720	1,800
United States	2,890	4,630	2,960	1,730	830	1,280	1,450
Cameroon..........	20	440	370	210	250	350	340
Other countries..........	2,125	70	5,300	6,440	4,110	6,080	3,710
Subtotal	12,380	13,080	17,280	16,530	13,080	19,760	17,520
Imports under the plan..........	n.a.	3,200	3,300	2,400	3,000	n.a.	n.a.
Total imports	n.a.	16,280	20,580	18,930	16,080	n.a.	n.a.

298

Recorded Exports[5]

EEC[4]	2,910	2,120	2,150	2,250	3,170	2,760	2,810
United Kingdom...	520	520	520	110	10	...	...
Norway	1,750	1,880	1,980	2,470	2,520	2,120	2,070
Yugoslavia	220	570	860	350	240	180	110
Soviet Union.....	310	530	620	950	1,110	1,470	1,420
Other Eastern Europe	890	670	850	780	620	1,050	1,060
People's Republic of China (PRC)	20	40	90	250	520	650	590
United States	1,780	2,960	2,960	1,240	530	470	350
Cameroon	1,410	1,480	540	740	1,240	1,270	1,120
Other countries[6]	5,660	2,560	3,750	3,460	4,110	2,380	3,340
Total exports.....	15,470	13,330	14,320	12,600	14,070	12,350	12,870

... means none; n.a. means not available.

[1] Guinea's reporting year ends September 30.

[2] For value of the Guinean franc—see Glossary.

[3] Imports are valued c.i.f. (cost, insurance, and freight included).

[4] The old six-member European Economic Community (Common Market) comprising France, Italy, Belgium, the Netherlands, Luxembourg, and the Federal Republic of Germany (West Germany).

[5] Exports are valued f.o.b. (free on board—excluding insurance and freight beyond borders).

[6] Notably alumina exports to Spain.

EEC, the only Western European countries listed.

The trend of trade may have partly reflected crop conditions and prices (see ch. 11). It also reflected shifts in foreign policy designed to steer an independent course between East and West. Much trade in the years 1960 through 1962 was under bilateral agreements concluded while reliance on communist aid was heavy and policy inclined in their favor through 1961. This aid was mainly in the form of goods. The Soviet Union gave short-term commercial credits amounting to more than 20 percent of total foreign exchange resources. In December 1961 the Soviet ambassador was expelled on grounds of propaganda activity. This coincided with a Soviet moratorium on all new foreign aid commitments from late 1961 to late 1963, and in the years 1963 through 1965 Guinea received no new capital commitments from communist countries (see ch. 10). During these years there was substantial balance-of payments support and food aid from the United States, and reliance on aid from the West increased. In 1965 there was again an effort to stress relations with the East, until the renewal in 1967 of cooperation with both East and West (see ch. 9).

Some observers professed to see economic motives behind the political reasons cited for expelling the Soviet ambassador in 1961 and the West German ambassador in 1971: both countries had become major creditors. Guinea was unable to repay a US$10 million portion of the Soviet debt that fell due in 1965 and 1966. In the early years of uncoordinated imports and faulty internal distribution there had been some problems with imports from the Soviet Union, including oversized industrial installations, equipment adapted to arctic rather than tropical conditions, cement left on the docks to harden in the rain, and other comparable difficulties. Some Soviet-sponsored projects were not self-liquidating but required continuing financial support, so that the debt accumulated rapidly but the productive capacity from which to repay it did not keep pace. Work on Soviet aid projects was halted in the spring of 1963 but resumed in the fall. In 1967 and 1968 Soviet shipments of petroleum products were cut back. Beginning in 1975, however, the remaining Soviet debt was to be repaid out of bauxite shipments from the new Kindia mine.

The United States share of unplanned imports showed considerable variation. In the years 1964 through 1966 it ranged from 17 percent to as much as 35 percent of the total. These were the years when balance-of-payments support and Food for Peace shipments were at their height. In fiscal 1967 United States aid to Guinea was cut by 75 percent as part of a general reduction in aid to Africa and other areas but was later resumed. In the 1970s the Chinese Communists were supplying a growing share of rice imports. In 1972 the United States was furnishing only 8.2 percent of unplanned imports and taking 2.7 percent of exports.

Import trade with France has fluctuated in accordance with the current status of diplomatic relations, but export trade has shown a steadily declining trend. In 1959 France took about 75 percent of recorded exports, but its approximate share dropped to 5.7 percent in 1965 and to less than 1 percent in 1972. The statistical series from which these estimates are taken is given in United States dollars and is not comparable with the Guinean data used elsewhere. It shows that imports from France dropped by 77 percent between 1959 and 1961, reflecting the reorientation of policy toward Eastern Europe and the government's takeover of the trade monopoly formerly exercised by the great French colonial trading houses. Thereafter imports from France slowly increased again until in 1965 they were at 36 percent of their 1959 level, reflecting the gradual improvement of relations between the French and Guinean governments (see ch. 9). After a break with France in 1965, imports fell off sharply, and contacts were resumed in 1970. Although little progress was made on the diplomatic front, imports from France doubled in dollar value to an average of US$23 million in the years 1970 through 1973, or 60 percent of their 1959 level. Some of these imports may have been destined for the mining complex at Fria, which is managed by a French firm.

In 1971, before the break with West Germany, about 52.2 percent of imports from the EEC countries were coming from France, 18.5 percent from Italy, and 10.9 percent from West Germany. Only 5.1 percent of exports to the EEC were destined for France. Some 76.8 percent went to West Germany and 8.9 percent to Italy.

As a signatory to the Lomé Convention of February 28, 1975, Guinea was to enter for the first time into the benefit of concessions extended to developing countries by the EEC. At the break with France in 1958, Guinea had lost the preferences extended to French-speaking African countries on the French market. These former French preferences had gradually been converted to preferences on the entire EEC market for the other former colonies of France and Italy, under the provisions of the Treaty of Rome of 1957, the first Yaoundé Convention of 1963, and the second Yaoundé Convention of 1969. Because of its earlier break with France, Guinea had not become one of the eighteen African countries associated with the EEC under the Yaoundé conventions. It is difficult to judge whether Guinea had thus lost any significant trade advantage in the past. Its principal exports to Western Europe, bauxite and alumina, had not been materially affected by preferences, and its production of bananas and other tropical exports that might have benefited had failed to reach even the levels provided for under agreements with the communist countries.

The Lomé agreement had extended the benefits provided by EEC from the eighteen former associates to forty-six African, Caribbean, and Pacific (ACP) countries exporting tropical products, so that the margin of competitive advantage involved was somewhat narrowed. Beneficial new provisions, however, had been introduced. Ninety percent of the agricultural exports of the ACP countries were to be admitted duty free. No reciprocal concessions would be required. A new fund was to provide compensation for fluctuations in prices and production levels of certain tropical exports, including coffee, bananas, palm kernels, groundnuts (peanuts), iron ore, and many more of less immediate importance to Guinea. The thirty-four poorest ACP countries, including Guinea, would not have to repay this compensation.

Composition of Trade

After the alumina plant at Fria entered production in 1960, it began to account for a growing share of export earnings. By 1972 minerals were accounting for more than 70 percent of export value, and crop exports were of declining importance (see table 11). There was little incentive for the peasants to meet the government's crop export targets, and quantities of coffee, beef cattle, and other agricultural products were being smuggled out, as were diamonds, formerly a sizable export. Coffee and bananas had also become subject to increasing competition on free markets as consumers became more demanding. The government was trying to substitute pineapple for banana production, as pineapples brought a higher price and were less subject to spoilage and to high packing and transport costs (see ch. 11).

Most imports were unidentified. About 19 percent of recorded imports in 1969 and 6 percent in 1968 consisted of rice, textiles, and clothing, in all of which Guinea could be potentially self-sufficient. Some of the imports concealed under the "other" category, such as sugar, could probably also be replaced by domestic production. The fragmentary data availalbe suggest that an inadequate proportion of imports was going into increasing the country's productive capacity. Suret-Canale also pointed out that the foreign exchange received for the estimated GF2 billion in yearly smuggled exports was probably being used for consumer goods, hoarding, or flight capital and thus constituted a drain on the country's productive development.

TRANSPORTATION

In 1974 the principal functioning arteries of transportation were designed to carry bauxite, alumina, or other major exports to the ports (see fig. 10). These few routes were modern and well maintained, but the remainder of the transport system was said to be in poor condition. Data on road mileage and maintenance, motor vehicles in operation, and other transport features were fragmentary and conflicting (see table 12). There were usually said to be between 2,000 and 3,000 miles of improved main road, of which about 500 miles had been asphalt surfaced by 1974. Paved highways included one from Conakry to Forécariah and the main national highway from Conakry via Mamou to Kissidougou. In 1971 an agreement was signed to pave the remaining 217 miles to Nzérékoré in the course of the ensuing four years. Other highways were under construction from Boké to Mali and from Mamou to Kankan.

Railroad Transport

Officially there were 500 miles of meter-gauge railroads and 165 or 175 miles of standard-gauge lines. The old 410-mile single-track meter-gauge railroad from Conakry to Kankan, however, had been built between 1900 and 1914 and was never adequately renewed. According to some reports, it was rarely or never in use in 1974. The country's more modern railroad construction had been associated with mineral development. This made it possible to obtain share subscriptions from foreign investors or to furnish economic justification for loans from foreign governments or financial institutions. The debt incurred for construction could thus be repaid out of eventual ore production.

The first mining railroad had been a ten-mile standard-gauge line from the port of Conakry to the iron mine at Kaloum, which ceased operation after the mine was closed in 1966. The railroad from the Fria mine had been in operation since the end of 1959. It was meter gauge, because it joined the old meter-gauge line at a point between Dubréka and Conakry. The Fria line was variously described in different sources as being seventy, eighty, or ninety-three miles long, possibly depending on whether the last segment to Conakry was included. This line was modern and efficient but had always been reserved for the transport of ore, alumina, or supplies for the mine and alumina plant. The eighty-five-mile standard-gauge railroad from the Sangarédi bauxite mine to Kamsar and Port-Kakandé had been in operation since August 1973, and the seventy-mile standard-gauge line built by Soviet engineers from Conakry to Kindia (Débelé) was officially inaugurated in April 1974. There was also some difference of opinion on the precise length of these two lines.

As of 1974 the government's plans called for eventual construction of the costly 745-mile standard-gauge Trans-Guinean Railroad that would extend the newly constructed Conakry-Kindia line for another 675 miles to the iron ore deposits of Simandou and Nimba in the extreme southeast. Much of the proposed new line would parallel the existing meter-gauge line from Conakry to Kankan, which was officially deemed unsuitable for ore transport. Built over difficult terrain and with inadequate funds for use by pre-World War I steam locomotives, the single-track line was poorly graded, and the track had had too many years of wear and was too lightweight to stand up under use by modern diesel locomotives, heavier rolling stock, and longer trains. Even before independence it had been judged hopelessly superannuated, and its owners had reportedly decided that the least costly solution would be to close it down altogether.

Since independence the old Conakry-Kankan line had been operated at a mounting annual deficit by a semiautonomous government enterprise,

Table 11. Guinea, Composition of Trade, Selected Years, 1965–72[1]

(in millions of Guinean francs)[2]

	1965	1967	1968	1969	1970	1971	1972
Recorded Exports[3]							
Alumina and bauxite	7.7	8.1	8.4	8.4	8.6	8.9	9.1
Iron ore	1.0	0.2	..	..	..	..	..
Pineapples	..	..	0.7	1.0	1.2	1.2	0.9
Bananas	1.2	1.0	0.7	1.0	0.5	0.4	0.3
Coffee	0.5	1.2	1.5	1.5	1.5	0.7	0.7
Palm kernels	0.7	0.7	0.7	1.0	0.7	0.7	0.7
Other agricultural products	0.4	1.0	1.0	0.5 }	1.4	0.4	1.2
Other minerals	1.6	0.4	0.1	0.6 }			
Total	13.3	12.6	13.1	14.0	13.9	12.3	12.9

Unplanned Imports[4]

Rice	1.5	1.0	0.7	1.5	1.7	2.0	2.4
Textiles and clothing	1.2	0.7	0.5	1.5	2.5	1.6	1.5
Petroleum products	0.2	1.2	0.7	1.7	2.5	2.6	2.7
Metals and machinery	1.2	2.2	0.7	1.0	1.0	1.2	2.1
Other	9.0	11.4	12.5	7.4	9.6	12.3	8.8
Subtotal	13.1	16.5	15.1	13.1	17.3	19.7	17.5
Imports under the plan	3.2	2.4	4.7	3.0	n.a.	n.a.	n.a.
Total imports	16.3	18.9	19.8	16.1	n.a.	n.a.	n.a.
Imports for Fria[5]	(2.9)	(1.6)	(1.8)	(1.8)	n.a.	n.a.	n.a.

... means none; n.a. means not available.

[1] Guinea's reporting year ends September 30.

[2] For value of the Guinean franc—see Glossary.

[3] Exports are valued f.o.b. (free on board—insurance and freight beyond the border excluded).

[4] Unplanned imports exclude goods imported under development plan, which are given separately for the years 1965 through 1969. Imports are valued c.i.f. (cost, insurance, and freight included).

[5] Imports for Fria are included in unplanned imports.

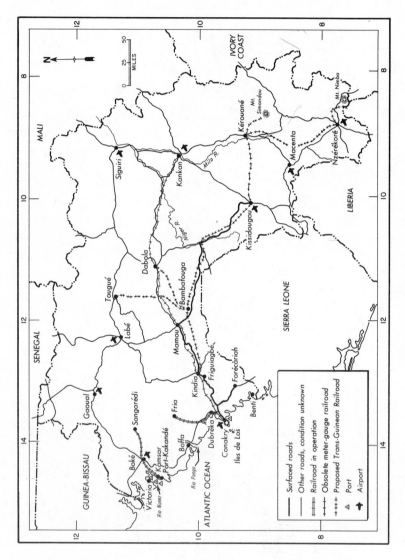

Figure 10. Guinea, Transportation System, 1974

Table 12. Guinea, Transport Data, Selected Years, 1964–72[1]

	1964	1965	1966	1968	1969	1971	1972
Road Mileage[2]							
"Improved" but poorly maintained	n.a.	6,525	n.a.	7,700	n.a.	3,705	n.a.
Impassable in rainy season	n.a.	(1,565)	n.a.	n.a.	n.a.	n.a.	n.a.
Main national roads	n.a.	n.a.	n.a.	(2,160)	n.a.	n.a.	n.a.
Paved	n.a.	n.a.	n.a.	(320)	n.a.	n.a.	n.a.
Unimproved local tracks	n.a.	n.a.	n.a.	7,500	n.a.	9,900	n.a.
Total roads and tracks	n.a.	n.a.	n.a.	14,900	n.a.	n.a.	17,650
Road Motor Vehicles Registered							
Passenger cars and taxicabs	8,100	9,300	8,500	7,600	8,000	7,400	7,200
Trucks, buses, and vans	12,600	13,500	12,500	11,300	12,000	11,900	10,700
Total	20,700	22,800	21,000	18,900	20,000	19,300	17,900
Railroad Traffic, Conakry-Kankan Line							
Eastbound freight (in long tons)	50,932	47,515	36,332	31,803	36,544	n.a.	n.a.
Westbound freight (in long tons)	43,795	40,608	38,650	16,382	17,435	n.a.	n.a.
Both ways (in million long ton-miles)	23,985	20,909	18,493	12,549	13,660	n.a.	n.a.
Passengers, Conakry suburbs	n.a.	n.a.	486,001	452,432 ⎫	97,115	n.a.	n.a.
Passengers, remaining line	n.a.	n.a.	152,876	114,712 ⎭		n.a.	n.a.
Conakry Port Traffic (in thousand metric tons)							
Goods loaded	1,580	1,471	n.a.	975	1,260	n.a.	n.a.
Goods unloaded	586	544	n.a.	435	510	n.a.	n.a.
Total	2,166	2,015	1,766	1,410	1,770	1,372	1,183

n.a. means not available.

[1] Guinea's reporting year ends September 30.

[2] Not intended to add to totals. Estimates for different years are from different sources and are not comparable over time.

the National Railroad Office of Guinea (Office National des Chemins de Fer de Guinée—ONCFG). In 1966 the deficit had surpassed GF250 million. On several occasions plans were formulated to rebuild the old line and convert it to standard gauge. A Soviet-sponsored project to this effect was reportedly rejected by the Guinean government as too costly. Negotiations with the PRC for the same project were reported in 1969 and 1971 but came to nothing.

A French business weekly reported in 1971 that the line had been reduced to operating only one passenger train a week, between Conakry and Kankan, and that freight traffic had been greatly reduced except for a few trains at harvesttime from the banana-growing regions around Coyah, Kindia, and Mamou. The line was heavily subsidized at one time by the Banana Equalization Fund, which covered the high transport costs for banana exports.

Other press reports alleged that in the years 1972 through 1974 operation of the old line had been confined largely to commuter shuttle service between Conakry and the suburb of Dixinn. The line's difficulties were attributed to its steep gradients, the poor condition of the rails, lack of diesel locomotives in operating condition, inadequate signals and communications, and inadequately trained maintenance and management personnel.

The suburban passenger service in Conakry was subsidized by the government as a matter of deliberate policy, in order to permit low fares for urban workers. As the urban population grew in the 1960s, this service had absorbed a growing portion of the line's operating deficit, necessitating reductions in service on the remainder of the line.

For the products of the Forest Region in the southeast, the cheapest export route was the railroad built by the Lamco mining company from its mine on the Liberian side of the Nimba range to the Liberian port of Buchanan. For bulk products of low unit value, this route was less costly than the Liberian road from Ganta to Monrovia. Guinean use of this line was permitted under an agreement with the Liberian government, which was renewed in the early 1970s. This agreement did not cover eventual exports of iron ore, which were the subject of continuing negotiations with Lamco (see Mining, this ch.). In the late 1960s imports by this route had included petroleum products for the Forest Region, and exports included logs, sawn timber, palm kernels, and a little coffee.

It was estimated that the proposed Trans-Guinean Railroad would cost a minimum of US$490 million, in addition to some US$60 million for the associated deepwater ore port of Conakry. Some critics therefore dismissed the plan as unrealistic. Others maintained that the roundabout route proposed could not pay its way or that rail is an outmoded method of transportation and that moving the ore by road would be more economical. Suret-Canale acknowledged that the project would be extremely high cost and that even the relatively modern railroads of France were obliged to operate at a deficit but defended the trans-

Guinean project as justified on political and strategic grounds. He also argued that it would eventually derive economic justification from the iron ore production of Simandou.

At a conference in Conakry in September 1974, finance minister Ismail Touré announced that a four-year preliminary feasibility study of the railroad had been completed by the Japanese engineering firm Nippon Koei, which had recommended its construction. Details of the proposed route were not published, but the minister said that the first phase of construction would be from Conakry to Bambafouga, where two separate spurs to the bauxite deposits at Dabola and Tougué would connect with the main line. Bambafouga is located southeast of Mamou. Presumably construction could begin at Kindia, as a new standard-gauge railroad from Conakry to Kindia had been completed in 1974. Phase II would continue the main line from Bambafouga to Nimba by way of Nzérékoré and Simandou. A more detailed feasibility survey had already been completed for Phase I and was about to begin on Phase II.

For some years the press had reported at intervals that financing for the Trans-Guinean Railroad had been obtained from one foreign source or another, but these reports proved to be premature. When Nippon Koei was first engaged to survey the route, it had been reported to be contributing the financing for the entire railroad; later it was said to be seeking to interest Japanese steel firms in the undertaking. Other reported sponsors of the project had ranged from Abu Dhabi to United States Steel. In October 1974 a number of press sources reported that a Canadian Engineering firm, Dynam, had been engaged to undertake a feasibility study for the line. The Canadian government was lending 500,000 Canadian dollars to finance the study. Some of these reports added that Canada was also providing the required funds for actual construction of the line, to be begun at once by a Canadian firm. This report remained to be confirmed in late 1974.

Road Motor Transport

In the early 1970s President Touré made a speech in which he denounced the country's national road system as being in an advanced state of deterioration. He attributed its systematic neglect in the past to sabotage by fifth-column elements but acknowledged that road mainte-nance equipment had generally been inefficiently used and inadequately maintained. As the eventual solution, he called for better coordination of responsibilities for building and maintaining the roads among local, regional, and national authorities.

A French business weekly surmised in 1971 that only about one-third of the motor vehicles reported in the statistics were actually in operating condition. Difficult roads, inadequate maintenance, and a lack of imported replacement parts were the reasons cited. Imports of passenger cars and parts had been severely restricted and were further curtailed after 1969. Pervasive government controls also meant that those most familiar with the specifications of needed parts were unable to order them freely as required, so that items authorized might not correspond with actual needs. Delays were sometimes so long that equipment deteriorated from disuse while awaiting parts.

Most of the trucks and other utility vehicles were of Soviet or other Eastern European makes, but French-made passenger cars predominated. Fria maintained about 200 French-made vehicles. A large shipment of American buses was imported in 1970. There had been a Mack truck assembly plant in Conakry, but it had ceased operation by 1970. It had produced altogether about 500 trucks, of which about 200 were thought to be still in operating condition. Many of the trucks produced had had Mack chassis with motors recovered from disused Soviet trucks.

Ports and Waterways

Few of the country's rivers were navigable for more than short distances. The Niger River usually was said to be navigable from July to November from the rapids of Kouroussa to Bamako in Mali. Suret-Canale, however, writing in 1968, found that traffic was limited to July and August. The old steamer service to Bamako had closed down in 1948, and only about 2,000 tons of freight a year were being carried on shallow-draft barges. On the Milo, the largest southern tributary of the Niger, shallow-draft boats could be used during the season as far as the rail terminus at Kankan. Elsewhere in the Niger basin within Guinea, traffic was limited to poled barges and canoes.

Conakry had one of the best natural harbors in West Africa, protected by the offshore Iles de Los. Conakry's harbor was badly subject to silting, however; and when costly regular dredging operations were neglected, ships had to await the tides to enter the port. For this reason and because of frequent delays in loading and unloading, some shipping lines refused to call at Conakry. In the early 1970s some sources cited Conakry's modern equipment, but others said that the equipment had been poorly maintained and operated. Friguia maintained its own ore-loading facilities, and the Soviet mining project at Kindia had renovated the ore docks abandoned by the old Kaloum iron-mining operation. The bauxite-mining enterprise at Sangarédi had also constructed its own ore port at Kamsar in the north.

Foreign trade took place almost entirely through the port of Conakry or the new ore port at Kamsar, except for such limited trade as moved through the Liberian port of Buchanan or the small declining banana ports at Benti and Forécariah. There had formerly been some coastal trade between Conakry and the smaller ports at Boké, at Boffa on the Rio Pongo estuary, and at Benti on the Mélikhouré River. In the late 1960s the lighters used in the coastal trade were no longer in operating condition, and any trade that took place was confined to canoes or motorized barks. Coastal trade was important, however, as a lower cost alternative to the difficult road transport, and the Five Year Development Plan (1973–78) called for the purchase of two coastal transport lighters for each of the major coastal regions to serve the smaller ports and the offshore islands.

Air Transport

The country had an airport of international standard at Conakry-Gbessia and eight smaller airfields at Labé, Boké, Kankan, Kissidougou, Nzérékoré, Siguiri, Macenta, and Gaoual. The landing facilities at Conakry-Gbessia airport had been enlarged and renovated with Soviet aid, and it could take aircraft the size of a Boeing 707 or a Russian 220-passenger TU–114. It was served by scheduled flights of six international airlines, including Air Afrique and the national airlines of the Soviet Union, Czechoslovakia, and the German Democratic Republic (East Germany).

The laterite landing strips at the domestic airfields were to have been asphalt surfaced under the Seven Year Plan (1964–71), but it was not clear how many had been completed by 1974. New strips at Macenta and Nzérékoré were completed in mid-1971. When Cuban engineers finished enlarging and renovating the military and civilian airfield at Labé in October 1973, it was said to be the country's third airport that could take small, medium-range aircraft the size of a Soviet IL–18 and was equipped for night landings. In 1975 the Cubans were to rebuild the airfield at Kankan.

Air Guinea had been founded in 1960. In the late 1960s it had four flights a week to Kankan, three to Boké and Labé, two to Kissidougou and Nzérékoré, and one flight a week to Siguiri. At that time the landing strip at Gaoual was still under construction, and the laterite strip at Macenta could be used only in the dry season. After two abortive agreements with United States firms, Air Guinea had continued using Soviet aircraft. It had three AN–24s, a twin-turboprop transport that could carry forty-four passengers. These were used for domestic service. Two AN–2 biplanes had been used by the banana service. Air Guinea also had two IL–18s that had hitherto been used only for special overseas flights by officials or student groups or for flights of pilgrims to Mecca. The airline also made occasional unscheduled flights to neighboring capitals: Bamako, Freetown, and Monrovia. In 1974 some critics alleged that Air Guinea no longer operated scheduled domestic flights and that passengers sometimes had to wait up to three days for a domestic flight to leave.

COMMUNICATIONS

Before independence the postal, telegraph, and telephone system had some of its matériel and management in Dakar. Moreover, the scorched earth policy pursued by many French expatriates in Guinea at independence had been particularly unfortunate in its effect on the telecommunications system. French personnel manning telephone and telegraph facilities departed abruptly, often taking with them equipment instruction manuals and other documents or even equipment. In appealing to the International Telecommunications Union for assistance in 1973, the Guineans stated that, despite accelerated training programs for Guinean personnel, the deficiencies in communication services resulting from the events of 1959 had not yet been overcome. Suret-Canale had reported in 1968 that interruptions of service were still frequent and that telegrams announcing the forthcoming arrival of visitors were usually delivered after their departure.

After independence several countries offered communications assistance to fill the vacuum left by the French. Some of this assistance involved radio installations (see ch.7). Construction of a radiotelephone transmission station begun by Czechoslovak technicians was abandoned because of disagreements, and Polish experts also left after encountering obstacles. Hungary supplied carrier equipment for overhead lines for domestic long-distance communication. The Siemens Company of West Germany had obtained quasi-exclusive rights for automatic telephone and telex offices and had proposed a long-term plan for installation of an automatic long-distance dialing system.

In 1963 a vocational school was opened in Conakry for postal and financial services and telecommunications. It trained operational personnel, equipment personnel, linemen, inspectors, and construction supervisors. Before 1963 Guinean personnel were trained at the vocational school at Rufisque in Senegal. Africanization of the services has made considerable progress.

A new training program, as well as a program for the expansion and modernization of telecommunications facilities, was drafted in 1973 by the Guinean government and a mission from the International Telecommunications Union. In February 1974 a loan equivalent to US$4.8 million was received for this program from the African Development Bank. The project was to take 3½ years and was to be carried out under the supervision of the Ministry of Posts and Telecommunications. Its aim was to link up the national telecommunications system to those of neighboring countries. The project included installation of a high-capacity microwave relay system, which would also serve as a support for television, along the road from Conakry to Forécariah (toward Sierra Leone); the road from Conakry to Mali via Kindia, Mamou, and Labé; and the road from Conakry toward Mali via Mamou, Faranah, and Kankan. It also provided for expansion of the automatic telephone exchanges of Conakry, Kankan, Kassa, and Sonfonya, increasing their capacity from 5,500 to 9,500 lines.

In 1971 there were thought to be about 7,000 telephones installed throughout the country. Theft of telephone and telegraph lines, a not uncommon problem in African countries, was a particularly acute one in Guinea because of the chaotic conditions created by depreciation of the currency. Some observers have reported that these same conditions obliged postal and communications personnel to leave their work frequently in the search for food and the necessities of existence, so that the postal system was functioning poorly.

SECTION IV. NATIONAL SECURITY

CHAPTER 13

DEFENSE AND PUBLIC ORDER

Since shortly after independence the country has existed in an atmosphere of perennial conspiracy and threats of coups d'etat. This has been substantiated by the multiplicity of purges that have spared neither government officials, members of the army, nor high-ranking officials of the Democratic Party of Guinea (Parti Démocratique de Guinée—PDG). Moreover, in early 1975 it was underlined by the fact that, aside from two separate one-day trips to Liberia, President Ahmed Sékou Touré had left Guinea only once since 1967. Endless accusations have been made in broadcasts by President Touré concerning the discovery of new plots against the regime, some attributed to dissidents within the country, others to exile opposition groups operating outside Guinea, and still others to nameless international forces of "imperialism and neo-colonialism."

Largely because of the government's general determination to isolate Guinean affairs from the watchful eyes of outside observers, little information on matters relating to contemporary national security has been published. This has been particularly true of data regarding the military and other security forces, especially since the threat to the governing regime inherent in the invasion of Conakry in November 1970 by exile opposition units backed by elements of the Portuguese military. Few foreign newsmen have been granted authorization to visit the country, and most of the available information on contemporary Guinean security affairs has come from broadcasts by the Voice of the Revolution, as the government-owned radio station in Conakry is called (see ch. 7).

Despite the government-imposed embargo on information, it seemed clear that the norms of Guinean public order and internal security in early 1975 were measured by standards adopted by the PDG and influenced to some degree by the doctrines of the Communist-oriented countries that have provided assistance to Guinea since its independence in 1958. Although public order was concerned with ordinary criminal activity, much greater emphasis was accorded adherence to the dictates and regulations of the party-state and its emphasis on the goals of the "Guinean revolution." Internal security meant the security of the regime in power and its programs of national development. Any opposition to, or even disagreement with, the doctrines of the government and the party was deemed contrary to the state's revolutionary aims and was subject to sanctionative measures of increasing severity.

The Guinean security establishment appeared to consist of three major elements, namely, the regular armed forces, various police services, and a growing militia of the PDG whose responsibilities in matters of security extended to the lowest structural levels of the society. According to estimates of the International Institute for Strategic Studies in London, the military component consisted of a force of some 5,500 officers and men comprising an army, an air force, and a small naval element. The police services, numbering roughly 3,500 officers and men, included the Gendarmerie, the Sûreté Nationale (National Police), and the Garde Républicaine (Republican Guard). The Cuban-style militia was growing in size and authority. This force had assumed an ever-increasing responsibility for national defense, particularly after its popularly credited role in the defeat of the 1970 invaders.

The army as a purely military force apparently had lost favor in the eyes of the president and the PDG leadership after a number of high-ranking military officials were accused of complicity in attempted coups d'etat. Consequently there have been indications that the governing regime has regarded the army with a measure of distrust. Since 1967 most of the army's activities have been directed to civic-action projects rather than to traditional military training exercises. The expansion of the militia as a paramilitary force reflected President Touré's concern over latent threats to his government, and he had introduced an element of counterbalance against the military and police services. To assure loyalty to the governing power, all three elements of the security establishment had been politicized and were completely subordinate to the party-state apparatus.

THE STATE OF INTERNAL SECURITY

Since 1960 a number of attempts have been made to overthrow the government of President Touré by assassination, coup d'etat, and invasion. It would be difficult to define the exact number of times such threats have occurred as the government has been almost ceaseless in its accusations that efforts either were being planned or were under way. Generally the accusations have been aimed at foreign powers—singly or in concert—who allegedly were supporting or formulating moves to institute a new political order in Guinea. The list of countries accused at various times has stretched across the political spectrum from Portugal, Guinea's more conservative African neighbors, France, and the United States to the Soviet Union and the People's Republic of China (PRC) (see ch. 9).

Despite such accusations, most of the threats were clearly the work of Guinean dissidents. The one obvious major exception was the seaborne invasion of Conakry in November 1970, which was at least partially motivated by something more than a desire to overthrow the government. A number of incidents labeled by the government as coup attempts appeared to have been only peaceful efforts at public protest.

Although the party-state has been unstinting in its efforts to develop a national consciousness throughout Guinea and to unite under the leadership of one political party, since independence there have been indications that all traces of opposition have not been completely eliminated. In the early 1960s, for example, it was known that certain ethnic, regional, occupational, or other groups held grievances—real or imaginary—against the government or animosities toward each other.

As the 1960s progressed, an apparently increasing number of Guineans bore strong animosities toward the government and resented many of its policies. Particularly disliked were some of the economic practices and the concentration of political leadership in a single party. At times there have been indications of ethnic rivalries within the governing party, particularly between the aggressive Malinké, conspicuous in the party and the government, and the Peul, proud of their origin and military history. Personal rivalries also have played a considerable role.

From the beginning of national sovereignty Guinean political leaders have regarded resistance to government policies as entirely without justification. The party-state, with its pervasive organization, has sought to indoctrinate the people to believe that any attempt to overthrow the existing order can come only from agents of "imperialistic" powers. During the early period after independence the majority of Guineans, therefore, seemed to be convinced that the PDG was their only safeguard against forces that sought to subject the country once more to colonial rule.

The government has regarded all individuals or groups opposing or criticizing its policies as actual or potential subversive elements, and subversion has been ruled a crime deserving of harsh and summary punishment. Accordingly party elements—including the militia and other security forces—were charged with keeping in close contact with the people in their areas of jurisdiction. They sought to prevent the development of situations from which opposition to party policies and projects might arise. The party has sought to avoid the formation of social classes or conflicts of interest between groups and has tried—with some success—to eliminate any special loyalties associated with ethnic origins, regional groupings, or religious beliefs. In implementing these policies, the government has made special appeals to the workers, to the villagers, to women, and to young people (see ch. 8).

The PDG has sought to make the weekly meetings called by local party units in every village and in all town wards effective instruments against subversion. These meetings are usually attended by most able-bodied Guineans.

The first overt manifestation of latent insecurity was disclosed in April 1960, less than fifteen months after independence, when PDG agents reportedly discovered a plot to overthrow the government by armed force. The Guinean High Court of Justice subsequently tried more than forty people for treason, sentencing nineteen to death (eight in absentia) and twenty-two to long prison terms at hard labor. Eight French nationals were expelled or fled to Senegal.

According to the PDG, the instigators of the plot were Guinean citizens who used funds from foreign sources, allegedly French, and possessed arms smuggled in from Senegal and Ivory Coast. Also included were explosives, radio equipment, subversive pamphlets urging the people to revolt, and correspondence outlining plans to hire some 5,000 saboteurs. A network of spies, President Touré explained to the National Assembly, had been set up in Conakry and in some of the towns and villages. The PDG reacted vigorously and called on all its members for increased vigilance to detect and root out all traitors and "imperialist agents."

In November 1961 an event occurred, still having repercussions in the 1970s, that demonstrated that opposition to the government could come from those who felt that PDG policies were not bringing about change fast enough as well as those for whom change was too fast. A strike over working conditions by the teacher's union, supported by students, was termed a left-wing coup attempt and was put down with considerable severity. Five leaders of the teacher's union were executed, and the Soviet embassy in Conakry was accused of supporting the teachers; the Soviet ambassador was expelled from Guinea. The readiness of the government to use force against opposition was demonstrated again in late 1965. Accusations of plotting to bring about the downfall of the government led to the arrest of the leaders of a group publicly attempting to form a legal opposition political party, as allowed by the Constitution.

By 1969 tension had risen further as the flight of opponents into exile continued and as the government took cognizance of the military coups d'etat that were occurring in other African countries. President Touré adopted a policy aimed at increasing PDG control in order to avoid a situation in Guinea similar to the events in neighboring Mali, where the friendly government had been overthrown by its army in November 1968. In February 1969, after military dissatisfaction over the creation of party control elements within each army unit, the Guinean government moved against the army's deputy chief of staff and a former minister of defense and security. Attention was directed to the army garrison at Labé, the center of the Peul homeland in Middle Guinea, which had originally been an area noted for its opposition to the PDG. The government initially alleged that a Peul group planned to assassinate President Touré and seize national power or, failing that, to bring about the secession of Middle Guinea. These accusations were later broadened to include other groups, and the charge of a specific Peul connection was dropped. More than 1,000 Guineans were arrested throughout the country in this so-called Labé plot. Thirteen of those arrested were executed, and twenty-seven were imprisoned; among them were three former cabinet ministers, including one of the key members of the party's left wing, Fodéba Kéita.

While the army's capabilities to act independently were reduced by weakening it, efforts to strengthen PDG control over the country were increased. Nevertheless violent opposition persisted. In June 1969 a crowd of onlookers witnessed one of several reported attempted assassinations of President Touré. This occurred as he drove in an open car with former Ghanaian leader Kwame Nkrumah and President Kenneth Kaunda of Zambia. The would-be assassin was captured and lynched by the crowd, and three other men were arrested and accused of complicity. According to the government radio, the man who tried to kill President Touré had been a member of the Guinean National Liberation Front (Front pour la Libération Nationale de Guineé—FLNG), an element of the exile opposition (see ch. 8). Allegedly the assassination team had trained in Ivory Coast, although the government of that country denied any involvement. Additional vague charges were made by President Touré against "imperialist powers," foreign embassies in Conakry, and certain foreign companies operating in Guinea. The attempt on the president's life appeared to have been connected with the earlier Labé plot.

The most serious attack on the government of President Touré was mounted in November of 1970 in the form of a seaborne invasion of Conakry conducted under cover of darkness. According to a wide variety of reports, considerable confusion existed regarding the size and composition of the force as well as the invaders' intentions. A subsequent United Nations (UN) mission—dispatched to Conakry to investigate the situation—clarified to some degree what had actually occurred, although the report of the mission of inquiry and the procedures followed in producing it were open to question by some observers.

According to the UN mission of inquiry, two unmarked World War II landing craft of the LST class and a 5,000-ton cargo vessel, with the aid of several small motorized boats, landed an infantry force of 250 to 300 men on Conakry's beaches. Wearing uniforms identical to those of the Guinean army, the invading force rapidly attacked several key targets throughout the city and beyond, including the city's power station. Although President Touré's summer villa was attacked and destroyed, only a minimal effort was directed at the presidential palace, where he was spending the night. The main attacking force reached but ignored the airport and apparently attacked what they thought was the operative radio station, unaware that its use had been discontinued when replaced earlier by a new station.

The invaders concentrated on destroying the headquarters of the African Party for the Independence of Guinea-Bissau and the Cape Verde Islands (Partido Africano da Independência da Guiné e do Cabo-

Verde—PAIGC) in an unsuccessful attempt to capture PAIGC leader Amilcar Cabral, who was in Europe at the time. Others seized the political prison camps and liberated a number of prisoners, including Portuguese soldiers and airmen who had been captured earlier by PAIGC forces and turned over to the Guineans for safekeeping; some had been held captive in these camps for as long as seven years. At this point, half of the invading force withdrew with the released prisoners to the waiting ships, leaving the task of overthrowing the Guinean government to a force estimated at fewer than 150 men. This group apparently hoped for an uprising by the population, but such a reaction failed to occur. Outside observers have speculated that public support was not achieved because the invaders failed to seize the right radio station, which continued to operate under government control. Moreover, most important government or party officials avoided capture.

During the first hours after the invasion, limited Guinean resistance was mounted. PAIGC personnel defending their headquarters and Guinea's Garde Républicaine, in whose camps the political prisoners were located, bore the brunt of the fighting. After the disquieting events of 1969, most of the Guinean army troops had been dispersed throughout the country and the few military units that remained in or near the capital did not have sufficient combat capability to participate in its defense.

The following day the PDG rallied considerable resistance to the remaining invaders. Apparently the brunt of the fighting was borne by the Guinean militia and other security force units. By evening the invasion ships had withdrawn, and most of the remaining invaders had been killed; at least sixty were taken prisoner, including six Portuguese. Guinean authorities reported that other forces from Portuguese Guinea had attempted an invasion by land just after the seaborne landings but had been driven back.

Fearing a continuation of the attacks, the Guinean government appealed to the UN and to other African states for military forces to aid in Guinea's defense. No troop response was forthcoming, but a number of countries offered other support. For example, Egyptian transport planes carrying light arms donated by Egypt and Nigeria landed at Conakry-Gbessia airport shortly after the president's appeal. The mission of inquiry, which was the UN response to President Touré's plea for assistance, later concluded that the vessels and about half of the invading force were under the control of the Portuguese army and that their mission had been limited to the liberation of Portuguese prisoners and the crippling of the PAIGC. The rest of the force, according to the UN mission, was composed of military members of Guinean exile opposition groups bent on a coup d'etat. The Portuguese government subsequently denied any connection with the invading force, but the Assembly of Guineans in Europe (Régroupement des Guinéens en Europe—RGE) claimed full credit for the operation, stating that they had hired the ships in Europe and had embarked from training bases in Sierra Leone, unknown to that country's government. The RGE insisted, however, that its only objective had been the liberation of 400 political prisoners.

In the aftermath of the invasion an extensive purge of the Guinean political and administrative elite was carried out in three stages. When it was concluded, sixteen of the twenty-four members of the cabinet, five former government ministers, thirteen of the country's twenty-nine governors of administrative regions, several Guinean ambassadors, and the Roman Catholic archbishop of Conakry had fallen. Many of those arrested, including the archbishop, were among President Touré's oldest friends and closest supporters.

Only a few military and police officers were among those seized in the initial purge. In this move ninety-two persons were sentenced to death (thirty-four in absentia) including four former cabinet members and the chief of state security. A further seventy-two persons were sentenced to imprisonment for life at hard labor. Even in the first wave of the purge, at least as many Guinean officials as captured invaders were involved.

In the second wave of arrests, in July 1971, the army's officer corps bore the brunt of the accusations. Those convicted included General Noumandian Keita, chief of the Combined Arms General Staff, and a majority of the field-grade army officers. A number of junior officers and noncommissioned personnel were also charged. Eight officers were sentenced to death.

All of the resulting trials took a highly irregular form. No use was made of the regular courts, the military court, or the existing revolutionary tribunal of the party. Instead the National Assembly was constituted by presidential appointment as the Supreme Revolutionary Tribunal. The accused were not given the right to counsel, to defend themselves, or even to appear at their own trials. Instead, after long periods in jail, tape recordings of detailed confessions were released. These confessions generally implicated others as members of a vague fifth column, which was defined as including anyone accused of not acting effectively in instituting the policies of the government. The failure of the Seven Year Plan (1964–71), therefore, could be blamed on sabotage by "enemies of the people" through such "counter revolutionary acts" as the ordering of wrong spare parts or the unwise assignment of equipment. Such acts were presumed to be treasonable because collectively they influenced the people and alienated them from the government. Accusations of fifth column activity were accordingly lumped together and defined as part of a plot to discredit and weaken the government.

According to the government prosecutors, this fifth column had supported either a Portuguese invasion or even vaguer programs to overthrow the government, allegedly sponsored by a number of countries in Africa and Europe. Most notable among the countries accused was the Federal Republic of Germany (West Germany). Generally the people accused testified that they had succumbed to bribes, often from varying and conflicting sources. General Keita, for example, claimed he had been paid a large sum of money to join the West German ambassador's spy networks with duties as varied as organizing plans for Guinea's invasion and creating discord among army units.

The recorded confessions were broadcast over the government radio and published, page after page, in the country's only daily newspaper for months. Local party units were instructed to study the testimony and then to decide the fate of the accused. Their verdicts were tabulated by the regional upper echelons of the party and eventually passed for ratification to the National Assembly, acting as the Supreme Revolutionary Tribunal. The number of people convicted, even from among the army, was never released, but those publicly convicted numbered some 250. A number of reports by outside observers estimated that, in all, about 10,000 arrests were made.

After a period of relative calm in 1972, new accusations of plots against the government were voiced loudly in 1973. In April of that year a number of cabinet ministers were accused of being implicated in an effort allegedly aimed at the overthrow of the governments of Guinea and Sierra Leone. According to President Touré this plot was supported by Portugal, Belgium, France, Great Britain, Rhodesia, and South Africa.

Some outside observers have speculated that President Touré's apparent preoccupation with plots against his government may be conditioned in part by a firm desire to instill a sense of vigilance within the Guinean people. In each instance he has broadcast his warnings of impending threats over the government radio in addition to exhortations that are dispensed to the lowest levels of the party organization. For example, in his address welcoming Nigerian head-of-state General Yakubu Gowon to Guinea in February 1974, President Touré advised Guineans who had gathered for the occasion in the Conakry stadium and those who were listening to the radiobroadcast:

At this very moment, there are 1,500 mercenaries stationed on the two borders of our national territory ready to attack us again. . . . They say they have already acquired three warships for the purpose. They also say that they will carry out maneuvers to divert the attention of our troops so that their ships can land the mercenaries in Guinea to accomplish their cowardly assignment. They say they will attack Conakry airport and seize the Alpha Yaya military barracks in Conakry because, according to them, our arms and ammunition are stored there and once they seize it our people will be without arms and ammunition. According to them, when this happens they will then prevent troops from friendly countries from coming to our assistance. . . . Let these mercenaries come. . . . The Guinean armed forces are always ready. Their tomb is in each Guinean home, workshop, and road junction. They will be given a first class burial. The Guinean revolution will triumph over their machinations. We say this in the presence of the current president of the Organization of African Unity; he can himself speak to the mercenaries who have returned from the Ivory Coast and Senegal. Among the mercenaries are Ivorians, Guineans, Senegalese, and foreigners. The OAU president can question them himself, and he will see the truth of what we have been saying about the anti-Guinean plot. . . . Long live the Federal Republic of Nigeria! Long live General Gowon! Down with imperialist lackeys! Down with colonialism and imperialism! Honor to struggling peoples! Ready for revolution!

CRIME AND PUNISHMENT

In early 1975 the scope of criminal activity was not known with any reasonable degree of accuracy because the government had not produced official statistical reports on crime in Guinea since the establishment of the nation as an independent republic. Despite the lack of publicly available statistical reporting, however, certain trends in criminal activity have been reflected in speeches made by President Touré, in warnings published in the government press, and in the activities of the security forces that have been reported by a number of observers.

Treason and other major offenses against the state were regarded by the government as the most serious crimes. Theft, arson, and embezzlement involving state property or funds were generally dealt with more severely than the same offenses against private property. Those charged with treasonable acts usually were tried promptly and, if convicted, could expect to be executed or to be given maximum prison sentences. The death sentence also could be expected in convictions for offenses viewed as sabotage of the national economy.

During the colonial period smuggling developed into a flourishing trade, and controls by law enforcement agencies were largely ineffective against this illegal activity. Some enterprises in Conakry specialized in smuggling and moved commodities through distribution points in the larger towns to local tradesmen.

Since independence, smuggling and black-marketing have continued on a large scale, despite efforts of the customs service, the police, the army, and the militia. The trade, which apparently has been both into and out of the country, has involved a wide variety of consumer goods and food products (see ch. 6; ch. 11; ch. 12). The clandestine shipment of diamonds from the Forest Region to the coast through Liberia and Sierra Leone has been of great concern because it has affected an important source of government revenue.

Economic problems faced by Guinea over the years since independence, including rapid inflation, loss of confidence in the national currency, and the shortage of consumer goods, have bolstered the prevalence of smuggling and black-market activity. These illegal practices have been widely pursued or supported in all areas of the country and on a number of occasions have been controlled or exploited by government officials or influential members of the PDG.

Black-marketing and smuggling have been denounced repeatedly by President Touré as a serious threat to governmental economic planning. Members of the political party's National Political Bureau (Bureau Politique National—BPN) gave special attention to the effectiveness of frontier surveillance and the measures taken against violations of customs laws. The PDG has passed resolutions calling on all members for increased vigilance in the struggle against illegal speculations, frontier traffic, money transactions, and black-marketing. Security units operating as frontier guards have been instructed to disrupt illegal border crossings with force, and the militia has been given authority to ferret out illicit traders in the markets throughout the country.

At the village level, militia members are seen touring the markets checking for merchants who use nonstandard measures and those who attempt to sell their wares without payment of the required market taxes. They also attempt to apprehend local producers who engage in selling their goods en route to market, thus avoiding the inspections and forced adherence to government regulations. The task of suppressing black-market operations has been a difficult one, however, as most people have tended to protect the illicit dealers who provide goods that are often unobtainable through regular channels. In the case of smuggling, suppressive measures have been at best difficult, considering the expanse of often poorly defined borders and the remoteness of certain rural areas.

To combat smuggling and black-market activities, new articles were adopted and added to the country's penal code in December 1968. The new additions provided for criminal prosecution for "abuse of power by state officials and employees, illicit acquisition of wealth through border trade, and the growing influence of foreign merchants." The PDG's intent of putting a stop to fraud and corruption within the governing administration was implicit in the new criminal law provisions.

Despite these governmental sanctions the illicit activities continued, and in late 1972 a number of influential officials were tried on charges of "economic sabotage." To handle what the president termed "serious lapses in foreign exchange dealings," PDG and government officials were charged with corruption and tried before tribunals in various parts of the country. Party federations were also organized to "wage war on profiteers" in a nationwide campaign begun in 1972 to "change the mentality of exploitation" by traders. Asserting that a large share of Guinean-produced goods was taken illegally into neighboring countries, particularly Sierra Leone, the president condemned the activities of Lebanese and Syrian traders. As a deterrent to this practice he forbade traders to operate a market within sixteen miles of a border. A renewed campaign against an apparently rising incidence of theft was also instituted.

The government's continuing concern with these problems was reflected in a speech by President Touré broadcast by the government radio in Conakry in early 1975. According to the broadcast, the president called on members of the PDG to step up efforts to suppress the illegal traffic in goods. Speaking to party members in Kankan Administrative Region, President Touré warned, "if a peddler arrives with goods, seize those goods because they belong to you; throw him in prison and, if necessary, kill him. And do it the way the Koran prescribes for the sheep sacrifice."

The president's outspoken statement followed the arrest of three

324

prominent people on the charge of illegal traffic in goods. Charged were the governor of Kankan Administrative Region, a regional party official, and the secretary general of a state-owned commercial firm. According to President Touré, top civil servants and PDG officials were involved in illegal trading through connections with people in Conakry and certain outlying administrative regions. Launching what he described as a "holy war on (illicit) trafficking," which he termed "the new prototype of Satan in 1975," the president threatened that government or PDG officials caught in such illegal activities would be executed. He also announced that the army had been mobilized to ferret out hoarders, whom he blamed for the rising prices of certain basic foods, such as rice, meat, and sugar.

Illegal currency transactions have also plagued Guinea since independence; and since the introduction of the Guinean franc in 1960, currency has been under black-market rule (see ch. 10). In March 1963 the government announced without warning that all people holding Guinean currency would have four days to exchange it for new issues. After the deadline the old money would cease to be legal tender and could not be exchanged. Concurrently all paper money outside the country was decreed worthless. In announcing the move President Touré stated that the reform was intended to combat the widespread practice of smuggling Guinean francs to neighboring countries where they were sold for less than face value. The money received was then used to purchase goods produced in Guinea that had been smuggled into the neighboring areas. The obvious intent of these illegal commercial transactions was to avoid Guinean taxes and to escape the higher costs caused by Guinean inflation.

Efforts to combat a sizable traffic in counterfeit currency also were of considerable concern to the government. The introduction of the syli in October 1972 was part of a concerted effort to stem the circulation of counterfeit notes introduced by foreign operators. This action as well as moves to reduce the volume of illicit foreign exchange dealings appeared to have been effective (see ch. 10). For illegally smuggling counterfeit Malian currency into Guinean, one Guinean was sentenced to death by public hanging.

In early 1975 the government's efforts to establish and maintain public order were based on the concept of a legal system developed "in conformity with the interests of the republic" (see ch. 8). The system of criminal law was statutory and was based largely on a penal code of 1965 (amended in 1968) and a companion code of criminal procedure. The penal code was divided into three books. Book I defined three categories of offenses, namely, *crimes* (felonies), *délits* (misdemeanors), and *contraventions* (violations). Book II of the penal code established the general principles to be followed by Guinean courts in judging criminal responsibility, particularly with regard to minors, accomplices, mitigating circumstances, and offenders who were adjudged insane. Persons under the age of thirteen years could not be tried for *crimes or délits*.

Extenuations that precluded charging anyone with a *crime* or *délit* were invoked if the accused was in a state of impaired mentality at the time the offense was committed, if he was compelled by a force he could not resist, if he acted under the order of legitimate authority, or if the act was committed in self-defense or in defense of another person. Punishments for specific crimes were outlined in Book III of the code.

The most common punishments were fines, imprisonment, and confinement at hard labor. The death penalty was invoked for a number of offenses, particularly in cases of serious offenses against the state or the principles of the "Guinean revolution," but there were indications that such sentences were not always carried out.

Little information was available regarding the country's penal system, but it was known that facilities established by the French during the colonial era had been taken over and used by the Guineans at independence. Shortly afterward the prison service was reorganized, and a similar action was taken in 1972. From 1958 to 1960 general supervision of the prison service was a responsibility of the Ministry of Justice. The reorganization reflected in the *Journal Officiel de la République de Guinée* in late 1972 indicated that a new penal administration had been created that year under the supervision of the Ministry of Interior and Security.

State-supported penal facilities were classified according to three kinds of institution: Camayeene Central Prison in Conakry; local prisons, of which there was one in each administrative region; and undefined lockups maintained at *arrondissement* (district) level. According to the government's official journal, persons arrested on suspicion of having committed a violation of law could be detained in any of Guinea's penal facilities. Having been charged with a violation, the accused could be retained in the same facility and, if convicted by a court of law, could remain in the same institution. Political offenders were usually sent to a number of security force installations for confinement while awaiting disposition of their cases. In the early 1970s at least three such camps were known to exist in the Conakry area, namely, Camp Mamadou Boiro, Camp Almamy Samory, and Camp Alpha Yaya.

Many of the officials appointed to supervise penal facilities throughout the country had at one time served as police commissioners in the same administrative regions. Information regarding the efficiency of prison administration, the treatment of prisoners, or their living conditions was not available in early 1975.

The widespread use of penal labor and the hardships endured in work camps had been the sources of bitter complaints against the colonial administration. Nonetheless, the use of penal labor appeared to have continued into the postindependence period, on a reduced scale, at various places throughout the country. According to President Touré, the criminal was often put to useful work while being given the punishment he deserved, and his humiliation before society would cause him to reform. Modern rehabilitation practices within penal institutions appeared to be lacking in most instances, although the need for them was recognized. The Three Year Development Plan (1960–63) envisaged the construction of a prison having facilities for the reeducation of convicts. It was likely that the Camayenne facility in Conakry was that called for in the plan, but in early 1975 that assumption could not be corroborated on the basis of available information.

SECURITY FORCES

Before Guinean independence maintenance of public order and internal security was the responsibility of the French governor of Guinea in Conakry, who was directly subordinate to the governor general of French West Africa in Dakar, Senegal. Police units consisted mainly of locally recruited African personnel, supervised by French cadres and serving under overall French command. They were organized, equipped, and trained by the French, along lines similar to those of comparable units in other French colonies of West Africa. Qualified Guineans in many instances became noncommissioned officers and, in exceptional cases, held commissions. Trained in French procedures, many of them by the end of World War II were serving with French police units in other territories of French West Africa.

Similarly, before Guinean sovereignty territorial defense was the responsibility of Metropolitan France, which deployed units of its army on a regional basis throughout its African territories for this purpose. During the colonial period roughly 50,000 Guinean soldiers served in French army units composed entirely of Africans. A large number of these soldiers served in Europe and Indochina during World War II; others saw action in Algeria and other parts of Africa. When Guinea rejected membership in the proposed French Community in 1958 and chose complete independence instead, General Charles de Gaulle reacted to the rebuff by cutting all political, economic, and military ties with the new republic. In rapid order the French dismantled their military installations, removing all movable equipment and supplies as well as all French military technicians. The usual military assistance provided other former French colonies was denied Guinea. In addition France began immediately to repatriate Guinean soldiers then serving in its army. Of the approximately 22,000 Guineans in French uniform in 1958, about 10,000 of those serving outside Guinea chose to remain in the French army. The remaining 12,000 were demobilized and returned home.

The new government of President Touré recognized that returning veterans, imbued with French traditions inspired by long association with the army of France, might represent a latent political force of disruptive potential to PDG aims. The party leadership recalled that Guinean veterans of French military service before World War II, particularly the Peul of the Fouta Djallon area, had tended to find themselves at odds with the people in their home communities. They had been critical of the local administration and were themselves criticized as having become outsiders who favored European ways. Many of them had used the knowledge acquired during their French military service to exploit their compatriots. Faced with the inability to provide jobs for a large group of returning veterans in 1959, PDG leaders were apprehensive about the possibility of trouble from the ex-soldiers, some of whom were expected to enlist in the new Guinean army for the purpose of inciting insurrection and bringing back French rule.

The solution adopted by the new government was in essence a resolution of the dual problems of building a national army while at the same time neutralizing a large, potentially dangerous group of Guineans trained in the art of military warfare by the former colonial power. After a process of careful screening to determine political reliability, some were chosen to join with members of the former territorial Gendarmerie to form the People's Army of Guinea (L'Armée Populaire de Guinée). By the end of January 1959 the new army had achieved a personnel strength of approximately 2,000 officers and men. The remaining veterans of French service were urged to join the PDG and to take an active part in the new republic's national development programs. All were included in party efforts to instill a sense of zeal for the country's new revolutionary mission.

Among the measures taken to assure the loyalty of the ex-servicemen who were not taken into the Guinean army was the formation early in February 1959 of the National Veterans Association; almost all veterans became members. According to an American observer who did research in Guinea in 1959 and again during the 1960s, the veterans were given roles in local affairs, responsibilities in human investment projects, and assignments in administrative and party activities. Although on occasion President Touré had directed the people to increase their vigilance over the activities of the ex-servicemen and resolutely to oppose any threat by them or their supporters, by 1963 most veterans had returned to their villages, quietly resuming their former lives.

The problems of creating, training, and equipping a national military establishment from scratch, together with similar requirements for a police system, were not easily resolved. Numerous solutions were tried, and continuing reforms and frequent changes in the responsibilities of each element ensued. Growing reliance on a paramilitary militia as a primary instrument of national defense has resulted, according to President Touré's statements, from recognition that Guinea cannot afford to recruit, train, equip, and maintain the large standing army he feels it needs. Outside observers generally agree, however, that this move has been conditioned primarily by the real or imagined threats to security that have preoccupied the government. After discovery of its involvement in the so-called Labé plot of 1969, the army was regarded by the governing party as a hotbed of subversion. Subsequently steps already under way were speeded up to reduce the army's ability to mount

328

a coup d'etat, and the militia became a counterforce against a possible military threat.

The Military Establishment

Armed Forces and the Government

The Constitution empowers the president of the republic as commander in chief of the armed forces. At cabinet level, responsibility for supervision of the military and the other security forces has varied considerably. At times the entire security establishment has been under a minister of national defense and security, with a separate secretary of state in charge of each of the different elements. Since the reorganization of the government in 1972, responsibility for the military element has been assigned to the Ministry of the People's Army under the Domain of the Prime Minister (see ch. 8).

Since then the minister of the people's army has supervised the Combined Arms General Staff, which devised military policy and directed its implementation at service level. Until early 1971 the chief of this general staff was General Noumandian Keita, the military establishment's most senior officer. But after he was charged with treason in the purges that followed the 1970 invasion, he was replaced by the army's chief of staff, Namory Keita, who was promoted to the rank of general.

In early 1975 there was little information available on the operation of the Combined Arms General Staff. The commanders of all three military services were among its membership, and certain high-level civilians of the Ministry of the People's Army also may have been represented. According to earlier information, the general staff directed the activities of the National Bureau of Recruitment, which compiled the statistical records of the annual contingent of young Guineans liable for military service. Another important function of the general staff was to administer the procurement of military equipment and supplies. This responsibility included the procurement of armament through foreign military assistance programs. The general staff also collaborated with foreign military advisers in Guinea regarding training programs and organizational policies.

In other African countries government control of military establishments often has depended on some kind of ethnic or regional balance among servicemen, particularly in armies. In Guinea, however, President Touré has relied on a system in which national objectives have been inculcated through political indoctrination. The army has been associated intimately with the aims and philosophies of the governing political party, and a PDG element functions in each separate military unit. At every level military personnel and those of the other security units are expected to participate in PDG activities.

At the highest level the civil and military leadership has been merged, and military officers are frequently drawn into PDG conferences. For example, the ranking officials are included in the group of top-level government officials who attend the annual PDG conferences. Even though a large number of military officers have been removed from office in the series of government purges that have occurred, those promoted to fill the primary positions have continued to be included in all key functions. The party's ideology, therefore, has taken precedence over all other considerations.

The military establishment is constantly reminded by the PDG leadership that it is expected to play a significant role in instilling nationalism in the Guinean people, particularly among its own recruits. Despite the close relationship between the military services and the political party, however, this relationship has not always been regarded by the government as one of complete agreement between two equals sharing common interests. Aware of the latent power potential of military forces, the party has maintained tight control over the army just as it has over all other national institutions. The policy of regarding the military as a functional entity of the party has been in large part successful. The PDG units within each military and police service have been intended to develop reliable contacts between party functionaries and military personnel, in part to detect discontent within the services.

The cumulative effect of the so-called Labé plot in 1969 involving certain elements of the military establishment and the purges that followed the 1970 invasion was a decimation of the upper ranks of the army. In plans announced by President Touré to "purify and reconvert" the army of its inherited colonial structure, those who were not wholehearted supporters of PDG policies were to be removed. In addition 900 officers and men who had reached a certain age were to be forced to retire from active duty; this group presumably included most, if not all, of those who had served in the French army before Guinean independence. According to one outside observer, many of these officers were opposed to the leftward turn in PDG policies, which was blamed on the influence of Chinese Communists. These officers also were displeased with the growing power of the militia, which had been strengthened as a counterbalance to the army after the spate of military coups in other African countries.

In a move unique in Africa and unusual anywhere, Guinean soldiers were integrated into the civil service in 1970 in order that they could be assigned to civilian occupations within the governmental structure, particularly to economic development tasks. They were henceforth to be known as "militants in uniform."

To further assure control of the security establishment, President Touré issued a decree in August 1974 establishing a body known as the Military and Paramilitary Unity Committee. According to the presidential directive, such a committee would be established within each of the military services, all police organizations, and the national militia. Each committee was assigned the same mission of assuring complete harmony between the activities of its parent service on the one hand, including the conduct of all personnel, and the party line and government directives on the other. Each committee was directed to assure that the duties assigned to its parent service were fulfilled in the best possible way and to strive for constant improvement in service efficiency in all areas of its assigned missions. The chairman of each committee was charged with responsibility for all political activities of the service to which his unit was attached.

Mission, Organization, and Operations

In early 1975 the Guinean military establishment consisted of an army of about 5,000 officers and men, an air force with a personnel strength of approximately 300, and a naval element of about 200 officers and men. The army was organized into four infantry battalions, one armored battalion, and one engineer battalion. Information was not available regarding the organizational structure of the air force and the navy.

At its inception in 1958 the army was assigned a threefold mission: ensuring domestic order, guarding life and property, and defending the nation's sovereignty. It was, in effect, a reserve force held in readiness to support the Gendarmerie, the Sûreté Nationale, and the Garde Républicaine in emergencies. In addition the army was increasingly called upon to participate in the human investment program by aiding in the construction of new roads, bridges, and buildings; in the creation of new plantations; and in the cultivation of crops, particularly on state farms. Military units were also expected to respond as emergency relief missions to areas stricken by fire, floods, or other disasters.

In the years since independence, however, the army's mission has undergone a noticeable shift in emphasis. Particularly since the Labé affair in 1969, publicity about army units and their leaders has been focused on their contribution to the economic development programs, rather than on their traditional military function. Emphasis on army personnel as "militants in uniform" and on their obligation of loyalty to the government and service to the nation underscore the primacy of their civic action mission. With the shift in defense responsibilities to the militia, some observers have reported that sections of the army have been deprived of arms and that the emphasis on civic action tasks has undoubtedly been made at the expense of military training and, consequently, combat effectiveness.

According to the published documents of the International Institute for Strategic Studies in 1974, the army's armored battalion could draw upon a modest inventory of Soviet medium tanks manufactured in the late 1940s and Soviet armored personnel carriers of comparable vintage. Other heavy arms consisted of field artillery guns ranging in caliber from 85-mm to 122-mm. Much of the more complicated equipment was of questionable or inoperable condition because of age and a lack of spare parts. According to some reports, however, a considerable amount of newer Soviet equipment was received after the 1970 invasion in order to lessen the possibility of a second attack and to improve Soviet-Guinean relations. This equipment was believed to be in good order, but much of it may have been distributed to the militia rather than to the army.

All Guinean ethnic groups have been represented in the army since its inception. In an effort to subordinate regional or ethnic ties to loyalty to the nation and in order to protect the service from family or local pressures, army personnel of all ranks are frequently transferred on an individual basis from one station to another and are generally not stationed in their home regions.

In the early 1970s the country was organized into four military zones, each corresponding to one of the four geographic regions (see ch. 3). One of the four infantry battalions was assigned to each of the military zones. The zone headquarters was also battalion headquarters, serving as the supervisory element for units of company and platoon size that were assigned to each of the country's twenty-nine administrative regions. Thus the only concentrations of army troops in the vicinity of the national capital appeared to be the armored battalion and elements of the engineer battalion.

Apart from its tacit role of defending territorial integrity, which in reality was an ancillary mission, the army was expected to play a larger part in civic action and as an economic production unit. In 1967 the army's command structure included a directorate of economic action, which was divided into a number of departments that were responsible for the different elements of the civic action mission. Army battalions at field level were organized into services corresponding to these supervisory departments.

Within the Agricultural Production Service certain battalions were responsible for growing crops on communal land and for livestock raising. The Industrial Service was assigned to operate the military factory in Conakry built by West Germany in the 1960s, where army personnel manufactured uniforms and shoes and repaired vehicles. The Transport Service was responsible for shipment of the crops and manufactured items produced by the Agricultural Production Service and the Industrial Service. The Engineering Service, which consisted of the army engineering battalion, engaged in the construction of buildings and roads and in the maintenance of streets in Conakry and other large towns. Engineering companies were assigned to Conakry, Kankan, and Boké. In all of its production activities, the army was expected not only to achieve self-sufficiency but also to make a profit for government expenditure in the national development program.

In early 1975 little information was available regarding the air force and the navy apart from what could be surmised from their equipment inventories and the sporadic bits and pieces gleaned from government documents and media releases. According to the inventory attributed to the Guinean air force by the International Institute for Strategic Studies, its mission apparently consisted of providing air support to ground

332

forces, aerial defense of national territory, and aerial resupply and transport services.

In addition to a squadron of Soviet-built jet fighters of mid-1950s vintage, the air force had in its aircraft inventory a few Soviet trainers of a similar but older design and several Czechoslovak advanced trainers, all of which had a potential for serving as ground attack aircraft. In addition it had several Soviet piston-engine trainers and Soviet light transports. Two seventy-five passenger Soviet turboprop transports were variously reported as belonging to the air force or to Air Guinea. The civil airline had a small number of other Soviet light and medium transport aircraft that, given the close links between the airline and the air force, could be used for military missions if needed. Several Soviet helicopters were also available. The air force was totally dependent upon Soviet assistance for logistics and training and upon Soviet personnel for aircraft maintenance. There were apparently more than enough Guinean pilots for the limited number of aircraft, although all lacked combat experience. Units of the air force were based primarily at Conakry-Gbessia airport, but some may have been dispersed to a second jet-capable airfield built near Labé by Cuban engineers in 1973 (see ch. 12).

The navy, which came into existence in about 1967, provided limited coastal and river patrol services. In 1974 its modest inventory of vessels included Soviet-built motor torpedo boats of the eighty-five-foot, sixty-ton class; similar vessels built by the PRC; Soviet ninety-eight-foot motor patrol boats; and small utility landing craft. The condition of the vessels on hand was poor, and several may not have been operational in early 1975. The navy was entirely dependent upon the Soviets or the Chinese Communists for logistics and training.

Manpower and Training

After independence the number of voluntary applications to serve in the armed forces far exceeded available vacancies. A presidential ordinance published in October 1959 nevertheless created a conscription system generally patterned after that established in 1912 by the French colonial administration. The ordinance stipulated that all able-bodied male citizens between the ages of nineteen and forty-nine were liable for military service. It prescribed three methods for obtaining recruits: by conscription of annual contingents; by enlistment; and by reenlistment. Over the years, however, the inducements of military service have proved attractive enough to have made it unnecessary for the government to resort to conscription to meet established manpower requirements. Nonetheless, compulsory service in an element of the security establishment for a period of two years appears to have continued into the 1970s. Apparently this service commitment could be fulfilled by duty in any of the military units, the militia, or any of the police services.

Little information was available in early 1975 regarding the existence of a military reserve force. In the early 1960s, however, military obligations had entailed a lengthy reserve req 'rement after completion of actuve duty in the army. In the national in᾽ ,est, reserve duty at that time was usually devoted to work on economic development projects. In December 1970 after the invasion of Conakry, the government announced that, because of its fear of a second invasion, reservists released from active duty from 1966 through 1969 were being recalled to duty.

At independence most of the officers and men who entered the new Guinean army had received training in basic military subjects during their duty with French colonial units. Many of them had attended French noncommissioned officer schools or had been given specialized training courses. Some Guinean soldiers presumably had attended the military preparatory school at Saint-Louis in Senegal or one of the other military schools in French West Africa, and a few had trained at military schools in France. All ranks participated in regular French troop-training programs, which included instruction in such basics as the use and maintenance of weapons and tactical exercises for small units. Army recruits were trained at Camp Soundiata near Kankan.

In early 1960 the National Military Academy (Ecole Nationale Militaire) was opened at Camp Alpha Yaya in Conakry. Designed to train selected noncommissioned officers to become commissioned officers, the school's first class studied for one year before graduating. Two-year and four-year courses were envisaged for succeeding classes. Instruction in military subjects was offered, but primary emphasis was placed on "training in accordance with the requirements of the Guinean revolution." In the early 1970s information on the status of the national military academy and other military training camps was not available.

Throughout the 1960s training was provided to elements of the military establishment by foreign military advisory missions, including those of the Soviet Union, Czechoslovakia, West Germany, and the PRC (see Foreign Assistance, this ch.). In addition members of the armed forces received military training in schools in the communist countries.

Since 1969 army training considerations of a strictly military nature apparently have been overshadowed by the service's civic action role. According to information contained in the PDG newspaper *Horoya* in August 1974, the government was making a concerted effort to eliminate a widespread rate of illiteracy within the army ranks. An element of each new Military and Paramilitary Unity Committee was charged with the operation of a literacy campaign aimed at teaching all "militants in uniform" to read, write, and perform mathematical calculations in the shortest possible time.

Little additional information was available to permit an assessment of the quality of Guinean military manpower. Apart from those who served in the provisional battalion that was sent briefly to the Congo (Zaïre) in 1960—under the command of a Guinean politician awarded the rank of general—and those who served in a protective role in Sierra Leone between 1971 and 1974, the army had little field experience of a truly military nature. Moreover, all of the military services were untested in battle.

Defense Costs

During the first few years of independence, expenditures for defense were relatively modest because of the outright grants of military aid and supplies by Czechoslovakia and the Soviet Union. Because of the increases in size of the military establishment after 1964 and the arming and reorganizing of the militia, the Guinean contribution to the country's defense outlay had to be increased. According to figures published by the United States Arms Control and Disarmament Agency, the defense budget voted by the Guinean National Assembly rose from an equivalent of US$4 million in 1961 to US$14.4 in 1965 and climbed steadily to US$18.6 in 1972, when it was equivalent to between 4 and 5 percent of Guinea's gross national product (GNP). Data on actual expenditures, which were said to differ from those authorized in the voted budgets, were not made public. The voted military budgets, which included the armed forces and the militia, were roughly the same size as those voted for the three police services; in 1971 the combined military and police budgets constituted about 11.5 percent of total current expenditures voted by the National Assembly. There was no information indicating whether the people regarded this as a heavy drain on the struggling economy.

The Police System

The functions of the various police organizations, like all other governmental activities, fit into the context of the political goals of the national leadership. The police are used, whenever needed, to stop acts or agitations that are thought to undermine the prestige of the PDG or to oppose its policies. Without creating a rule of terror, the police have, on occasion, acted promptly and brusquely against those suspected of damaging or opposing government programs. Suspected offenders have been subjected to intense surveillance. Moreover, the laws, decrees, and ordinances that the police are called upon to enforce have been, in effect, legalized enactments of PDG policies.

By presidential decree the police carry out the policies of the General Directorate of Security Services, which is attached to the Ministry of Interior and Security. The directorate is charged with assisting the minister of interior and security in the direction and administration of all the police services, which in early 1975 consisted of three major elements: the Sûreté Nationale (National Police), the Gendarmerie, and the Garde Républicaine (Republican Guard). Much of the equipment and training was similar, and elements of organizational structure were common to all services; nevertheless, they formed three distinct organizations.

The directorate, located in Conakry, consisted of six bureaus that were responsible for criminal investigation, state security, economic law enforcement, traffic management, public safety, and technical services. This centralized police service, headed by a general director and assisted by a deputy, was responsible for the discipline of all police personnel and for making inspection tours of all the police services throughout the country. Details regarding the organization, operation, and complete duties of the directorate were not available in early 1975.

As the governor of each administrative region was responsible for law enforcement and the maintenance of peace and order in his area, both he and the ministry were concerned with security problems. The definition of their respective responsibilities was unclear, but the ministry appeared to be responsible for the overall command and administration of the security forces and the control of security matters of national interest, whereas the regional and local administrations were responsible for the distribution of security forces in local areas and for their commitment in local disturbances.

There have been no indications that recruitment for police duty has ever presented any problem. In the past applicants were given competitive examinations to determine eligibility for enrollment in the national police school at Kankan. Aside from considerations of economy, the concentration of training in one school permitted uniformity of basic instruction in all of the police services. Little information has been available regarding the duration of the course, the subjects included, training facilities, or the capacity of the school. In 1960 Czechoslovak police specialists were on duty at the school, presumably to give technical advice and to assist in organizing the curriculum. As most of the older Guinean officers and noncommissioned officers assigned to the school at its inception had experienced service with French security units, some tradition of French police methods had survived, at least until the arrival of the Czechs or other foreign security specialists who have provided aid to the Guinean security establishment (see Foreign Assistance, this ch.).

Sûreté Nationale

Sûreté Nationale is the designation given to the civil police forces in all cities and towns. In the early 1970s the International Institute for Strategic Studies estimated that this urban police service had a strength of about 1,000 officers and men. Recruitment, direction, administration, and training of the urban police are responsibilities of the centralized General Directorate of Police Services.

Although the urban police are under the overall control of the central government, they function under the general supervision of the governors of the administrative regions to which they are assigned. Each governor has attached to his staff a chief of police who is in charge of all the regional police and their operations. The number of police in an administrative region depends upon the size and importance of its urban centers. The police organization may be subdivided into precincts or town quarter detachments and these, in turn, into police posts that are responsible for maintaining local peace and order. Besides being charged with protecting the lives, rights, and property of the people, the Sûreté Nationale also has a countersubversive mission. According to President Touré, it may be called upon as needed to stop sabotage, agitation, and all subversive activity and to help protect the "achievements of the revolution."

A special section of the Sûreté Nationale is charged with checking on the activities of foreigners in the country, including their entry and departure. Detachments from this section have performed their duties in Conakry at the port and at the international airport and, presumably, at the customary border crossing points. Agents from this section are responsible for examining the passports and other identification papers of incoming and outgoing people and the questionnaires they are required to fill out upon entry or exit.

The strong influence of the PDG on the Sûreté Nationale has been evident on numerous occasions. Homage to the party's BPN and to the government have been noted in official police statements emphasizing the educational role of the police in the republic and stressing the role of the police as protectors of the people instead of "oppressors as under colonial rule."

The ranks and grades of the Sûreté Nationale resemble those of the military forces but with different titles. The police in the capitals of administrative regions and in other large towns are under the supervision of a police commissioner *(commissaire de police)*. He is usually assisted by a deputy *(adjoint au commissaire de police)* and by one or more police inspectors *(inspecteur de police)*. Lower grades include senior sergeant major *(brigadier-chef)*, sergeant major *(adjudant)*, sergeant *(brigadier)*, corporal *(assistant de police)*, and private *(agent de police)*.

Gendarmerie

The Gendarmerie, with an estimated strength of approximately 900, is charged with the enforcement of law and with the maintenance of public safety and security in the rural areas where more than 80 percent of the population lives. It is a paramilitary force.

The main force of the Gendarmerie is organized into so-called brigades, at least one of which is assigned to each administrative region. A brigade is composed of six to thirty-six gendarmes, depending upon the importance of its responsibilities. It is ordinarily commanded by a lieutenant who is appointed to his post by presidential decree. In some instances, however, decrees have designated a senior noncommissioned officer for this post.

Besides the regular brigades assigned to administrative regions, some additional units—designated as frontier gendarmerie brigades—are distributed among the administrative regions on the country's borders. The primary mission of the frontier brigades is to assist the Customs Service in its efforts to prevent smuggling and illegal border crossing, issues of key significance in the government's view. The Customs Service itself is a separate organization under the Ministry of Finance. Although the frontier gendarmerie cooperates with the Customs Service, the latter agency apparently has some law enforcement units of its own that work in close cooperation with customs officials. According to the government radio in April 1974, the tenth National Congress of the PDG had requested a reorganization of the Customs Service and improvements in its operating techniques.

Conakry has at least three Gendarmerie brigades—the port, the airport, and the city brigades. Another kind of Gendarmerie unit is the mobile detachment *(peloton mobile)*. The detachments apparently operate under the direct control of the Gendarmerie commander and assist him in supervising and coordinating the activities of the various Gendarmerie units throughout the country. There are also two so-called criminal brigades, one for the Fouta Djallon area and one for Conakry. Members of the criminal brigades make investigations of important cases, but regular Gendarmerie brigade members are frequently designated to act as special investigators. These personnel are authorized to take depositions, collect fines, and make special reports in connection with specific infractions.

The system of ranks and grades in the Gendarmerie corresponds to that of the army. Lower ranks include senior sergeant major *adjudant-chef)*, sergeant major *(adjudant)*, sergeant *(maréchal des logis chef)*, corporal *(gendarme troisième classe)*, private first class *(gendarme deuxième classe)* and private *(gendarme)*.

Garde Républicaine

Like the Gendarmerie, the Garde Républicaine is a paramilitary organization with an estimated strength of about 1,600 officers and men. It reinforces the Gendarmerie in the administrative regions. In Conakry, besides guarding the president's residence, it provides the band and the motorcycle escort that are used in the official welcoming ceremonies for visiting dignitaries. One company guards the portion of Camp Alpha Yaya, an installation near the Conakry-Gbessia airport, that is used as a political prison.

The Militia

The militia is an organization born of the need to strengthen the country's defense establishment while at the same time providing employment in activities that will assist national development. Since its inception the organization has been completely subservient to the doctrine and aims of the PDG.

Guinea's initial efforts to form a militia system in early 1961 grew out of a PDG decision to form "committees for the defense of the revolution" on a workplace basis. Party leaders continually urged the people to be constantly alert and ready to "protect the achievements of the revolution." The rank and file were exhorted to report or oppose any dishonest practices, such as theft of property, embezzlement of funds, or

338

any other willful act harmful to the national economy. Members of the party's youth movement, the Youth of the African Democratic Revolution (Jeunesse de la Révolution Démocratique Africaine—JRDA), were especially encouraged to report derelictions of duty and infractions of the laws to party authorities or to the police. Some organizations formed units of volunteers who assumed limited police functions, such as detecting violations and tracking down suspects. According to government announcements, these efforts proved effective and drew high praise from party officials. As the PDG increased its demands for vigilance against such economic crimes as black-marketing and smuggling, and as it began to label all of its opponents traitors, the militia's role expanded.

Although composed of unpaid volunteers, members of the Popular Militia (Milices Populaires) were given distinctive uniforms and assigned definite tasks during the early and middle 1960s. The zeal with which the militia performed its mission, however, soon led to obvious excesses, and in 1966 a growing public demand for its dissolution began. Instead, at a session of the National Council of the Revolution held in Labé, President Touré reemphasized the militia's role and outlined improvements in its organization and personnel structure. New emphasis was placed on linking the militia's methods of recruitment and training with those of an organized civic service composed of young men and women between the ages of seventeen and thirty under the leadership and guidance of Guinean army personnel and Cuban advisers. With a claimed membership of 15,000, the civic service could be found at work on development programs throughout the country, serving as the core of the government's effort to resuscitate its earlier human investment program (see ch. 5). Soon thereafter these civic service groups began to be referred to as part of the militia.

By 1969 the government announced that the militia was being given a role equivalent to the army, an implicit attempt to lessen the possibility of a military coup d'etat. The element of the militia assigned to the Conakry area was given small arms and military training.

In 1974 the political leaders of Guinea spent much effort defining the role of what had become known as the National and Popular Militia, a dual name that reflected a new attempt at reorganization. The president announced that the country could not afford the large standing force needed to deter what he regarded as a constant threat of invasion. The militia, therefore, was to be organized as a reserve force at several levels throughout the country to assure national defense.

At the national level in Conakry, the militia was to become a regular full-time force. Although a part of the national element was to be organized into combat units, its major role appeared to be defined as that of a staff and cadre for the reserve militia units at the village, industrial, and school levels. The national element was to have status equal to that of the military and police forces.

At the level of the administrative regions, the permanent militia cadre were to circulate among the villages, spending three months in each one in a training program for local militia members. The goal of this effort, as enunciated by President Touré, would be to provide an ultimate paramilitary strength of 100 men in each of the country's 4,000 villages. Similarly, units of militia reserves would be created in factories and schools. As arms became available, they would be distributed to village depots, from which they would be issued as needs arose.

The extent to which this planned reorganization and expansion of the militia had been effected was unclear in early 1975, but the program described by President Touré was to be phased in as part of the Five Year Development Plan (1973–78). Militia training, particularly the use of small arms provided by the Chinese Communists, was being given to university students in Conakry as well as to those in all secondary schools.

Militia members, readily distinguishable by the red, yellow, and green belts worn with their khaki uniforms, guarded the country's frontiers and such installations as industrial projects, harbors, airfields, banks, radiobroadcasting stations, and gasoline dumps. Several outside observers have described them as a second police force, fighting against prostitution, black-market operations, and other economic crimes and even directing vehicular traffic. There is no reported evidence that the regular police have acted in any way to restrict militia performance. In the eyes of the party faithful, the militia has become a reliable and exemplary model of militant response to PDG goals. In 1974 the government announced that henceforth anyone wishing to enter the armed forces, the police services, or the civil service must have performed satisfactory duty with the militia.

FOREIGN ASSISTANCE

In early 1975 all of Guinea's security forces were completely dependent upon foreign sources of supply for weapons, ammunition, and most other equipment. Shortly after independence Czechoslovakia supplied Guinea with several thousand small arms, forging a fist link with the communist world. Since then, however, the vast majority of military, police, and militia equipment has been provided by the Soviet Union; the PRC, Cuba, and Czechoslovakia have provided smaller amounts. Most advanced training in the use of complicated items of military hardware has been provided by military assistance personnel from the donor countries. In addition a large number of Guinean officers and technical personnel have been sent to those countries for training. Soviet military aid between independence and 1970, for example, amounted to the equivalent of US$25 million.

The influence of Western nations on the Guinean security establishment, however, has been much less pronounced. The army as well as the police forces, nonetheless, have retained some semblance of the French colonial heritage, such as organizational forms and rank structures. Some of the older personnel, who had served in French police units before 1958, were still on active duty in early 1975. Between 1963 and 1967, a period in which Soviet political influence in Guinea had declined temporarily, the United States provided a limited amount of military equipment. During the same period, West Germany provided the equivalent of about US$7 million in equipment and training for three Guinean army engineer companies whose primary mission was the construction of transportation routes. Any friendly Guinean sentiments toward West Germany and France in these earlier periods, however, had been countered subsequently by political propaganda campaigns of the PDG that accused those European countries of planning and encouraging efforts to overthrow President Touré's government.

Foreign suppliers, primarily the Soviet Union and the PRC, have shipped weapons and other military equipment to Guinea for transshipment to neighboring Mali. Other weapons and supplies were given to Guinea for redistribution to PAIGC forces in Guinea-Bissau to aid in expelling the Portuguese from their colonial enclave.

Large numbers of Soviet and Cuban military assistance personnel in Guinea have been reported by foreign observers. The Soviet technicians have been associated particularly with the Guinean air force, and the Cubans have been active among the militia and in civic action training programs. The PRC also has maintained a military mission of significant size, although it was smaller than those of the Soviet Union and Cuba. The Chinese Communists have been notably active in training Guinean navy personnel in the operation of the patrol boats donated by the PRC.

After the defeat of the November 1970 invasion force, a number of African countries—some not always among Guinea's diplomatic supporters–reacted with military aid, such as the arms received from Egypt and Nigeria. Several others, including Sierra Leone and later Libya, signed mutual defense treaties with the Guinean government (see ch. 9). The treaty with Sierra Leone was invoked by that country's government in 1971, and 300 Guinean army troops were sent to Freetown to serve as a guard force against the threat of a military coup d'etat. The Guineans also provided a helicopter. This force was shortly reduced to 100 men and then to fifty; the last Guinean troops were withdrawn in 1974.

Although Guinea's air and port facilities for military use were still limited in 1975, the republic's geographic position on the shores of West Africa remained of strategic interest to the Soviet Union. Guinea's geographic vantage point was readily discernible when viewed in terms of its proximity to countries of the Western Hemisphere across the Atlantic Ocean's narrowest point. In the early 1960s Soviet technicians completed a major improvement of the Conakry-Gbessia airport, lengthening the runway to 10,000 feet in order to permit it to handle international flights of modern jet aircraft. In return for this and for Soviet military aid, the Guinean government permitted the Soviet air force to retain a portion of the airfield for its own use as a servicing point for reconnaissance aircraft on patrol over the southern and mid-Atlantic shipping lanes. Guinea, however, had refused to let the Soviets use the airfield in flights to Cuba during the missile crisis involving the United States and the Soviet Union in October 1962.

Since the 1970 invasion of Conakry, Soviet ships have been on almost constant patrol off the Guinean coast. In return for this screen against a possible repeat of the seaborne invasion, Guinea has provided bunkering and other port privileges at Conakry for Soviet vessels. It has been reported that the Soviet Union has sought permission to establish a naval base in the vicinity of Conakry, but apparently Guinea has not granted the request.

Dependence on the communist countries for training of Guinean security force personnel has been pronounced. In 1972 alone at least sixty-five Guinean air force personnel and five Air Guinea employees were sent to schools in the Soviet Union for training as pilots, navigators, and technicians. Five of the ten officers and four of the sergeants were to be trained as pilots. During the same year 331 military personnel from all the services were sent to the PRC. Another group of significant size was sent to Cuba, largely for training in specialties usable in Guinean civic action programs.

BIBLIOGRAPHY

Section I. Social

Adamolekun, Lapido. "Administrative Training in the Republic of Guinea, 1957–1970," *Journal of Administration Overseas* [London], XI, No. 4, October 1972, 233–252.

Ainslie, Rosalynde. *The Press in Africa*. New York: Walker, 1967.

Ajayi, J. F. Ade, and Crowder, Michael (eds.). *History of West Africa*, I. London: Longman, 1971.

Ameillon, B. *La Guinée: Bilan d'une Indépendance*. Paris: F. Maspero, 1964.

Appia, B. "Les Forgerons du Fouta-Djalon," *Journal de la Société des Africanistes* [Paris], XXXV, No. 2, 1965, 317–352.

Attwood, William. *The Reds and the Blacks*. New York: Harper and Row, 1967.

Balanghien, Etienne. "Voie des ancêtres chez les Malinké," *Vivant Univers* [Namur], No. 267, 1970, 22–31.

Barbé, Raymond. *Les Classes Sociales en Afrique Noire*. Paris: Editions Sociales, 1964.

Berg, Eliot J. "Education and Manpower in Senegal, Guinea, and the Ivory Coast." Pages 232–267 in Frederick Harbison and Charles A. Myers (eds.), *Manpower and Education: Country Studies in Economic Development*. New York: McGraw Hill, 1965.

————. "French West Africa." Pages 186–259 in Walter Galenson (ed.), *Labor and Economic Development*. New York: John Wiley and Sons, 1959.

Binet, F. "Groupes socio-professionnels en Guinée," *Le Monde Non-Chrétien* [Paris], XXXIV, No. 74, April-June 1965, 76–83.

Bolibaugh, Jerry B. *Educational Development in Guinea, Mali, Senegal, and Ivory Coast*. Washington: GPO, 1972.

Bravmann, René A. *Islam and Tribal Art in West Africa*. London: Cambridge University Press, 1974.

Brench, Anthony C. *The Novelists' Inheritance in French Africa*. London: Oxford University Press, 1967.

Camara, Djigui. "A la veille des examens de fin de cycle dans nos CER," *Horoya* [Conakry], No. 2124, June 20, 1974, 4.

Carter, Gwendolen M. (ed.) *African One-Party States*. Ithaca: Cornell University Press, 1962.

Charles, Bernard. "Cadres politiques et administratifs dans la construction nationale en Guinée," *Revue de l'Institut de Sociologie* [Brussels],

IV, No. 2–3, 1967, 345–353.

―――. *Guinée*. Lausanne: Editions Rencontre, 1963.

Church, R. J. Harrison. *West Africa*. (6th ed.) New York: John Wiley and Sons, 1968.

Cohen, William B. *Rulers of Empire: The French Colonial Service in Africa*. Stanford: Hoover Institution Press, Stanford University, 1971.

Conil-Lacoste, Michel, and Tracoré, Kamori. "No More Secret Languages," *New Africa* [London], IX, No. 3–4, 1967, 14.

Cournanel, Alain. "Situation de la classe ouvrière en République de Guinée," *Partisans* [Paris], No. 61, September-October 1971, 119–136.

Cowan, L. Gray. "Guinea." Pages 149–236 in Gwendolen M. Carter (ed.), *African One-Party States*. Ithaca: Cornell University Press, 1962.

Daget, J. *Les Poissons du Fouta Dialon et la Basse Guinée*. (Mémoires de l'Institut Français d'Afrique Noire, No. 65.) Dakar: Institut Français d'Afrique Noire, 1962.

Dalby, David. "Distribution and Nomenclature of the Manding People and Their Languages." Pages 1–13 in Carleton T. Hodge (ed.), *Papers on the Manding*. Bloomington: Indiana University, 1971.

Davidson, Basil. "Guinea: Past and Present," *History Today* [London], IX, No. 6, June 1959, 392–398.

―――. *A History of West Africa to the Nineteenth Century*. (Anchor Books.) Garden City: Doubleday, 1966.

Davies, Oliver. *West Africa Before the Europeans: Archaeology and Prehistory*. London: Methuen, 1967.

Decker, Henry de. *Nation et Développement Communautaire en Guinée et au Sénégal*. Paris: Mouton, 1967.

Demographic Yearbook, 1959. New York: United Nations, Department of Economic and Social Affairs, Statistical Office, 1959.

Demographic Yearbook, 1973. United Nations, Department of Economic and Social Affairs, Statistical Office. New York: 1974.

Derman, William. *Serfs, Peasants and Socialists: A Former Serf Village in the Republic of Guinea*. Berkeley: University of California Press, 1973.

Diallo, Alpha Amadou. "Die Gruendung eines Institutes fuer traditionelle Heilkunde," *Afrika Heute* [Bonn], No. 14, July 15, 1967, 217–218.

Diallo, Ousmane Poreko. "Evolution sociale chez les Peuls du Fouta-Djalon," *Recherches Africaines* [Conakry], No. 4, October-December 1961, 73–94.

Diaré, Ibrahim Khalil. "Musique guinéenne: audience et prestige," *Horoya* [Conakry], No. 2098, March 24, 1974, 7.

―――. "Les orchestres modernes aux compétitions régionales," *Horoya* [Conakry], No. 1935, September 28, 1972, 2.

Dobert, Margarita. "Guinea, the Role of Women," *Africa Report*, XIV,

No. 7, October 1970, 26–28.

Doré, Michel Blecko. "Institut Polytechnique de Kankan," *Horoya* [Conakry], December 20, 1973, 3.

"Dossier Guinée," *Remarques Africaines* [Brussels], XIII, No. 388, November 25, 1971, 414–419.

Du Bois, Victor D. "Guinea Educates a New Generation," *Africa Report*, VI, No. 7, July 1961, 3–4, 8.

——. *Guinea's Prelude to Independence: Political Activity, 1945–58.* (American Universities Field Staff Reports, West Africa Series, Guinea, V, No. 6.) New York: AUFS, 1962.

——. *The Guinean Vote for Independence: The Maneuvering Before the Referendum of September 28, 1958.* (American Universities Field Staff Reports, West Africa Series, Guinea, V, No. 7.) New York, AUFS, 1962.

——. *The Independence Movement in Guinea: A Study in African Nationalism.* Doctoral dissertation. Princeton: Princeton University, 1963.

——. *The Problems of Independence: The Decolonization of Guinea.* (American Universities Field Staff Reports, West Africa Series, Guinea, V, No. 8.) New York: AUFS, 1962.

——. *The Rise of an Opposition to Sékou Touré, Part I: Reform and Repression by the Parti Démocratique de Guinée.* (American Universities Field Staff Reports, West Africa Series, IX, No. 1.) New York: AUFS, March 1966.

——. *Thaw in the Tropics: France and Guinea Move Toward a Rapprochement.* (American Universities Field Staff Reports, West Africa Series, Guinea, VI, No. 2.) New York: AUFS, 1963.

Dupire, Marguerite. *Organisation Sociale des Peul.* Paris: Librairie Plon, 1970.

Fage, J. D. *An Atlas of African History.* London: Edward Arnold, 1958.

——. *A History of West Africa: An Introductory Survey.* Cambridge: Cambridge University Press, 1969.

"Les films guinéens remportent la médaille d'or," *Horoya* [Conakry], No. 1979, March 11, 1973, 2.

France. Ministère de la France d'Outre-Mer. Service de Statistique. *Documents et Statistiques, L'Enquête Démographique de Guinée, 1954–1955: Résultats Provisoires.* Paris: n.d.

France. Service des Statistiques Chargé des Relations et de la Coopération avec les Pays d'Outre-Mer. *Etude Démographique par Sondage in Guinée, 1954–1955: Résultats Définitifs,* I and II. Paris: n.d.

"French Guinea." Pages 56–58 in *Encyclopedia of World Art.* New York: McGraw-Hill, 1959.

Furon, Raymond. *The Geology of Africa.* (Trans., A. Hallam and L. A. Stevens.) New York: Hafner, 1963.

Germain, J. "Extrait d'une monographie des habitants du Cercle de

N'Zérékoré (Guerzé, Kono, Manon)," *Etudes Guinéennes* [Conakry], No. 13, 1955, 3–54.

Gessain, Monique. "A propos de l'évolution actuelle des femmes Coniagui et Bassari," *Journal de la Société des Africainistes* [Paris], XXXIV, No. 11, 1964, 258–276.

Gifford, Prosser, and Louis, William Roger (eds.). *France and Britain in Africa: Imperial Rivalry and Colonial Rule.* New Haven: Yale University Press, 1971.

Gigon, Fernand. *Guinée, Etat-Pilote.* Paris: Plon, 1959.

Greenberg, Joseph H. *The Languages of Africa.* (3d ed.) Bloomington: Indiana University, 1970.

Guery, André. "Les classes sociales en Guinée," *Remarques Africaines* [Brussels], XXI, No. 365, November 5, 1970, 390–397.

Guinea. Laws, Statutes, etc.

"Décret No. 246 PRG du 20 Septembre 1972," (concerning the taking of a general population census), *Journal Officiel de la République de Guinée* [Conakry], 14th year, No. 21, November 1, 1972, 182.

"Decret No. 145 PRG du 2 Juillet 1973" (concerning the result of the December 1972 general population census), *Journal Officiel de la République de Guinée* [Conakry], 15th year, No. 18, September 1, 1973, 187.

"Decret No. 0047 PRG du 8 Mars 1974" (concerning creation of a single teacher cadre), *Journal Officiel de la République de Guinée* [Conakry], 16th year, No. 5, March 1, 1974, 64–66.

Guinea. Le Haut Commissariat à l'Information au Tourisme et à L'I.N.R.D.G. *Chefs d'Oeuvre de l'Art Guinéen et Africain: Catalogue.* Conakry: Institut National de Recherches et de Documentation, 1967.

Guinea. Office of the Secretary of State for Information and Tourism. *Guinea and its People.* Conakry: Office of the Secretary of State for Information and Tourism, 1965.

"Guinée: aujourd'hui, la révolution culturelle," *Jeune Afrique* [Paris], No. 405, October 7, 1968, 37–38.

Hachten, William A. *Muffled Drums: The News Media in Africa.* Ames: Iowa State University Press, 1971.

Hair, P. E. H. "Ethnolinguistic Continuity on the Guinea Coast," *Journal of African History* [London], VIII, No. 2, 1967, 247–268.

Hance, William A. *The Geography of Modern Africa.* New York: Columbia University Press, 1964.

Hanry, Pierre. *Erotisme Africain*, I. Paris: Payot, 1970.

Hapgood, David. *Africa: From Independence to Tomorrow.* New York: Atheneum, 1965.

Harbison, Frederick, and Myers, Charles A. (eds.). *Manpower and Education: Country Studies in Economic Development.* New York: McGraw-Hill, 1965.

Hargreaves, John D. "British and French Imperialism in West Africa, 1885–1898." Pages 261–282 in Prosser Gifford and William Roger Louis (eds.), *France and Britain in Africa: Imperial Rivalry and Colonial Rule*. New Haven: Yale University Press, 1971.

——. *Prelude to the Partition of West Africa*. New York: St. Martin's Press, 1966.

——. *West Africa: The Former French States*. Englewood Cliffs: Prentice-Hall, 1967.

Harris, Joseph E. "Protest and Resistance to the French in Fouta Diallon," *Genève-Afrique* [Geneva], VIII, No. 1, 1969, 3–18.

Hazard, John N. "Guinea's Non-Capitalist Way," *Columbia Journal of Transnational Law*, V, No. 2, 1966, 231–262.

Heine, Bernard. *Status and Use of African Lingua Franca*. Munich: Weltforum Verlag, 1970.

Henebelle, Guy. "Côte d'Ivoire, Sénégal, Guinée: six cinéastes Africains parlent," *L'Afrique Littéraire et Artistique* [Paris], No. 8, December 1969, 58–70.

Hennebelle, Guy, et al. (eds.) *Les Cinémas Africains en 1972*. Paris: Société Africaine d'Edition, 1972.

Herdeck, Donald E. *African Authors: A Companion to Black African Writing, 1300–1973*. Washington: Black Orpheus Press, 1973.

Hodge, Carleton T. (ed.) *Papers on the Manding*. Bloomington: Indiana University, 1971.

Holt, P. M.; Lambton, Ann K. S.; and Lewis, Bernard (eds.). *The Cambridge History of Islam: Volume II, The Further Islamic Lands, Islamic Society and Civilization*. Cambridge: Cambridge University Press, 1970.

Houis, M. "Que sont les Soso?" *Etudes Guinéennes* [Conakry], VI, 1950, 77–79.

Hughes, John. "Communist Focus on Guinea," *New Leader*, XLII, No. 27, July 6, 1959, 3–4.

Johnson, R. W. "The PDG and the Mamou Deviation." Pages 347–369 in Christopher Allen and R. W. Johnson (eds.), *African Perspectives*. Cambridge: Cambridge University Press, 1970.

Kitchen, Helen (ed.). *The Educated African*. New York: Praeger, 1962.

Knight, Roderic. "Record Reviews (Musique malinké: Guinée; and Musique d'Afrique occidentale: Musique malinké, musique baoulé)," *Ethnomusicology* XVIII, No. 2, May 1974, 337–339.

Krueger, Heinz, and Umann, Joachim. *Blende auf fuer Guinea*. Leipzig: F. A. Brochkaus Verlag, 1961.

Laude, Jean. *The Arts of Black Africa*. Berkeley: University of California Press, 1971.

Lestrange, Monique de. *Les Coniagui et les Bassari*. Paris: Presses Universitaires de France, 1955.

Leunda, Xavier. "La réforme de l'enseignement et son incidence sur l'évolution rurale en Guinée," *Civilisations* [Brussels], XXII, No.2, 1972, 232–262.

Leuzinger, Elsy. *Africa: The Art of the Negro Peoples* (Trans., Ann E.

Keep) (2d ed.) New York: Crown, 1967.

Levtzion, Nehemia. *Ancient Ghana and Mali.* (Studies in African History, No. 7.) London: Methuen, 1973.

————. "The Early States of the Western Sudan to 1500." Pages 120–157 in J.F. Ade Ajayi and Michael Crowder (eds.), *History of West Africa*, I. London: Longman, 1971.

Lewis, I.M. (ed.) *Islam in Tropical Africa.* London: Oxford University Press, 1966.

McCall, Daniel F. "The Cultural Map and Time-Profile of the Mande-Speaking Peoples." Pages 27–98 in Carleton T. Hodge (ed.), *Papers on the Manding.* Bloomington: Indiana University, 1971.

Marcum, John A. "Report from Guinea," *New Leader*, XLI, No. 44, December 1, 1958, 3–7.

May, Jacques Meyer, and McLellan, Donna L. *The Ecology of Malnutrition in the French-Speaking Countries of West Africa and Madagascar.* New York: Hafner, 1968.

Mengrelis, Thanos. "Esquisse sur l'habitat Guerzé," *Africa* [London], XXXIII, No. 1, January 1963, 45–53.

Morgan, W.B., and Pugh, J.C. *West Africa.* London: Methuen, 1969.

Morrison, Donald G., et al. *Black Africa: A Comparative Handbook.* New York: Free Press, 1972.

Morrow, John H. *First American Ambassador to Guinea.* New Brunswick: Rutgers University Press, 1968.

Mortimer, Edward. *France and the Africans, 1944–1960: A Political History.* New York: Walker, 1969.

Mountjoy, Alan B., and Embleton, Clifford. *Africa: A New Geographical Survey.* New York: Praeger, 1967.

Murdock, G.P. *Africa: Its Peoples and Their Cultural History.* New York: McGraw-Hill, 1959.

N'Diaye, Bokar. *Groupes Ethniques au Mali.* Bamako: Editions Populaires, 1970.

Neres, Philip. *French-Speaking West Africa: From Colonial Status to Independence.* London: Oxford University Press, 1962.

Niane, Djibril Tamsir. "Mise en place des populations de la Haute-Guinée," *Recherches Africaines* [Conakry], No. 2, 1960, 40–53.

————. *Recherches sur L'Empire du Mali au Moyen Age.* (Mémoires de L'Institut National de Recherches et de Documentation, No. 2.) Conakry: Institut National de Recherches et de Documentation, 1962.

Okpaku, Joseph. "Les Ballets Africains Sont Belles: Guinea's National Ensemble in San Francisco," *Journal of the New African Literature and the Arts.* Issue No. Fall 1967, June 1968, 65–67.

Oliver, Roland, and Fage, J.D. *A Short History of Africa.* (Penguin African Library, AP2.) Baltimore: Peguin Books, 1962.

Ottenberg, Simon, and Ottenberg, Phoebe. *Cultures and Societies of Africa.* New York: Random House, 1960.

Panikkar, Kavalan Madhusudan. *Revolution in Africa.* Bombay: Asia

Publishing House, 1961.

Paulme, Denise. *Les Civilisations Africaines*. Paris: Presses Universitaires de France, 1959.

──────. *Les Gens du Riz*. Paris: Plon, 1954.

──────. "La notion de sorcier chez les Baga," *Bulletin de l'IFAN* [Dakar], XX, Series B, Nos. 1–2, January-April 1958, 406–416.

──────. "La Société Kissi: son organisation politique," *Cahiers d'Etudes Africaines* [Paris], I, No. 1, January 1960, 75–85.

──────. "Structures sociales en pays Baga," *Bulletin de l'IFAN* [Dakar], XVIII, Series B, Nos. 1–2, January-April 1956, 98–116.

Phillips, John. *Agriculture and Ecology in Africa*. New York: Praeger, 1960.

Pretty, Margaret. "L'éducation en Guinée, 1878–1962," *West African Journal of Education* [Ibadan], XII, No. 2, June 1968, 134–136.

"Rapport de la Commission des Programmes," *Horoya*[Conakry], No. 1893, May 5, 1972, 3–4.

Ray Autra (Mamadou Traoré). *Connaissance de la République de Guinée*. Dakar: A. Diop, 1960.

"Recommandations du Conseil Supérieur de l'Education," *Horoya* [Conakry], No. 1993, April 28, 1973, 2–3.

"Révolution culturelle en Guinée: Création de Centre d'Enseignement Révolutionnaire," *Afrique Nouvelle* [Dakar], No. 1097, August 15–21, 1968, 4.

Rivière, Claude. "Bilan de l'Islamisation," *Afrique Documents* [Dakar], No. 5–6, 1960, 319–359.

──────. "Dixinn-Port, enquête sur un quartier de Conakry," *Bulletin de l'IFAN* [Dakar], XIX, Nos. 1–2, January-April 1967, 425–452.

──────. "Dynamique des systèmes foncières et inégalités sociales: le cas Guinéen," *Cahiers Internationaux de Sociologie* [Paris], No. 20, 1973, 61–94.

──────. "Fétichisme et démystification: l'exemple Guinéen," *Afrique Documents* [Dakar], Nos. 102 and 103, 1969, 131–168.

──────. "Guinée: la difficile émergence d'un artisanat caste," *Cahiers d'Etudes Africaines* [Paris], IX, No. 36, 1969, 600–625.

──────. "Les incidents sociologiques du développement," *Développement et Civilisations* [Paris], No. 30, June 1967, 55–69.

──────. *Mutations Sociales en Guinée*. Paris: Editions Marcel Rivière, 1971.

──────. "Les résultats d'un ensiegnement révolutionnaire en Guinée," *Revue Française d'Etudes Politiques Africaines* [Paris], No. 52, April 1970, 35–36.

──────. "Les travailleurs de Wassa-Wassa: enquête sur l'Entreprise Nationale de Tabacs et Allumettes," *Canadian Journal of African Studies* [Montreal], II, No. 1, Spring 1968, 81–96.

Roberts, Stephen H. *History of French Colonial Policy (1870–1925)*, I. London: P.S. King, 1929. Reprinted London: Frank Cass, 1963.

Rudin, Harry R. "Guinea Outside the French Community," *Current History*, XXXVII, No. 215, July 1959, 13–16.

Shaw, Thurstan. "The Prehistory of West Africa." Pages 33–37 in J.F. Ade Ajayi and Michael Crowder (eds.), *History of West Africa*, I. London: Longman, 1971.

Skogan, Wesley. *Bibliography on Party Politics in Guinea, 1950–1962*. Evanston: Northwestern University, International Comparative Political Parties Project, 1967.

"Statistics: Vital Rates," *Population Index*, XL, No. 3, July 1974, 596–608.

Stern, T Noel. "Political Aspects of Guinean Education," *Comparative Education Review*, VIII, No. 1, June 1964, 98–103.

Stride, G.T., and Ifeka, Caroline. *Peoples and Empires of West Africa: West Africa in History, 1000–1800*. New York: Africana Publishing, 1971.

Suret-Canale, Jean. "The End of Chieftaincy in Guinea." Pages 96–117 in Irving L. Markovitz (ed.), *African Politics and Society*. New York: Free Press, 1970.

––––––. "La fin de la chefferie en Guinée," *Journal of African History* [London], VII, No. 3, 1970, 459–494.

––––––. *French Colonialism in Tropical Africa, 1900–1945*. (Trans., Till Gottheiner.) New York: Pica Press, 1971.

––––––. *La République de Guinée*. Paris: Editions Sociales, 1970.

––––––. "Touba in Guinea: Holy Place of Islam." Pages 53–81 in Christopher Allen and R.W. Johnson (eds.), *African Perspectives*. New York: Cambridge University Press, 1970.

Tagliaferri, Aldo, and Hammacher, Arno. *Fabulous Ancestors: Stone Carvings from Sierra Leone and Guinea*. New York: Africana Publishing, 1974.

Teel, William. *An Outline of African Art*. Cambridge, Massachusetts: University Prints, 1970.

Thompson, Virginia, and Adloff, Richard. *French West Africa*. Stanford: Stanford University Press, 1958.

"Les travaux du CNR: Rapport de la Commission de la Culture et de l'Education," (première partie) *Horoya* [Conakry], No. 1925, August 18, 1972, 3–4.

"Les travaux du CNR: Rapport de la Commission de la Culture et de l'Education," (dernière partie) *Horoya* [Conakry], No. 1926, August 21, 1972, 5–7.

Trimingham, J. Spencer. *A History of Islam in West Africa*. London: Oxford University Press, 1962.

––––––. "The Phases of Islamic Expansion and Islamic Culture Zones in Africa." Pages 127–143 in I. M. Lewis (ed.), *Islam in Tropical Africa*. London: Oxford University Press, 1966.

United Nations. "Population and Vital Statistics: Data Available as of 1 October 1974," *Population and Vital Statistics Report*, XXVI, No. 4,

1974, 6–7.

United Nations Educational, Scientific and Cultural Organization. *Survey on the Scientific and Technical Potential of the Countries of Africa*. Paris: UNESCO, 1970.

———. *World Survey of Education, V: Educational Policy, Legislation, and Administration*. Paris: UNESCO, 1971.

U.S. Department of Commerce, Bureau of the Census. *World Population: 1973*. Washington: 1973.

U.S. Department of Commerce. Office of Technical Services. Joint Publications Research Service—JPRS (Washington). The following item is from the JPRS series *Translations on Africa*:

"President Touré Reviews Information Organs, Suggests Improvements," *Horoya-Hebdo* [Conakry], February 26–March 3, 1972, 3–27. (JPRS: 55,603, Series No. 1139, March 31, 1972).

U.S. Department of Health, Education, and Welfare. *Social Security Programs Throughout the World*. Washington: GPO, 1973.

Voss, Joachim. *Guinea*. Bonn: Schroeder, 1968.

Webster, J.B., and Boahen, A.A. *History of West Africa: The Revolutionary Years–1815 to Independence*. New York: Praeger, 1970.

Weinstein, Brian. "Guinea's School of Public Administration," *Journal of Local Administration Overseas* [London], IV, No. 4, October 1968, 239–243.

World Radio-TV Handbook, 1974, (Ed., J.M. Frost.) Hvidovre, Denmark: World Radio-TV Handbook, 1974.

(Various issues of the following periodicals have also been used in the preparation of this section: *Horoya* [Conakry], January 1972-June 1974; *Horoya-Hebdo* [Conakry], December 1970-December 1974.)

Section II. Political

Adamolekun, Lapido. "Administrative Training in the Republic of Guinea, 1975–1970," *Journal of Administration Overseas* [London], XI No. 4, October 1972, 233–252.

———. "Politics and Administration in West Africa: The Guinean Model," *Journal of Administration Overseas* [London], VIII, No. 4, October 1969, 235–242.

Adrian, Charles F. "Political Thought of Sékou Touré." Pages 101–135 in W. A. E. Skurnik (ed.), *African Political Thought*. Denver: University of Denver, 1968.

Attwood, William, and Loeb, James I. "Africa and Acts of Dissent," *Washington Post*, December 12, 1971, 21.

Bornstein, R. "Organization of Senegal River States," *Journal of Modern African Studies* [London], X, No. 2, July 1972, 267–283.

Charles, Bernard. "Cadres politiques et administratifs dans la construction nationale en Guinée," *Revue de l'Institut de Sociologie* [Brussels], IV, No. 2–3, 1967, 345–353.

———. *La République de Guinée*. Paris: Berger-Levrault, 1972.

Craene, Philippe de. " 'Le dialogue avec Conakry se poursuit' déclare Président Houphouet-Boigny," *Le Monde* [Paris], July 28, 1972, 1.

Dobert, Margarita. "Civic and Political Participation of Women in French Speaking West Africa." Unpublished doctoral dissertation. Washington: George Washington University, 1970.

Du Bois, Victor D. *The Decline of the Guinean Revolution, Part I: The Beginnings of Disillusionment*. (American Universities Field Staff Reports, West Africa Series, VIII, No. 7.) New York: AUFS, November 1965.

———. *The Decline of the Guinean Revolution, Part II: Economic Development and Political Expediency*. (American Universities Field Staff Reports, West Africa Series, VIII, No. 8.) New York: AUFS, December 1965.

———. *The Decline of the Guinean Revolution, Part III: The Erosion of Public Morality*. (American Universities Field Staff Reports, West Africa Series, VIII, No. 9.) New York: AUFS, December 1965.

———. *The Rise of an Opposition to Sékou Touré, Part I: Reform and Repression by the Parti Démocratique de Guinée*. (American Universities Field Staff Reports, West Africa Series, IX, No. 1.) New York: AUFS, March 1966.

———. *The Rise of an Opposition to Sékou Touré, Part II: The Estrangement Between the Leaders and the People of Guinea*.

(American Universities Field Staff Reports, West Africa Series, IX, No. 2.) New York: AUFS, March 1966.

——. *The Rise of an Opposition to Sékou Touré, Part III: The Plot Against the Government and the Accusations Against the Council of the Entente and France.* (American Universities Field Staff Reports, West Africa Series, IX, No. 3.) New York: AUFS, March 1966.

——. *The Rise of an Opposition to Sékou Touré, Part IV: The Entente's Reactions to the Guinean Accusations.* (American Universities Field Staff Reports, West Africa Series, IX, No. 4.) New York: AUFS, April 1966.

——. *The Rise of an Opposition to Sékou Touré, Part V: The Formation of a Common Front Against Guinea by the Ivory Coast and Ghana.* (American Universities Field Staff Reports, West Africa Series, IX, No. 5.) New York: AUFS, April 1966.

——. *The Rise of an Opposition to Sékou Touré, Part VI: The Activation of the Guinean Exiles: The Front de Libération Nationale de Guinée (F.L.N.G.).* (American Universities Field Staff Reports, West Africa Series, IX, No. 7.) New York: AUFS, July 1966.

Foucault, Bertrand F. de. "Vers un réaménagement des relations entre les riverains du fleuve Sénégal," *Revue de Defense Nationale* [Paris], XXVIII, No. 2, February 1972, 244–257.

"Guinea." Pages 376–389 in *Africa South of the Sahara, 1974.* London: Europa Publications, 1974.

Hazard, John N. "Guinea's Non-Capitalist Way," *Columbia Journal of Transnational Law,* V, No. 2, 1966, 231–262.

Henderson, Gregory. "Guinea." Pages 317–339 in Gregory Henderson (ed.), *Public Diplomacy and Political Change: Four Case Studies.* New York: Praeger, 1973.

Johnson, R. W. "The PDG and the Mamou Deviation." Pages 347–369 in Christopher Allen and R. W. Johnson (eds.), *African Perspectives.* Cambridge: Cambridge University Press, 1970.

"Justice in Guinea," *Review of the International Commission of Jurists* [Geneva], No. 7, December 1971, 4–8.

Legum, Colin (ed.). *Africa Contemporary Record: Annual Survey and Documents, 1970–1971,* III. London: Rex Collings, 1971.

——. *Africa Contemporary Record: Annual Survey and Documents, 1971–1972,* IV. New York: Africana Publishing, 1972.

——. *Africa Contemporary Record: Annual Survey and Documents, 1972–1973,* V. New York: Africana Publishing, 1973.

——. *Africa Contemporary Record: Annual Survey and Documents, 1973–1974,* VI. New York: Africana Publishing, 1974.

Legum, Colin, and Drysdale, John (eds.). *Africa Contemporary Record: Annual Survey and Documents, 1968–1969,* I. London: Africa Research, 1969.

——. *Africa Contemporary Record: Annual Survey and Documents, 1969–1970,* II. Exeter: Africa Research, 1970.

Legvold, Robert. *Soviet Policy in West Africa*. Cambridge: Harvard University Press, 1970.

Parti Démocratique de Guinée. *Status du P.D.G.* (1969 ed.) Conakry: PDG, 1969.

"Les P.R.L." *Horoya-Hebdo* [Conakry], July 13–20, 1974, 34–41.

"Réorganisation de la Justice," *Horoya* [Conakry], August 25, 1973, 4–7.

Rivière, Claude. "La mobilisation politique de la jeunesse Guinéenne," *Revue Française d'Etudes Politiques Africaines* [Paris], No. 42, June 1969, 67–89.

———. "La politique étrangère de la Guinée," *Revue Française d'Etudes Politiques Africaines* [Paris], No. 68, August 1971, 37–68.

———. "Purges et complots au sein du PDG," *Revue Française d'Etudes Politiques Africaines* [Paris], No. 95, November 1973, 31–45.

Salacuse, Jeswald W. *An Introduction to Law in French-Speaking Africa, I: French-Speaking Africa South of the Sahara*. Charlottesville: Michie, 1969.

Stokke, Baard Richard. *Soviet and Eastern European Trade and Aid in Africa*. New York: Praeger, 1967.

Suret-Canale, Jean. "The End of Chieftaincy in Guinea." Pages 96–117 in Irving L. Markovitz (ed.), *African Politics and Society*. New York: Free Press, 1970.

———. "Les relations internationales de la République de Guinée." Pages 259–276 in K. Ingham, *Foreign Relations of African States*. London: Butterworths, 1974.

U.S. Department of Commerce. Office of Technical Services. Joint Publications Research Service—JPRS (Washington). The following items are from the JPRS series *Tranlations on Africa:*

"Causes, Effects of Guineans' Exodus Discussed," *Remarques Africaines* [Paris], November 25, 1971. (JPRS: 55,002, Series No. 1107, January 21, 1972).

"Communique Describes 2d Session of PDG Central Committee," *Horoya* [Conakry], May 27, 1972, 2, 4. (JPRS: 56,414, Series No. 1178, July 3, 1972).

"Eighth District Officials Purged," *Horoya* [Conakry], August 31–September 7, 1974. 38–39. (JPRS: 63,083, Series No. 1524, September 27, 1974).

"Isolation of Guinea Makes Assessment of Nation Difficult," *Le Monde* [Paris], October 3, 1973, 1. (JPRS: 60,300, Series No. 1383, October 12, 1973).

"Kissidougou Federal Bureau Purged and Reorganized," *Horoya* [Conakry], June 13, 1974, 1–2. (JPRS: 62,639, Series No. 1498, August 3, 1974).

"Organization, Motivating Forces of Society Discussed," *Révolution Africaine* [Algiers], October 22–28, 1971. 28–34, 37–38. (JPRS: 54,523, Series No. 1080, November 18, 1971).

U.S. Department of State. Bureau of Intelligence and Research.

Communist States and Developing Countries: Aid and Trade in 1973. (Research Studies No. INR RS–20.) Washington: October 10, 1974, 1–15.

————. *World Strength of Communist Party Organizations, 1971.* Washington: 1971.

————. *World Strength of Communist Party Organizations, 1972.* Washington: 1972.

"Vers la normalisation des rapports Franco-Guinéens," *Marchés Tropicaux et Méditerrannéens* [Paris], January 31, 1975, 249–250.

"Violemment mis en cause par M. Sékou Touré: Sénégal et Côte d'Ivoire," *Le Monde* [Paris], September 20, 1973, 1–8.

Whiteman, Kaye. "Guinea in West African Politics," *The World Today* [London], XXVII, No. 8, August 1971, 350–358.

Section III. Economic

Amin, Samir. "Guinea: Economy." Pages 397–404 in *Africa South of the Sahara, 1973*. London: Europa Publications, 1973.

Cournanel, Alain. "Situation de la classe ouvrière en République de Guinée," *Partisans* [Paris], No. 61, September-October 1971, 119–136.

Decker, Henry de. *Nation et Développement Communautaire en Guinée et au Sénégal*. Paris: Mouton, 1967.

Edwards, John. "Bauxite Supplies Concern," *Financial Times* [London], September 24, 1974, 18.

Germany, Federal Republic of. Statistisches Bundesamt. *Länderberichte: Guinea*. (Series Allgemeine Statistik des Auslandes.) Stuttgart: Kohlhammer, 1967.

Goldman, Marshall I. *Soviet Foreign Aid*. New York: Praeger, 1967.

Hain, Werner von. "Die Landwirtschaft der Republik Guinea," *Geographische Berichte* [Berlin], IX, No. 3, 1964, 179–193.

Hazard, John N. "Guinea's Non-Capitalist Way," *Columbia Journal of Transnational Law*, V, No. 2, 1966, 231–262.

Hodgkinson, Edith. "Guinea: Economy." Pages 378–384 in *Africa South of the Sahara, 1974*. London: Europa Publications, 1974.

Karst, J. "L'achèvement du projet de Boké," *Industrie et Travaux d'Outre-Mer* [Paris], XX, No. 242, January 1974, 38–43.

Legum, Colin (ed.). *Africa Contemporary Record: Annual Survey and Documents, 1971–1972*, IV. New York: Africana Publishing, 1972.

———. *Africa Contemporary Record: Annual Survey and Documents, 1973–1974*, VI. New York: Africana Publishing, 1974.

May, Jacques Meyer, and McLellan, Donna L. *The Ecology of Malnutrition in the French-Speaking Countries of West Africa and Madagascar*. New York: Hafner, 1968.

O'Connor, Michael. "Guinea and the Ivory Coast: Contrast in Economic Development," *Journal of Modern African Studies* [London], X, No. 3, October 1972, 409–426.

Organisation for Economic Cooperation and Development. *Development Cooperation: 1972 Review*. Paris: OECD, 1972.

———. *Development Cooperation: 1973 Review*. Paris: OECD, 1973.

———. *Geographical Distribution of Financial Flows to Less-Developed Countries*. Paris: OECD, 1965.

Pick's Currency Yearbook, 1973. (Ed., Franz Pick.) New York: Pick Publishing, 1973.

Production Yearbook, 1972. Rome: United Nations Food and Agriculture Organization, 1973.

Rivière, Claude. "Les conséquences de la réorganisation des circuits commerciaux en Guinée," *Revue Française d'Etudes Politiques Africaines* [Paris], No. 66, June 1971, 74–96.

———. "Les coopératives agricoles en Guinée," *Revue Française d'Etudes Politiques Africaines* [Paris], No. 59, November 1970, 55–64.

———. "La politique étrangère de la Guinée," *Revue Française d'Etudes Politiques Africaines* [Paris], No. 68, August 1971, 37–68.

Statistical Yearbook, 1973. (25th ed.) New York: United Nations, Department of Economic and Social Affairs, Statistical Office, 1974.

Stokke, Baard Richard. *Soviet and Eastern European Trade and Aid in Africa.* New York: Praeger, 1967.

Suret-Canale, Jean. *La République de Guinée.* Paris: Editions Sociales, 1970.

Swindell, K. "Industrialization in Guinea," *Geography* [London], 54 No. 245, November 1969, 456–458.

United Nations. Economic Commission for Africa. *Summaries of Economic Data.* Fifth Year, No. 14 (Guinea), Addis Ababa: ECA, December 1973.

U.S. Agency for International Development. *Africa Data Book.* Washington: AID, December 1973.

U.S. Department of Commerce. Office of International Marketing. *Market Profiles for Africa.* (Overseas Business Reports, OBR 72–074.) Washington: GPO, December 1972.

U.S. Department of State. Bureau of Intelligence and Research. *Communist States and Developing Countries: Aid and Trade in 1973.* (Research Studies, No. INR RS–20.) Washington: October 10, 1974, 1–15.

Voss, Joachim. *Guinea.* Bonn: Schroeder, 1968.

———. *Der Progressistische Entwicklungstaat: Das Beispiel der Republik Guinea* (Vol. 81 of the papers of the Friedrich Ebert Foundation.) Hannover: Verlag für Literatur und Zeitgeschehen, 1971.

(Various issues of the following periodicals have been used in the preparation of this section: *Africa: An International Business, Economic and Political Monthly* [London], January 1973–October 1974; *Africa Research Bulletin* [London], January 1971–November 1974, *African Development* [London], January 1972–September 1974; *Direction of Trade* [Washington], annual issues No. 5, 1963–1967 through No. 8, 1968–1972; and monthly issues January–October 1974; *Europe-Outremer* [Paris], January 1972–April 1974; *Industries et Travaux d'Outre-Mer* [Paris], January 1972–July 1974; *Quarterly Economic Review: Senegal, Mali, Mauritania, and Guinea* [London], No. 2, 1963 to No. 3, 1974; *West Africa* [London], January 1972–November 1974; *World Agricultural Economics and Rural Sociology Abstracts* [Oxford], 1970–1974.)

Section IV: National Security

"Air Forces of the World, Part 5: North and West Africa," *Interavia* [Geneva], XXIV, No. 1, January 1974, 71–74.

Bell, M. J. V. *Army and Nation in Sub-Saharan Africa.* (Adelphi Papers, No. 21.) London: International Institute for Strategic Studies, August 1965.

——. *Military Assistance to Independent African States.* (Adelphi Papers, No. 15.) London: International Institute for Strategic Studies, 1970.

Booth, Richard. *The Armed Forces of African States.* (Adelphi Papers No. 67.) London: International Institute for Strategic Studies, 1970.

Cruise O'Brien, Donal. "Guinea: Recent history." Pages 377–378 in *Africa South of the Sahara, 1974.* London: Europa Publications, 1974.

Derman, William. *Serfs, Peasants and Socialists: A Former Serf Village in the Republic of Guinea.* Berkeley: University of California Press, 1973.

Dobert, Margarita. "Who Invaded Guinea?" *Africa Report,* XVI, No. 3, March 1971, 16–18.

Du Bois, Victor D. "The Role of the Army in Guinea," *Africa Report,* VIII, No. 1, January 1963, 3–5.

Dupuy, Trevor N. (ed.) *The Almanac of World Military Power.* Dunn Loring, Virginia: T. N. Dupuy Associates, 1970.

Guinea. Office of the Secretary of State for Information and Tourism. *Guinea and Its People.* Conakry: Office of the Secretary of State for Information and Tourism, 1965.

Lee, J. M. *African Armies and Civil Order.* New York: Praeger, 1969.

Legum, Colin (ed.). *Africa Contemporary Record: Annual Survey and Documents, 1970–1971,* III. London: Rex Collings, 1971.

——. *Africa Contemporary Record: Annual Survey and Documents, 1971–1972,* IV. New York: Africana Publishing, 1972.

——. *Africa Contemporary Record: Annual Survey and Documents, 1972–1973,* V. New York: Africana Publishing, 1973.

——. *Africa Contemporary Record: Annual Survey and Documents, 1973–1974,* VI. New York: Africana Publishing, 1974.

Legum, Colin, and Drysdale, John (eds.). *Africa Contemporary Record: Annual Survey and Documents, 1968–1969,* I. London: Africa Research, 1969.

——. *Africa Contemporary Record: Annual Survey and Documents, 1969–1970,* II. Exeter: Africa Research, 1970.

The Military Balance, 1971–1972. London: International Institute for

Strategic Studies, 1971.

The Military Balance, 1973–1974. London: International Institute for Strategic Studies, 1973.

The Military Balance, 1974–1975. London: International Institute for Strategic Studies, 1974.

Quarterly Economic Review: Senegal, Mali, Mauritania, and Guinea. No. 4. London: The Economist, December 1974.

Salacuse, Jeswald W. *An Introduction to Law in French-Speaking Africa, I: French-Speaking Africa South of the Sahara.* Charlottesville: Michie, 1969.

Stokke, Baard Richard. *Soviet and Eastern European Trade and Aid in Africa.* New York: Praeger, 1967.

Suret-Canale, Jean. *La République de Guinée.* Paris: Editions Sociales, 1970.

U.S. Arms Control and Disarmament Agency. *World Military Expenditure and Arms Trade, 1963–1973.* Washington: GPO, 1975.

―――. *World Military Expenditures, 1971.* Washington: GPO, July 1972.

U.S. Department of Commerce. Office of Technical Services. Joint Publications Research Service—JPRS (Washington). The following items are from the JPRS series *Translations on Africa:*

"Airmen Going to USSR for Training Courses," *Journal Officiel de la République de Guinée* [Conakry], February 15, 1972, 26–27. (JPRS: 55,723, Series No. 1144, April 17, 1972).

"Decree Establishes Police Services Bureau," *Journal Officiel de la République de Guinée* [Conakry], July 1, 1974, 161. (JPRS 62,755, Series No. 1506, August 19, 1974).

"Military Men to USSR," *Journal Officiel de la République de Guinée* [Conakry], October 1, 1972, 167–168. (JPRS: 58,226, Series No. 1264, February 13, 1973).

"Military-Paramilitary Committees' Duties Defined," *Horoya* [Conakry], August 10–17, 1974, 43–44. (JPRS 63,144, Series No. 1529, October 7, 1974).

"President Describes Army's Social and Economic Role," *Horoya* [Conakry], February 19, 1974, 1–2. (JPRS: 61,663, Series No. 1455, April 4, 1974).

"President Sékou Touré's Address Welcoming Gen. Gowon," Conakry Radio, February 18, 1974. (JPRS: 61,368, Series No. 1439, March 1, 1974).

"Touré Discusses Militia Organization," *Horoya* [Conakry], March 31, 1974, 3–4. (JPRS: 61,941, Series No. 1469, May 8, 1974).

Voss, Joachim. *Guinea.* Bonn: Schroeder, 1968.

Weeks, George. "The Armies of Africa," *Africa Report,* IV, No. 1, January 1964, 11.

(Various issues of the following periodicals were also used in the preparation of this section:*Africa* [London], July–December 1974; *Africa*

Research Bulletin [London], January 1968–March 1975; *Le Monde* [Paris], November 1970–April 1973; *Marchés Tropicaux et Méditerranéens* [Paris], March 1974–February 1975; *New York Times*, November 1970–October 1974; *Washington Post*, November 1970–March 1975; *West Africa* [London], April 1973–March 1975.)

GLOSSARY

AOF—Afrique Occidentale Française (French West Africa). Federation of French West African territories established in 1894; replaced by the French Community *(q.v.)* beginning in 1958; AOF ceased to exist officially on January 21, 1959.

CER—Centre de'Education Révolutionnaire (Center of Revolutionary Education). Term used generally as a synonym for school in Guinea; based on a change of educational concepts in the late 1960s whereby all schools were to be transformed into institutions that provided a work-study program, combining production and education.

extended family—A kin group consisting of two or more related nuclear families *(q.v.)*. For example, a man, his wife or wives, his unmarried children, his married sons, their wives and children.

franc area—The monetary area formed by the states of the former French Community *(q.v.)* with the exception of French Somaliland but with the addition of Tunisia, Togo, and Cameroon. The currencies of these countries are tied to the French franc and are freely transferable. Also know as the franc zone.

French Community—A politicoeconomic association of France and its former overseas possessions. Formed in 1958, it replaced the French Union, which was the successor of the French colonial empire. Of the French overseas territories, Guinea alone rejected membership in the French Community and chose independence instead.

GDP—Gross domestic product. The total value of productive activity occurring within the national border, theoretically obtained by adding up the estimated value added by each productive sector of the economy. The value added by each producer is equivalent to actual or imputed wages, profits, and other incomes payable for factor services. GDP differs from gross national product (GNP), which excludes the value of net factor payments to nonresidents (interest, profits, and salary remittances). Monetary GDP excludes the imputed value of subsistence production.

GNP—Gross national product. *See* GDP.

griot—A member of a traditional caste of musicians, genealogists, and praise singers; the term may be applied in the modern context to anyone who regularly sings another's praises.

Guinean franc—Guinean currency from March 1, 1960, to October 2, 1972. Until introduction of the Guinean franc (GF), currency was the African Financial Community franc (Communauté Financière Africaine franc—CFAF) tied to the French franc (CFAF50 equaled one

French franc); exchange rate per US$1 was CFAF246.8 from 1958 through February 1960. After introduction of the Guinean franc, official exchange rate per US$1 was GF246.8 from March 1, 1960, through December 31, 1971, and GF227.365 from January 1, 1972, through October 1, 1972; Guinean syli (q.v.) introduced on October 2, 1972.

Guinean syli—Guinean currency, adopted on October 2, 1972; one Guinean syli (GS1) consists of 100 cauris. Official exchange rate per US$1 was GS22.7 from October 2, 1972, through February 13, 1973, and subsequently GS20.46. Syli, a Soussou word meaning elephant, has been redefined by President Touré as "the will of the people of Guinea to destroy colonialism, neocolonialism, and imperialism."

harmattan—Hot, dry wind from the Sahara Desert that blows from the northeast and prevails over much of West Africa during the dry seasons.

jihad—A religious duty imposed on Muslims by the sharia (q.v.) for the spread of Islam. Popularly known as "holy war," it is waged against unbelievers and enemies of the faith. Followers may fulfill their jihad duty in four different ways: by the heart, the tongue, the hand, and the sword.

lineage (patrilineage, matrilineage)—A group of people who can trace their descent from a known common ancestor; a patrilineage if descent is traced only through males, a matrilineage if descent is traced only through females.

loi-cadre—Legislation passed by French Parliament in 1956, setting up a new structural framework for governing the overseas territories. It granted universal suffrage and gave broad legislative powers to the territorial assemblies.

nuclear family—A kin group consisting of a man, his wife, and their unmarried children.

PDG—Parti Démocratique de Guinée (Democratic Party of Guinea). Since the republic's establishment in 1958, this has been the only political party permitted by the governing administration.

PRL—Pouvoir Révolutionnaire Local (Local Revolutionary Power); basic unit of local government. Operates at village and town-ward level with politicoeconomic responsibilities; completely enmeshed with the apparatus of the PDG (q.v.).

sharia—The body of formally established, sacred Islamic law. It is based primarily on Allah's commandments as found in the Koran. In theory it governs religious matters and also regulates political, economic, civil, criminal, ethical, social, and domestic affairs in Muslim countries. In practice it is commonly supplemented by the customary law of a region and by government legislation and administrative practice. Courts applying this law are called shariat courts.

The Sudan—General term for the broad zone of Africa between the southern edge of the Sahara Desert and the upper limit of the tropical rain forests. The zone extends from the Atlantic coast of Guinea eastward to Ethiopia and the Red Sea. The term derives from "Bilad as Sudan" (Land of the Blacks), which originated with medieval Arab writers.

World Bank Group—Consists of the International Bank for Reconstruction and Development (IBRD, commonly known as the World Bank) and its two financial affiliates, the International Finance Corporation (IFC), which became operational in 1956, and the International Development Association (IDA), which became operational in 1960. IFC works specifically with the private sector in developing countries, and IDA operates in the same sectors and with the same policies as the IBRD but provides credits only to the poorer developing countries and on easier terms than conventional IBRD loans.

INDEX

Abu Dhabi (country): 196, 230, 309
administrative hierarchy. *See* political subdivisions
adult education: 142–143; under French rule, 29
Africa: v, 144, 149, 150, 156, 173, 199, 235, 243, 245, 255, 300, 312–313, 327, 329; coups d'etat, 177; and ethnicity, 62; food potential, 244; foreign relations with Guinea, 182, 183–190, 341; pan-Africanism, v, 181, 182, 183, 186; values, 87
Africa, Black: 4
Africa, French Black: 10, 31, 33, 35
Africa, French Equatorial: 34, 35, 38
Africa, French West: 4, 6, 12, 18, 19, 22, 53, 126, 256, 237; decree of 1895, 24; Supreme Council for the Colonies, 24; territorial administration, 24–38
Africa, North: 11, 14, 16, 31
Africa Socialist Movement (Mouvement Socialiste Africain—MSA): 36
Africa, West (*see also* empires and kingdoms): v, 1, 9, 10, 12, 16, 17, 24, 66, 68, 147, 163, 203, 236, 255, 260, 288, 310, 341; and Islam, 89–90; languages of, 72
African, Caribbean, and Pacific (ACP) countries: 301–302
African Democratic Rally (Rassemblement Démocratique Africain—RDA): 34, 73, 163, 170, 185
African Financial Community franc (Communauté Financière Africaine franc—CFAF): viii, 232
African Maritime Fishing Company (Société Africaine des Pêches Maritimes—Afrimar): 270
African Party for the Independence of Guinea-Bissau and the Cape Verde Islands (Partido Africano da Independência da Guiné e do Cabro-Verde—PAIGC): 187–188, 319–320, 341
African Peoples Congress (APC): 186
africanization. *See* Christianity; civil service; communications; education; Fria mining complex; industry; nationalization; trade, domestic
Afrique-Asie: 132

Agricultural Production Service: 332
agriculture (*see also* cattle; cooperatives; collectivization; crops; cultivators; dairy products; droughts; exports; farms and farming; fertilizers; fish and fishing; floods; food processing; food supply; forests and forestry; herding; imports; irrigation; livestock; oxplow; slash-and-burn technique; soil; tractors): 6, 46, 235–271; disincentives, 235, 243–245; and economy, 201, 207, 208, 221, 222; and government policy, 241; schools, 134, 139, 236, 241; subsistence consumption, 198; targets set, 250, 263
Ahmadu: 18
air force: ix, 331, 332–333, 341, 342
Air Guinea: ix, 311, 333
air transportation (*see also* transportation): ix, 311; airfields, 55, 194; Soviet aircraft, 221
Algeria: 24, 142, 147, 208, 223, 226, 230, 283, 284, 327
Algiers: 29
almamy: 15, 20, 21
Almoravids. *See* Muslims
alumina (*see also* Fria mining complex; mining): viii, 48, 49, 194, 196, 197, 198, 199, 202, 210, 276, 277, 279, 296, 301, 304; Halco, 195, 281–282; Harvey Aluminum, 195, 281, 287
aluminum: 209, 231, 276–277, 278, 280; processing, 233
Amaria (town): 289, 291
amulets: 95, 97; and folk medicine, 116
Arabs: 14, 181, 196, 223, 230; pan-Arabism, 97
aristocracy (*see also* social stratification): 27; and Islam, 14, 15; Peul, 78, 83
armed forces (*see also* air force; army, militia; navy; police): 329–335; Combined Arms General Staff, 329; enlistments, 333; and the government, 329–331; military appointments, 152; and the PDG, 167; reserves, 333–334, 339; and subversion, 317–318; training, 334
army: ix, 157, 316, 331; and civil service, 330, 332; and disaster relief missions, 331;

in labor force, 331, 332; and party loyalty, 177; purges, 315, 318, 321, 322, 330; and subversion, 328

artisans: 65, 81, 84, 200, 287; blacksmiths, 65, 103, 110; carvers, 102; ironsmiths, 67; potters, 67, 102, 128, 130

artisti expression. *See* cultural life

Asia: 182

Assembly of Guineans in Europe (Régroupement des Guinéens en Europe—RGE) (*see also* emigration of political exiles): 320–321

Association of Guineans in France (Association des Guinéens en France—AGF): 178

Atlantic Ocean: 341

Australia: 276, 281, 284

Austria: 287

Ayekoé partnership: and bauxite, 283

Bafing River (*see also* Sénégal River): 43, 46, 288

Baga group: 54, 62–64, 65, 66, 84, 91, 97; Baga Foré, 65; and cultivating, 260; fishermen, 269; language, 72, 73

Bahrain: 196, 230

Bakoye River: 12, 43

balafon: 125

balance of payments: 208, 213–215; and the United States, 300

Balandier, Georges: 131

Ballets Africains: 107, 122, 126–127

Bamako: 19, 34

Bambafouga (town): 309

bananas: viii, 4, 42, 46, 74, 205, 212, 253, 257, 259, 266, 267–268, 301, 302, 304, 308; Banana Equalization Fund, 308

Banankoro (town): 286

Banéa (town): 289

banks and banking: 203, 207, 221, 231–232; central bank, 203, 205, 206, 231, 232; French, 293; nationalization of, 293; specialized banks, 231, 232

Barry, Diawadou: 35

Barry, Ibrahima: 35

Barry III: 35

Bassari group: language, vii

bauxite (*see also* Boké bauxite project; Fria mining complex; International Bauxite Association; mining): viii, 6, 41, 48, 49, 194, 195, 196, 275, 276, 277, 278–283, 301, 304; and economy, 197, 198, 199, 202, 209, 210, 214, 223, 224, 225, 226, 230, 296; and France, 190, 274; potential, 279; and Soviet Union, 193; and transportation, 309

Bauxite Company of Guinea (Compagnie des Bauxites de Guinée—CBG): 282

Béavogui, Louis Lansana: 155, 181, 182, 189, 196

Bekkaye, Sidi Ahmad al: 91

Belgium: 142, 271, 277, 286; and security of Guinea, 322

Belle Vue National School of Fine Arts: 128

Benard, Jean: 200

Benti (town): 18, 310

Berbers: 11, 12

Bettelheim, Charles: 220, 293

beverages: 112–113; beer, 112; palm wine, 112–113

Beyla region: xiv, 46, 49, 58, 264–265, 285

birthrate: 55–56; infant mortality, 56

Bissandougou: 19

black markets: 99, 100, 104, 106, 107, 197, 201–202, 203, 206, 245; currency, 325; foreign exchange, 233–234; and national security, 323, 324; produce, 209, 269

Boffa region: xiv; 28, 58, 92, 250, 252, 310

Boisson, Pierre: 29

Boké bauxite project: 195, 212, 222, 281–282, 289

Boké Improvement Office (Office d'Aménagement de Boké—OFAB): 282

Boké region: xiv, 17, 18, 20, 43, 48, 49, 58, 92, 195, 252, 288, 290, 310, 311

books (*see also* education; mass communication): 145

Bordo (town): 139

Bouré area: 12, 19, 49, 54

bourgeoisie (*see also* middle group): 74, 84

Brazil: 284

Brazzaville Conference: 30, 31

British Broadcasting Corporation (BBC): 147

budget: 215, 216, 217, 218–219; education, 136, 218, 219; under French rule, 220; and legislature, 153; military, 335; planning, 215; and state enterprises, 217

Bulgaria: 142, 288

bureaucracy: 3

cabinet (*see also* ministries; prime minister): 152, 154–156, 165, 170, 178; and the Central Committee, 169; and economy, 200, 207; and party organization, 170, 172; punishment of members, 249–250, 321

Cabral, Amilcar: 320

Camayenne Peninsula: 42, 43, 49

Cameroon: 277, 297; and trade, 298, 299

Camp Almany Samory: 326

Camp Alpha Yaya: 322, 326; and National Military Academy, 333

Camp Mamadou Boiro: 326

Camp Soundiata: 334

368

power, 318, 319; revolutionary tribunals, 162; sections, 168; and security, 316, 320, 325, 328, 329–330, 335, 337, 341; and smuggling, 339; village committees, 157, 168
dentists: 115
Diakhanké group: 63, 67–68, 91; language, 72, 73
Diallo, Saïfoulaye: 35
Diallo, Siradiou: 293
Diallo, Yacine: 31, 33, 34, 35
Dialonké group (see also Soussou group): 15, 62, 63, 65, 66, 67, 70, 73, 82; language, 72
diamonds: vii, 49, 275, 279, 285–286; nationalization of mines, 274, 285, 286; smuggling, 285, 286, 302, 323
Diane, Lansana: 172
Diani falls: 291
dictatorship: 175
Diecké Forest: 270
diet (see also beverages, disease; food supply; health): 111–113, 206; fish, 52, 111; and hungry season, 111, 112; inadequate harvests, 100–102; malnutrition, viii; meat, 268; rice, 111
Dinguiraye region: xiv, 18, 49, 54, 58
Dinguiraye (town): 289
disease: viii, 112, 113–114; cholera, 113; leprosy, 113; malaria, 113, 114; malnutrition, viii; schistosomiasis, 114; tuberculosis, 113; venereal disease, 113
divorce: 85, 159
doctors:115
Dogome (village): 282
Donké stream: 289, 290
drainage: 46; canals, 261
drama: 126
droughts: 235, 254, 256
Dubreka region: xiv, 57, 58
Dumont, René: 241

economy (see also balance of payments; banks and banking; budget; currency; exports; Five Year Plan; foreign aid; foreign debt; foreign exchange; gross domestic product; gross national product; income; inflation; investments; Seven Year Plan; smuggling; taxation; trade, domestic; trade, foreign; wages and salaries): viii, 1, 6, 183, 197–234; capital formation, 202; central planning, 201, 213, 220; deficit, 219; and emigration, 3; and government controls, 1, 209, 221; information about, 200; malpractices, 207; and the PDG, 166; and production, 206–207, 208, 221; setbacks, 221, 222; subsistence, 74,
200
education (see also adult education; curriculum; enrollments; higher education; intellectual life; languages; schools; students; teachers; universities; vocational and technical training): vii–viii, 119, 133–143, 176; administration, 135–136; africanization, 119, 133; and French rule, 28; Higher Council of Education, 141, 143; and language, 73; for a national society, 87, 88; textbooks, 72, 75–76, 138, 145
Education and Culture Domain: 135
Egypt: 142, 147, 196, 226, 227, 283; and defense assistance, 320, 341
Eisenhower, Dwight D.: 194
elders (see also social system): 79, 82, 103; councils of, 81, 85; and rebellion, 86
electricity (see also hydroelectric power): 183, 199, 291; and budget, 223; Grades Chutes, 289; nationalization, 288; power potential, 288–289
elite (see also privileged class; social stratification): 87, 190; under French rule, 28, 33; intellectual, 178; Peul group, 78; and politics, 163, 167, 171
emigration (see also Assembly of Guineans in Europe): of intelligentsia, 78, 178; in 1960's, 42; of political exiles, 149, 166, 171, 177, 178, 183, 187, 315, 319; restrictions, 178
empires and kingdoms: 3, 9, 11–12, 19, 67, 69
employment: militia, 338; urban, 6, 99
Energo projekt (see also mining; Yugoslavia): 282–283, 284
Engineering Service: 332
enrollments: viii
ethnic groups: vii, 2, 5, 6, 61–76; and military, 332; social and political units, 81; tensions and rivalries, 73, 317
Europe (see also western nations): 9, 16–22, 27; early activities in Africa, 16–20; influences from, 5; and slave trade, 12
Europe, Eastern: 39, 147, 181, 191–192, 193, 225, 277; broadcasts, 147; economic aid, 204, 224, 227, 228; and mining, 280; and students, 141; and trade, 298, 299, 301
Europe, Western (see also western nations): 224, 226–227, 266–267; and students, 142; and trade, 297
European Economic Community (EEC): 196, 297, 298, 299, 301
évolvés: 28, 30
executive branch (see also cabinet; ministries; presidency; prime minister; Touré, President Ahmad Sékou): 152, 154–156;

371

French Press Agency (Agence France Presse—AFP): 144
French Sudan: 21–22
French Union: 1, 9, 22, 31–33, 37
Fria mining complex (*see also* Friguia): 49, 57, 106, 110, 190, 195, 199, 210, 211, 212, 273, 274, 275, 276, 278, 280, 301, 302, 303; africanization, 280; manufacturing, 286; nationalization, 275
Fria region: xiv, 49, 57, 58, 288, 290, 291
Frialco: 280, 281
Friguia: 280, 310
fruits (*see also* agriculture; bananas; cassava; crops; pineapples): 238, 253, 259; and canneries, 264, 287; citrus, 267
fuels: 50

Gamal Abdel Nasser Polytechnic Institute: 96, 115, 139, 141; Higher School of Administration, 139–140
Gambia, The: 57, 177, 187
Gambie River: 43, 46
Gaoual region: xiv, 58, 65, 253, 288, 290, 311
Garde Républicaine (Republican Guard) (*see also* police): 316, 320, 331, 335, 338–340
Gbinigko (town): 286
Gendarmerie (*see also* police): 316, 328, 331, 335, 337–338; brigades, 337; ranks and grades, 338
General Confederation of Labor (Confédération Generale du Travail—CGT): 4, 34
General Directorate of Police Services: 336
General Directorate of Security Services: 335
Georges Poiret School: 29
German Democratic Republic (East Germany): 142, 145, 146, 182, 195, 311
Germany, Federal Republic of (West Germany): 39, 146, 148, 192, 195–196, 287, 301, 332; and aid, 227, 229, 288; and communications, 312; and mining, 280, 297; and opposition to government, 321; and security of Guinea, 334, 341
Ghana: 11, 12, 14, 39, 188–189, 195; Empire, 13, 68; union with, 151, 188; Wagadu, 11
God: 89, 91, 92, 93
gold: 11, 12, 16, 17, 19, 49, 54
government (*see also* civil service; collectivization; cooperatives; Democratic Party of Guinea; executive branch; judiciary; legislative branch; political subdivisions; prime minister; privileged class): viii, 149–179; French rule, 24–37; Islamic, 15; opposition to, 175–179, 317, 318, 320, 322;

party leaders, 87–88; "revolutionary regime", 153; totalitarian controls, 166; trade monopoly, 210
government, local. *See* political subdivisions
governors: 157; and national security, 336; and purges, 321; and smuggling, 293, 325
Gowon, General Yakubu: 322
grains. *See* crops
Grandes Chutes: 289, 290, 291
Great Britain (*see also* United Kingdom): 18, 19, 21, 39; early economic interests, 16–17, 19; and mining, 280; and security of Guinea, 322
griots: 120, 121, 122, 127; and music, 125, 126
gross domestic product (GDP): 198, 199, 200, 201
gross national product (GNP): 199, 214, 225, 335
groundnuts: 45, 57, 102, 238, 242, 253, 260, 262, 265; oil mill, 287
Guéckédou region: xiv, 57, 58; and agriculture, 260
Guéckédou (town): 295
Guerze group: 63, 70, 75, 84, 93, 97; caricature drama, 126; language, vii, 72, 73; stilt dance, 124
Guinea Highlands: 43, 45, 46, 49
Guinea-Bissau: 1, 53, 75, 146, 179, 181, 186, 187–188
Guinea-Kuwait Fishing Company (Société Guinéo-Koweitienne de Pêche—Soguikop): 270
Guinean Diamond Exploitation Enterprise (Entreprise Guinéene d'Exploitation du Diamont—EGED): 286
Guinean franc (GF): ix, 203, 232, 294; counterfeited, 206
Guinean National Liberation Front (Front pour la Libération Nationale de Guinée—FLNG): 178, 319
Guinean Petroleum Company (Société Guinéenne de Pétrole—Soguip): 286
Guinean Press Agency (Agence Guinéenne de Presse—AGP): 144
Guinean syli (GS): ix
Guyana: 276, 277

handicrafts: 81, 129–130; basketweaving, 129; jewelry, 129–130; textiles, 130
harmattan: 47, 48, 256
health (*see also* diet; disease; food supply; sanitation): viii, 31, 113–117
Henry the Navigator, Prince: 16
herding (*see also* cattle, livestock, meat supply): 2, 235, 245, 268–269; and Malinke,

373

282–283; and nationalization, 274, 281
ministries (see also cabinet): 152, 153, 154,
155, 172, 210, 211, 217, 321; Defense and
Security, 318; Finance, 215, 278, 284, 309,
338; Financial Control, 215, 217; Financial
Trade, 207; Foreign Affairs, 181, 182;
Foreign Trade, 182, 207; Health, 114;
Higher Education and Scientific Re-
search, 135; Interior and Security, 157,
335, 336; Justice, 161; Labor and Social
Legislation, 117; People's Army, 329;
Planning, 202, 207, 215, 220; Posts and
Telecommunications, 312; Preuniversity
Education and Literacy, 135; Public
Works, Urban Affairs, and Housing, 116
missides: 82, 85
missions and missionaries: 28, 92–93; Ameri-
can, 92, broadcasts of, 97
Mmani group: 63, 65–66, 70; language, 72
Mobutu Sese Seko, President: 280
Monchon: 65
Morocco: 12, 14, 24, 226, 227, 274
mosques: 78, 82, 90
motion pictures: 107, 147–148; prizes, 148;
Soviet, 132
motor vehicles (see also transportation): 307,
309–310
Mount Nimba: vii, 43, 46; and iron ore, 283;
natural reserve, 131
Muhammad: 89
Musa, Ibrahim: 15
Musa, Mansa: 12
music: 121, 124–126, 127, 128; balafon, 125;
drums, 124–125; Gendarmerie Women's
Band, 127; jazz, 127–128; National Syli
Band, 127; songs, 124, 125–126
Muslims (see also Islam): 2, 67, 69, 87, 88, 97,
196, 264, 268; and age-groups, 81; almamy,
15, 20, 21; Almoravid group, 12, 14; and
folk medicine, 116; independent state of, 9;
and marriage, 80; ritual dance, 124; and
Syrians, 71

Nalou group: 17, 18, 62, 63, 65, 73; language,
72, 73
Napoleon III: 18
National and Popular Militia: 339
National Assembly (see also legislative
branch; PDG): viii, 151, 152, 153, 154, 156,
159, 162, 217; budget, 215, 216; and
government opposition, 318, 321, 322;
Permanent Commission, 153, 159
National Bureau of Recruitment: 329
National Confederation of Workers of
Guinea (Confédération Nationale des

Travailleurs de Guinée—CNTG): 145,
173–174
National Council of the Revolution (Conseil
National de la Révolution—CNR): 339;
and schools, 134, 136, 142, 168
National Economic Council: 210–211
National Electricity Company: 288
National Health School: 115
National Institute of Languages: 139
National Institute of Research and Docu-
mentation (Institut National de Recher-
ches et de Documentation—INRD): 131,
132
National Military Academy: 334
National Political Bureau (Bureau Politique
National—BPN): 140, 154, 155, 165, 169,
170, 171, 172; and surveillance, 323, 337
National Railroad Office of Guinea (Office
National des Chemins de Fer de Guinée—
ONCFG): 308
National Revolutionary Council: 162
National Savings Bank (Caisse Nationale
d'Epargne—CNE): 231
National Social Security Fund: 117
National Teaching Institute: 139
National Telecommunications School: 139,
312
National Veterans Association: 328
National Women's Committee (Comité
National des Femmes—CNF): 167, 168,
172
nationalism: v, 4, 30, 38, 75, 163, 174, 183,
330
nationalization. See banks; collectivization;
cooperatives; diamonds; electricity; Fria
mining complex; industry; mining; schools;
trade, domestic
navy: ix, 331, 333
Nénékhaly-Camara, Condetto: 122
nepotism: 75
Netherlands: and early commercial interests, 16; KLM fishing firm, 271
newspapers (see also mass communication;
press): ix, 115, 143, 144, 145; and politics,
174, 322
Niane, Djibril Tamsir: 122–123
Niger River: 12, 15, 19, 43, 46, 49, 53, 54, 55,
261, 288, 310; Upper Niger, 235, 258, 262,
288; valley, 11
Nigeria: 147, 186, 284, 322; and defense aid,
320, 341
Nimba Mountains: 43, 46, 49, 283
Nkrumah, Kwame: 188–189, 319
nomads: 66; seminomads, 74
North Atlantic Treaty Organization: 194

secret societies: 81, 94, 95; and dance, 123; Poro, 94; Sande, 94

security forces: 327–329; soldiers in colonial period, 327–328

security, national (*see also* armed forces; Conakry invasion; coups d'etat; fifth columnists; Labé plot; militia; purges, subversion): ix–x, 1, 7, 315–342

Senegal: 1, 3, 16, 17, 18, 20, 53, 57, 75, 183–184, 187, 217, 226, 381; Guinean exiles, 177, 184; Saint Louis military school, 334

Sénégal River (*see also* Bafing River): 18, 46, 255

Sénégal River Basin States 183–185; Development Commission, 184

Sénégal River Development Organization (Organisation pour la Mise en Valeur du Fleuve Ségégal—OMVS): 184

Senghor, Léopold-Sédar: 146, 177, 183–84

Sérédou (town): 270, 271, 290

serfs (*see also* slavery): 66, 82, 83, 103, 163; children, 82; and housing, 108; and land, 240

Seven Year Plan (1964–71): 201, 202, 216, 221, 222, 223, 287, 289, 311, 321; and agriculture, 240, 248, 261, 264, 265, 266

Sierra Leone: ix, 2, 16, 17, 19, 21, 46, 53, 75, 177, 185–186, 232, 259, 276, 320, 323, 334–335; and defense aid, 341

Siguiri region: xiv, 19, 49, 58, 252, 261–262; and agriculture, 252, 254

Siguiri (town): 33, 54, 288, 289, 290, 311; hospital, 115

Sikasso area: 19

Simandou Mountains: 43, 49, 283, 309

Sisters of Saint Joseph of Cluny: 28

slash-and-burn technique (*see also* soil, bush burnings): 254–255, 256

slavery (*see also* serfs): 4, 12, 16, 17, 27, 65, 66, 78, 81, 163; and the Diakhanké, 68; and the Dialonké, 67; end of domestic, 82; and the Peul, 67, 73, 81; and Samory Touré, 20

smuggling: viii, 197, 202, 204, 207, 233, 245, 273, 293, 295, 302; diamonds 285–286; exports, 204, 302; food, 236, 259, 261, 293; and national security, 323, 324; volume of, 296

snakes: 52; antivenins, 132

social security: 117; fringe benefits, 213

social stratification (*see also* aristocracy; bourgeoisie; elite; *évolués; indigenat;* peasants; privileged class; slavery): 3, 7, 78; feudal class and caste, 67; and government service, 77

social system: 77–88; age-groups, 81;

changing, 82–87; feudalism, 81; and the national society, 87–88; traditional 70–82

socialism and socialists (*see also* Marxism): 1, 31, 33, 36, 84, 119, 144, 151, 192; African, 174; French, 163

socialist cooperatives (*see also* cooperatives): 135

soil (*see also* rainfall): 41, 42, 45, 48–49, 54, 237, 254, 255, 260, 265; and bush burnings, 54, 100, 237, 238, 253, 254, 255, 262, 265; bush fallow rotation, 237; fertilizers, 238, 266; laterite, 48, 49, 54, manuring, 237, 238

Sonfonya (town): 271, 312

Songhai Empire: 12, 13, 14

Soninké group: 11, 12, 14, 67

Sori, Ibrahim: 15

Soso region: 12

Souapiti (town): 289, 291

Soussou group (*see also* Dialonke group): vii, 9, 33, 61–62, 63, 65, 66, 67, 73, 75, 80, 82, 84, 87, 88, 91, 171; fishermen, 269; language, vii, 72, 73

South Africa: 193; and security of Guinea, 323

Soviet Union: x, 39, 104, 132, 147, 225, 226, 242; and agriculture, 246, 263, 268, 269, 270; aid projects, 71, 139, 145–146, 192, 204, 221, 223, 224, 227, 228, 230, 289, 297; and airport, 311; books, 132; broadcasts, 147; cannery, 287–288; equipment, 192, 300; expulsion of Soviet ambassador, 300; 318; foreign relations with, 182, 191, 192–193, 194; and mining, 278, 286, 300; and railroads, 303, 308; and security of Guinea, 331–332, 333, 334, 335, 340, 341, 342; and students, 141, 142; and subversion in Guinea, 316; and trade, 298, 299, 300; and trucks, 310

Sow, Alpha: 122

Spain: and mining, 280, 284, 297

sports: 104, 144

Stevens, Siaka: 186

strikes: 34; absence of, 213; of teachers, 318

students: 131, 133, 135; abroad, 141–142, 174, 178, 192; and militia training, 340; seizure of, 189; and teacher's strike, 318; in United States, 227

subsistence existence. *See* cultivators; economy; farms and farming

subversion (*see also* fifth columnists): 317–318, 328; countersubversion, 337

Sudan (*see also* French Sudan): 9, 11, 12–13, 14, 18, 19, 69

suffrage. *See* voting

Sufism (*see also* Islam): 91

sugar. *See* crops
Sundiata: 12
Sundiata: 122–123
Supreme Council for Overseas France: 24
Supreme Revolutionary Tribunal: 162, 321, 322
Suret-Canale, Jean: 123, 204, 242, 244, 245, 249, 252, 269, 270, 281, 286, 287, 296, 302, 308–309, 310, 312
Sûreté Nationale (National Police) (*see also* police): 316, 331, 335, 336–337; ranks and grades, 337
Surinam: 276
Swiss-Guinean Mining Company: 283
Switzerland: 214, 229; and mining, 280, 283, 284
syli (*see also* currency): 206, 208, 232, 290–291, 325
Syli Cinema: 147
Syria: Syrians in Guinea, 71, 324

Tamara Island: 278, 281
"target 1980": 223, 273
tariffs: 30
taxation: 86, 215, 216, 218; under French rule, 21, 25–26; head tax, 216; local, 158; and produce, 237
Tchidimbo, Raymond: 97–98
tea. *See* crops
teachers: 72, 139, 141, 142, 192; under French rule, 29, 30, 38; qualifications, 138; strike, 318; training, 140–141
television (*see also* mass communication): 312
Télimélé region: xiv, 58
Télimélé (town): 59
Telli, Diallo: 196
Tenda group: 63, 68
Territorial School of Administration: 37
textiles (*see also* cotton): 130, 305
theater: 72
third world: 209
Three Year Development Plan (1960–1963): 105, 142, 201, 220, 221, 327; and agriculture, 240, 248, 262, 263; and manufacturing, 287
Tidjani, Si Ahmad ben Muhammad al: 91
Timbo: 21
Tinkisso River: 43, 289, 290
tobacco: 238, 262, 263; factory, 264
Tolo (town): 139
Toma group: 21, 63, 70, 71, 75, 84, 85, 96, 97; language, vii, 72, 73
Tominé River: 288
topography: vii, 146, 256; of Forest Region, 45–46

Toucouleur Empire: 18, 19
Tougué region: xiv, 49, 58; and agriculture, 262; and mining, 278, 280, 282, 283, 297
Touré, Ismail: 278, 284, 309
Touré, President Ahmed Sékou: (*see also* executive branch, purges): viii, 1, 4, 5, 6, 7, 10, 34–35, 36, 37, 38, 39, 79, 122, 132, 133, 144, 146, 149–150, 151, 152, 154, 155, 165, 177; and agriculture, 236, 237, 242, 249, 251, 268; assassination plots, 318, 319, 322; and courts, 162; and "debunking" campaign, 96–98, 116; and economy, 200, 203, 204, 206, 208; and education, 119–120, 133, 134, 142; and ethnic differences, 73, 74; and foreign relations, 181, 182, 183, 185, 186, 187, 188–189, 190–191, 194; and industry, 276; and internal security, 316, 318, 324–325, 326–327, 328, 330–331, 337, 339, 340; and living conditions, 99, 103; and medical services, 114–115; opposition to, 178, 315, 316, 318, 319, 341; philosophy, 174, 175, 178; and the political party, 162, 164, 165, 166–167, 169, 170, 171, 172, 174; and social change, 85, 86; and trade, 297; and transportation, 309; writings and speeches, 121, 145, 156, 174, 201, 206–207
Touré, Sadan Moussa: 122
Touré Samory: 9, 19–20, 21, 69, 89
towns: 54, 55, 59; and electricity, 288
tractors (*see also* agriculture): 236, 239, 240, 247, 250, 252, 261, 263; tractor bourgeoisie, 236, 239, 247, 261
trade, domestic (*see also* black markets; *comptoirs*; consumerism; food supply; inflation; smuggling): 176, 248, 273, 289–296; africanization, 295; barter, 295–296; middlemen, 294, 295; Muslims, 14; nationalization of, 273, 293, 295; private traders, 294–295
trade, foreign (*see also* black markets; smuggling): 192, 193, 203, 293, 296–302, 304, 310; bilateral, 300; caravan, 11; and communist countries, 191, 296; early European, 16, 17, 18, 19, 27; self-sufficiency potential, 302; state control of, 210, 211, 221, 293; trends, 296–302
tradition (*see also* secret societies): circumcision, 91; and contemporary society, 77, 243; cultural, 76; and ethnicity, 62; and inheritance problems, 80; initiation rites, 85, 96; of Islam, 92; rural, 247–248; social, 79–82, trading, 248, 249
transportation (*see also* air transportation; motor vehicles; ports; railroads; roads): ix, 197, 271, 273, 302–311; early caravans, 11;

381

wildlife: 52–53
William Ponty School: 170
witchcraft and sorcery: 95; and folk medicine, 116
women (*see also* lineage, matrilineal): 81, 145, 176; and arts, 126, 127, 129, 130; and birthrate, 56; clothing, 110–111; cultivating and gardening chores, 101, 102, 238; and food preparation, 112; and housing construction, 108; and initiation rites, 85; and Islam, 90; and maternity care, 116, 117; and militia, 339; and politics, 35, 77, 86–87, 154, 157, 164, 165, 167, 169, 172–173; and population, 56; potters, 67, 81, 102; serfs, 82, 83; and trading, 103, 105–106, 295
word of mouth (*see also* mass communication): 120
World Bank. *See* International Bank for Reconstruction and Development (IBRD)

World Health Organization: 113, 114
World War II: 9–10; and inherent rights of people 163
Yaounde Conventions: 301
Yomou region: xiv, 58, 260
youth: 177; groups, 77; and militia, 339; and nationalism, 76; in politics, 35, 83, 86, 97, 154, 164
Youth of the African Democratic Revolution (Jeunesse de la Révolution Démocratique Africaine—JRDA): 126, 128, 167, 168, 172, 173, 177; and policing, 339
Yugoslavia: 142, 214, 225, 276, 287; aid projects, 71, 223, 230, 289; Energo project, 282–283, 284; and mining, 278, 283, 284, 297; and trade, 198, 299
Zaire: 280, 284, 334
Zambia: 319
Ziama Forest: 270, 271

PUBLISHED AREA HANDBOOKS

550–65	Afghanistan		550–69	Ivory Coast
550–98	Albania		550–30	Japan
550–44	Algeria		550–34	Jordan
550–59	Angola		550–56	Kenya
550–73	Argentina		550–50	Khmer Republic (Cambodia)
550–169	Australia		550–81	Korea, North
550–170	Belgium		550–41	Korea, South
550–66	Bolivia		550–58	Laos
550–20	Brazil		550–24	Lebanon
550–168	Bulgaria		550–38	Liberia
550–61	Burma		550–85	Libya
550–83	Burundi		550–163	Malagasy Republic
550–166	Cameroon		550–172	Malawi
550–96	Ceylon		550–45	Malaysia
550–159	Chad		550–161	Mauritania
550–77	Chile		550–79	Mexico
550–60	China, People's Rep. of		550–76	Mongolia
550–63	China, Rep. of		550–49	Morocco
550–26	Colombia		550–64	Mozambique
550–67	Congo, Democratic Republic of (Zaire)		550–35	Nepal, Bhutan and Sikkim
			550–88	Nicaragua
550–91	Congo, People's Republic of		550–157	Nigeria
550–90	Costa Rica		550–94	Oceania
550–152	Cuba		550–48	Pakistan
550–22	Cyprus		550–46	Panama
550–158	Czechoslovakia		550–156	Paraguay
550–54	Dominican Republic		550–92	Peripheral States of the Arabian Peninsula
550–155	East Germany			
550–52	Ecuador		550–42	Peru
550–150	El Salvador		550–72	Philippines
550–28	Ethiopia		550–162	Poland
550–167	Finland		550–160	Romania
550–29	Germany		550–84	Rwanda
550–153	Ghana		550–51	Saudi Arabia
550–87	Greece		550–70	Senegal
550–78	Guatemala		550–86	Somalia
550–174	Guinea		550–93	South Africa, Republic of
550–82	Guyana		550–171	Southern Rhodesia
550–164	Haiti		550–95	Soviet Union
550–151	Honduras		550–27	Sudan, Democratic Republic of
550–165	Hungary		550–47	Syria
550–21	India		550–62	Tanzania
550–154	Indian Ocean Territories		550–53	Thailand
550–39	Indonesia		550–89	Tunisia
550–68	Iran		550–80	Turkey
550–31	Iraq		550–74	Uganda
550–25	Israel		550–43	United Arab Republic (Egypt)

550–97	Uruguay	550–55	Vietnam, South
550–71	Venezuela	550–99	Yugoslavia
550–57	Vietnam, North	550–75	Zambia